*Taming Text*

# Taming Text

### How to Find, Organize, and Manipulate It

GRANT S. INGERSOLL
THOMAS S. MORTON
ANDREW L. FARRIS

MANNING
SHELTER ISLAND

For online information and ordering of this and other Manning books, please visit
www.manning.com. The publisher offers discounts on this book when ordered in quantity.
For more information, please contact

>  Special Sales Department
>  Manning Publications Co.
>  20 Baldwin Road
>  PO Box 261
>  Shelter Island, NY 11964
>  Email: orders@manning.com

Manning Publications Co.
20 Baldwin Road
PO Box 261
Shelter Island, NY 11964

Development editor: Jeff Bleiel
Technical proofreader: Steven Rowe
Copyeditor: Benjamin Berg
Proofreader: Katie Tennant
Typesetter: Dottie Marsico
Cover designer: Marija Tudor

ISBN 9781933988382
Printed in the United States of America
5 6 7 8 9 10 – MAL – 18 17 16 15 14

# brief contents

# contents

# *foreword*

At a time when the demand for high-quality text processing capabilities continues to grow at an exponential rate, it's difficult to think of any sector or business that doesn't rely on some type of textual information. The burgeoning web-based economy has dramatically and swiftly increased this reliance. Simultaneously, the need for talented technical experts is increasing at a fast pace. Into this environment comes an excellent, very pragmatic book, *Taming Text*, offering substantive, real-world, tested guidance and instruction.

Grant Ingersoll and Drew Farris, two excellent and highly experienced software engineers with whom I've worked for many years, and Tom Morton, a well-respected contributor to the natural language processing field, provide a realistic course for guiding other technical folks who have an interest in joining the highly recruited coterie of text processors, a.k.a. natural language processing (NLP) engineers.

In an approach that equates with what I think of as "learning for the world, in the world," Grant, Drew, and Tom take the mystery out of what are, in truth, very complex processes. They do this by focusing on existing tools, implemented examples, and well-tested code, versus taking you through the longer path followed in semester-long NLP courses.

As software engineers, you have the basics that will enable you to latch onto the examples, the code bases, and the open source tools here referenced, and become true experts, ready for real-world opportunites, more quickly than you might expect.

LIZ LIDDY
DEAN, ISCHOOL
SYRACUSE UNIVERSITY

# *preface*

Life is full of serendipitous moments, few of which stand out for me (Grant) like the one that now defines my career. It was the late 90s, and I was a young software developer working on distributed electromagnetics simulations when I happened on an ad for a developer position at a small company in Syracuse, New York, called TextWise. Reading the description, I barely thought I was qualified for the job, but decided to take a chance anyway and sent in my resume. Somehow, I landed the job, and thus began my career in search and natural language processing. Little did I know that, all these years later, I would still be doing search and NLP, never mind writing a book on those subjects.

My first task back then was to work on a cross-language information retrieval (CLIR) system that allowed users to enter queries in English and find and automatically translate documents in French, Spanish, and Japanese. In retrospect, that first system I worked on touched on all the hard problems I've come to love about working with text: search, classification, information extraction, machine translation, and all those peculiar rules about languages that drive every grammar student crazy. After that first project, I've worked on a variety of search and NLP systems, ranging from rule-based classifiers to question answering (QA) systems. Then, in 2004, a new job at the Center for Natural Language Processing led me to the use of Apache Lucene, the de facto open source search library (these days, anyway). I once again found myself writing a CLIR system, this time to work with English and Arabic. Needing some Lucene features to complete my task, I started putting up patches for features and bug fixes. Sometime thereafter, I became a committer. From there, the floodgates opened. I got more involved in open source, starting the Apache Mahout machine learning project with Isabel Drost and Karl Wettin, as well as cofounding Lucid Imagination, a company built around search and text analytics with Apache Lucene and Solr.

Coming full circle, I think search and NLP are among the defining areas of computer science, requiring a sophisticated approach to both the data structures and algorithms necessary to solve problems. Add to that the scaling requirements of processing large volumes of user-generated web and social content, and you have a developer's dream. This book addresses my view that the marketplace was missing (at the time) a book written for engineers by engineers and specifically geared toward using existing, proven, open source libraries to solve hard problems in text processing. I hope this book helps you solve everyday problems in your current job as well as inspires you to see the world of text as a rich opportunity for learning.

GRANT INGERSOLL

I (Tom) became fascinated with artificial intelligence as a sophomore in high school and as an undergraduate chose to go to graduate school and focus on natural language processing. At the University of Pennsylvania, I learned an incredible amount about text processing, machine learning, and algorithms and data structures in general. I also had the opportunity to work with some of the best minds in natural language processing and learn from them.

In the course of my graduate studies, I worked on a number of NLP systems and participated in numerous DARPA-funded evaluations on coreference, summarization, and question answering. In the course of this work, I became familiar with Lucene and the larger open source movement. I also noticed that there was a gap in open source text processing software that could provide efficient end-to-end processing. Using my thesis work as a basis, I contributed extensively to the OpenNLP project and also continued to learn about NLP systems while working on automated essay and short-answer scoring at Educational Testing Services.

Working in the open source community taught me a lot about working with others and made me a much better software engineer. Today, I work for Comcast Corporation with teams of software engineers that use many of the tools and techniques described in this book. It is my hope that this book will help bridge the gap between the hard work of researchers like the ones I learned from in graduate school and software engineers everywhere whose aim is to use text processing to solve real problems for real people.

THOMAS MORTON

Like Grant, I (Drew) was first introduced to the field of information retrieval and natural language processing by Dr. Elizabeth Liddy, Woojin Paik, and all of the others doing research at TextWise in the mid 90s. I started working with the group as I was finishing my master's at the School of Information Studies (iSchool) at Syracuse University. At that time, TextWise was transitioning from a research group to a startup business developing applications based on the results of our text processing research. I stayed with the company for many years, constantly learning, discovering new things, and working with many outstanding people who came to tackle the challenges of teaching machines to understand language from many different perspectives.

Personally, I approach the subject of text analytics first from the perspective of a software developer. I've had the privilege of working with brilliant researchers and transforming their ideas from experiments to functioning prototypes to massively scalable systems. In the process, I've had the opportunity to do a great deal of what has recently become known as data science and discovered a deep love of exploring and understanding massive datasets and the tools and techniques for learning from them.

I cannot overstate the impact that open source software has had on my career. Readily available source code as a companion to research is an immensely effective way to learn new techniques and approaches to text analytics and software development in general. I salute everyone who has made the effort to share their knowledge and experience with others who have the passion to collaborate and learn. I specifically want to acknowledge the good folks at the Apache Software Foundation who continue to grow a vibrant ecosystem dedicated to the development of open source software and the people, process, and community that support it.

The tools and techniques presented in this book have strong roots in the open source software community. Lucene, Solr, Mahout, and OpenNLP all fall under the Apache umbrella. In this book, we only scratch the surface of what can be done with these tools. Our goal is to provide an understanding of the core concepts surrounding text processing and provide a solid foundation for future explorations of this domain.

Happy coding!

DREW FARRIS

# acknowledgments

A long time coming, this book represents the labor of many people whom we would like to gratefully acknowledge. Thanks to all the following:

- The users and developers of Apache Solr, Lucene, Mahout, OpenNLP, and other tools used throughout this book
- Manning Publications, for sticking with us, especially Douglas Pundick, Karen Tegtmeyer, and Marjan Bace
- Jeff Bleiel, our development editor, for nudging us along despite our crazy schedules, for always having good feedback, and for turning developers into authors
- Our reviewers, for the questions, comments, and criticisms that make this book better: Adam Tacy, Amos Bannister, Clint Howarth, Costantino Cerbo, Dawid Weiss, Denis Kurilenko, Doug Warren, Frank Jania, Gann Bierner, James Hatheway, James Warren, Jason Rennie, Jeffrey Copeland, Josh Reed, Julien Nioche, Keith Kim, Manish Katyal, Margriet Bruggeman, Massimo Perga, Nikander Bruggeman, Philipp K. Janert, Rick Wagner, Robi Sen, Sanchet Dighe, Szymon Chojnacki, Tim Potter, Vaijanath Rao, and Jeff Goldschrafe
- Our contributors who lent their expertise to certain sections of this book: J. Neal Richter, Manish Katyal, Rob Zinkov, Szymon Chojnacki, Tim Potter, and Vaijanath Rao
- Steven Rowe, for a thorough technical review as well as for all the shared hours developing text applications at TextWise, CNLP, and as part of Lucene

- Dr. Liz Liddy, for introducing Drew and Grant to the world of text analytics and all the fun and opportunity therein, and for contributing the foreword
- All of our MEAP readers, for their patience and feedback
- Most of all, our family, friends, and coworkers, for their encouragement, moral support, and understanding as we took time from our normal lives to work on the book

### Grant Ingersoll

Thanks to all my coworkers at TextWise and CNLP who taught me so much about text analytics; to Mr. Urdahl for making math interesting and Ms. Raymond for making me a better student and person; to my parents, Floyd and Delores, and kids, Jackie and William (love you always); to my wife, Robin, who put up with all the late nights and lost weekends—thanks for being there through it all!

### Tom Morton

Thanks to my coauthors for their hard work and partnership; to my wife, Thuy, and daughter, Chloe, for their patience, support, and time freely given; to my family, Mortons and Trans, for all your encouragement; to my colleagues from the University of Pennsylvania and Comcast for their support and collaboration, especially Na-Rae Han, Jason Baldridge, Gann Bierner, and Martha Palmer; to Jörn Kottmann for his tireless work on OpenNLP.

### Drew Farris

Thanks to Grant for getting me involved with this and many other interesting projects; to my coworkers, past and present, from whom I've learned incredible things and with whom I've shared a passion for text analytics, machine learning, and developing amazing software; to my wife, Kristin, and children, Phoebe, Audrey, and Owen, for their patience and support as I stole time to work on this and other technological endeavors; to my extended family for their interest and encouragement, especially my Mom, who will never see this book in its completed form.

# about this book

*Taming Text* is about building software applications that derive their core value from using and manipulating content that primarily consists of the written word. This book is not a theoretical treatise on the subjects of search, natural language processing, and machine learning, although we cover all of those topics in a fair amount of detail throughout the book. We strive to avoid jargon and complex math and instead focus on providing the concepts and examples that today's software engineers, architects, and practitioners need in order to implement intelligent, next-generation, text-driven applications. *Taming Text* is also firmly grounded in providing real-world examples of the concepts described in the book using freely available, highly popular, open source tools like Apache Solr, Mahout, and OpenNLP.

## Who should read this book

Is this book for you? Perhaps. Our target audience is software practitioners who don't have (much of) a background in search, natural language processing, and machine learning. In fact, our book is aimed at practitioners in a work environment much like what we've seen in many companies: a development team is tasked with adding search and other features to a new or existing application and few, if any, of the developers have any experience working with text. They need a good primer on understanding the concepts without being bogged down by the unnecessary.

In many cases, we provide references to easily accessible sources like Wikipedia and seminal academic papers, thus providing a launching pad for the reader to explore an area in greater detail if desired. Additionally, while most of our open source tools and examples are in Java, the concepts and ideas are portable to many other programming languages, so Rubyists, Pythonistas, and others should feel quite comfortable as well with the book.

This book is clearly not for those looking for explanations of the math involved in these systems or for academic rigor on the subject, although we do think students will find the book helpful when they need to implement the concepts described in the classroom and more academically-oriented books.

This book doesn't target experienced field practitioners who have built many text-based applications in their careers, although they may find some interesting nuggets here and there on using the open source packages described in the book. More than one experienced practitioner has told us that the book is a great way to get team members who are new to the field up to speed on the ideas and code involved in writing a text-based application.

Ultimately, we hope this book is an up-to-date guide for the modern programmer, a guide that we all wish we had when we first started down our career paths in programming text-based applications.

## Roadmap

Chapter 1 explains why processing text is important, and what makes it so challenging. We preview a fact-based question answering (QA) system, setting the stage for utilizing open source libraries to tame text.

Chapter 2 introduces the building blocks of text processing: tokenizing, chunking, parsing, and part of speech tagging. We follow up with a look at how to extract text from some common file formats using the Apache Tika open source project.

Chapter 3 explores search theory and the basics of the vector space model. We introduce the Apache Solr search server and show how to index content with it. You'll learn how to evaluate the search performance factors of quantity and quality.

Chapter 4 examines fuzzy string matching with prefixes and *n*-grams. We look at two character overlap measures—the Jaccard measure and the Jaro-Winkler distance—and explain how to find candidate matches with Solr and rank them.

Chapter 5 presents the basic concepts behind named-entity recognition. We show how to use OpenNLP to find named entities, and discuss some OpenNLP performance considerations. We also cover how to customize OpenNLP entity identification for a new domain.

Chapter 6 is devoted to clustering text. Here you'll learn the basic concepts behind common text clustering algorithms, and see examples of how clustering can help improve text applications. We also explain how to cluster whole document collections using Apache Mahout, and how to cluster search results using Carrot[2].

Chapter 7 discusses the basic concepts behind classification, categorization, and tagging. We show how categorization is used in text applications, and how to build, train, and evaluate classifiers using open source tools. We also use the Mahout implementation of the naive Bayes algorithm to build a document categorizer.

Chapter 8 is where we bring together all the things learned in the previous chapters to build an example QA system. This simple application uses Wikipedia as its knowledge base, and Solr as a baseline system.

Chapter 9 explores what's next in search and NLP, and the roles of semantics, discourse, and pragmatics. We discuss searching across multiple languages and detecting emotions in content, as well as emerging tools, applications, and ideas.

## Code conventions and downloads

This book contains numerous code examples. All the code is in a `fixed-width font like this` to separate it from ordinary text. Code members such as method names, class names, and so on are also in a fixed-width font.

In many listings, the code is annotated to point out key concepts, and numbered bullets are sometimes used in the text to provide additional information about the code.

Source code examples in this book are fairly close to the samples that you'll find online. But for brevity's sake, we may have removed material such as comments from the code to fit it well within the text.

The source code for the examples in the book is available for download from the publisher's website at www.manning.com/TamingText.

## Author Online

The purchase of *Taming Text* includes free access to a private web forum run by Manning Publications, where you can make comments about the book, ask technical questions, and receive help from the authors and from other users. To access the forum and subscribe to it, point your web browser at www.manning.com/TamingText. This page provides information on how to get on the forum once you are registered, what kind of help is available, and the rules of conduct on the forum.

Manning's commitment to our readers is to provide a venue where a meaningful dialogue between individual readers and between readers and authors can take place. It's not a commitment to any specific amount of participation on the part of the authors, whose contribution to the forum remains voluntary (and unpaid). We suggest you try asking the authors some challenging questions, lest their interest stray!

The Author Online forum and archives of previous discussions will be accessible from the publisher's website as long as the book is in print.

# about the cover illustration

The figure on the cover of *Taming Text* is captioned "Le Marchand," which means merchant or storekeeper. The illustration is taken from a 19th-century edition of Sylvain Maréchal's four-volume compendium of regional dress customs published in France. Each illustration is finely drawn and colored by hand. The rich variety of Maréchal's collection reminds us vividly of how culturally apart the world's towns and regions were just 200 years ago. Isolated from each other, people spoke different dialects and languages. In the streets or in the countryside, it was easy to identify where they lived and what their trade or station in life was just by their dress.

Dress codes have changed since then and the diversity by region, so rich at the time, has faded away. It is now hard to tell apart the inhabitants of different continents, let alone different towns or regions. Perhaps we have traded cultural diversity for a more varied personal life—certainly for a more varied and fast-paced technological life.

At a time when it is hard to tell one computer book from another, Manning celebrates the inventiveness and initiative of the computer business with book covers based on the rich diversity of regional life of two centuries ago, brought back to life by Maréchal's pictures.

# Getting started
# taming text

If you're reading this book, chances are you're a programmer, or at least in the information technology field. You operate with relative ease when it comes to email, instant messaging, Google, YouTube, Facebook, Twitter, blogs, and most of the other technologies that define our digital age. After you're done congratulating yourself on your technical prowess, take a moment to imagine your users. They often feel imprisoned by the sheer volume of email they receive. They struggle to organize all the data that inundates their lives. And they probably don't know or even care about RSS or JSON, much less search engines, Bayesian classifiers, or neural networks. They want to get answers to their questions without sifting through pages of results. They want email to be organized and prioritized, but spend little time actually doing it themselves. Ultimately, your users want tools that enable

1

them to focus on their lives and their work, not just their technology. They want to control—or tame—the uncontrolled beast that is *text*. But what does it mean to tame text? We'll talk more about it later in this chapter, but for now taming text involves three primary things:

- The ability to find relevant answers and supporting content given an information need
- The ability to organize (label, extract, summarize) and manipulate text with little-to-no user intervention
- The ability to do both of these things with ever-increasing amounts of input

This leads us to the primary goal of this book: to give you, the programmer, the tools and hands-on advice to build applications that help people better manage the tidal wave of communication that swamps their lives. The secondary goal of *Taming Text* is to show how to do this using existing, freely available, high quality, open source libraries and tools.

Before we get to those broader goals later in the book, let's step back and examine some of the factors involved in text processing and why it's hard, and also look at some use cases as motivation for the chapters to follow. Specifically, this chapter aims to provide some background on why processing text effectively is both important and challenging. We'll also lay some groundwork with a simple working example of our first two primary tasks as well as get a preview of the application you'll build at the end of this book: a fact-based question answering system. With that, let's look at some of the motivation for taming text by scoping out the size and shape of the information world we live in.

## 1.1   Why taming text is important

Just for fun, try to imagine going a whole day without reading a single word. That's right, one whole day without reading any news, signs, websites, or even watching television. Think you could do it? Not likely, unless you sleep the whole day. Now spend a moment thinking about all the things that go into reading all that content: years of schooling and hands-on feedback from parents, teachers, and peers; and countless spelling tests, grammar lessons, and book reports, not to mention the hundreds of thousands of dollars it takes to educate a person through college. Next, step back another level and think about how much content you *do* read in a day.

To get started, take a moment to consider the following questions:

- How many email messages did you get today (both work and personal, including spam)?
- How many of those did you read?
- How many did you respond to right away? Within the hour? Day? Week?
- How do you find old email?
- How many blogs did you read today?
- How many online news sites did you visit?

- Did you use instant messaging (IM), Twitter, or Facebook with friends or colleagues?
- How many searches did you do on Google, Yahoo!, or Bing?
- What documents on your computer did you read? What format were they in (Word, PDF, text)?
- How often do you search for something locally (either on your machine or your corporate intranet)?
- How much content did you produce in the form of emails, reports, and so on?

Finally, the big question: how much time did you spend doing this?

If you're anything like the typical information worker, then you can most likely relate to IDC's (International Data Corporation) findings from their 2009 study (Feldman 2009):

> Email consumes an average of 13 hours per week per worker... But email is no longer the only communication vehicle. Social networks, instant messaging, Yammer, Twitter, Facebook, and LinkedIn have added new communication channels that can sap concentrated productivity time from the information worker's day. The time spent searching for information this year averaged 8.8 hours per week, for a cost of $14,209 per worker per year. Analyzing information soaked up an additional 8.1 hours, costing the organization $13,078 annually, making these two tasks relatively straightforward candidates for better automation. It makes sense that if workers are spending over a third of their time searching for information and another quarter analyzing it, this time must be as productive as possible.

Furthermore, this survey doesn't even account for how much time these same employees spend creating content during their personal time. In fact, eMarketer estimates that internet users average 18 hours a week online (eMarketer) and compares this to other leisure activities like watching television, which is still king at 30 hours per week.

Whether it's reading email, searching Google, reading a book, or logging into Facebook, the written word is everywhere in our lives.

We've seen the individual part of the content picture, but what about the collective picture? According to IDC (2011), the world generated *1.8 zettabytes* of digital information in 2011 and "by 2020 the world will generate 50 times [that amount]." Naturally, such prognostications often prove to be low given we can't predict the next big trend that will produce more content than expected.

Even if a good-size chunk of this data is due to signal data, images, audio, and video, the current best approach to making all this data findable is to write analysis reports, add keyword tags and text descriptions, or transcribe the audio using speech recognition or a manual closed-captioning approach so that it can be treated as text. In other words, no matter how much structure we add, it still comes back to text for us to share and comprehend our content. As you can see, the sheer volume of content can be daunting, never mind that text processing is also a hard problem on a small scale, as you'll see in a later section. In the meantime, it's worthwhile to think about what the ideal applications or tools would do to help stem the tide of text that's engulfing us. For many, the answer lies in the ability to quickly and efficiently hone in on the answer to our questions, not just a list of possible answers that we need to then sift through. Moreover, we wouldn't need to jump through hoops to ask our questions; we'd just be able to use our own words or voice to express them with no need for things like quotations, AND/OR operators, or other things that make it easier on the machine but harder on the person.

Though we all know we don't live in an ideal world, one of the promising approaches for taming text, popularized by IBM's Jeopardy!-playing Watson program and Apple's Siri application, is a question answering system that can process natural languages such as English and return *actual* answers, not just pages of *possible* answers. In *Taming Text*, we aim to lay some of the groundwork for building such a system. To do this, let's consider what such a system might look like; then, let's take a look at some simple code that can find and extract key bits of information out of text that will later prove to be useful in our QA system. We'll finish off this chapter by delving deeper into why building such a system as well as other language-based applications is so hard, along with a look at how the chapters to follow in this book will lay the foundation for a fact-based QA system along with other text-based systems.

## 1.2  *Preview: A fact-based question answering system*

For the purposes of this book, a QA system should be capable of ingesting a collection of documents suspected to have answers to questions that users might ask. For instance, Wikipedia or a collection of research papers might be used as a source for finding answers. In other words, the QA system we propose is based on identifying and analyzing text that has a chance of providing the answer based on patterns it has seen in the past. It won't be capable of inferring an answer from a variety of sources. For instance, if the system is asked "Who is Bob's uncle?" and there's a document in the collection with the sentences "Bob's father is Ola. Ola's brother is Paul," the system wouldn't be able to infer that Bob's uncle is Paul. But if there's a sentence that directly states "Bob's uncle is Paul," you'd expect the system to be able to answer the question. This isn't to say that the former example can't be attempted; it's just beyond the scope of this book.

A simple workflow for building the QA system described earlier is outlined in figure 1.1.

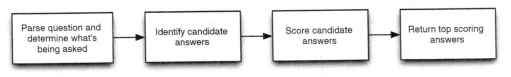

**Figure 1.1  A simple workflow for answering questions posed to a QA system**

Naturally, such a simple workflow hides a lot of details, and it also doesn't cover the ingestion of the documents, but it does allow us to highlight some of the key components needed to process users' questions. First, the ability to parse a user's question and determine what's being asked typically requires basic functionality like identifying words, as well as the ability to understand what kind of answer is appropriate for a question. For instance, the answer to "Who is Bob's uncle?" should likely be a person, whereas the answer to "Where is Buffalo?" probably requires a place-name to be returned. Second, the need to identify candidate answers typically involves the ability to quickly look up phrases, sentences, or passages that contain potential answers without having to force the system to parse large quantities of text.

Scoring implies many of the basic things again, such as parsing words, as well as a deeper understanding of whether a candidate actually contains the necessary components to answer a question, such as mentioning a person or a place. As easy as some of these things sound given the ease with which most humans *think* they do these things, they're not to be taken for granted. With this in mind, let's take a look at an example of processing a chunk of text to find passages and identify interesting things like names.

### 1.2.1 *Hello, Dr. Frankenstein*

In light of our discussion of a question answering system as well as our three primary tasks for working with text, let's take a look at some basic text processing. Naturally, we need some sample text to process in this simple system. For that, we chose Mary Shelley's classic *Frankenstein.* Why *Frankenstein?* Besides the authors' liking the book from a literary standpoint, it also happens to be the first book we came across on the Gutenberg Project site (http://www.gutenberg.org/), it's plain text and nicely formatted (which you'll find is a rarity in your day-to-day life with text), and there's the added bonus that it's out of copyright and freely distributable. We've included a full copy in our source tree, but you can also download a copy of the book at http://www.gutenberg .org/cache/epub/84/pg84.txt.

Now that we have some text to work with, let's do a few tasks that come up time and time again in text applications:

- Search the text based on user input and return the relevant passage (a paragraph in this example)
- Split the passage into sentences
- Extract "interesting" things from the text, like the names of people

To accomplish these tasks, we'll use two Java libraries, Apache Lucene and Apache OpenNLP, along with the code in the com.tamingtext.frankenstein.Frankenstein Java file that's included with the book and also available on GitHub at http:// www.github.com/tamingtext/book. See https://github.com/tamingtext/book/blob /master/README for instructions on building the source.

The high-level code that drives this process can be seen in the following listing.

**Listing 1.1  Frankenstein driver program**

```
Frankenstein frankenstein = new Frankenstein();
frankenstein.init();
frankenstein.index();
String query = null;
while (true) {
  query = getQuery();
  if (query != null) {
    Results results = frankenstein.search(query);
    frankenstein.examineResults(results);
    displayResults(results);
  } else {
    break;
  }
}
```

Make content searchable.

Prompt user for query.

Perform search.

Parse results and show interesting items.

In the driver example, you first index the content. Indexing is the process of making the content searchable using Lucene. We'll explain this in more detail in the chapter on search later in the book. For now, you can think of it as a quick way of looking up where words occur in a piece of text. Next you enter a loop where you ask the user to enter a query, execute the search, and then process the discovered results. For the purposes of this example, you treat each paragraph as a searchable unit. This means that when you execute a search, you'll be able to know exactly which paragraph in the book matched the query.

After you have your paragraphs, you switch over to using OpenNLP, which will take each paragraph, split it into sentences, and then try to identify the names of people in a sentence. We'll forgo examining the details of how each of the methods are implemented, as various sections in the remainder of the book cover the concepts. Instead, let's run the program and try a query and look at the results.

To run the code, open a terminal window (command prompt and change into the directory containing the unpacked source code) and type bin/frankenstein.sh on UNIX/Mac or bin/frankenstein.cmd on Windows. You should see the following:

```
Initializing Frankenstein
Indexing Frankenstein
Processed 7254 lines.  Paragraphs: 722

Type your query.  Hit Enter to process the query \
(the empty string will exit the program):
>
```

At this point, you can enter a query, such as "three months". A partial listing of the results follows. Note that we've inserted [...] in numerous places for formatting purposes.

```
>"three months"
Searching for: "three months"
Found 4 total hits.
---------------------------------
Match: [0] Paragraph: 418
Lines: 4249-4255
```

```
     "'Do you consider,' said his companion to him, ...
     ----- Sentences ----
         [0] "'Do you consider,' said his companion to him, ...
         [1] I do not wish to take any unfair advantage, ...
-----------------------------------
Match: [1] Paragraph: 583
Lines: 5796-5807
     The season of the assizes approached.  ...
     ----- Sentences ----
...      [2] Mr. Kirwin charged himself with every care ...
         >>>> Names
             Kirwin
...      [4] ... that I was on the Orkney Islands ...
         >>>> Locations
             Orkney Islands

-----------------------------------
Match: [2] Paragraph: 203
Lines: 2167-2186
     Six years had elapsed, passed in a dream but for one indelible trac
e, ...
     ----- Sentences ----
... [4] ... and represented Caroline Beaufort in an ...
         >>>> Names
             Caroline Beaufort

...      [7] While I was thus engaged, Ernest entered:  ...   "Welcome
, my dearest Victor," said he.   "Ah!
         >>>> Names
             Ah

         [8] I wish you had come three months ago, and then you would ha
ve found us all joyous and delighted.
         >>>> Dates
             three months ago

         [9] ... who seems sinking under his misfortune; and your pers
uasions will induce poor Elizabeth to cease her ...
         >>>> Names
             Elizabeth


         ...
```

This output shows the results of fetching the top paragraphs that mention "three months" as a phrase (four paragraphs in all) along with a few examples of the sentences in the paragraph, as well as lists of any names, dates, or locations in that text. In this example, you can see samples of the sentence detection as well as the extraction of names, locations, and dates. A keen eye will also notice a few places where the simple system is clearly wrong. For instance, the system thinks *Ah* is a name, but that *Ernest* isn't. It also failed to split the text ending in "... said he. "Ah!" into separate sentences. Perhaps our system doesn't know how to properly handle exclamation points or there was some odd formatting in the text.

For now, we'll wave our hands as to why these failed. If you explore further with other queries, you'll likely find plenty of the good, bad, and even the ugly in processing text. This example makes for a nice segue into our next section, which will touch on some of these difficulties in processing text as well as serve as motivation for many of the approaches we take in the book.

## 1.3  *Understanding text is hard*

Suppose Robin and Joe are talking, and Joe states, "The bank on the left is solid, but the one on the right is crumbling." What are Robin and Joe talking about? Are they on Wall Street looking at the offices of two financial institutions, or are they floating down the Mississippi River looking for a place to land their canoe? If you assume the former, the words *solid* and *crumbling* probably refer to the state of the banks' finances, whereas the latter case is an assessment of the quality of the ground on the side of a river. Now, what if you replaced the characters' names with the names *Huck* and *Tom* from *The Adventures of Tom Sawyer*? You'd likely feel pretty confident in stating it's a river bank and not a financial institution, right? As you can see, context is also important. It's often the case that only with more information from the surrounding context combined with your own experiences can you truly know what some piece of content is about. The ambiguity in Joe's statement only touches on the surface of the complexity involved in understanding text.

Given well-written, coherent sentences and paragraphs, knowledgeable people seamlessly look up the meanings of words and incorporate their experiences and knowledge of their surroundings to arrive at an understanding of content and conversations. Literate adults can (more or less) effortlessly dissect sentences, identify relationships, and infer meaning nearly instantaneously. And, as in the Robin and Joe example, people are almost always aware when something is significantly out of place or lacking from a sentence, paragraph, or document as a whole. Human beings also feed off others in conversation, instantly adapting tone and emotions to convey thoughts on subjects ranging from the weather to politics to the role of the designated hitter. Though we often take these skills for granted, we should remember that they have been fine-tuned through many years of conversation, education, and feedback from others, not to mention all the knowledge passed down from our ancestors.

At the same time, computers and the fields of information retrieval (IR) and natural language processing (NLP) are still relatively young. Computers need to be capable of processing language on many different levels in order to come close to "understanding" content like people do. (For an in-depth discussion of the many factors that go into NLP, see Liddy [2001].) Though full understanding is a tall order for a computer, even doing basic tasks can be overwhelming given the sheer volume of text available and the variety with which it occurs.

There's a reason the saying goes "the numbers don't lie" and not "the text doesn't lie"; text comes in all shapes and meanings and trips up even the smartest people on a regular basis. Writing applications to process text can mean facing a number of technical and nontechnical challenges. Table 1.2 outlines some of the challenges text applications face, each row increasing in difficulty from the previous.

**Table 1.1  Processing text presents challenges at many levels, from handling character encodings to inferring meaning in the context of the world around us.**

| Level | Challenges |
|---|---|
| Character | – Character encodings, such as ASCII, Shift-JIS, Big 5, Latin-1, UTF-8, UTF-16.<br>– Case (upper and lower), punctuation, accents, and numbers all require different treatments in different applications. |
| Words and morphemes[a] | – Word segmentation: dividing text into words. Fairly easy for English and other languages that use whitespace; much harder for languages like Chinese and Japanese.<br>– Assigning part of speech.<br>– Identifying synonyms; synonyms are useful for searching.<br>– Stemming: the process of shortening a word to its base or root form. For example, a simple stemming of *words* is *word*.<br>– Abbreviations, acronyms, and spelling also play important roles in understanding words. |
| Multiword and sentence | – Phrase detection: *quick red fox*, *hockey legend Bobby Orr*, and *big brown shoe* are all examples of phrases.<br>– Parsing: breaking sentences down into subject-verb and other relationships often yields useful information about words and their relationships to each other.<br>– Sentence boundary detection is a well-understood problem in English, but is still not perfect.<br>– Coreference resolution: "Jason likes dogs, but he would never buy one." In this example, *he* is a coreference to Jason. The need for coreference resolution can also span sentences.<br>– Words often have multiple meanings; using the context of a sentence or more may help choose the correct word. This process is called *word sense disambiguation* and is difficult to do well.<br>– Combining the definitions of words and their relationships to each other to determine the meaning of a sentence. |
| Multisentence and paragraph | At this level, processing becomes more difficult in an effort to find deeper understanding of an author's intent. Algorithms for summarization often require being able to identify which sentences are more important than others. |
| Document | Similar to the paragraph level, understanding the meaning of a document often requires knowledge that goes beyond what's contained in the actual document. Authors often expect readers to have a certain background or possess certain reading skills. For example, most of this book won't make much sense if you've never used a computer and done some programming, whereas most newspapers assume at least a sixth-grade reading level. |
| Multidocument and corpus | At this level, people want to quickly find items of interest as well as group related documents and read summaries of those documents. Applications that can aggregate and organize facts and opinions and find relationships are particularly useful. |

a. A *morpheme* is a small linguistic unit that still has meaning. Prefixes and suffixes are examples of morphemes.

Beyond these challenges, human factors also play a role in working with text. Different cultures, different languages, and different interpretations of the same writing can leave even the best engineer wondering what to implement. Merely looking at some sample files and trying to extrapolate an approach for a whole collection of documents is often problematic. On the other side of the coin, manually analyzing and annotating large sets of documents can be expensive and time consuming. But rest assured that help is available and text can be tamed.

## 1.4    *Text, tamed*

Now that you've seen some of the challenges you're about to face, take heart knowing that many tools exist both commercially and in the open source community (see http://www.opensource.org) to tackle these topics and many more. One of the great things about the journey you're embarking on is its ever-changing and ever-improving nature. Problems that were intractable 10 years ago due to resource limits are now yielding positive results thanks to better algorithms, faster CPUs, cheaper memory, cheaper disk space, and tools for easily harnessing many computers into a single virtual CPU. Now, more than ever, quality open source tools exist that can form the foundation for new ideas and new applications.

This book is written to bring real-world experience to these open source tools and introduce you to the fields of natural language processing and information retrieval. We can't possibly cover all aspects of NLP and IR nor are we going to discuss bleeding-edge research, at least not until the end of the book; instead we'll focus on areas that are likely to have the biggest impact in taming your text.

By focusing on topics like search, *entity identification* (finding people, places, and things), grouping and labeling, clustering, and summarization, we can build practical applications that help users find and understand the important parts of their text quickly and easily.

Though we hate to be a buzzkill on all the excitement of taming text, it's important to note that there are no perfect approaches in working with text. Many times, two people reviewing the same output won't agree on the correctness of the results, nor will it be obvious what to fix to satisfy them. Furthermore, fixing one problem may expose other problems. Testing and analysis are as important as ever to achieving quality results. Ultimately, the best systems take a human-in-the-loop approach and learn from user feedback where possible, just as smart people learn from their mistakes and from their peers. The user feedback need not be explicit, either. Capturing clicks, and analyzing logs and other user behaviors can provide valuable feedback on how your users are utilizing your application. With that in mind, here are some general tips for improving your application and keeping your sanity:

- Get to know your users. Do they care about certain structures like tables and lists, or is it enough to collect all the words in a document? Are they willing to give you more information in return for better results, or is simplicity the rule? Are they willing to wait longer for better results, or do they need a best guess immediately?

- Get to know your content. What file formats (HTML, Microsoft Word, PDF, text) are used? What structures and features are important? Does the text contain a lot of jargon, abbreviations, or different ways of saying the same thing? Is the content focused on a single area of interest or does it cover a number of topics?
- Test, test, and test some more. Take the time (but not too much time) to measure the quality of your results and the cost of obtaining them. Become practiced in the art of arbitration. Every nontrivial text-based application will need to make trade-offs in regards to quality and scalability. By combining your knowledge of your users and your content, you can often find the sweet spot of quality and performance that satisfies most people most of the time.
- Sometimes, a best guess is as good as it gets. Look for ways to provide confidence levels to your users so they can make an informed decision about your response.
- All else being equal, favor the simpler approach. Moreover, you'll be amazed at how good simple solutions can be at getting decent results.

Also, though working in non-native languages is an interesting problem in itself, we'll stick to English for this book. Rest assured that many of the approaches can be applied to other languages given the right resources.

It should also be pointed out that the kinds of problems you might wish to solve range in difficulty from relatively straightforward to so hard you might as well flip a coin. For instance, in English and other European languages, tokenization and part of speech tagging algorithms perform well, whereas tools like machine translation of foreign languages, sentiment analysis, and reasoning from text are much more difficult and often don't perform well in unconstrained environments.

Finally, text processing is much like riding a roller coaster. There will be highs when your application can do no wrong and lows when your application can do no right. The fact is that none of the approaches discussed in this book or in the broader field of NLP are the final solution to the problem. Therein lies the ultimate opportunity for you to dig in and add your signature. So let's get started and lay the foundation for the ideas to come in later chapters by setting the context that takes us beyond search into the wonderful world of natural language processing.

## 1.5 *Text and the intelligent app: search and beyond*

For many years now, search has been king. Without the likes of Google and Yahoo!, there's no doubt that the internet wouldn't be anywhere near what it is today. Yet, with the rise of good open source search tools like Apache Solr and Apache Lucene, along with a myriad of crawlers and distributed processing techniques, search is a commodity, at least on the smaller scale of personal and corporate search where huge data centers aren't required. At the same time, people's expectations of search engines are increasing. We want better results in less time while entering only one or two keywords. We also want our own content easily searched and organized.

Furthermore, corporations are under huge pressure to constantly add value. Every time some big player like Google or Amazon makes a move to better access information, the bar is raised for the rest of us. Five, ten, or fifteen years ago, it was enough to add search capabilities to be able to find data; now search is a prerequisite and the game-changing players use complex algorithms utilizing machine learning and deep statistical analysis to work with volumes of data that would take people years to understand. This is the evolution of the intelligent application. More and more companies are adopting machine learning and deep text analysis in well-defined areas to bring more intelligence to their applications.

The adoption of machine learning and NLP techniques is grounded in the reality of practical applications dealing with large volumes of data, and not the grandiose, albeit worthwhile, notion of machines "understanding" people or somehow passing the Turing Test (see http://en.wikipedia.org/wiki/Turing_Test). These companies are focused on finding and extracting important text features; aggregating information like user clicks, ratings, and reviews; grouping and summarizing similar content; and, finally, displaying all of these features in ways that allow end users to better find and use the content, which should ultimately lead to more purchases or traffic or whatever is the objective. After all, you can't buy something if you can't find it, right?

So, how do you get started doing all of these great things? You start by establishing the baseline with search (covered in chapter 3) and then examine ways of automatically organizing content using concepts that you employ in your daily life. Instead of doing it manually, you let the machine do it for you (with a little help when needed). With that in mind, the next few sections break down the ideas of search and organizing content into three distinct areas and propose an example that ties many of the concepts together, which will be explored more completely in the ensuing chapters.

### 1.5.1  *Searching and matching*

Search provides the starting point for most of your text taming activities, including our proposed QA system, where you'll rely on it both for indexing the input data as well as for identifying candidate passages that match a user's question. Even when you need to apply techniques that go beyond search, you'll likely use search to find the subset of text or documents on which to apply more advanced techniques.

In chapter 3, "Searching," we'll explore how to make documents available for searching, indexing, and how to retrieve documents based on a query. We'll also explore how documents are ranked by a search engine and use this information to improve the returned results. Finally, we'll examine faceted search, which allows searches to be refined by limiting results to a predefined category. The coverage of these topics will be grounded in examples using Apache Solr and Apache Lucene.

After you're familiar with the techniques of search, you'll quickly realize that search is only as good as the content backing that search. If the words and phrases that your users are looking for aren't in your index, then you won't be able to return a relevant result. In chapter 4, "Fuzzy string matching," we'll look at techniques for enabling query recommendations based on the content that's available via query spell-checking as well as how these same techniques can be applied to database- or record-linking tasks that go beyond simple database joins. These techniques are often used not only as part of search, but also for more complex things like identifying whether two user profiles are the same person, as might happen when two companies merge and their customer lists must be combined.

### 1.5.2    Extracting information

Though search will help you find documents that contain the information you need, often you need to be able to identify smaller units of information. For instance, the ability to identify proper names in a large collection of text can be immensely helpful in tracking down criminal activity or finding relationships between people who might not otherwise meet. To do this we'll explore techniques for identifying and classifying small selections of text, typically just a few words in length.

In chapter 2, "Foundations of taming text," we'll introduce techniques for identifying words that form a linguistic unit such as noun phrases, which can be used to identify words in a document or query which can be grouped together. In chapter 5, "Identifying people, places, and things," we'll look at how to identify proper names and numeric phrases and put them into semantic categories such as person, location, and date, irrespective of their linguistic usage. This ability will be fundamental to your ability to build a QA system in chapter 8. For both of these tasks we'll use the capabilities of OpenNLP and explore how to use its existing models as well as build new models that better fit the data. Unlike the problem of searching and matching, these models will be built from examining manually annotated content and then using statistical machine learning approaches to produce a model.

### 1.5.3    Grouping information

The flip side to extracting information from text is adding supplemental information to your text by grouping it together or adding labels. For example, think about how much easier it would be to process your email if it were automatically tagged and prioritized so that you could also find all emails that are similar to one another. This way, you could focus in on just those emails that require your immediate attention as well as find supporting content for emails you're sending.

One common approach to this is to group your text into categories. As it turns out, the techniques used for extracting information can also be applied to grouping text or documents into categories. These groups can often then be used as facets in your search index, supplemental keywords, or as an alternate way for users to navigate information. Even in cases where your users are providing the categories via tagging, these techniques can recommend tags that have been used in the past. Chapter 7, "Classification, categorization, and tagging," shows how to build models to classify documents and how to apply these models to new documents to improve user experience with text.

When you've tamed your text and are able to find what you're looking for, and you've extracted the information needed, you may find you have too much of a good thing. In chapter 6, "Clustering text," we'll look at how to group similar information. These techniques can be used to identify redundant information and, if necessary, suppress it. They can also be used to group similar documents so that a user can peruse entire topics at a time and access the relevancy of multiple documents at once without having to read each document.

### 1.5.4  An intelligent application

In our penultimate chapter, "Building an example question answering system," we'll bring a number of the approaches described in the early chapters together to build an intelligent application. Specifically, you'll build a fact-based question answering system designed to find answers to trivia-like questions in text. For instance, given the right content, you should be able to answer questions like, "Who is the President of the United States?" This system uses the techniques of chapter 3, "Searching," to identify text that might contain the answer to your question. The approaches presented in chapter 5, "Identifying people, places, and things," will be used to find these pieces of text that are often the answers to fact-based questions. The material in chapter 2, "Foundations of taming text," and chapter 7, "Classification, categorization, and tagging," will be used to analyze the question being asked, and determine what type of information the question is looking for. Finally, you'll apply the techniques for document ranking described in chapter 3 to rank your answers.

## 1.6  Summary

Taming text is a large and sometimes overwhelming task, further complicated by different languages, different dialects, and different interpretations. Text can appear as elegant prose written by great authors or the ugliest of essays written without style or substance. Whatever its form, text is everywhere and it must be dealt with by people and programs. Luckily, many tools exist both commercially and in open source to help try to make sense of it all. It won't be perfect, but it's getting better all the time. So far, we've taken a look at some of the reasons why text is so important as well as hard to process. We've also looked at what role text plays in the intelligent web, introduced the topics we'll cover, and gave a brief overview of some of the things needed to build a simple question answering system. In the next chapter, we'll kick things off by laying down the foundations of text analysis along with some basics on extracting raw text from the many file formats found in the wild today.

## 1.7  Resources

"Americans Spend Half of Their Spare Time Online." 2007. Media-Screen LLC. http://www.media-screen.com/press050707.html.

Feldman, Susan. 2009. "Hidden Costs of Information Work: A Progress Report." International Data Corporation.

Gantz, John F. and Reinsel, David. 2011. "Extracting Value from Chaos." International Data Corporation. http://www.emc.com/collateral/analyst-reports/idc-extracting-value-from-chaos-ar.pdf.

Liddy, Elizabeth. 2001. "Natural Language Processing." *Encyclopedia of Library and Information Science, 2nd Ed.* NY. Marcel Decker, Inc.

"Trends in Consumers' Time Spent with Media." 2010. eMarketer. http://www.emarketer.com/Article.aspx?R=1008138.

# Foundations of
# taming text

## In this chapter

- Understanding text processing building blocks like tokenizing, chunking, parsing, and part of speech tagging
- Extracting text from common file formats using the Apache Tika open source project

Naturally, before we can get started with the hard-core text-taming processes, we need a little warm-up first. We'll start by laying the ground work with a short high school English refresher where we'll delve into topics such as tokenization, stemming, parts of speech, and phrases and clauses. Each of these steps can play an important role in the quality of results you'll see when building applications utilizing text. For instance, the seemingly simple act of splitting up words, especially in languages like Chinese, can be difficult. Even in English, dealing with punctuation appropriately can make tokenization hard. Likewise, identifying parts of speech and phrases in text can also be difficult due to the ambiguity inherent in language.

We'll follow up the discussion on language foundations by looking at how to extract text from the many different file formats encountered in the wild. Though many books and papers wave their hands at content extraction, assuming users

16

have plain text ready to go, we feel it's important to investigate some of the issues involved with content extraction for several reasons:

- Text is often hard to extract from proprietary formats. Even commercial extraction tools often fail at extracting the proper content.
- In the real world, you'll spend a fair amount of time looking at various file formats and extraction tools and trying to figure out what's right. Real-world data rarely comes in simple string packages. It'll have strange formatting, random out-of-place characters, and other problems that will make you want to pull your hair out.
- Your downstream processing will only be as good as your input data. The old saying "garbage in, garbage out" is as true here as it is anywhere.

In the last part of this chapter, after you've refreshed your English knowledge and extracted content, we'll look at some foundational pieces that will make life easier for your applications and libraries. Without further ado, let's look at some language basics like how to identify words and how to separate them into useful structures like sentences, noun phrases, and possibly full parse trees.

## 2.1 Foundations of language

Are you pining for the good old days of grammar school? Perhaps you miss high school English class and diagramming sentences, identifying subject-verb relationships, and watching out for dangling modifiers. Well, you're in luck, because part of text analysis is recalling the basics of high school English and beyond. Kidding aside, the next few sections build the foundation you need for the applications we're discussing by taking a look at common issues that need to be addressed in order to analyze text. By explicitly building this foundation, we can establish a shared vocabulary that will make it easier to explain concepts later, as well as encourage thinking about the features and function of language and how to harness them in an application. For instance, when you build your QA system later in chapter 8, you'll need the ability to split raw strings up into individual words and then you'll need to understand what role each of those words plays in the sentence (part of speech) as well as how they relate to each other via things like phrases and clauses. Given this kind of information, you'll then be able take in a question like "Who is Bob's uncle?" and dissect it to know that the question requires the answer to be a proper name (which consists of words that have been tagged as nouns) and that it must occur in the same sentence as the words *Bob* and *uncle* (and likely in that order). Though we take these things for granted, the computer must be told to look for these attributes. And though some applications will need all of these building blocks, many others will only need one or two. Some applications will explicitly state their usage, whereas others won't. In the long run, the more you know about how language works, the better off you'll be in assessing the trade-offs inherent in any text analysis system.

In the first section, we'll describe the various categories of words and word groupings, and look at how words are combined to form sentences. Our brief introduction to the area known in linguistics as *syntax* will focus on the topics that we'll refer to later in the book. In the second section, we'll look inside the words themselves, called *morphology*. Though we won't be using morphology explicitly in this book, our basic introduction will help you understand some of the techniques we'll present. Finally, though syntax and morphology are studied as systems that can be applied to all spoken or natural languages, we'll limit our focus and examples to English.

### 2.1.1 Words and their categories

Words fall into a small number of lexical categories, or parts of speech. These categories include nouns, verbs, adjectives, determiners, prepositions, and conjunctions. Though you've probably been exposed to these categories at various points, you may not have seen them all at once or remember exactly what they mean. Basic familiarity with these concepts will be useful in upcoming chapters as we explore techniques that use these categories directly or at least are informed by them. Table 2.1 contains a chart of the basic lexical categories, a definition, and an example, after which we'll go into some additional details about these high-level categories.

**Table 2.1   Definitions and examples of commonly occurring lexical categories**

| Lexical categories | Definition[a] | Example (in *italics*) |
|---|---|---|
| Adjective | A word or phrase naming an attribute, added to or grammatically related to a noun to modify or describe it. | The *quick red* fox jumped over the *lazy brown* dogs. |
| Adverb | A word or phrase that modifies or qualifies an adjective, verb, or other adverb or a word group, expressing a relation of place, time, circumstance, manner, cause, degree, etc. | The dogs *lazily* ran down the field after the fox. |
| Conjunction | A word that joins together two words, phrases, or clauses. | The quick red fox *and* the silver coyote jumped over the lazy brown dogs. |
| Determiner | A modifying word that determines the kind of reference a noun or noun group has, for example *a*, *the*, *every*. | *The* quick red fox jumped over *the* lazy brown dogs. |
| Noun | A word used to identify any of a class of people, places, or things, or to name a particular one of these. | The quick red *fox* jumped over the lazy brown *dogs*. |
| Preposition | A word governing, and usually preceding, a noun or pronoun and expressing a relation to another word or element in the clause. | The quick red fox jumped *over* the lazy brown dogs. |
| Verb | A word used to describe an action, state, or occurrence, and forming the main part of the predicate of a sentence, such as *hear*, *become*, and *happen*. | The quick red fox *jumped* over the lazy brown dogs. |

a. All definitions are taken from the New Oxford American Dictionary, 2nd Edition.

These lexical categories are based on their syntactic usage rather than their meaning, but because some semantic concepts are more likely to be expressed with a particular syntactic construction, they're often defined based on these semantic associations. For instance, a noun is often defined as a person, place, or thing, or a verb as an action, but we use nouns such as *destruction* or usages of the verb *be*, as in "Judy is 12 years old," which don't convey the typical semantic relationships associated with nouns and verbs.

These high-level categories often have more specific subcategories, some of which will be used later in this book. Nouns are further classified into common nouns, proper nouns, and pronouns. Common nouns usually describe a class of entities such as *town*, *ocean*, or *person* and are distinguished from proper nouns, which represent unique entities and are typically capitalized such as *London, John,* or *Eiffel Tower*. Pronouns are nouns that reference other entities, usually mentioned previously, and include words such as *he*, *she*, and *it*. Many of the other lexical categories also contain subcategories and there are even additional subcategories of nouns, but these will be sufficient for the topics covered here. Additional information on these topics can be found in the many good references on grammar and language available by searching the web, and specifically Wikipedia, or from reading references like *The Chicago Manual of Style* or listening to podcasts like Grammar Girl (http://grammar.quickanddirtytips.com/).

### 2.1.2 *Phrases and clauses*

Most of the lexical categories for words listed in the previous section have corresponding structures for phrases that can consist of multiple words. The phrases are rooted by at least one word of a particular type, but can also consist of words and phrases of other types. For example the noun phrase *the happy girl* consists of a determiner (the) and an adjective (happy), and is rooted by the common noun *girl*. Examples of each of these phrases is shown in table 2.2.

**Table 2.2  Examples of commonly occurring phrasal categories**

| Phrasal types | Example (in *Italics*) | Comment |
|---|---|---|
| Adjective | The *unusually red* fox jumped over the *exceptionally lazy* dogs. | The adverbs *unusually* and *exceptionally* modify the adjectives *red* and *lazy*, respectively, to create adjectival phrases. |
| Adverb | The dogs *almost always* ran down the field after the fox. | The adverb *almost* modifies the adverb *always* to create an adverbial phrase. |
| Conjunction | The quick red fox *as well as* the silver coyote jumped over the lazy brown dogs. | Though this is somewhat of an exceptional case, you can see that the multiword phrase *as well as* performs the same function as a conjunction such as *and*. |
| Noun | The *quick red fox* jumped over *the lazy brown dogs*. | The noun *fox* and its modifiers *the*, *quick*, and *red* create a noun phrase, as does the noun *dogs* and its modifiers *the*, *lazy*, and *brown*. |

**Table 2.2   Examples of commonly occurring phrasal categories (continued)**

| Phrasal types | Example (in *Italics*) | Comment |
|---|---|---|
| Preposition | The quick red fox jumped *over the lazy brown dogs.* | The preposition *over* and the noun phrase *the lazy brown dogs* form a prepositional phrase that modifies the verb *jumped.* |
| Verb | The quick red fox *jumped over the lazy brown dogs.* | The verb *jumped* and its modifier the prepositional phrase *over the lazy brown dogs* form a verb phrase. |

Phrases can be combined together to form clauses, which are the minimal unit needed to construct a sentence. Clauses minimally consist of a noun phrase (the subject) and a verb phrase (the predicate), which often consists of a verb and another noun phrase. The phrase *The fox jumped the fence* is a clause consisting of the noun phrase, *The fox* (the subject), and the verb phrase, *jumped the fence,* which consists of the noun phrase, *the fence* (the object), and the verb *jumped.* The other types of phrases can optionally be added to the sentence to express other relationships. With these components, you can see that any sentence could be decomposed into a set of clauses, and those into sets of phrases, and those into sets of words with particular parts of speech. The task of determining the parts of speech, phrases, clauses, and their relationship to one another is called *parsing.* You may have performed this syntactic analysis yourself if you ever diagrammed a sentence. Later in this chapter we'll examine software that performs these tasks.

### 2.1.3   *Morphology*

*Morphology* is the study of the internal structure of words. In most languages, words consist of a *lexeme,* or root form, and various affixes (prefix, suffix) that mark the word based on how it's being used. In English, words are marked primarily with suffixes and the rules for these are based on the word's lexical category.

Common and proper nouns in English are inflected for number, and have two distinct forms, singular and plural. Singular nouns consist of a root form and plural nouns are usually marked with *s* at the end. Though common and proper nouns only consist of two forms, pronouns vary based on number, person, case, and gender. Pronouns, though, are a closed class of words, with only 34 distinct forms, so it's typically easier to enumerate them rather than modeling their morphological structure. Nouns that are derived from other lexical categories also contain suffixes marking these transformations. For nouns based on verbs or adjectives, these include the following suffixes, as described in tables 2.3 and 2.4.

Verbs have a more complex system of morphology consisting of eight possible inflected forms, but all regular verbs only contain four distinct forms. A number of irregular verbs can also be used with an *en* suffix when used as a past participle instead of the regular *ed* ending for this form. These forms are shown in table 2.5. The remaining three forms are only lexicalized distinctly for a few irregular verbs and don't use a common suffix.

Adjectives and adverbs can be marked for comparison and have a comparative and superlative form. The base form adjective *tall* can be inflected as comparative with the *-er* suffix to produce *taller* or as superlative with the *-est* suffix to produce *tallest*. Likewise, an adverb such as *near* can also be inflected as comparative with the *-er* suffix to produce *nearer* or as superlative with the *-est* suffix to produce *nearest*.

With a basic understanding of the relationships between words and the structure of the words themselves, we can get right to work on using software that uses these distinctions to tame text.

**Table 2.3  Examples of noun morphology when the noun is based on a verb**

| Suffix | Example | Verb |
|--------|---------|------|
| -ation | nomination | nominate |
| -ee | appointee | appoint |
| -ure | closure | close |
| -al | refusal | refuse |
| -er | runner | run |
| -ment | advertisement | advertise |

**Table 2.4  Examples of noun morphology when the noun is based on an adjective**

| Suffix | Example | Adjective |
|--------|---------|-----------|
| -dom | freedom | free |
| -hood | likelihood | likely |
| -ist | realist | real |
| -th | warmth | warm |
| -ness | happiness | happy |

**Table 2.5  Examples of regular verb morphology and common past participle ending for irregular verbs**

| Suffix | Example | Marked form |
|--------|---------|-------------|
| none | look | Base form |
| -ing | looking | Gerund form |
| -s | looks | Third person singular form |
| -ed | looked | Past tense form |
| -en | taken | Past participle form |

## 2.2  Common tools for text processing

Now that you have a basic understanding of the syntax and semantics of language, let's take a look at some tools to help you identify these and other important things in digital text. Some of these tools will be used all of the time, whereas others will only be used on occasion. The following sections start off with basics like string manipulation and then continue on to more complicated items such as full sentence parsing. Generally speaking, the basics will be used every day, whereas more complicated tools like full language parsers may only be used in certain applications.

### 2.2.1  String manipulation tools

Libraries for working with strings, character arrays, and other text representations form the basis of most text-based programs. Most programming languages contain libraries for doing basic operations like concatenation, splitting, substring search, and a variety of methods for comparing two strings. Learning a regular expression library like Java's `java.util.regex` package will further your capabilities (see *Mastering*

*Regular Expressions* by Jeffrey Friedl for a full accounting of regular expressions). It'll also pay to be intimately familiar with the `String`, `Character`, and `StringBuilder` classes, as well as the `java.text` package. With these tools, you can easily capture surface-level distinctions in text such as whether a word is capitalized, the length of a word, or whether it contains a number or non-alphanumeric character. Additionally, being familiar with parsing dates and numbers is also useful. In chapter 4, we'll look in greater detail at algorithms designed for working with strings. For now, let's consider attributes of text that are more linguistically motivated.

### 2.2.2 *Tokens and tokenization*

The first step after extracting content from a file is almost always to break the content up into small, usable chunks of text, called *tokens*. Tokens often represent single words, but as you'll soon see, what constitutes a small, usable chunk can be specific to an application. The most common first approach to tokenizing English is to split up a string based on the occurrence of whitespace such as spaces and line breaks, as in this simple tokenizer: `String[] result = input.split("\\s+");`. In this simplistic example, the input `String` is split into an array of `Strings` using the regular expression `\s+` (note that Java requires the escaping of the backslash), which breaks on whitespace. Though this approach mostly works, running this code on a sample sentence like

```
I can't believe that the Carolina Hurricanes won the 2005-2006 Stanley
Cup.
```

yields the tokens in table 2.6. You'd be correct in thinking the period at the end of the word *Cup* could be problematic.

**Table 2.6  Sentence split by whitespace**

| I | can't | believe | that | the | Carolina | Hurricanes | won | the | 2005-2006 | Stanley | Cup. |
|---|-------|---------|------|-----|----------|------------|-----|-----|-----------|---------|------|

Though splitting on whitespace works in some instances, most applications will need to handle punctuation, acronyms, email addresses, URLs, and numbers in order to provide the most benefit. Additionally, different applications often will have different tokenization requirements. For instance, in the Apache Solr/Lucene search library (covered in chapter 3), the `StandardTokenizer` accounts for commonly occurring items like punctuation and acronyms. In fact, running the preceding sentence about the Hurricanes through the `StandardTokenizer` drops the ending period, giving you the tokens shown in table 2.7.

**Table 2.7  Sentence split by Solr `StandardTokenizer`**

| I | can't | believe | that | the | Carolina | Hurricanes | won | the | 2005 | 2006 | Stanley | Cup |
|---|-------|---------|------|-----|----------|------------|-----|-----|------|------|---------|-----|

Now you might be thinking, "I didn't want to get rid of the period; I just didn't want it attached to *Cup*." This is a valid point and one that underscores the importance of thinking about what your tokenization needs are for your application. Since a search application like Lucene doesn't need sentence-ending periods in most cases, it's fine to drop them from the token results in this case.

For other types of applications, different tokenizations may be required. Processing the same sentence using OpenNLP's `english.Tokenizer` produces table 2.8.

**Table 2.8　Sentence split by OpenNLP `english.Tokenizer`**

| I | ca | n't | believe | that | the | Carolina | Hurricanes | won | the | 2005-2006 | Stanley | Cup | . |
|---|----|-----|---------|------|-----|----------|------------|-----|-----|-----------|---------|-----|---|

Note here that the punctuation is maintained and the contraction *can't* has been split up. In this case, OpenNLP is using tokenization as a precursor to performing grammatical processing. For this type of application, punctuation is useful for helping identify clause boundaries and *can* and *not* have distinct grammatical roles.

If you look at another type of processing available in OpenNLP and used for named-entity identification (discussed in chapter 5), you see another type of tokenization. Here the approach is to split strings up via token class: alphabetic, numeric, whitespace, and other. The output of the `SimpleTokenizer` for the same sentence is shown in table 2.9.

**Table 2.9　Sentence split by OpenNLP `SimpleTokenizer`**

| I | can | ' | t | believe | that | the | Carolina | Hurricanes | won | the | 2005 | - | 2006 | Stanley | Cup | . |
|---|-----|---|---|---------|------|-----|----------|------------|-----|-----|------|---|------|---------|-----|---|

In this example, you see that the date range has been split up. This allows the named-entity component to identify each of the dates in the date range individually as is required by this application.

As you saw earlier, tokenization decisions are influenced by what task is being performed. The unit of text that's appropriate for the task is influenced by the types of processing that will be performed on the text. Luckily, most libraries will provide tokenization capabilities that preserve what is needed for later processing or will provide a means for using your own tokenizer.

Other common techniques applied at the token level include these:

- *Case alterations*—Lowercasing all tokens can be helpful in searching.
- *Stopword removal*—Filtering out common words like *the, and,* and *a.* Commonly occurring words like these often add little value (note we didn't say *no* value) to applications that don't rely on sentence structure.
- *Expansion*—Adding synonyms or expanding acronyms and abbreviations in a token stream can allow applications to handle alternative inputs from users.
- *Part of speech tagging*—Assigning the part of speech to a token. Covered in more detail in the following section.
- *Stemming*—Reducing a word to a root or base form, for example, *dogs* to *dog.* Covered in more detail in section 2.2.4.

We'll skip over the simple cases of stopword removal, expansion, and case alterations as these are basic operations, usually involving simple lookups in a `Map` or basic method calls on a `String` object. In the next two sections, we'll cover part of speech tagging and stemming in more detail, before moving beyond the word to the sentence level.

### 2.2.3 *Part of speech assignment*

Identifying a word's part of speech (POS), such as whether it's a noun, verb, or adjective, is commonly used to enhance the quality of results in downstream processing. For instance, using part of speech can help determine what the important keywords are in a document (see Mihalcea [2004], among other examples) or to assist in searching for specific usages of a word (such as *Will* as a proper noun versus *will* the modal verb, as in "you will regret that"). There are many readily available, trainable part of speech taggers available in the open source community. One such tagger is the OpenNLP Maximum Entropy Tagger, available at http://opennlp.apache.org/. Don't worry too much about the phrase *maximum entropy*; it's just a way of saying it uses statistics to figure out which part of speech is most likely for a word. The OpenNLP English POS tagger uses part of speech tags from the Penn Treebank Project (http://www.cis.upenn.edu/~treebank) to label words in sentences with their part of speech. Table 2.10 has a sampling of the more common tags used in Penn Treebank. Many of these tags have related tags to mark the many different forms of a word, such as past and present tenses, and singular versus plural. For a complete listing, see http://repository.upenn.edu/cgi/viewcontent.cgi?article=1603&context=cis_reports.

**Table 2.10  Definitions and examples of commonly occurring parts of speech**

| Parts of speech | Penn Treebank tag name | Examples |
|---|---|---|
| Adjective, superlative adjective, comparative adjective | JJ, JJS, JJR | nice, nicest, nicer |
| Adverb, superlative adverb, comparative adverb | RB, RBR, RBS | early, earliest, earlier |
| Determiner | DT | a/the |
| Noun, plural noun, proper noun, plural proper noun | NN, NNS, NNP, NNPS | house, houses, London, Teamsters |
| Personal pronoun, possessive pronoun | PRP, PRP$ | he/she/it/himself, his/her/its |
| Infinitive verb, past-tense verb, past-participle verb, present-tense third person singular verb, present-tense other than third person verb, gerund or present participle verb | VB, VBD, VBN, VBZ, VBP, VBG | be, was, been, is, am, being |

Now that you're familiar with some of the POS tags we'll encounter, let's look at how the OpenNLP POS tagger works. The POS tagger works using a statistical model built by examining a *corpus*, or collection, of documents that have already been marked with POS tags. This model contains data to calculate the probability that a word has a certain part of speech. Luckily, you don't have to create the model (although you could); one has been provided for you. The next listing demonstrates how to load the model and related information and run the POS tagger.

**Listing 2.1  OpenNLP POS tagger example**

```
File posModelFile = new File(                          ⟵── Give path to POS model.
    getModelDir(), "en-pos-maxent.bin");
FileInputStream posModelStream = new FileInputStream(posModelFile);
POSModel model = new POSModel(posModelStream);

POSTaggerME tagger = new POSTaggerME(model);          │ Tokenize sentence
String[] words = SimpleTokenizer.INSTANCE.tokenize(   ⟵┘ into words.
    "The quick, red fox jumped over the lazy, brown dogs.");
String[] result = tagger.tag(words);                  ⟵┐ Pass in tokenized
for (int i=0 ; i < words.length; i++) {                │ sentence to be
  System.err.print(words[i] + "/" + result[i] + " ");  │ tagged.
}
System.err.println("n");
```

The output from running listing 2.1 is the following:

```
The/DT quick/JJ ,/, red/JJ fox/NN jumped/VBD over/IN the/DT lazy/JJ ,/,
brown/JJ dogs/NNS ./.
```

A quick check shows reasonable output: *dogs* and *fox* are nouns; *quick, red, lazy,* and *brown* are adjectives; and *jumped* is a verb. For now, that's all you need to know about part of speech tagging, although we'll revisit it in later sections and chapters.

### 2.2.4  *Stemming*

Imagine it's your job to read all the newspapers in your country (hope you've got coffee!) watching for articles on banks. So you get a search engine and you feed it all your newspapers and then you begin to search for bank, banks, banking, banker, banked, and so on. Being short on time, you think, "Gee, I wish I could just search for *bank* and it would find all the variations," and like that you realize the power of stemming (and synonyms, but that's a different topic). *Stemming* is the process of reducing a word to a root, or simpler form, which isn't necessarily a word on its own. Stemming is often used in text processing applications like search because users usually expect to find documents on banking when searching for the word *bank*. In most cases, users don't need an exact match for their keywords, unless they tell you otherwise.

There are many different approaches to stemming, each with their own design goals. Some are aggressive, reducing words to the smallest root possible, whereas others are lighter, preferring to do basic things like removing *s* or *ing* from words. The trade-off in search, for example, is almost always the classic match-up of quality versus quantity. Aggressive stemming usually leads to more results but lower quality, whereas light stemming can preserve some quality at the risk of missing some useful results. Stemming can also cause problems where words with different meanings are reduced to the same stem, thus losing the meaning, while other words that are related aren't reduced to the same stem (see Krovetz [1993]).

How should you pick a stemmer and when should you use one? As with most NLP applications, it depends. Running tests, making empirical judgments, and some trial and error will ultimately lead to the best practical answers to those questions. In the end, the best advice is to make it easy to change stemmers by coding to an interface. Then, start with a light stemmer and try to gather feedback from your testers or users. If your users think they're missing out on the variations, then you can stem more aggressively.

Now that you know some of the reasons to use stemming, let's look at using the Snowball stemmers (http://snowball.tartarus.org/) developed by Dr. Martin Porter and colleagues. Besides the friendly licensing terms, the Snowball stemmers support a variety of approaches and language coverage, including but not limited to these:

- Porter and Porter2 (named EnglishStemmer)
- Lovins
- Spanish
- French
- Russian
- Swedish

The following listing creates an English stemmer (sometimes called Porter2) and then loops through an array of tokens.

**Listing 2.2  Using the Snowball English stemmer**

```
EnglishStemmer english = new EnglishStemmer();              ◁— Set up
                                                               tokens
String[] test = {"bank", "banks", "banking", "banker", "banked",  ◁— to be
                "bankers"};                                         stemmed.
String[] gold = {"bank", "bank", "bank", "banker", "bank", "banker"};
for (int i = 0; i < test.length; i++) {
  english.setCurrent(test[i]);
  english.stem();
  System.out.println("English: " + english.getCurrent());    ◁— Do stemming.
  assertTrue(english.getCurrent() + " is not equal to " + gold[i],
          english.getCurrent().equals(gold[i]) == true);
}
```

*Define expectations for results.* → String[] gold

*Tell english what to stem.* → english.setCurrent

As expected by the unit test, the result of stemming is "bank", "bank", "bank", "banker", "bank", "banker". Note that *banker* (and *bankers*) didn't get reduced to *bank* according to the English stemmer rules. This isn't a bug in the English stemmer, just a matter of how the algorithm works. Not great for our newspaper reading job, but still better than having to run all the variations of *bank* through a search engine. Without a doubt, at some point when using stemming you'll have a user or tester complain that word *X* can't be found, or was stemmed incorrectly. If you truly believe it should be fixed, then your best bet is to use a protected words list that prevents that word from being stemmed instead of trying to correct the stemming algorithm itself (unless you control the code).

### 2.2.5 *Sentence detection*

Suppose you wanted to identify all the places the phrase *Super Bowl Champion Minnesota Vikings*[1] occurred in the news and you came across the following text:

> Last week the National Football League crowned a new Super Bowl Champion. Minnesota Vikings fans will take little solace in the fact that they lost to the eventual champion in the playoffs.

Tokenizing these sentences using the StandardTokenizer used in section 2.2.2 produces the following tokens:

```
..."a", "new", "Super", "Bowl", "Champion", "Minnesota", "Vikings", "fans",
"will", ...
```

If you were strictly looking for the occurrence of the tokens *Super, Bowl, Champion, Minnesota,* and *Vikings* next to each other, this would be a phrase match. But we know that this shouldn't be a match thanks to the occurrence of the period between *Champion* and *Minnesota.*

Computing sentence boundaries can help reduce erroneous phrase matches as well as provide a means to identify structural relationships between words and phrases and sentences to other sentences. With these relationships, you can then attempt to find meaningful pieces of information in the text. Java comes with the BreakIterator class that identifies sentences, but it often needs extra programming to handle special cases. For instance, a simple approach to BreakIterator results in this:

```
BreakIterator sentIterator =
                BreakIterator.getSentenceInstance(Locale.US);
String testString =
        "This is a sentence.  It has fruits, vegetables, etc. " +
        "but does not have meat.  Mr. Smith went to Washington.";
sentIterator.setText(testString);
int start = sentIterator.first();
int end = -1;
List<String> sentences = new ArrayList<String>();
while ((end = sentIterator.next()) != BreakIterator.DONE) {
  String sentence = testString.substring(start, end);
  start = end;
  sentences.add(sentence);
  System.out.println("Sentence: " + sentence);
}
```

The output from running the BreakIterator example is the following:

```
Sentence: This is a sentence.
Sentence: It has fruits, vegetables, etc. but does not have meat.
Sentence: Mr.
Sentence: Smith went to Washington.
```

---

[1] Sigh. A guy can dream, can't he?

Though the BreakIterator handled the inline *etc.*, it didn't properly handle *Mr.*. To fix this, you need to add to the program to properly handle special cases like abbreviations, quotes, and other sentence termination possibilities. A better option is to use a more robust sentence detection program like the one in OpenNLP, demonstrated next.

**Listing 2.3  OpenNLP sentence detection**

```
//... Setup the models
File modelFile = new File(modelDir, "en-sent.bin");          Create
InputStream modelStream = new FileInputStream(modelFile);    SentenceDetector
SentenceModel model = new SentenceModel(modelStream);        with en-sent.bin
SentenceDetector detector =                                  model.
  new SentenceDetectorME(model);
String testString =
  "This is a sentence. It has fruits, vegetables," +
  " etc. but does not have meat. Mr. Smith went to Washington.";
String[] result = detector.sentDetect(testString);          Invoke
for (int i = 0; i < result.length; i++) {                    detection
  System.out.println("Sentence: " + result[i]);              process.
}
```

Running listing 2.3 produces the correct output:

```
Sentence: This is a sentence.
Sentence: It has fruits, vegetables, etc. but does not have meat.
Sentence: Mr. Smith went to Washington.
```

### 2.2.6  *Parsing and grammar*

One of the more challenging aspects of our building blocks—parsing sentences into a meaningful, structured set or tree of relationships—is also one of the most useful. For example, identifying noun and verb phrases and their relationships to each other can help you determine the subject of a sentence along with the associated action the subject is taking. Parsing a sentence into a useful structure is difficult due to the ambiguity inherent in natural language. Parsing programs often have to decide between many different possible parses. For instance, figure 2.1 shows a parse of the following sentence:

```
The Minnesota Twins, the 1991 World Series Champions, are currently in
third place.
```

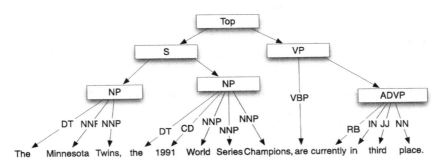

**Figure 2.1  Sample parsing of a sentence using the OpenNLP parser**

This parse tree was created using the OpenNLP Parser. The parser uses a syntax designed by the Penn Treebank project we discussed in section 2.2.3. The following code is used to perform the parse:

```
File parserFile = new File(modelDir, "en-parser-chunking.bin");
FileInputStream parserStream = new FileInputStream(parserFile);
ParserModel model = new ParserModel(parserStream);

Parser parser = ParserFactory.create(
        model,
        20, // beam size
        0.95); // advance percentage
Parse[] results = ParserTool.parseLine(
        "The Minnesota Twins , the 1991 World Series " +
        "Champions , are currently in third place .",
        parser, 3);
for (int i = 0; i < results.length; i++) {
  results[i].show();
}
```

In this code example, the key step is the invocation of the parseLine() method, which takes in the sentence to parse and the maximum number of possible parses to return. Running this code produces the following output (truncated for display purposes) where each line is a different parse:

```
(TOP (S (NP (NP (DT The) (NNP Minnesota) (NNS Twins)) (, ,) (NP (DT the)
...
(TOP (S (NP (NP (DT The) (NNP Minnesota) (NNPS Twins)) (, ,) (NP (DT the)
...
(TOP (S (NP (NP (DT The) (NNP Minnesota) (NNP Twins)) (, ,) (NP (DT the)
...
```

Close inspection of these results shows the subtlety of parsing, namely, in the tagging of the word *Twins*. The first instance tags *Twins* as a plural noun (NNS), the second as a plural proper noun, and the third as a singular proper noun. The outcome of this result can often be the difference between getting a good outcome or not, since if the word *Twins* is treated as a common noun (in the first case), then a tool that's trying to extract proper noun phrases (which are often very important in text) will miss the *Minnesota Twins* altogether. Though this may not seem critical in the context of an article on sports, imagine you're writing an application that needs to find people involved in crime by examining articles discussing key members of criminal groups.

Though we showed a full parse here, full (or deep) parses aren't always needed. Many applications will perform well using *shallow parsing*. Shallow parsing identifies the important pieces of a sentence, such as the noun and verb phrases, but doesn't necessarily relate them or define finer-grained structures. For example, in our earlier example of the Minnesota Twins, a shallow parse might only return *Minnesota Twins* and *1991 World Series Champions* or some variation of clauses like that.

Parsing is a rich and involved area of active research in the field, much of which is beyond the scope of this book. For our purposes, parsing is used in places like question answering to help identify the appropriate structure of a sentence so that we can extract an answer. For the most part, we'll treat parsing as a black box to be used when appropriate rather than delving into it more deeply.

### 2.2.7 Sequence modeling

The constructs presented thus far provide a means of identifying surface-level features as well as linguistically motivated attributes of text. We now consider modeling text based on the view of text as a sequence of words or characters. A common way to model a sequence is to examine each element in a sequence as well as some of the elements that immediately precede and follow it. How much or little of the surrounding context is considered varies by application, but in general you can think of this as a window of context where the size of the window is set based on how much of the context is to be considered. For instance, using sequences of characters can be useful for finding matches in searching data that has gone through an OCR (optical character recognition) process. It can also be useful when attempting to match phrases or for working with languages that don't have whitespace between words.

For example, a window size of 5 where the middle element is the one being modeled would examine the previous two elements in the sequence, as well as the subsequent two elements. Including the middle element, we're considering at most five elements in the sequence, which is the window size. As each element in the sequence is processed, the window can be thought to slide across the input sequence. In order to allow the entire window to be defined for all positions of the sentence, often boundary words are affixed to the sentence (see table 2.11).

**Table 2.11   An example *n*-gram window of size 5 at position 6 in a sentence**

| -2 | -1 | 0 | 1 | 2 | 3 | 4 | 5 | 6 | 7 | 8 | 9 | 10 | 11 | 12 | 13 | 14 | 15 |
|---|---|---|---|---|---|---|---|---|---|---|---|---|---|---|---|---|---|
| bos | bos | I | ca | n't | believe | that | the | Carolina | Hurricanes | won | the | 2005-2006 | Stanley | Cup | . | eos | eos |
| | | | | | | <- | - | window | - | -> | | | | | | | |

This type of modeling is often referred to as *n-gram modeling*. The idea is that the window is of size *n*, and the words within the window are *n-grams*. Table 2.12 shows some examples of some of the *n*-grams of various sizes for our example sentence.

**Table 2.12   N-grams of various sizes**

| Unigrams | believe | Stanley | the | Carolina |
|---|---|---|---|---|
| Bigrams | believe,that | Stanley,Cup | the,Carolina | |
| Trigrams | believe,that,the | 2005-2006,Stanley,Cup | | |
| four-grams | can't,believe,that,the | 2005-2006,Stanley,Cup,. | | |
| five-grams | that,the,Carolina,Hurricanes,won | | | |

The same idea can also be applied to modeling characters, where each character serves as an element in an *n*-gram window. This approach of using *n*-grams with characters will be used in chapter 4.

*N*-grams are also easily decomposed and thus lend themselves well to statistical modeling and estimation. In our example, we have a five-gram being used to model the context around the word *Carolina*. It's unlikely that we've seen that exact sequence of words, and difficult to make any estimation about how likely this sequence of words is. However, we're able to estimate a probability based on the trigram *the Carolina Hurricanes* or even the bigrams *the, Carolina* and *Carolina, Hurricanes*. This type of back-off estimation where a large context is used in conjunction with smaller, easier-to-estimate contexts is common in text processing approaches that use statistical methods to model ambiguity in text.

Most types of text processing use a combination of surface string characteristics, linguistic units, and sequence or *n*-gram modeling. For example, a typical part of speech tagger will use sentence and tokenization processing to determine what elements it's tagging, model prefixes and suffixes using string manipulation, and sequence modeling to capture the words that come before and after the word being tagged. Even though these techniques don't readily capture the meaning or semantics of text, they're surprisingly effective. This approach of combining these three types of processing will be used in chapter 5.

Now that you have a basic idea of the foundations of processing text, including string manipulation, linguistic processing, and *n*-gram sequence modeling, we can look at one of the most commonly asked and first-encountered questions for developers working with text: how to extract text from common file formats like HTML and Adobe PDF.

## 2.3 Preprocessing and extracting content from common file formats

In this section, we'll demonstrate extracting text from many common file formats. We'll discuss the importance of preprocessing and introduce an open source framework for extracting content and metadata from common file formats like HTML and Adobe PDF.

### 2.3.1 The importance of preprocessing

Imagine you're writing an application that allows a user to enter keywords to search all the files on their computer. In order to create this application, you need to figure out how to make these files available for searching. To get a better idea of what you need to do, you start looking around your own hard drive, quickly realizing that you have thousands, maybe even millions of files and they come in a variety of types. Some are Microsoft Word; some are Adobe Portable Document Format (PDF). Others are text-based like HTML and XML; still others are in some proprietary format that you don't have a clue about. Being the smart programmer that you are, you know that in order to make sense of all these file types, you need to transform them into a common format so that you only have to worry about one format internally. This process of standardizing the many different file types to a common text-based representation is called *preprocessing*. Preprocessing can also mean adding to or modifying the text to make it more usable by a library. For instance, certain libraries may expect the input to already have sentences identified. Ultimately, preprocessing includes any steps that must be undertaken before inputting data into the library or application for its intended use. As a primary example of preprocessing, we'll look at extracting content from common file formats.

Though many open source tools are available for extracting text from various file types (which will be covered shortly), this is one area where it may be worth the money to purchase a library of file converters to plug in to your application. Commercial file converters may pay licensing fees to companies like Microsoft and Adobe, allowing them access to documentation and programming libraries that open source file converters are unable to access. Additionally, they offer support and maintenance on a fairly routine basis. It isn't fair, but nobody said life is fair! But before paying for the commercial tool, make sure you get an evaluation copy and test it on your documents. We've tested at least one well-known commercial vendor head-to-head with an open source library on Adobe PDF files (which are often the hardest to extract text from) and the open source library was as good as, if not better than, the commercial vendor. Given the price of the commercial version, using the open source library was a no-brainer in this case. Your mileage may vary depending on your content.

Since this is a book about open source text tools, we'd be remiss if we didn't look at what tools are available for preprocessing. Table 2.13 lists some of the file formats you're likely to come across as well as one or more built-in or open source libraries for extracting text from that format. We can't cover all file formats in a book of this nature, so we'll focus on those you're most likely to encounter in your applications. Whatever your file types and whether or not you use open source libraries or commercial tools, most applications will want a simple, text-based representation to use internally. This allows you to use basic string manipulation libraries like those that come with Java, Perl, and most modern programming languages. Since there are many different libraries and many different approaches to content extraction, it's also best to either develop a framework for mapping file formats to content or to use an existing framework.

**Table 2.13   Common file formats**

| File format | MIME type | Open source library | Remarks |
|---|---|---|---|
| Text | plain/text | Built-in | |
| Microsoft Office (Word, PowerPoint, Excel) | application/msword, application/vnd.ms-excel, etc. | 1. Apache POI<br>2. Open Office<br>3. textmining.org | textmining.org is for MS Word only. |

**Table 2.13   Common file formats (continued)**

| File format | MIME type | Open source library | Remarks |
|---|---|---|---|
| Adobe Portable Document Format (PDF) | application/pdf | PDFBox | Text can't be extracted from image-based PDFs without first using optical character recognition. |
| Rich Text Format (RTF) | application/rtf | Built-in to Java using RTFEditorKit | |
| HTML | text/html | 1. JTidy<br>2. CyberNeko<br>3. Many others | |
| XML | text/xml | Many XML libraries available (Apache Xerces is popular) | Most applications should use SAX-based parsing instead of DOM-based to avoid creating duplicate data structures. |
| Mail | Not applicable (N/A) | Java Mail API, export mail to file, mstor | Your mileage may vary depending on your mail server and mail client. |
| Databases | N/A | JDBC, Hibernate, others, database export | |

Thankfully, several projects provide a framework for preprocessing. These projects wrap many of the libraries named in table 2.13. This approach lets you write your application using a single, unified interface for all of these libraries. One such open source project we use is called Apache Tika (http://tika.apache.org/), which will be introduced next.

### 2.3.2   *Extracting content using Apache Tika*

Tika is a framework for extracting content from many different sources, including Microsoft Word, Adobe PDF, text, and a host of other types. In addition to wrapping the various extraction libraries, Tika also provides MIME detection capabilities such that it's possible to have Tika autodetect the type of content and then parse it with the appropriate library.

Additionally, if you don't find your format in Tika, not to worry; a search of the web will often yield a library or application to work with your format that can be plugged in (and donated back to the project, we hope!) or handled separately. Even with a framework like Tika, it's recommended that you create interfaces to wrap the extraction process, as you'll most likely want to add a file format later that's not covered by the framework and will need a clean way of bringing it into your codebase.

At the architectural level, Tika works much like SAX (Simple API for XML; see http://www.saxproject.org/) parsers work for processing XML. Tika extracts information from the underlying content format (PDF, Word, and so on) and then provides callback events that can then be processed by the application. This callback mechanism is exactly the same as the SAX ContentHandler, and should be intuitive for anyone who has worked with SAX on other projects. Interacting with Tika is as simple as instantiating one of Tika's Parser classes, which then provides a single method:

```
void parse(InputStream stream, ContentHandler handler,
           Metadata metadata, ParseContext parseContext)
    throws IOException, SAXException, TikaException;
```

Using the parse method, you need only pass in content as an InputStream, and content events will be processed by the application's implementation of the ContentHandler. Metadata about the content will be filled into the Metadata instance, which is at its heart a hashtable.

At the Parser level, Tika comes with several implementations out of the box, including one for each of the specific MIME types supported by Tika, plus an AutoDetectParser that can identify the MIME type automatically. Tika also comes with several ContentHandler implementations based on common extraction scenarios such as only extracting the main body of a file.

Now that you know the basic philosophy behind Tika and have seen its basic interface, let's look at how to use it to find and extract text from many different file formats. Let's start with a basic case of extracting HTML and then we'll change things up a bit to show parsing of PDF files.

For starters, say you want to parse some rather simple HTML:

```
<html>
  <head>
    <title>Best Pizza Joints in America</title>
  </head>
  <body>
    <p>The best pizza place in the US is
      <a href="http://antoniospizzas.com/">Antonio's Pizza</a>.
    </p>
    <p>It is located in Amherst, MA.</p>
  </body>
</html>
```

In looking at this example, you'd most likely want to extract the title, the body, and possibly the links. Tika makes all of this simple, as can be seen in the following code.

**Listing 2.4 Extracting text from HTML with Apache Tika**

```
InputStream input = new ByteArrayInputStream(
                          html.getBytes(Charset.forName("UTF-8")));
ContentHandler text = new BodyContentHandler();
LinkContentHandler links = new LinkContentHandler();
ContentHandler handler = new TeeContentHandler(links, text);
Metadata metadata = new Metadata();
Parser parser = new HtmlParser();
ParseContext context = new ParseContext();
parser.parse(input, handler, metadata, context);
System.out.println("Title: " + metadata.get(Metadata.TITLE));
```

ContentHandler that will extract between body tags.

ContentHandler that knows about HTML links.

Where extracted metadata gets stored.

Wrap up ContentHandlers into one.

Input is HTML, so construct Parser for it.

Do the parse.

```
System.out.println("Body: " + text.toString());
System.out.println("Links: " + links.getLinks());
```

The output from running the HTML given through the code results in the following output:

```
Title: The Big Brown Shoe
Body: The best pizza place in the US is Antonio's Pizza.
It is located in Amherst, MA.

Links: [<a href="http://antoniospizzas.com/">Antonio's Pizza</a>]
```

The code used to parse the HTML involves two pieces: the construction of the ContentHandlers and the Metadata storage, and the creation and execution of the Parser, which, as the name implies, does the parsing. In the HTML example, you used an HTMLParser to parse the contents, but in most situations you'd likely want to use Tika's built-in AutoDetectParser, as demonstrated in this example, which parses a PDF file.

**Listing 2.5   Using the `AutoDetectParser` to identify and extract content**

```
InputStream input = new FileInputStream(
        new File("src/test/resources/pdfBox-sample.pdf"));    ⟵┐ Create
                                                                 │ InputStream
                                                                 │ to read in
                                                                 │ content.
ContentHandler textHandler = new BodyContentHandler();

Metadata metadata = new Metadata();

Parser parser = new AutoDetectParser();

ParseContext context = new ParseContext();

parser.parse(input, textHandler, metadata, context);    ⟵── Execute parse.

System.out.println("Title: " + metadata.get(Metadata.TITLE));
System.out.println("Body: " + textHandler.toString());
```

The Metadata object will hold metadata like author and title about the map's content.

AutoDetectParser will figure out the document's MIME type automatically when parse is called. Since you know the input is a PDF file, you could've used the PDFParser instead.

Get title from Metadata instance.

Print out body from ContentHandler.

In the PDF example, you input a PDF file as an InputStream, and construct one of Tika's included ContentHandlers and a Metadata object for storing ancillary information like author and number of pages about the document in a convenient place for use in the application. Finally, you create the Parser, parse the document, and then print out some information about the document. As you can see, the process is simple.

The fact that Tika can make working with all the different file formats easy is good news, but there's even better news: Tika is already integrated into Apache Solr through a contribution called the Solr Content Extraction Library (a.k.a. *Solr Cell*). In chapter 3, we'll show how easy it is to send all types of documents into Solr and have them indexed and searchable with little effort. Additionally, even if you don't use Solr for search, you could use it as an extraction server, as it has an option to send back the extracted form of a document without indexing it.

## 2.4   *Summary*

In this chapter, we looked at some of the basics of language like morphology, grammar, syntax, and semantics, as well as some tools for working with these. After that, we looked at the all-too-common task of preprocessing files to extract useful content from them. Though these pieces of the text puzzle aren't necessarily sexy, they're almost always necessary. For instance, many people gloss over the importance of content extraction from proprietary formats in order to get on to the text analysis, but extracting content into usable text is often time consuming and difficult to get right. Likewise, understanding the basics of how language works, as we introduced in this chapter, will go a long way to understanding the rest of this book and also understanding others in the field. With that in mind, it's time to take your first steps into finding and organizing your content by looking into what's often the foundation of many text analysis systems: search.

## 2.5   **Resources**

Hull, David A. 1966. Stemming Algorithms: A Case Study for Detailed Evaluation. *Journal of the American Society of Information Science*, volume 47, number 1.

Krovetz, R. 1993 "Viewing Morphology as an Inference Process." Proceedings of the Sixteenth Annual International (ACM) (SIGIR) Conference on Research and Development in Information Retrieval.

Levenshtein, Vladimir I. 1996. "Binary codes capable of correcting deletions, insertions, and reversals." *Doklady Akademii Nauk SSSR*, 163(4):845-848, 1965 (Russian). English translation in *Soviet Physics Doklady*, 10(8):707-710, 1966.

Mihalcea, Rada, and Tarau, Paul. 2004, July. "TextRank: Bringing Order into Texts." In Proceedings of the Conference on Empirical Methods in Natural Language Processing (EMNLP 2004), Barcelona, Spain.

"Parsing." Wikipedia. http://en.wikipedia.org/wiki/Parsing.

Winkler, William E., and Thibaudeau, Yves. 1991. "An Application of the Fellegi-Sunter Model of Record Linkage to the 1990 U.S. Decennial Census." *Statistical Research Report Series RR91/09*, U.S. Bureau of the Census, Washington, D.C.

# Searching

**In this chapter**

- Understanding search theory and the basics of the vector space model
- Setting up Apache Solr
- Making content searchable
- Creating queries for Solr
- Understanding search performance

Search, as a feature of an application or as an end application in itself, needs little introduction. It's part of the fabric of our lives, whether we're searching for information on the internet or our desktop, finding friends on Facebook, or finding a keyword in a piece of text. For the developer, search is often a key feature of most applications, but especially so in data-driven applications where the user needs to sift through large volumes of text. Moreover, search often comes in prepackaged solutions like Apple Spotlight on the desktop or via an appliance like the Google Search Appliance.

Given the ubiquity of search and the availability of prepacked solutions, a natural question to ask is, why build your own search tool using an open source solution? There are at least a few good reasons:

- *Flexibility*—You can control most, if not all, aspects of the process.
- *Cost of development*—Even when buying a commercial solution, you need to integrate it, which requires a lot of work.
- *Who knows your content better than you?*—Most shrink-wrap solutions make assumptions about your content that may not be appropriate.
- *Price*—No license fees. 'Nuff said.

Beyond these reasons, the quality of open source search tools is staggering. More than any other tool discussed in this book, open source search tools like Apache Lucene, Apache Solr, and others are stable, scalable, and ready for prime time, as they're used in a large multitude of places. For this book, we'll build on the Apache Solr search project to enable fast search of content under your control. You'll start by learning some of the basic search concepts behind many search engines, including Lucene and Solr. We'll then explore how to set up and configure Solr, and then proceed to index and search content we've added to Solr. We'll finish up with some tips and techniques for improving search performance, both in general and for Solr.

First, let's get started by taking a look at what's fast becoming a standard search feature in online stores like Amazon.com and eBay: search and faceting. By grounding the later sections in this easy-to-understand, real-world example, you can begin to formulate how to leverage the capabilities of Amazon and others into your own applications. By the end of this chapter, you should understand not only the basic concepts of search, but also how to set up and run a real search engine, and develop some insight on how to make it fast.

## 3.1  Search and faceting example: Amazon.com

We've all been there. You're searching some shopping site and can't quite nail down the exact keywords to find the thing you're looking for without haphazardly wading through hundreds of results. At least, you can't on sites that don't have faceted search capabilities. As an example, assume you're searching for a brand new, Energy Star, well-reviewed, 50-inch LCD TV on Amazon.com, so you type in *LCD TV* and get back something like what's shown in figure 3.1. Naturally, the first page of results isn't what you want, nor should you expect it to be, since you put in such a generic query. So you begin to narrow your search. On systems without faceted browsing, you'd do this by adding keywords to your queries; for example your query could become *50 inch LCD TV* or *Sony 50 inch LCD TV*. But since you aren't exactly sure what you want, and have only an idea, you begin to explore the facets that Amazon provides. *Facets* are categories derived from the search results that are useful for narrowing a search. In Amazon's case, in figure 3.1, they're displayed on the left side under the heading Category and have values like Electronics (4,550) and Baby (3). Facets almost always come with a count of how many items are in that category, to further enable users to decide what might be interesting.

Continuing with this sample query, you know that a TV is electronic, so you click the Electronics facet and arrive at the facets shown in figure 3.2. Note how the facets

**Figure 3.1　Snippet of search results for the query "LCD TV" from Amazon.com. Image captured 9/2/2012.**

have changed to reflect your new selections. Once again, the categories listed are pertinent to both your search terms and previously chosen facets. Furthermore, every category listed is guaranteed to return results because the actual data exists in the results.

Finally, clicking some more facets, you can add Portable Audio & Video, 4 stars and up, and a price range of $50 to $100 to arrive at a page that has results that are easily

**Figure 3.2　Facets for the search term "LCD TV" after choosing the Electronics facet. Image captured 9/2/2012.**

**Figure 3.3   Search results for "LCD TV" narrowed down by several facets. Captured 9/2/12**

managed, as seen in figure 3.3. From here, you can easily make your choice from what's available.

The Amazon example demonstrates that search with faceting is a powerful device for sites that have a combination of structured (metadata) and unstructured (raw text) data like e-commerce sites, libraries, and scientific content, among others. Calculating facets requires looking at the metadata associated with a set of search results, and then grouping it together and counting it. (Luckily, Solr does all this work for you out of the box.) Beyond facets, it should be obvious that if your users can't find something, they can't buy it or fix it or learn what features it offers. So improving your search capabilities isn't some esoteric exercise in programming; it can be a real boost to your bottom line. In order to understand how to add and improve your search, let's first take a step back and look at basic search concepts, after which we'll get into the workings of adding and enhancing search.

## 3.2   *Introduction to search concepts*

Before we get started with actual search concepts, wipe the slate clean and forget all you know about web-based search (at least for a while). Forget about Google. Forget about Yahoo! and Bing. Forget about PageRank (if you're familiar with it), data centers, and thousands of CPUs scouring every corner of the internet, collecting every available byte for inclusion in some online search engine. Peel back all those layers so you can look at the core concepts of search. At its most basic, search can be described in four parts:

1  *Indexing*—Files, websites, and database records are processed to make them searchable. Indexed files are called *documents* from this point forward.

2  *User input*—Users enter their information need through some form of user interface.

3  *Ranking*—The search engine compares the query to the documents in the index and ranks documents according to how closely they match the query.

4 *Results display*—The big payoff for the user: the final results are displayed via a user interface, whether it's at the command prompt, in a browser, or on a mobile phone.

The next four sections will further break down each of the indexing, query input, and ranking processes.

### 3.2.1 Indexing content

Regardless of your user input mechanism and ranking algorithms, if you don't have a good understanding of the structure and type of content in your collection, no amount of math is going to give better results than a search engine that understands what's important in a document. For instance, if all your documents have a title attribute and you know that title matches are often the most informative, you may be able to inform your search engine to give extra weight to documents that have title matches, thus boosting them higher in the results. Likewise, if you deal a lot with dates and numbers or people and phrases, you may need to do extra work to properly index your content. On the negative side, imagine how poor a search engine would be if it indexed all the HTML tags present in an online news site and couldn't distinguish between the tags and the actual content. Obviously, this is a toy example, but it underscores the need to develop an iterative approach to creating and improving applications to be more responsive to users' needs. The first task of anyone implementing search is to gain some knowledge of the content to be indexed. This research should cover both the typical structure of the document as well as a look at the actual contents.

After a preliminary understanding of the content is obtained, the process of making it searchable, called *indexing*, can begin. Indexing is the search engine process of making one or more documents searchable. In order to make a document searchable, the indexing process must analyze the content of the document. Document analysis usually consists of splitting the document up into tokens and, optionally, making one or more changes to each token to create a normalized token, called a *term*. Changes applied to tokens to produce terms may include stemming, downcasing, or complete removal. Applications are usually responsible for making the decision on what changes to apply. Some applications may not make any changes, whereas others may make extensive changes. In some cases, the search engine won't offer much in the way of controlling analysis. Though this lack of control is easier to work with at first, it'll most likely come back to haunt you later when the results aren't up to standard. Table 3.1 describes some common approaches to transforming tokens into terms for indexing.

After terms have been extracted from the document, usually they're stored in a data structure, called an *inverted index*, that's optimized to quickly find the documents that contain a term. When a user enters a term to search, the search engine can quickly look up all the documents that contain the term. In figure 3.4, a sample inverted index shows the links between words in the index (sometimes called a *vocabulary*) and the

**Table 3.1   Common analysis techniques**

| Technique | Description |
| --- | --- |
| Tokenization | Process of breaking up a string into tokens to be indexed. Proper, consistent handling of punctuation, numbers, and other symbols is important. For instance, tokenizing *microprocessor* might mean outputting several tokens (micro, processor, and microprocessor) so that user queries for variations are more likely to succeed. |
| Downcasing | All words are converted to lowercase, making it easy to do case-insensitive search. |
| Stemming | Strips words of suffixes, and so on. Described in chapter 1. |
| Stopword removal | Remove commonly occurring words like *the*, *and*, and *a* that occur in most documents. Originally done to save space in the index, but some newer search engines no longer remove stopwords since they can help in more advanced queries. |
| Synonym expansion | For each token, synonyms are looked up in a thesaurus and added to the index. This is often done on the query terms instead of the index terms, since updates to the synonym list can be accounted for dynamically at query time without the need to re-index. |

documents that they occur in. Many search engines go beyond simple term-to-document indexing and store the position of the terms in the document as well. This makes it easier to do phrase and other more advanced queries where position information is needed to calculate whether two or more terms are near each other.

In addition to storing the term to document relationships, the indexing process often calculates and stores information about the importance of the terms in relation to other terms in the document. This calculation of importance plays a vital role in the engine's ability to make the leap from a simple Boolean matching model (does the term exist in the document or not?) to a ranking model that can return documents deemed more relevant ahead of those that are less relevant. As you can guess,

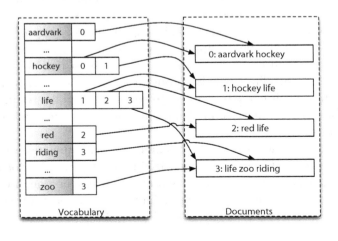

Figure 3.4   The inverted index data structure maps terms to the documents they occur in, enabling fast lookup of query terms in a search engine. The left side represents a sampling of the vocabulary in the documents and the right side represents the documents. The inverted index tracks where terms occur in documents.

the ability to rank documents by relevance is a huge leap forward when it comes to dealing with large quantities of information, as it allows users to focus in on only highly relevant content. Moreover, by calculating as much of this information as possible during indexing, the engine can enable fast lookup and ranking during search time. We'll cover more of how this is done later in the chapter. For now, that's pretty much all you need to know about the gory details of indexing. Now let's take a look at the types of things that searchers usually want to do with an index.

### 3.2.2 User input

Search systems generally capture the user's information need through a user interface (UI) that takes one or more inputs such as keywords, document types, language, and date ranges, and returns a ranked list of documents that are deemed most relevant to the user's query. Many web-based search engines rely on a simple keyword-based approach, as seen in figure 3.5, but they often also provide a more advanced query input mechanism, as (partially) pictured in figure 3.6.

**Figure 3.5   http://search.yahoo.com presents a simple user interface to search users.**

When deciding what type of input mechanisms to use, it's important to keep in mind who your users are and what their comfort level is with different input mechanisms. Web searchers are more likely to be accustomed to simple keyword-based interfaces, whereas sophisticated power users may expect more advanced tools that let them precisely define their information need to obtain better results. In many cases, it's wise to have both a simple keyword-based interface and a more advanced interface for power users.

**Figure 3.6   http://search.yahoo.com has an advanced search entry screen (under the More link) to allow users to fine-tune their results.**

Over the years, the query capabilities of search engines have steadily grown, allowing users to input complex queries using phrases, wildcards, regular expressions, and even natural language entries. Additionally, many general-purpose search engines utilize a set of operators like AND, OR, NOT, quotes for phrases, and so forth that allow for the creation of complex queries to narrow results. Proprietary implementations may go even further and provide specific operators designed to deal directly with internal data structures, file formats, and query needs. Table 3.2 contains a listing of common query types and operators used in search engines. Search engines may implicitly create any one of these query types without the user ever knowing such actions are taking place. For example, natural language–based search engines (the user enters full sentences, even paragraphs, as queries) often automatically identify phrases during the query processing stage and go on to submit phrase queries to the underlying engine. Likewise, Google Canada's advanced search interface provides simple text boxes that allow users to create complex phrase and Boolean queries, as can be seen in figure 3.7, without ever entering a quote or special operator. Moreover, many search engines will also perform multiple queries for every user query and then collate the results for presentation back to the user. This approach allows the engine to use multiple strategies to find the best results.

**Table 3.2   Common query types and operators in search**

| Query types and operators | Description | Example |
|---|---|---|
| Keyword | Each term is a separate lookup in the index. | dog<br>programming<br>baseball |
| Phrase | Terms must occur next to each other, or at least within some user-specified distance. Double quotes are usually used to mark the beginning and end of the phrase. | "President of the United States"<br>"Manning Publications"<br>"Minnesota Wild Hockey"<br>"big, brown, shoe" |
| Boolean operators | AND, OR, and NOT are often used to join two or more keywords together. AND indicates both terms must be present for a match; OR says at least one must be present. NOT means the following term can't be present for a match. Parentheses often can be used to control scope and provide nesting capabilities. Many search engines implicitly use AND or OR if no operator is specified in a multiterm query. | franks AND beans<br>boxers OR briefs<br>(("Abraham Lincoln" AND "Civil War") NOT ("Gettysburg Address")) |

**Table 3.2 Common query types and operators in search** *(continued)*

| Query types and operators | Description | Example |
|---|---|---|
| Wildcard and regular expression | Search terms can contain wildcard operators (? and *) or full-blown regular expressions. These query types usually consume more CPU resources than simpler queries. | bank?—Find any word starting with *bank* and ending with any character: banks. bank*—Find any word starting with *bank* and ending with any number of characters: banks, banker. aa.*k—Matches words starting with *aa* containing any character in between followed by a *k*: aardvark. |
| Structured | Structured queries rely on the structure of the indexed document to be searched. Common structures in documents include title, date published, author, uniform resource locator (URL), user ratings, and so on. | Date range—Find all documents between two dates. Find specific authors. Restrict results to one or more internet domains. |
| Similar documents | Given one or more already found documents, find other documents that are similar to the chosen documents. Sometimes called *relevance feedback* or *more like this*. | Google used to provide a Similar Pages link for most results. Clicking automatically generated a query from the chosen document and searched the index with the new query. |
| Guided search | Guided search, or faceted browsing, is an increasingly popular mechanism that provides users with suggestions to refine their query through guaranteed valid categories. | Amazon.com uses faceted browsing to allow searchers to restrict by price range, manufacturer, and other queries. Facet counts show how many entries are in each category. |

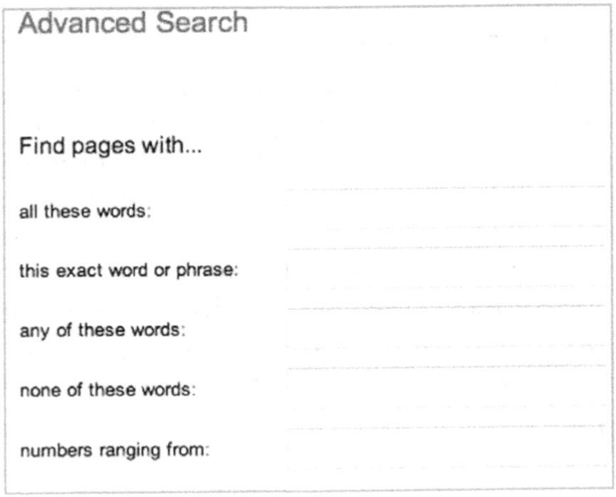

Advanced Search

Find pages with...

all these words:

this exact word or phrase:

any of these words:

none of these words:

numbers ranging from:

**Figure 3.7 Google Canada's Advanced Search UI automatically builds complex phrase and Boolean queries without requiring the user to know specific reserved words like AND, OR, NOT or quoting phrases.**

Some engines will even go so far as to try to classify the kind of query used and then choose different scoring parameters depending on the type of query used. For instance, it's common in e-commerce for searches to fall into one of two query types: known item and category/keyword. A *known item* search happens when a user specifically knows the name of the item (or close to it) and just needs to know where that item is in the store. For example, a search for *Sony Bravia 53-inch LCD TV* is a known item search, as there are likely only one or two matches for that search. A category search is much more general and often involves only a few keywords: *televisions* or *piano music*. In the case of known item search, failing to return the specific item in the top few results is considered a failure of the system. For category search, there's more wiggle room in what to return since the terms are often fairly general.

After submission to the search engine, query tokens are normally processed using the same analysis that index tokens go through in order to produce similar transformations from tokens to terms. For example, if tokens are stemmed in the index, then query tokens should also be stemmed. Many search engines also choose to do synonym expansion at query time. *Synonym expansion* is an analysis technique where each token is looked up in a user-defined thesaurus. If a match occurs, then new tokens, representing the synonyms, are added into the list of tokens. For instance, if the original query term is *bank,* analysis might add additional tokens for *financial institution* and *credit union* into the query, unbeknownst to the user. Synonym expansion can also be done at index time, but it often results in large increases in index size and requires the content be re-indexed whenever the synonym list is updated.

Now that we've covered some of the basic user issues involved in search, let's discuss the vector space model and learn the basics of what makes search work. Having this understanding will help you better judge the trade-offs between the various search approaches, allowing you to make informed decisions about which approach will meet your needs.

### 3.2.3  *Ranking documents with the vector space model*

Though search (or information retrieval) is a relatively mature field compared to some of the other topics we'll discuss, this doesn't mean the field has settled on one perfect way of finding information. There are many different ways of modeling the search task, each with its own merits. We'll focus on the vector space model (VSM), since it's the model used in our search libraries of choice and one of the most popular ways of ranking documents given user queries. If you want to read more on the other models, including the probabilistic model, see section 3.7.4, *Modern Information Retrieval* by Baeza-Yates and Ribeiro-Neto (Baeza-Yates 2011), or *Information Retrieval: Algorithms and Heuristics (2nd Edition)* by Grossman and Frieder (Grossman 1998).

#### A QUICK LOOK INSIDE THE VECTOR SPACE MODEL

The vector space model, first introduced in 1975 (Salton 1975), is an algebraic model that maps the terms in a document into an *n*-dimensional linear space. That was a mouthful, so what does it mean? Imagine you have a set of documents with a restricted language and thus can only contain the words *hockey* or *cycling*. Now imagine plotting these documents on a two-dimensional graph, with *hockey* as the vertical axis and *cycling* as the horizontal axis. Then, a document with both words present could be represented by an arrow (a vector, or term-vector) at a 45-degree angle between the two axes, as illustrated in figure 3.8.

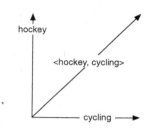

Though visualizing a two-dimensional space is easy, it isn't that much harder to extrapolate the notion to many dimensions. In this way, you can represent all documents as vectors in an *n*-dimensional linear space. In this representation, each word in the collection of documents represents a dimension. For instance, suppose you have two documents in your collection with the following content in each:

**Figure 3.8   An example of the vector space model for a document containing two words: hockey and cycling**

- Document 1: The Carolina Hurricanes won the Stanley Cup
- Document 2: The Minnesota Twins won the World Series

You could then represent these documents in your vector space by numbering each unique word. For instance, the word *the* would be given an index of 1, *carolina* of 2, *hurricanes* of 3, and so on through all words in all documents. These numbers correspond to the dimensions in your vector space. You can see that when two documents have the same word, they'll overlap in that dimension. Figure 3.9 illustrates this concept by mapping the two example documents into a 10-dimensional vector space where the presence of a word in a document means that dimension of the vector has a value of 1 stored in it.

In the real world, search engines work with a very high number of dimensions (*n* is often greater than 1 million) and so the simple model presented by the two-document example must be altered both for storage and quality reasons. For storage, search engines only store the presence of a term, not its absence—hence the inverted index data structure. This saves you from storing a lot of zeros, as most documents don't contain most words. For quality, instead of simply storing a 1 indicating the presence

---

Index    1 2      3        4   1  5     6

Doc 1:  The Carolina Hurricanes won the Stanley Cup

Index    1  7       8    4   1  9     10

Doc 2:     The Minnesota Twins won the World Series

Doc 1 Vector:   <1, 1, 1, 1, 1, 1, 0, 0, 0, 0>

Doc 2 Vector:   <1, 0, 0, 1, 0, 0, 1, 1, 1, 1>

Legend: A "1" in the vector means the word for that index number is present in the document; a "0" means it is not present in the document, e.g., "The" is in both documents, while "Carolina" is only in the first.

**Figure 3.9   Two documents represented as vectors in a 10-dimensional vector space**

of a word, most engines store some type of weight that's intended to capture the importance of that term relative to all the other terms. In math terms, you're scaling the vector. In this manner, you can start to see that if you compare the terms in a query to the terms, and their weights, in the documents that contain the query terms, you could produce a formula as to how relevant a document is to a query, which we'll come back to in a moment.

Though many different weighting schemes are available, the most common is often called the *term frequency-inverse document frequency model*, or *TF-IDF* for short. The essential insight of the TF-IDF model is that terms that occur frequently in a document (TF) relative to the number of times they occur in the overall collection (IDF) are more important than terms that commonly occur in a large number of documents. Think of TF and IDF as the yin and yang of search, each one balancing the other. For instance, *the* is a common word in most English text, giving it a very high document frequency (or small IDF), resulting in a very small contribution of any occurrence to the overall weight when scoring documents. This isn't to say that *the* and other common words, often referred to as *stopwords*, aren't useful in search, as they can be useful in phrase matching and other more advanced capabilities beyond the scope of the current discussion. At the opposite end of the spectrum, a word that occurs multiple times in a document (has a high TF value), while rarely occurring in the rest of the collection, is a valuable word and will contribute significantly to the weight assigned the document in question given a query with that term. Returning to the two-document example, the word *the* occurs twice in the first document and twice in the second document. Its total document frequency is four, which means the weight of the word *the* in the first document would be $2/4 = 1/2 = 0.5$. Similarly, *Carolina* only occurs once in the first document and thus once overall in the collection, so it would have a weight of $1/1 = 1$. Applying this for all terms would then result in a complete set of weighted vectors. Document 1 in the example would look like this:

```
<0.5, 1, 1, 0.5, 1, 1, 0, 0, 0, 0>
```

Given our representation of documents in the vector space, the next logical question is, how does the VSM match queries to documents? To start, queries can be mapped into the same vector space as the documents. Next, note that if you align the tail of the query vector to the tail of the document vector, an angle is formed. Remembering high school trigonometry, taking the cosine of this angle gives you a value between -1 and 1, which you can use to rank the documents in comparison to the query. It's easy to see that if the angle between the two vectors is zero degrees, then you have an exact match. Since the cosine of zero is one, your ranking measure confirms this understanding. Figure 3.10 visualizes this concept, with $\Theta$ as the angle formed between the two vectors, one being the document vector ($d_j$), and the other being a query vector ($q$). The tuple associated with each vector at the bottom of the figure represents the weights used in creating each vector, similar to the two-document example described earlier. Finally, doing this for all documents in the collection will yield a ranked list of results that can be returned to the user. In practice, search engines don't normally score all documents, focusing instead on only those documents that contain one or more terms in common between the query and the document. Additionally, most search engines supplement pure VSM scoring with other features and capabilities, such as document length, average document length of all documents in the collection, as well as algorithms that can give more weight to one document over another, or even one section of a document over another.

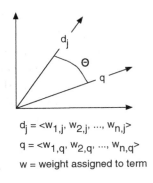

$d_j = <w_{1,j}, w_{2,j}, ..., w_{n,j}>$

$q = <w_{1,q}, w_{2,q}, ..., w_{n,q}>$

w = weight assigned to term

**Figure 3.10  Vector space–based comparison between a user's query, q, and the jth document in the collection**

Naturally, search engine writers have also figured out efficient mechanisms for calculating these scores, such that it's possible, using the vector space model, to search millions (even billions) of documents in subsecond time on commodity hardware. The trick is to make sure those documents that are returned are relevant to the user's search. Both search speed and relevance are the topics of section 3.6. For now, let's assume these are a given and move on to look at some ideas on displaying search results.

### 3.2.4  *Results display*

If you're like us, results display is usually the last thing on your mind. After all, what's wrong with throwing up the top ten hits in order and providing a way to go to the next results? Truth be told, nothing is wrong with this approach if your users are happy with it; simplicity is a noble design goal and something more people should keep in mind. But spending the extra time to determine the best ways to display your results can greatly enhance the quality of your user interactions. But beware: cleverly engineered results displays don't always provide the most useful information even if they look great, so make sure you spend some time thinking about usability and your target user's comfort level with such interfaces. Some additional questions to keep in mind concerning results display are these:

- What parts of the document should be displayed? The title is usually a given, if there is one. How about a summary or access to the original content?
- Should you highlight keywords from the query in the display?
- How do you handle duplicate, or near-duplicate, results?
- What navigation links or menus can you provide to enhance your user's experience?
- What if the user doesn't like the results or needs to expand or narrow the scope of their search?

These questions can only be answered by you and will be specific to your application. Our advice is to focus on what your target audience is most likely used to seeing and make sure, at a minimum, you provide that display capability. Then, you can try out alternate displays by sampling a subsection of your users and providing them with a chance to use alternate displays to see how they respond.

Through analysis of your most common queries and your users' behavior, you can make decisions on not only how to display your ranked list of results, but also what information to supply so users can quickly find what they need. With this in mind, let's analyze some techniques that can help organize results.

Figure 3.11 shows the results of a search on Google for *Apple*. Note that in the first result Google adds links to common Apple destination pages, stock quotes, store locations (even a map), related people and more. Further down (not in the screenshot) are links and related searches.

Note also in figure 3.11 how none of the entries are actually about apple, the fruit, as in Granny Smith and Gala? (There is one further down the page, but Google chooses to devote most of its primary screen real estate to the company.) Obviously, Apple Inc. should be the top-ranked site given its popularity, but what if you could separate your results into groups based on related items? This is the reasoning behind the increasing popularity of faceted browsing and the closely related notion of *clustering* (covered in chapter 6). With each of these techniques, the results of a search are grouped into buckets based on document attributes. In the case of faceted browsing, documents are usually preassigned categories, whereas clustering determines the similarity of the documents dynamically based on the returned results. In both cases, users can refine or restrict the results displayed based on guaranteed valid categories. In other words, by choosing one of the buckets, the user knows that there are results available related to that category.

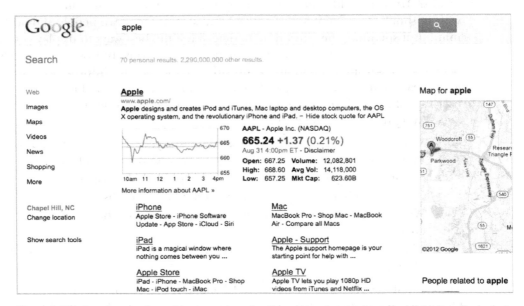

**Figure 3.11  Google search provides a number of options beyond a simple ranked list when displaying search results.**

Search results clustering can also improve display results. For instance, Carrot Search (http://www.carrotsearch.com) provides a mechanism (see the "Live Demo" off the main page) for clustering the results of a large number of different search engines. Figure 3.12 shows the results of running the same Apple search as in figure 3.11. On the left side of the Carrot Search display are the clusters that the results have been grouped into. With this type of display, it's easy to narrow a search to specific clusters, like apple pie instead of Apple Inc., as is shown in figure 3.12. We'll look at how to use Carrot clustering for your results later in chapter 6.

Before we move on to Apache Solr, know that there are many excellent books on information retrieval, as well as websites, special interest groups, whole communities, and volumes of academic papers on how to do search. So if you're looking for some special type of search engine or just want to know more, start at your favorite web search engine and search for *information retrieval*. Also, the Association for Computing Machinery (ACM) has an excellent special interest group called SIGIR that holds an annual conference where many of the best and brightest in the field go to share knowledge.

Enough of the high-level concepts, already, right? Let's take a look at how to incorporate a real search engine into an application by taking a look at Apache Solr.

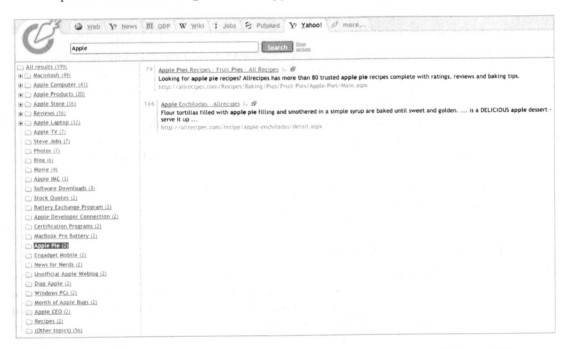

**Figure 3.12  Clustering can be a useful way of showing the results from ambiguous search terms, in this case Apple, which can mean, among other things, Apple Inc. or apple the fruit.**

## 3.3    *Introducing the Apache Solr search server*

Apache Solr (http://lucene.apache.org/solr) is an industrial-strength, high performance, thread-safe search server based on Apache Lucene. Solr was first built at CNET and was donated to the Apache Software Foundation in early 2006. Since that time, it has grown to include many new capabilities and a large and active community committed to adding new features, fixing issues, and improving performance. Solr provides many key features that make it a top-of-the-line search server, including these:

- Easy, HTTP-based protocols for indexing and searching, as well as clients for Java, PHP, Ruby, and other languages
- Advanced caching and replication to increase performance
- Easy configuration
- Faceted browsing
- Hit highlighting
- Administration, logging, and debugging facilities designed to take the guesswork out of using Solr
- Distributed search
- Spell-checking
- Content extraction using Apache Tika
- Quality documentation

One of Solr's best features is its use of Apache Lucene. Like Solr, Lucene has an active community and a reputation as a rock-solid search library (as opposed to Solr, which is a search server) delivering quality results and performance. Originally written by Doug Cutting, Apache Lucene has developed into a fast and powerful library for enabling text-based search. If you're looking for more details on Lucene, check out *Lucene In Action* (Second Edition) by Erik Hatcher, Otis Gospodnetić, and Mike McCandless. It's an excellent resource on all the workings of Lucene, many of which apply to Solr.

Now that you know some of the great things Solr has to offer, let's look at setting up Solr and using it, since Solr turns many of the things that you have to program in Lucene into configuration items.

### 3.3.1    *Running Solr for the first time*

The entire Apache Solr source and examples are included with the source distribution from this book. Otherwise, Solr can be downloaded from the Solr website at http://lucene.apache.org/solr by clicking the Download link on the front page and following the download instructions. Solr requires Java JDK 1.6 or greater. It comes with the Jetty servlet container, but should work with most modern servlet containers like Apache Tomcat. For this book, we're using the version bundled with the Taming Text source, but you may choose to use a later version if available, so the instructions given here may be slightly different. See the Solr website for official instructions on

Figure 3.13   The Solr welcome screen
demonstrates that the Solr application
started up correctly.

usage. In the *Taming Text* source distribution (tamingText-src directory), give the
example application a try by following these steps on the command line:

1   `cd apache-solr/example`
2   `java -jar start.jar`—This command should start up Jetty with Solr deployed
    as a web application within it on port 8983.
3   Point your browser at http://localhost:8983/solr/, where you should see the
    window in figure 3.13. If the welcome screen doesn't show up, refer to the Solr
    website for troubleshooting help.
4   In a separate command-line window, change into the example directory as in
    step 1.
5   In this new command-line window, type `cd exampledocs`.
6   Send the example documents contained in the directory to Solr by running the
    post.jar Java application: `java -jar post.jar *.xml`.
7   Switching to your browser and the Solr welcome screen, click through to the
    Solr Administration screen, as seen in figure 3.14.
8   In the query box, enter a query such as `Solr` and submit to see the results.

That's all there is to getting Solr off the ground and running. But to configure Solr for
your particular application, you'll need to set up the Solr Schema (schema.xml) and,
possibly, the Solr configuration (solrconfig.xml). For the purposes of this book, only

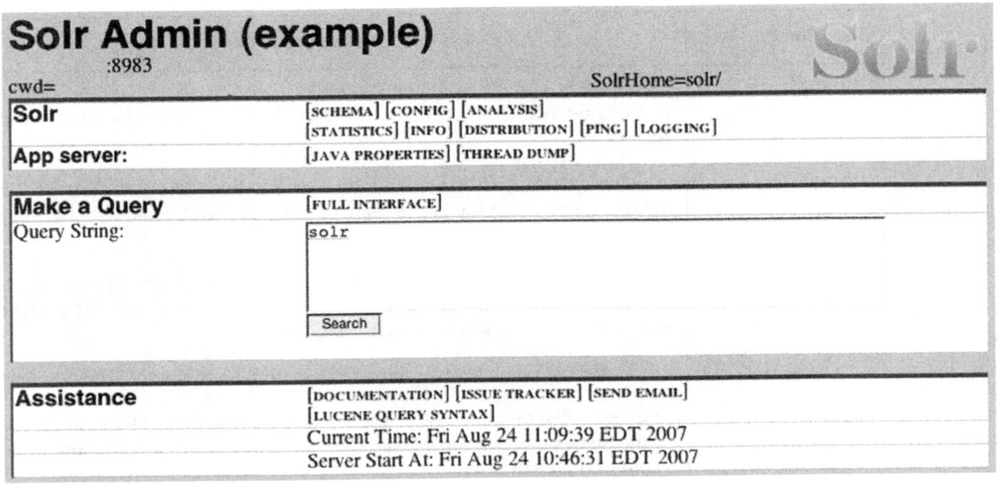

## Solr Admin (example)
:8983

cwd=                                                          SolrHome=solr/

| Solr | [SCHEMA] [CONFIG] [ANALYSIS]<br>[STATISTICS] [INFO] [DISTRIBUTION] [PING] [LOGGING] |
|---|---|
| **App server:** | [JAVA PROPERTIES] [THREAD DUMP] |

| **Make a Query** | [FULL INTERFACE] |
|---|---|
| Query String: | solr |
| | Search |

| **Assistance** | [DOCUMENTATION] [ISSUE TRACKER] [SEND EMAIL]<br>[LUCENE QUERY SYNTAX] |
|---|---|
| | Current Time: Fri Aug 24 11:09:39 EDT 2007 |
| | Server Start At: Fri Aug 24 10:46:31 EDT 2007 |

Figure 3.14   Screenshot of the Solr administration screen

certain parts of these files will be highlighted in the coming sections and chapters, but the complete example files are located in the book source under the apache-solr example configuration directory (`apache-solr/example/solr/conf`). Additionally, the Solr website (http://lucene.apache.org/solr) has many resources, tutorials, and articles on how to configure and use Solr for your particular needs.

### 3.3.2    *Understanding Solr concepts*

Since Solr is a web-based search service, most operations take place by sending HTTP GET and POST requests from a client application to the Solr server. This flexibility allows many different applications to work with Solr, not just Java-based ones. In fact, Solr provides client code for Java, Ruby, Python, and PHP, as well as the standard XML responses that can easily be handled by any application.

When Solr receives a request from the client, it parses the URL and routes the request to the appropriate `SolrRequestHandler`. The `SolrRequestHandler` is then responsible for processing the request parameters, doing any necessary computation, and assembling a `SolrQueryResponse`. After a response has been created, a `Query-ResponseWriter` implementation serializes the response and it's sent back to the client. Solr supports many different response formats, including XML and JSON, as well as formats that are easily used by languages like Ruby and PHP. Finally, custom `Query-ResponseWriters` can be plugged in to provide alternate responses when needed.

With regard to content processing, Solr shares much of its terminology and capabilities for indexing and searching with Lucene. In Solr (and Lucene), an index is built of one or more `Documents`. A `Document` consists of one or more `Fields`. A `Field` consists of a name, content, and metadata telling Solr/Lucene how to handle the content. These metadata options are described in table 3.3.

**Table 3.3   Solr `Field` options and attributes**

| Name | Description |
| --- | --- |
| indexed | Indexed `Fields` are searchable and sortable. You can also run Solr's analysis process on indexed `Fields`, which can alter the content to improve or change results. |
| stored | The contents of a stored `Field` are saved in the index. This is useful for retrieving and highlighting the contents for display but isn't necessary for the actual search. |
| boost | A `Field` can be given more weight than others by setting a boost factor. For instance, it's common to boost title `Fields` higher than regular content since matches in titles often yield better results. |
| multiValued | Allows for the same `Field` to be added multiple times to a document. |
| omitNorms | Effectively disables the use of the length of a field (the number of tokens) as part of the score. Used to save disk space when a `Field` doesn't contribute to the score of a search. |

Solr is slightly more restrictive than Lucene in that it imposes a schema definition (written in XML, stored in a file called schema.xml) on top of the `Field` structure to allow for much stronger typing of `Field`s through the declaration of `FieldType`s. In this manner, it's possible to declare that certain fields are dates, integers, or plain strings and what attributes the `Field`s contain. For example, the `dateFieldType` is declared as

```
<fieldType name="date" class="solr_DateField"
         sortMissingLast="true" omitNorms="true"/>
```

**Short for
org.apache.solr.schema.DateField**

Solr also lets you require that each `Document` have a unique `Field` value associated with it.

If a `Field` is indexed, then Solr can apply an analysis process that can transform the content of that `Field`. In this way, Solr provides a means to stem words, remove stopwords, and otherwise alter the tokens to be indexed as we discussed earlier in section 3.2.1. This process is controlled via the Lucene `Analyzer` class. An `Analyzer` consists of an optional `CharFilter`, a required `Tokenizer`, and zero or more `TokenFilter`s. A `CharFilter` can be used to remove content while maintaining correct offset information (such as stripping HTML tags) for things like highlighting. Note that in most cases, you won't need a `CharFilter`. A `Tokenizer` produces `Token`s, which in most cases correspond to words to be indexed. The `TokenFilter` then takes `Token`s from the `Tokenizer` and optionally modifies or removes the `Token`s before giving them back to Lucene for indexing. For instance, Solr's `WhitespaceTokenizer` breaks words on whitespace, and its `StopFilter` removes common words from search results.

As an example of a richer `FieldType`, the example Solr schema (apache-solr/example/solr/conf/schema.xml) contains the following declaration of the `text-FieldType` (note, this evolves over time, so it may not be exactly the same):

```
<fieldType name="text" class="solr.TextField"
         positionIncrementGap="100">
  <analyzer type="index">
   <tokenizer
       class="solr.WhitespaceTokenizerFactory"/>
    <filter class="solr.StopFilterFactory" ignoreCase="true"
         words="stopwords.txt"/>

    <filter class="solr.WordDelimiterFilterFactory"
       generateWordParts="1" generateNumberParts="1" catenateWords="1"
          catenateNumbers="1" catenateAll="0"
        splitOnCaseChange="1"/>

    <filter class="solr.LowerCaseFilterFactory"/>
    <filter class="solr.EnglishPorterFilterFactory"
         protected="protwords.txt"/>
```

**This analyzer is used only during document indexing, as indicated by the type="index" attribute. If the same exact approach is to be used during both indexing and querying, then only one analyzer need be declared and the type attribute can be dropped.**

**Create tokens based on whitespace. Note: every Tokenizer and TokenFilter is wrapped inside of a Factory that produces the appropriate instance of the analysis class.**

**Remove commonly occurring stopwords. See the stopwords.txt file in the Solr conf directory for the default list.**

**Split up words that contain mixed case, numbers, etc. For example, iPod becomes iPod and i, Pod.**

**Stem words using Dr. Martin Porter's stemmer. See http://snowball.tartarus.org.**

```
      <filter class="solr.RemoveDuplicatesTokenFilterFactory"/>
    </analyzer>
    <analyzer type="query">
      <tokenizer class="solr.WhitespaceTokenizerFactory"/>
      <filter class="solr.SynonymFilterFactory"
          synonyms="synonyms.txt" ignoreCase="true" expand="true"/>
      <filter class="solr.StopFilterFactory" ignoreCase="true"
          words="stopwords.txt"/>
      <filter class="solr.WordDelimiterFilterFactory"
          generateWordParts="1"
          generateNumberParts="1" catenateWords="0"
          catenateNumbers="0" catenateAll="0"
          splitOnCaseChange="1"/>
      <filter class="solr.LowerCaseFilterFactory"/>
      <filter class="solr.EnglishPorterFilterFactory"
          protected="protwords.txt"/>
      <filter class="solr.RemoveDuplicatesTokenFilterFactory"/>
    </analyzer>
  </fieldType>
```

*This analyzer is only used for queries, as indicated by the type="query" attribute. It's slightly different from the index analyzer due to the use of synonyms, but otherwise the tokens will look the same, which is important for matching.*

*Expand any query term that appears in the synonym file named synonyms.txt (in the Solr conf directory).*

From this example, it should be clear that applications can mix and match their own approach to analysis by simply declaring the type of `Tokenizers` and `TokenFilters` to be used, and their ordering.

With these two `FieldType` declarations, you could declare several `Fields` like this:

```
<field name="date" type="date" indexed="true" stored="true"
        multiValued="true"/>

<field name="title" type="text" indexed="true"
        stored="true"/>

<field name="generator" type="string" indexed="true"
        stored="true" multiValued="true"/>

<field name="pageCount" type="sint"
        indexed="true" stored="true"/>
```

*A date Field that's indexed and stored can be used for searching and sorting documents by date.*

*The title Field is a TextField that's indexed and stored. TextFields are tokenized and analyzed using the associated Analyzer declared in the Solr schema.*

*The generator Field is a StrField that Solr indexes and stores exactly as it's passed in.*

*Stores the pageCount of a document as a sortable integer, meaning the value isn't human readable, but is optimized for sorting.*

### DESIGNING A SOLR SCHEMA

As is true in the design of any text analysis system, careful attention needs to be paid to how to enable search for users. The Solr schema syntax provides a rich set of capabilities ranging from advanced analysis tools for tokenization and stemming, to spell-checkers and custom sorting possibilities. All of these capabilities are specified in the Solr schema (schema.xml) and Solr configuration. As a general rule, when starting a new Solr project, start with the example schema and configuration from Solr and examine it to see what to keep and what to remove. This approach works well because the example schema is well documented, carefully explaining each concept in detail.

The Solr schema can be broken down into three distinct sections:

- Field type declaration
- Field declaration
- Miscellaneous declaration

The field type declaration tells Solr how to interpret the content contained in a field. Types defined in this declaration can then be used later in the field declaration section. But just because a type is declared doesn't mean it must be used. Currently, Solr includes many types, most notably `IntField`, `FloatField`, `StrField`, `DateField`, and `TextField`. Furthermore, applications can easily implement their own `FieldType` to extend the typing capability of Solr.

The `Field` declaration section is where the rubber meets the road. In this section of the schema, applications declare exactly how documents are going to be indexed and stored inside of Solr by declaring their name, type, and other metadata that lets Solr know how to treat indexing and search requests.

Lastly, the miscellaneous section comprises a grab-bag of declarations identifying items like the name of the `Field` to use as a unique key for each document or the default search field. Additional declarations tell Solr to copy the contents of one `Field` to another `Field`. By copying from one `Field` to another, Solr can efficiently analyze the same content in multiple ways, making for more options when searching. For instance, it's often beneficial to allow users to search in a case-sensitive manner. By creating a `<copyField>` that copies the contents of one `Field` to another `Field` that's set up to preserve case, case-sensitive searching can be enabled.

In designing a schema, the temptation is often to throw in everything, including the kitchen sink, and then generate large queries that search all of these different fields. Though this can be done in Solr, it's better to think about which fields need to be stored and indexed and which don't because the information is already available elsewhere. Often, most simple queries can be handled by creating an "all" `Field` that contains the content of all the other searchable `Fields`. With this strategy, you can quickly search the content without generating queries across multiple `Fields`. Then, when more restrictive searching is needed, the individual `Fields` can be searched.

In Solr, the analysis process is easily configured and often requires no programming whatsoever. Only in special cases where the existing Lucene and Solr `CharFilters`, `Tokenizers`, and `TokenFilters` aren't sufficient (people have contributed many analysis modules to Lucene and Solr) will there be a need to write new analysis code.

Now that you have a basic understanding of how content needs to be structured for Solr, we can delve into how to add the content to Solr to make it searchable. The next section will cover how to formulate `Documents` and send them to Solr for indexing, and from there we'll look into searching that content.

## 3.4 Indexing content with Apache Solr

Solr has several ways to index content, ranging from posting XML or JSON messages, CSV files or common office MIME types, to pulling data from a database via SQL commands or RSS feeds. We'll cover the basics of indexing using XML messages and common office types here, but we'll leave the others to the Solr documentation. Specifically, if you want more information on indexing CSV files, see http://wiki.apache.org/solr/UpdateCSV. Finally, to learn more about indexing content from a database and RSS feeds, see the Data Import Handler at http://wiki.apache.org/solr/DataImportHandler.

Before we cover XML indexing, we should note that there are four types of indexing activities you can perform with Solr:

- *Add/update*—Allows you to add or update a document to Solr. Additions and updates aren't available for searching until a commit takes place.
- *Commit*—Tells Solr that all changes made since the last commit should be made available for searching.
- *Delete*—Allows you to remove documents either by ID or by query.
- *Optimize*—Restructures Lucene's internal structures to improve performance for searching. Optimization, if done at all, is best done when indexing has completed. In most cases, you need not worry about optimization.

### 3.4.1  *Indexing using XML*

One way of indexing in Solr involves constructing an XML message from preprocessed content and sending it as an HTTP POST message. This XML message might look something like this:

```
<add>
  <doc>
    <field name="id">solr</field>
    <field name="name" boost="1.2">
        Solr, the Enterprise Search Server
    </field>
    <field name="mimeType">text/xml</field>
    <field name="creator">Apache Software Foundation</field>
    <field name="creator">Yonik Seeley</field>

    <field name="description">An enterprise-ready, Lucene-based search
      server.  Features include search, faceting, hit highlighting,
      replication and much, much more</field>
  </doc>
</add>
```

In the example XML, you can see a simple structure wherein you declare the <add> command and then include it in one or more <doc> entries. Each document specifies the Fields associated with it and an optional boost value. This message can then be POSTed to Solr just as any web browser or HTTP client POSTs. For more information on using XML commands for Solr see the Solr wiki at http://wiki.apache.org/solr/UpdateXmlMessages.

Luckily, Solr has an easy-to-use client-side library called SolrJ that handles all of the work involved in creating Solr XML messages. The following listing demonstrates using SolrJ to add documents to Solr.

**Listing 3.1   Example usage of the SolrJ client library**

**Create an HTTP-based Solr Server connection.** →

```
SolrServer solr = new CommonsHttpSolrServer(
                new URL("http://localhost:" + port + "/solr"));

SolrInputDocument doc = new SolrInputDocument();

doc.addField("id", "http://tortoisehare5k.tamingtext.com");   ←

doc.addField("mimeType", "text/plain");

doc.addField("title",
            "Tortoise beats Hare!  Hare wants rematch.", 5);   ←

Date now = new Date();

doc.addField("date",
                DateUtil.getThreadLocalDateFormat().format(now));

doc.addField("description", description);

doc.addField("categories_t", "Fairy Tale, Sports");   ←

solr.add(doc);                                         ←

solr.commit();                                         ←
```

The schema used for this instance of Solr requires a unique field named id.

Add a Title field to the document and boost it to be 5 times as important as other fields.

**Dates must be formatted in a specific way for Solr.** →

A dynamic field allows for the addition of unknown fields to Solr. The _t tells Solr this should be treated as a text field.

Send the newly created document to Solr. Solr takes care of creating a correctly formatted XML message and sending it to Solr using Apache Jakarta Commons HTTPClient.

After you've added all your documents and wish to make them available for searching, send a commit message to Solr.

To index your content, you need to send Solr add commands for each SolrInput-Document. Note that multiple SolrInputDocuments can be included in a single add; just use the SolrServer add method that takes in a Collection. This is encouraged for performance reasons. You might be thinking that the overhead of HTTP will be costly to indexing performance, but in reality the amount of work needed for managing connections is small compared to the cost of indexing in most cases.

There you have it, the basics of Solr indexing using XML. Now let's look at indexing common file formats.

### 3.4.2   *Extracting and indexing content using Solr and Apache Tika*

In order to extract content from documents and index them in Solr, you have to leverage several concepts that you learned in this chapter and in chapter 1 that go beyond putting a search box in the user interface. First and foremost, you have to design your Solr schema to reflect the information that's extracted from the content you're making searchable. Since you're using Tika for extraction capabilities, the application needs to map the metadata and content produced by Tika into your schema fields.

To view the full Solr schema, open the solr/conf/schema.xml file in your favorite editor. There isn't much to add to the design factors of the schema, other than that we tried to make sure we were mapping the right types from Tika to the proper Field-Types in Solr. For example, the page count is an integer, so we made it an integer in the Solr schema. For this field and the other fields, we iteratively looked at a sampling of documents and the information extracted from them. To do this, we took advantage of the fact that the Solr Tika integration allows you to extract content without indexing it. Using a tool called curl (available on most *NIX machines and for Windows at http://curl.haxx.se/download.html), you can send files and other HTTP requests to Solr. If Solr isn't running already, use the commands in chapter 1 to start it. Once Solr is up and running, you can index some content. In this case, we sent the following command to Solr asking it to extract the content in a sample file:

```
curl "http://localhost:8983/solr/update/extract?&extractOnly=true" \
    -F "myfile=@src/test/resources/sample-word.doc"
```

The input to this command is a sample Word document located under the src/test/resources directory in the book's source code, but you can try any Word or PDF file. For curl to locate the sample document properly, you should run the curl command from the top directory of the book's code. The output will contain the extracted content along with the metadata and looks like this (some content has been removed for brevity):

```
<?xml version="1.0" encoding="UTF-8"?>
<response>
  <lst name="responseHeader">
    <int name="status">0</int>
    <int name="QTime">8</int>
  </lst>
  <str name="sample-word.doc">&lt;?xml version="1.0"
                  encoding="UTF-8"?&gt;
  &lt;html xmlns="http://www.w3.org/1999/xhtml"&gt;
  &lt;head&gt;
  &lt;title&gt;This is a sample word document&lt;/title&gt;
  &lt;/head&gt;
  &lt;body&gt;
  &lt;p&gt;This is a sample word document.&amp;#xd;
  &lt;/p&gt;
  &lt;/body&gt;
  &lt;/html&gt;
  </str>
  <lst name="sample-word.doc_metadata">
    <arr name="Revision-Number">
      <str>1</str>
    </arr>
    <arr name="stream_source_info">
      <str>myfile</str>
    </arr>
    <arr name="Last-Author">
      <str>Grant Ingersoll</str>
    </arr>
```

```
     <arr name="Page-Count">
       <str>1</str>
     </arr>
     <arr name="Application-Name">
       <str>Microsoft Word 11.3.5</str>
     </arr>
     <arr name="Author">
       <str>Grant Ingersoll</str>
     </arr>
     <arr name="Edit-Time">
       <str>600000000</str>
     </arr>
     <arr name="Creation-Date">
       <str>Mon Jul 02 21:50:00 EDT 2007</str>
     </arr>
     <arr name="title">
       <str>This is a sample word document</str>
     </arr>
     <arr name="Content-Type">
       <str>application/msword</str>
     </arr>
     <arr name="Last-Save-Date">
       <str>Mon Jul 02 21:51:00 EDT 2007</str>
     </arr>
   </lst>
</response>
```

From this output, you can see the kind of information that Tika returns and then plan your schema accordingly.

After the schema is defined, the indexing process is handled by sending documents to Solr's ExtractingRequestHandler, which provides the necessary infrastructure for leveraging Tika to extract the content. In order to use the ExtractingRequestHandler, you must set it up in the Solr configuration file. In this case, your solrconfig.xml contains the following:

```
<requestHandler name="/update/extract"
    class="org.apache.solr.handler.extraction.ExtractingRequestHandler">
  <lst name="defaults">
    <str name="fmap.Last-Modified">last_modified</str>
    <str name="fmap.Page-Count">pageCount</str>
    <str name="fmap.Author">creator</str>
    <str name="fmap.Creation-Date">created</str>
    <str name="fmap.Last-Save-Date">last_modified</str>
    <str name="fmap.Word-Count">last_modified</str>
    <str name="fmap.Application-Name">generator</str>
    <str name="fmap.Content-Type">mimeType</str>
    <!-- Map everything else to ignored -->
    <bool name="uprefix">ignored_</bool>
  </lst>
</requestHandler>
```

Since this is already packaged into the tamingText-src Solr setup, you're all set to index the content. At this point, all you need to do is send some documents to Solr.

For our purposes, we'll rely on `curl` again, but for real applications, a crawler or some code to get documents from a storage repository (CMS, DB, and so on) and into Solr via a Solr client like SolrJ will be more appropriate.

To demonstrate via `curl`, you can modify the extract-only command by dropping the `extract.only` parameter and adding in a few others, as in the following:

```
curl "http://localhost:8983/solr/update/extract?

  literal.id=sample-word.doc&defaultField=fullText&commit=true" \
  -F "myfile=@src/test/resources/sample-word.doc"
```

Besides the specification of the file to upload (`-F` parameter), there are two important pieces to this command:

- You send the file to the /update/extract URL instead of just /update. This tells Solr that you want to use the `ExtractingRequestHandler` you configured earlier.
- The parameters you pass in, in this case:
  - `literal.id=sample-word.doc`—This tells Solr to add the literal value `sample-word.doc` as a `Field` to the `Document` with the name id. In other words, this is your unique ID.
  - `defaultField=fullText`—Where possible, Solr will automatically match up the extracted content names to Solr `Field` names. If no field name matches, this value specifies the default field to use to index the content. In this case, all unmapped and unmatched content will go into the `fullText` field.
  - `commit=true`—This instructs Solr to immediately commit the new document to its index so that it will be searchable.

That command covers the basics of using the `ExtractingRequestHandler`. To learn about more advanced features, see http://wiki.apache.org/solr/ExtractingRequest-Handler.

Running the indexing commands against your set of files should produce similar results—adjusted, naturally, to what's located in your directories. Given this simple index, you can now look into what kind of results can be obtained by querying the index using Solr's built-in administration tool.

> **TIP**   When working with Lucene and Solr indexes, Luke is your best friend for understanding what's in your index. Written by Andrzej Bialecki, Luke is useful for discovering how terms were indexed and what documents are in the index, as well as other metadata like the top 50 terms by frequency in a field. Luke is freely available at http://code.google.com/p/luke/.

Now that you have some content in your index, we get to the big payoff by looking at how search works in Solr. In the next section, you'll use SolrJ to send search requests to Solr and also look at the results.

## 3.5 *Searching content with Apache Solr*

Much like indexing, search is accomplished by sending HTTP requests to Solr that specify the user's information needs. Solr contains a rich query language that enables users to use terms, phrases, wildcards, and a number of other options. The options seem to grow with every release. Not to worry: the Solr website (http://lucene.apache.org/solr) does a good job of documenting any new features and so should be consulted for the latest and greatest query capabilities.

To understand how search works in Solr, let's take a step back and look at how Solr processes requests. If you remember from section 3.3.2, Solr examines incoming messages and routes the request to an instance of the `SolrRequestHandler` interface. Fortunately, Solr comes with many useful `SolrRequestHandlers` so that you don't have to implement your own. Table 3.4 lists some of the more common `SolrRequestHandlers` and their functionality.

**Table 3.4  Common `SolrRequestHandlers`**

| Name | Description | Sample query |
|------|-------------|--------------|
| `StandardRequestHandler` | As you might guess by the name, the `Standard-RequestHandler` is the default `SolrRequest-Handler`. It provides mechanisms for specifying query terms, fields to search against, number of results to retrieve, faceting, highlighting, and relevance feedback. | `&q= description%3Awin+OR+ description%3Aall &rows=10`—Queries the description field for the terms *all* or *win*, returning a maximum of 10 rows |
| `MoreLikeThisHandler` | Returns documents that are "More Like This"—similar to a given document. | `&q=lazy&rows=10&qt=%2Fmlt&qf= title^3+des cription^10` |
| `LukeRequestHandler` | The `LukeRequestHandler` is named in reference to the handy Lucene/Solr index discovery tool named Luke. Luke is a simple yet powerful GUI tool that provides insight into the structure and contents of an existing index. The `Luke-RequestHandler` mimics much of the functionality of Luke by providing metadata about the index in the form of query responses that can be used by applications to display information about an index. | `&show=schema`—Returns information about the schema of the current index (field names, storage and indexing status, and so on) |

Though a `RequestHandler` can generically handle any request, a derivative class, the `SearchHandler`, is responsible for actually handling the search requests. A `Search-Handler` is composed of one more `SearchComponents`. `SearchComponents` plus a query parser do the majority of heavy lifting when it comes to search. Solr has many `Search-Components` as well as a few different query parsers available. These are also pluggable if you wish to add your own components or query parser. To better understand this issue and other Solr input parameters, let's take a closer look at these capabilities.

### 3.5.1 Solr query input parameters

Solr provides a rich syntax for expressing input parameters and output processing. Table 3.5 covers the seven different input categories, providing descriptions and common or useful parameters. Since Solr is almost always improving, consult the Solr website for the authoritative list of parameters.

**Table 3.5  Common Solr input parameters**

| Key | Description | Default | Supported by | Example |
|-----|-------------|---------|--------------|---------|
| q | The actual query. Syntax varies depending on the `SolrRequestHandler` used. For the `Standard-RequestHandler`, the supported syntax is described at http://wiki.apache.org/solr/SolrQuerySyntax. | N/A | `StandardRequestHandler,` `DisMaxRequestHandler,` `MoreLikeThisHandler,` `SpellCheckerRequest-` `Handler` | q=title:rabbit AND description:"Bugs Bunny" q=jobs:java OR programmer |
| sort | Specify the `Field` to sort results by. | score | Most `SolrRequestHandlers` | q=ipod&sort=price desc q=ipod&sort=price desc,date asc |
| start | The offset into the results set to return results from. | 0 | Most `SolrRequestHandlers` | q=ipod&start=11 q=ipod&start=1001 |
| rows | The number of results to return. | 10 | Most `SolrRequestHandlers` | q=ipod&rows=25 |
| fq | Specify a `FilterQuery` to restrict results by. A `FilterQuery` is useful, for instance, when restricting results to a given date range or all documents with an *A* in the title. `FilterQuerys` are only useful when performing repeated queries against the restricted set. | N/A | Most `SolrRequestHandlers` | q=title:ipod&fq= manufacturer:apple |

**Table 3.5  Common Solr input parameters** *(continued)*

| Key | Description | Default | Supported by | Example |
|-----|-------------|---------|--------------|---------|
| facet | Request facet information about a given query. | N/A | Most `SolrRequestHandlers` | q=ipod&facet=true |
| facet.field | The `Field` to facet on. This `Field` is examined to build the set of facets. | N/A | Most `SolrRequestHandlers` | q=ipod&facet= true&facet.field=price& facet.field= manufacturer |

Naturally, with all of the options outlined in table 3.5 and the many more described online comes the difficult decision of what to make available in your application. The key is to know your users and how they want to search. In general, things like highlighting and More Like This, though nice features, can slow searches down due to extra processing (especially if using combinations of these). On the other hand, highlighting is useful when users want to quickly zero in on the context of the match. Next, let's look at how to access Solr programmatically, as that will be the main mechanism for integrating Solr into your application.

> **NOTE**  All this discussion of input parameters has no doubt left you wondering about the reward from all of this work. Namely, what do the results look like and how can you process them? To that end, Solr provides a pluggable results handler based on derivations of the Query-ResponseWriter class. Similar to the various implementations of the Solr-RequestHandler, there are several implementations of QueryResponse-Writer, one of which should satisfy your output needs. The most common (and default) responder is the XMLResponseWriter, which is responsible for serializing the search, faceting, and highlighting (and any other) results as an XML response that can then be handled by a client. Other implementations include the JSONResponseWriter, PHPResponseWriter, PHPSerializedResponseWriter, PythonResponseWriter, RubyResponseWriter, and the XSLTResponseWriter. Hopefully, the names of these are pretty self-explanatory, but if not, have a look at the Solr website for more details. Additionally, if you need to interface with a legacy system or output your own binary format, implementing a QueryResponseWriter is relatively straightforward with plenty of examples available in the Solr source code.

### PROGRAMMATIC ACCESS TO SOLR

Up to now, you've seen a number of different inputs to Solr, but what about some real code that does searching?

Solr also provides some more advanced, though common, query capabilities. For instance, the DismaxQParser query parser provides a simpler query syntax than the LuceneQParser query parser and also gives preference to documents where clauses occur in separate fields. The sample code in the next listing demonstrates how to call a RequestHandler that uses the DismaxQParser for query parsing.

**Listing 3.2   Example Solr query code**

DisMax parser
searches across
fields given by the
qf parameter and
boosts terms
accordingly.

```
queryParams.setQuery("lazy");
queryParams.setParam("defType", "dismax");
queryParams.set("qf", "title^3 description^10");
System.out.println("Query: " + queryParams);
response = solr.query(queryParams);
assertTrue("response is null and it shouldn't be", response != null);
documentList = response.getResults();
assertTrue("documentList Size: " + documentList.size() +
    " is not: " + 2, documentList.size() == 2);
```

Tell Solr to use the
DisMax Query Parser
(named dismax in
solrconfig.xml).

Another common search technique is to allow the user a quick and easy way to find documents that are similar to a document in the current search results. This process is often called Find Similar or More Like This. Solr comes with More Like This capabilities built-in; they just need to be configured. For example, in solrconfig.xml, you can specify the /mlt request handler as

```
<requestHandler name="/mlt" class="solr_MoreLikeThisHandler">
  <lst name="defaults">
    <str name="mlt.fl">title,name,description,fullText</str>
    </lst>
</requestHandler>
```

In this simple configuration, you're specifying that the MoreLikeThisHandler should use the title, name, description, and fullText fields as the source for generating a new query. When a user requests a More Like This query, Solr will take the input document, look up the terms in the specified Fields, figure out which are the most important, and generate a new query. The new query will then be submitted to the index and the results returned. To query your new request handler, you can use the code shown next.

**Listing 3.3   More Like This example code**

Specify
document
results should
be similar to.

```
queryParams = new SolrQuery();
queryParams.setQueryType("/mlt");
queryParams.setQuery("description:number");
queryParams.set("mlt.match.offset", "0");
queryParams.setRows(1);
queryParams.set("mlt.fl", "description, title");
response = solr.query(queryParams);
assertTrue("response is null and it shouldn't be", response != null);
SolrDocumentList results =
        (SolrDocumentList) response.getResponse().get("match");
assertTrue("results Size: " + results.size() + " is not: " + 1,
        results.size() == 1);
```

Create search to find
similar documents.

Specify field to
generate query.

Of course, one of Solr's most popular features is its built-in support for faceting, which is covered in the next section.

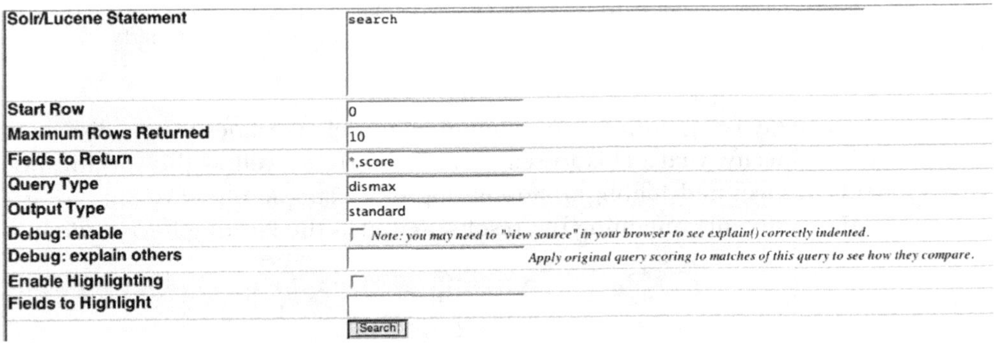

| Solr/Lucene Statement | search |
|---|---|
| Start Row | 0 |
| Maximum Rows Returned | 10 |
| Fields to Return | *,score |
| Query Type | dismax |
| Output Type | standard |
| Debug: enable | ☐ *Note: you may need to "view source" in your browser to see explain() correctly indented.* |
| Debug: explain others | *Apply original query scoring to matches of this query to see how they compare.* |
| Enable Highlighting | ☐ |
| Fields to Highlight | |
| | [Search] |

**Figure 3.15   Solr query interface**

### 3.5.2   *Faceting on extracted content*

Earlier, in section 3.4.2, we indexed some sample MS Word files using Solr and Tika. For this part, we added in some more of our own content, so your results may vary based on your content. But now that you have a deeper understanding of how searching works using the `SolrRequestHandler`, you can use Solr's simple administrative query interface to run a variety of searches. In our earlier example, we had Solr running on port 8983 of our local machine. Pointing a web browser at http://localhost:8983/solr/admin/form.jsp should yield a web page that looks like figure 3.15.

In this example, we're using the dismax `SolrRequestHandler`, which is defined in the solrconfig.xml configuration file and looks like this:

```
<requestHandler name="dismax" class="solr_DisMaxRequestHandler" >
  <lst name="defaults">
  <str name="echoParams">explicit</str>
  <float name="tie">0.01</float>
  <str name="qf">
     name title^5.0 description keyword fullText all^0.1
  </str>
  <str name="fl">
     name,title,description,keyword,fullText
  </str>
   <!-- Facets -->
   <str name="facet">on</str>
   <str name="facet.mincount">1</str>
   <str name="facet.field">mimeType</str>
   <str name="f.categories.facet.sort">true</str>
   <str name="f.categories.facet.limit">20</str>
   <str name="facet.field">creator</str>
  <str name="q.alt">*:*</str>
  <!-- example highlighter config, enable per-query with hl=true -->
  <str name="hl.fl">name,title,fullText</str>
  <!-- for this field, we want no fragmenting, just highlighting -->
  <str name="f.name.hl.fragsize">0</str>
  <!-- instructs Solr to return the field itself if no query terms are
       found -->
```

```
        <str name="f.name.hl.alternateField">name</str>
        <str name="f.text.hl.fragmenter">regex</str> <!-- defined below -->
      </lst>
  </requestHandler>
```

To make querying simpler, we've put in many default values for the dismax query handler to specify what fields to search and return, as well as the specification of what fields to facet and highlight. Submitting our example query to Solr, we get back an XML document containing the results, as well as the faceting information.

**Listing 3.4  Example Solr search results**

```
<response>

<lst name="responseHeader">                          ◀──────  Response header
 <int name="status">0</int>                                  section returns
 <int name="QTime">4</int>                                   metadata about
 <lst name="params">                                         input parameters and
  <str name="explainOther"/>                                 the search.
  <str name="fl">*,score</str>

  <str name="indent">on</str>
  <str name="start">0</str>
  <str name="q">search</str>
  <str name="hl.fl"/>
  <str name="wt">standard</str>
  <str name="qt">dismax</str>

  <str name="version">2.2</str>                      <result> section gives
  <str name="rows">10</str>                          information about the
 </lst>                                              documents that matched
</lst>                                               based on the query, the
<result name="response" numFound="2" start="0"       configuration, and the
         maxScore="0.12060823">               ◀───── input parameters.
 <doc>
  <float name="score">0.12060823</float>
  <arr name="creator">...</arr>

  <arr name="creatorText">...</arr>
  <str name="description">An enterprise-ready, Lucene-based
          search server.  Features include search,
          faceting, hit highlighting, replication and much,
          much more</str>
  <str name="id">solr</str>
  <str name="mimeType">text/xml</str>
  <str name="name">Solr, the Enterprise Search Server</str>
 </doc>

 <doc>
  <float name="score">0.034772884</float>
  <arr name="creator">...</arr>
  <arr name="creatorText">...</arr>
  <str name="description">A Java-based search engine library
          focused on high-performance, quality results.</str>
  <str name="id">lucene</str>
  <str name="mimeType">text/xml</str>
```

```
      <str name="name">Lucene</str>
    </doc>
  </result>
<lst name="facet_counts">
 <lst name="facet_queries"/>
 <lst name="facet_fields">
  <lst name="mimeType">
    <int name="text/xml">2</int>

  </lst>
  <lst name="creator">
    <int name="Apache Software Foundation">2</int>
    <int name="Doug Cutting">1</int>
    <int name="Yonik Seeley">1</int>
  </lst>
 </lst>

 <lst name="facet_dates"/>
</lst>
</response>
```

The facet_fields list section provides details on the facets found in the search results. In this example, the mimeType facet indicates four of the nine results are image/tiff, another four are text/plain, and one is image/png.

Listing 3.4 shows an abbreviated set of results (some field information was intentionally left out for display purposes) for the sample query, along with facet information. Though we relied on the default values specified in the dismax configuration, you could also pass in parameters via the URL that override the default parameters to return more results, highlight information, or query different fields.

That about covers the core of what you need to get started with Solr. Exploring the Solr website will provide more detail on all of these topics and more advanced topics like caching, replication, and administration. Next, let's take a step back and look at some general performance issues, along with some specific to Solr, and see how these factors can influence your search implementation.

## 3.6 *Understanding search performance factors*

At a high level, search performance is a measure of how well a search system works at producing results. It can be further broken down into two main categories: quantity and quality. Quantity refers to how fast you can return results (how many results you can return in a given amount of time), whereas quality refers to how relevant those results are to the search. It's often (but not always) the case that the two are opposing forces, requiring practitioners to constantly evaluate making trade-offs between greater speed and better results. In this section, we'll examine many of the tips and techniques that modern search engines employ to improve both quantity and quality. After that, we'll look at some Solr-specific tweaks to enable it to perform better. Before either of these topics, let's take a quick look at judging speed and relevancy since, without either of them, you have no way of knowing if you've succeeded.

### 3.6.1 *Judging quality*

As a user of a search engine, nothing is more frustrating than entering a query and getting back a list of results that are only vaguely relevant, if at all. What follows is almost always a trial-and-error approach of adding or subtracting keywords followed by a quick scan of the top 10 results. Often, it seems like you could find what you were looking for if you could just get the right combination of keywords. Other times, it feels like you should give up.

On the other side of the equation, search engine creators are constantly struggling with trade-offs between the quality of results, ease of use, and speed. Since by their nature queries are incomplete expressions of a user's information needs, search engines often employ complex algorithms that attempt to fill the gap between the user's incomplete query and what they really want.

In between the users and the creators is a fuzzy thing called *relevance*. Relevance is the notion of how appropriate a set of results is for a user's query. The reason it's fuzzy is because no two users will agree in all cases as to what's appropriate. And though judging relevance is a subjective task, many people have tried to come up with systematic approaches to determining relevance. Some have even gone so far as to organize conferences, complete with standard document collections, queries, and evaluation tools. Participants run the queries against the collection and submit their results to the conference, which then gathers the results and evaluates and ranks the groups according to how well they did. The granddaddy of these conferences, held annually, is called *TREC*, or the Text REtrieval Conference, and is run by the US National Institute of Standards and Technology (NIST).

Many of these conferences rely on two metrics of evaluation to determine which engines provide the best results. The first metric, *precision*, measures the number of relevant documents in the list of documents provided by the engine. As a refinement, precision is often looked at in the context of number of results returned. For instance, precision at 10 (often labeled P@10) measures how many relevant documents were returned in the top 10 results. Since most users only look at the first 10 results or the first page of results, it's often most useful to only look at precision at 10. The second metric, *recall*, measures the number of relevant documents found out of all the relevant documents in the collection. Note that perfect recall is attainable by returning all documents in the collection for every query, as dumb as that would be to do. In many situations, trade-offs are made between precision and recall. For example, precision can often be increased by requiring many, if not all, of the terms in a query to be present in a document. But on smaller collections, this may mean some queries return no results. Likewise, recall can often be increased by adding any and all synonyms for every query term into the query. Unfortunately, due to the ambiguity of many words, documents that rely on alternate meanings of a word might find their way into the final results, thus lowering precision.

So how should you evaluate the quality of your system? First and foremost, be aware that every technique has its strengths and weaknesses. More than likely, you should use more than one technique. Table 3.6 contains a list of some evaluation techniques; undoubtedly others may also prove useful for specific systems.

**Table 3.6  Common evaluation techniques**

| Technique | Description | Cost | Trade-offs |
|---|---|---|---|
| Ad hoc | Developers, Quality Assurance, and other interested parties informally evaluate the system and provide feedback on what works and what doesn't. | Low initially, but probably much higher in the long run. | Not formally repeatable unless logs are kept. Hard to know how changes affect other parts of system. Probably too narrow in focus to be effective. Risks tuning for a specific set of queries. At a minimum, all testers should try the same collection for the test. |
| Focus group | Groups of users are invited to use the system. Logs are kept of queries, documents chosen, etc. Users can also be asked to explicitly identify relevant and nonrelevant documents. Statistics can then be used to make decisions about search quality. | Depends on number of participants, cost of setting up evaluation system. | Can be useful, depending on number of participants. Can also provide feedback on usability. Logs can be saved to create a repeatable test. |
| TREC and other evaluation conferences | TREC provides a number of tracks for evaluating information retrieval systems, including those focused on web, blogs, and legal documents. | Fee required to obtain data; formal participation (submitting results) in TREC can be time consuming and costly. Questions and judgments are available for free and, with the data, can be run offline as needed. | Good for comparing to other systems and getting a general feel for quality, but data may not be representative of your collection, so results may not be all that useful for your system. |
| Query log analysis | Logs are taken from the production system and the top 50 queries are extracted, as well as 10-20 random samples. Analysts then judge the top 5 or 10 results from each query as relevant, somewhat relevant, not relevant, and embarrassing. Results are correlated and analyzed for underperforming queries. Over time, the goal is to maximize the relevant, minimize the nonrelevant, and eliminate the embarrassing. Additionally, searches returning zero results are analyzed for possible improvements. Further analysis may involve examining which results were | Depends on size of logs and number of queries used. | Best suited for testing your data with your users. Requires effective planning on what to log and when and how to collect it. Best done during beta testing and as an ongoing task of a production system. Risk of having lower-quality results early in process. |

**Table 3.6   Common evaluation techniques** *(continued)*

| Technique | Description | Cost | Trade-offs |
|---|---|---|---|
| Query log analysis *(continued)* | chosen (click-through analysis) and how long users spent on each page. The assumption is that the longer a person spends on a given result, the more relevant it is to their need. | | |
| A/B testing | Similar to query log analysis and focus group testing, a live system is used, but different users may receive different results. For example, 80% of the users receive results based on one approach, whereas the other 20% of users receive results from an alternate approach. Logs are then analyzed and compared to see whether users with common queries between the two groups preferred one approach to the other. This can be applied across any part of the system, ranging from how indexing is done to how results are displayed. Just make sure to thoroughly document the differences between the A and B groups. | Requires deploying and supporting two systems in production. Also depends on the number of queries and the size of the logs. | Well suited for testing with real users. Best done in non-peak times for limited periods of time. In other words, don't do it three weeks before Christmas if you're a shopping site! |

Ad hoc, focus group, TREC, and, to a lesser extent, log analysis and A/B testing all run the risk of producing a system optimized for the evaluation while not performing as well in the wild. For instance, using the TREC documents, queries, and evaluations (called *relevance judgments*) may mean your system does well on TREC-style queries (which are of a specific nature), and doesn't do well on queries that your users are likely to ask.

From a practical standpoint, most applications intended for a significantly sized audience will want to, at a minimum, do ad hoc testing and query log analysis. If you have sufficient funding, focus groups and TREC-style evaluations can give you more data points to evaluate your system. Log analysis and A/B testing will produce the most practical, usable results, and are the preferred methods of the authors.

Naturally, relevance tuning should never be viewed as a do-it-once-and-forget-about-it kind of task. Likewise, you shouldn't obsess about the quality of any one result, unless it's one of the most frequently asked queries. Moreover, you should rarely worry about why one result is ranked at position 4 and another is ranked at position 5. The only time, possibly, is when editorial decisions (someone paid money for a position) require a document to be at a specific position. At the end of the day, if a certain result should be the number-one hit for a query, then hardcode it as the number one hit for the query. Trying to tweak your system's various configuration parameters to make it appear as the first result via the normal search process is asking for headaches and will more than likely break other searches. Knowing when to use a hammer and when to use a screwdriver is half the battle in keeping your customers happy.

### 3.6.2 Judging quantity

There are numerous metrics for judging how well a search system performs in terms of quantity. Some of the more useful are listed here:

- *Query throughput*—The number of queries the system can process in a given time unit. Usually measured in queries per second (QPS). Higher is better.
- *Popularity versus time*—Charts how long each query takes, on average, by the frequency of the query. This is especially useful for showing where to spend time in improving the system. For instance, if the most popular query is also the slowest, the system is in trouble, but if only rarely asked queries are slow, it may not be worth the effort to investigate.
- *Average query time*—How long does the average query take to process? Related statistics show the distribution of queries over time. Smaller is better.
- *Cache statistics*—Many systems cache query results and documents and it's useful to know how often the cache is hit or missed. If there are routinely few hits, it may be faster to turn off caching.
- *Index size*—Measures how effective the indexing algorithm is at compressing the index. Some indexes may be as small as 20% of the original. Smaller is better, but disk is cheap so don't obsess too much over it.
- *Document throughput*—The number of documents indexed per time unit. Usually measured as documents per second (DPS). Higher is better.
- *Number of documents in index*—When an index size becomes too large, it may need to be distributed.
- *Number of unique terms*—Very high-level metric that provides a basic idea of the size of the index.

Additionally, the usual suspects like CPU, RAM, disk space, and I/O should play a role in judging how well a system is performing. The key to these metrics is that they should be monitored over time. Many systems (including Solr) provide administrative tools that make it easy for administrators to keep an eye on what's going on.

With a basis for understanding how your system is performing in place, the next section will examine a variety of tips and techniques for actually improving performance. This section will examine a wide variety of techniques ranging from hardware considerations to the trade-offs between various search and indexing options.

## 3.7    *Improving search performance*

From the early days of search engines, researchers and practitioners have been tuning their systems with a number of different goals in mind. Some want better relevancy; others want better compression; still others want better query throughput. Nowadays, we want all of these things and then some, but how do we obtain them? The following sections will hopefully provide a bevy of options to think about and try.

Before we begin, a warning is in order: tuning a search engine can take up large chunks of time and result in no measurable improvement. It's best to double-check that improvements are needed by monitoring both the quality and quantity aspects of a system before undertaking any tuning. Also, the advice contained here won't work in all situations. Depending on the search engine, some or all of the tips contained here may not even be applicable or may require a deep understanding of the engine in order to implement. Finally, be sure the problem really is in the search engine, and not the application, before spending too much time tuning.

With our metrics in place and the warnings out of the way, let's look at how we can improve search performance. Some performance issues are indexing time issues, whereas others are search time issues. Some issues relate only to the quantity or quality of results, whereas others will affect both. Let's start by taking a look at some hardware considerations, and then progress to software solutions like improving analysis and writing better queries.

### 3.7.1    *Hardware improvements*

One of the easiest and most cost-effective tuning options available to all search engines is to upgrade the hardware. Search engines usually like a lot of RAM, and they like to have the CPU all to themselves. Furthermore, in large systems that don't fit completely in RAM, improvements in the I/O system will also reap rewards. Of particular interest on the query side are solid state drives (SSDs), which greatly reduce seek times, but may be slower to write out data.

Single machine improvements can take you only so far. At some point, depending on the size of the data, machine, and number of users, there may come a time when the workload must be distributed across two or more machines. This can generally be handled in one of two ways:

1  *Replication*—A single index that fits on one machine is copied to one or more machines that are load balanced. This is often the case for online stores that don't have a particularly large index, but have a very high query volume.
2  *Distribution/sharding*—A single index is distributed across several nodes or *shards* based on a hash code or some other mechanism. A master node sends incoming queries to each of the shards and then collates the results.

As an alternative to splitting an index based on a hash code, it's often possible to logically separate an index and queries to separate nodes. For example, in multilingual search it can be useful (but not always) to split the indexes by language such that one node serves English queries and documents while another node serves Spanish queries and documents.

Naturally, hardware improvements can give you some nice gains, but only offer so much in terms of speedups, and can't offer anything in terms of relevance. It makes sense to look at some time-tested tips and techniques for speeding up and improving the quality of search, even if the gains may be harder to come by.

### 3.7.2 Analysis improvements

All search engines, whether closed or open source, must define a mechanism for converting the input text into tokens that can be indexed. For example, Solr does this through the `Analyzer` process where an `InputStream` is split into an initial set of tokens, which are then (optionally) modified. It's during this analysis process that the stage is often set for how well indexing performs in terms of speed and relevancy. Table 3.7 contains a repeat of some of the common analysis techniques offered earlier in the chapter, plus some new ones, and adds notes on how they help, and sometimes hurt, performance.

Table 3.7  Common performance-improving analysis techniques

| Name | Description | Benefits | Downsides |
|---|---|---|---|
| Stopword removal | Commonly occurring words like *the*, *a*, and *an* are removed before indexing, saving on index size. | Faster indexing, smaller index. | Lossy process. Better to index stopwords and handle them at query time. Stopwords are often useful for better phrase search. |
| Stemming | Tokens are analyzed by a stemmer and possibly transformed to a root form. For example, *banks* becomes *bank*. | Improves recall. | Lossy process that can limit ability to do exact match searches. Solution: keep two fields, one stemmed and one unstemmed. |
| Synonym expansion | For each token, 0 or more synonyms are added. Usually done at query time. | Improves recall by retrieving documents that don't contain the query keywords, but are still related to the query. | Ambiguous synonyms can retrieve unrelated documents. |
| Lowercasing tokens | All tokens are put into lowercase. | Users often don't properly case queries; lowercasing at query and index time allows for more matches. | Prevents case-sensitive matches. Many systems will keep two fields, one for exact matches, and one for inexact. |
| External knowledge as payloads | Some external source is consulted that provides additional info about the importance of a token, which is then encoded as a payload with the token in the index. Examples include font weight, link analysis, and part of speech. | Usually allows for more meaning to be stored about a particular token, which can enhance search. For example, link analysis is at the heart of Google's PageRank algorithm (Brin 1998). | Can significantly slow down the analysis process and increase the index size. |

Another useful but less-common technique that can help produce results in difficult situations is called *n-gram analysis,* which is a form of the sequence modeling we discussed earlier in the book. An *n-gram* is a subsequence of one or more characters or tokens. For example, the character-based one-gram (unigram) of *example* is *e, x, a, m, p, l, e,* whereas the bigrams are *ex, xa, am, mp, pl, le.* Likewise, token-based *n*-grams will produce pseudo-phrases. For example, the bigrams for *President of the United States* are *President of, of the, the United, United States.* Why are *n*-grams useful? They come in handy in approximate matching situations, or when the data isn't particularly clean such as OCR'ed data. In Lucene, the spell-checker component uses *n*-grams to produce candidate suggestions, which are then scored. When searching languages like Chinese, where it's often difficult for algorithms to determine tokens, *n*-grams are used to create multiple tokens. This approach doesn't require any knowledge about the language (Nie 2000). Word-based *n*-grams are useful when searching with stopwords. For example, assume a document contains the two sentences:

- John Doe is the new Elbonian president.
- The United States has sent an ambassador to the country.

This document is then (possibly) transformed, after analysis using stopwords, to these tokens: *john, doe, new, elbonian, president, united, states, sent, ambassador, country.* If the input query is then *President of the United States,* after analysis, the query is transformed to *president united states,* which would then match the Elbonian example since those three tokens coincide in the analyzed document. But if stopwords are kept during indexing, but only used to produce phrase-like *n*-grams on the query side, you can reduce the chances of false matches by generating a query like *President of the,* and *the United States,* or some other variation depending on the type of *n*-gram produced, which is more likely to match only on a sentence containing that exact phrasing. In some cases, it's useful to produce multiple grams. Again, using our example, you could produce bigrams up through five-grams and be more likely to exactly match *President of the United States.* Of course, this technique isn't perfect and can still cause problems, but it can help take advantage of the information in stopwords that would otherwise be lost.

In addition to the techniques in table 3.7 and *n*-grams, each application will have its own needs. This underscores one of the main advantages of open source approaches: the source is available to extend. Remember that the more involved the analysis is, the slower the indexing. Since indexing is often an offline task, it may be worthwhile to do more complicated analysis if measurable gains are to be had, but the general rule is to start simple and then add features if they solve a problem.

With analysis out of the way, we can now look at improving query performance.

### 3.7.3  *Query performance improvements*

On the query side of the coin, there are many techniques for improving both the speed and accuracy of search. In most situations, the difficulty in providing good results lies in underspecification of the information need by the user. It's the nature of the beast. And Google's simple interface that encourages one- or two-keyword queries has significantly raised the bar not only for other web-scale search engines, but for smaller engines as well. Though the big internet engines have access to the same material as Google, smaller systems generally don't have access to massive query logs or document structures such as HTML links and other user feedback mechanisms that can provide valuable information about what's important to a user. Before spending time building anything complex, try to address two key items that can help improve results:

1  *User training*—Sometimes users need to be shown how much better their results can be by learning a few key syntax tips, like phrases, and so forth.

2  *External knowledge*—Is there anything about one or more of the documents that makes it more important than another? For example, maybe it's written by the CEO, or maybe 99 out of 100 people marked it as being useful, or maybe your profit margin on the item described is five times that of another comparable item. Whatever it is, figure out how to encode that knowledge into the system and make it a factor during search. If the search system doesn't allow that, it may be time for a new system!

Beyond user training and the use of a priori knowledge about indexes, many things can be done to improve the speed and accuracy of queries. First and foremost, in most situations, query terms should be ANDed together, not ORed. For instance, if the user input was `Jumping Jack Flash`, then the query, assuming you aren't detecting phrases, should be translated into the equivalent of *Jumping AND Jack AND Flash* and not *Jumping OR Jack OR Flash*. By using AND, all query terms must match. This will almost certainly raise precision, but may lower recall. It will definitely be faster, as well, since there will be fewer documents to score. Using AND may result in a zero-result query, but it's then possible to fall back to an OR query, if desired. About the only time AND may not produce enough useful results for simple queries is if the collection is very small (roughly speaking, less than 200,000 documents).

**NOTE**  The use of AND here isn't meant to signify that all search engines support that syntax, but it's what Solr uses, so we kept it that way for simplicity of explanation.

Another useful query technique that can produce big gains in precision is to either detect phrases or automatically induce phrases using token *n*-grams. In the former case, analysis of the query is done to determine whether the query contains any phrases, and those are then translated into the system's internal phrase query representation. For example, if the user input is `Wayne Gretzky career stats`, a good phrase detector should recognize Wayne Gretzky as a phrase and produce the query `"Wayne Gretzky" career stats`, or even `"Wayne Gretzky career stats"`. Many search systems also offer a position-based *slop* factor when specifying phrases. This slop factor specifies how many positions apart two or more words can be and still be considered a phrase. Often it's also the case that the closer the words are, the higher the score.

As for improving the speed of queries, fewer query terms usually result in faster searches. Likewise, commonly occurring words are going to slow down queries since a large number of documents must be scored in order to determine the relevant ones, so it may be worthwhile to remove stopwords at query time. Obviously, encouraging your users to avoid ambiguous or commonly occurring words will also help, but it isn't likely to be practical unless your audience is mostly expert users.

Finally, a commonly used technique for improving quality, but not speed since it involves submitting at least two queries per user input, is called *relevance feedback*. Relevance feedback is the technique of marking one or more results, either manually or automatically, as relevant, and then using the important terms to form a new query. In the manual form of relevance feedback, users provide some indication (a check box or by clicking a link) that one or more documents are relevant, and then the important terms in those documents are used to create a new query which is then submitted to the system automatically, and the new results are returned. In the automatic case, the top 5 or 10 documents are automatically chosen as relevant, and the new query is formed from those documents. In both cases, it's also possible to identify documents that aren't relevant, and have those terms removed from the query or weighted less. In many cases, the new query terms that are kept are weighted differently from the original query and input parameters can be used to specify how much weight to give the original query terms or the new query terms. For instance, you may decide that the new terms are worth twice as much as the original terms, and multiply the new terms' weights by two. Let's look at a simple example of how this feedback process may look. Let's assume you have four documents in your collection, as described in table 3.8.

Now, let's assume the user was interested in what sports are played in Minnesota, so they query `minnesota AND sports`. A perfectly reasonable query, yet against this admittedly trivial example, without relevance feedback, only document 0 will be returned. But if you employ automatic relevance feedback and use the top result for query expansion, your system would create a new query, such as `(minnesota AND sports) OR (vikings OR dome OR football OR minneapolis OR st. paul)*2`. This new feedback query would bring back all the documents (how convenient!). It almost goes without saying that relevance feedback rarely works this well, but it usually does help, especially if the user is willing to provide judgments. To learn more about relevance feedback, see *Modern Information Retrieval* (Baeza-Yates 2011) or *Information Retrieval: Algorithms and Heuristics* (Grossman 1998). Moving along, let's take a quick look at some alternative scoring models to get an idea of some other approaches to search.

**Table 3.8  Example document collection**

| Document ID | Terms |
|---|---|
| 0 | minnesota, vikings, dome, football, sports, minneapolis, st. paul |
| 1 | dome, twins, baseball, sports |
| 2 | gophers, football, university |
| 3 | wild, st. paul, hockey, sports |

### 3.7.4 *Alternative scoring models*

Earlier, we focused on the vector space model (VSM) for scoring, specifically Lucene's model, but we'd be remiss if we didn't mention that there are many different ways of scoring with the VSM, as well as many different models for scoring beyond the VSM, some of which are listed in table 3.9. Most of these alternatives are implemented in research-oriented systems or are covered by patents and are inaccessible or impractical for users of open source in production. But some are now implemented under-the-hood in Lucene and are a configuration option away in Solr. In fact, much of Lucene's scoring capabilities are now pluggable in what will be (or is, depending on when we go to print) Lucene and Solr 4.0. Because we're using an earlier version, we won't cover using these models here. One way of improving query performance is by switching out the underlying scoring model.

Finally, note that much research on improving query performance is happening, via different models and different query formulations. Many good and interesting studies are published via the ACM Special Interest Group in Information Retrieval (SIGIR) at the annual conference. Monitoring their publications is a great way to stay current on new techniques for improving results. At any rate, the information here should give you enough to get started. Now, let's take a look at Solr performance techniques for some concrete improvements you can make on your system.

**Table 3.9  Alternative scoring methods and models**

| Name | Description |
| --- | --- |
| Language modeling | An alternative probabilistic model that turns the IR question on its head, sort of like the TV show Jeopardy, where the answer is given and the contestant must come up with the question. Instead of measuring whether a given document matches the query, it measures the likelihood that a given document would create the query. |
| Latent semantic indexing | A matrix-based approach which attempts to model documents at the conceptual level using singular value decomposition. Covered by patent, so of little use to open source users. |
| Neural networks and other machine learning approaches | In these approaches, the retrieval function is learned, over time, through a training set and feedback from the user. |
| Alternate weighting schemes | Many researchers have proposed modifications to the weighting schemes used in many of the models. Some of the modifications center around the use of document length and average document length as a scoring factor (Okapi BM25, pivoted document length normalization, among others). The basic premise is that longer documents will likely have higher TF values for a keyword than shorter, but the benefit of these repeated terms diminishes as the document gets longer. Note that this length normalization factor is usually not linear. |
| Probabilistic models and related techniques | Use statistical analysis to determine the likelihood that a given document is a match for the query. Related techniques include inference networks and language modeling. |

### 3.7.5   *Techniques for improving Solr performance*

Though Solr is highly capable out of the box, there are many best practices that you should follow to give Solr the chance to really show what it's made of in regard to performance. To properly address performance, we can break the problem down into two subsections, the first covering indexing performance and the second covering search. Before we begin, often the simplest way to get more performance is to upgrade to the latest released version. The community is active and new improvements are coming in all the time.

#### IMPROVING INDEXING PERFORMANCE

Indexing performance considerations can be divided into three parts:

- Schema design
- Configuration
- Submission methods

Good schema design, as discussed earlier, comes down to figuring out what fields are needed, how they're analyzed, and whether or not they need to be stored. Searching many `Fields` is going to be slower than searching one `Field`. Likewise, retrieving documents with a lot of stored `Fields` is going to be slower than documents without a lot stored `Fields`. Furthermore, complex analysis processes will adversely affect indexing performance due to time spent doing complex tokenization and token filtering procedures. Often, depending on your users, you may be able to sacrifice some quality for more speed.

The Solr configuration provides many levers for controlling performance; among them are controls for telling Lucene (the underlying library powering search) how to create and write the files for storing the index. These factors are specified in the solr-config.xml`<indexDefaults>` section, which the following is an example of:

**Using Lucene's compound file format saves on file descriptors at the cost of slower searching and indexing.**

```
<useCompoundFile>false</useCompoundFile>
```

**The mergeFactor controls how often Lucene merges internal files. Smaller numbers (< 10) use less memory than the default at the cost of slower indexing. In most cases, the default is sufficient, but you may wish to experiment.**

```
<mergeFactor>10</mergeFactor>
```

**maxBufferedDocs controls how many documents are buffered internally before flushing to disk. Larger numbers require more memory and speed up indexing, whereas smaller numbers use less memory.**

```
<maxBufferedDocs>1000</maxBufferedDocs>
```

**maxMergeDocs specifies the largest number of documents ever merged by Lucene. Smaller numbers (< 10,000) are better for systems with frequent updates; larger numbers are better for batch indexing and speed up searches.**

```
<maxMergeDocs>2147483647</maxMergeDocs>
```

**maxFieldLength specifies the maximum number of Tokens from a single Field that will be indexed. Increase this value (and your Java heap size) if you expect to have large documents with a lot of tokens.**

```
<maxFieldLength>10000</maxFieldLength>
```

Finally, how an application sends documents to Solr can greatly affect indexing performance. Best practices suggest sending multiple documents at a time when using the HTTP POST mechanism. Further increases in performance can be gained by using several threads to send multidocument requests, increasing throughput and minimizing HTTP costs. Solr will take care of all of the synchronization issues, so rest assured your data will be properly indexed. The following section lists these categories and describes the issues related to Solr performance.

**SEARCH PERFORMANCE**

Search performance can be broken down into a number of different categories, each offering different levels of performance (see table 3.10).

**Table 3.10  Search performance categories**

| Category | Description |
|---|---|
| Query type | Solr supports a rich query language, allowing for anything from simple term queries to wildcard and range queries. Complex queries using wildcards and searching ranges will be slower than simpler queries. |
| Size | Both query size (number of clauses) and index size play an important role in determining performance. The larger the index, the more terms to search (it's usually sublinear in the number of documents). More query terms usually means more documents and Fields to check. More Fields, can also mean more content to check if the query accesses all of those Fields. |
| Analysis | Just as in indexing, complicated analysis processes will be slower than simpler processes, but it's usually negligible for all but really long queries or when doing extensive synonym or query expansion. |
| Caching and warming strategies | Solr has advanced mechanisms for caching queries, documents, and other important structures. Furthermore, it can automatically populate some of these structures before making new index changes available for searching. See the solrconfig.xml for information on caching. Query log analysis and the Solr administration interface can help determine whether caching is helpful during search. If it's not helpful (high cache misses), it's better to turn it off. |
| Replication | High query volume can be addressed by replicating the Solr indexes out to several load-balanced servers, thus spreading queries out across several machines. Solr provides a suite of tools for synchronizing indexes between servers. |
| Distributed search | Large indexes can be split up (sharded) across several machines. A master node broadcasts the incoming query to all the shards and then collates the results. In combination with replication, large, fault-tolerant systems can be built. |

In the end, as with most optimization strategies, what works for one application may not work for another. The preceding guidelines provide general rules of thumb for using Solr, but pragmatic testing and profiling on your data and servers is the only way to know what works best for your situation. Next, let's take a look at some alternatives to Solr for both Java and other languages.

## 3.8    *Search alternatives*

One of the great things about open source is that anyone can cook up a project and make it available for others to use (naturally, this is also a disadvantage, as it becomes difficult to know what's good and what isn't). A number of open source search libraries are available for use in your product, many of which have different design goals. Some strive to be the fastest, whereas others are great for testing out new search theories and are more academic-oriented.

Though all of the authors have used Solr and Lucene extensively and are biased toward those solutions, table 3.11 provides alternative approaches or alternative language implementations.

**Table 3.11    Alternative search engines**

| Name | URL | Features | License |
|---|---|---|---|
| Apache Lucene and variants | http://lucene.apache.org/ | Low-level search library, requiring more engineering, but also providing more flexibility with more control over footprint, memory, etc. Similarly, there are other implementations of Lucene's APIs for .NET, Python (PyLucene), and Ruby (Ferret), each providing some level of compatibility with Lucene Java. | Apache Software License (ASL) |
| Apache Nutch | http://lucene.apache.org/nutch/ | A full-service crawler, indexer, and search engine built on Apache Hadoop and Lucene Java. | Apache Software License (ASL) |
| ElasticSearch | http://elasticsearch.com | A Lucene-based search server. | Apache Software License (ASL) |
| Minion | https://minion.dev.java.net/ | An open source search engine from Sun Microsystems. | GPL v2.0 |
| Sphinx | http://www.sphinxsearch.com/ | Search engine focused on indexing content stored in SQL database. | GNU Public License v2 (GPL) |
| Lemur | http://www.lemurproject.org/ | Uses an alternate ranking formula, called *language modeling*, instead of the vector space model. | BSD |
| MG4J—Managing Gigabytes for Java | http://mg4j.dsi.unimi.it/ | Search engine based on the excellent book *Managing Gigabytes* (Witten 1999). Aims to be scalable and fast. Also provides alternate ranking algorithms. | GPL |
| Zettair | http://www.seg.rmit.edu.au/zettair/ | Designed to be compact and fast, allowing you to index/search HTML and TREC collections. | BSD |

Though plenty of other search engines are available, the list in table 3.11 provides a nice sampling of tools across several languages and with several different licenses.

## 3.9 Summary

Searching your content is a rich and complex landscape. Providing better access to your content is the first step in gaining control of all of the data inundating your life. Furthermore, search is now one of those must-have components in almost any customer-facing application. The likes of Amazon, Google, Yahoo!, and others have successfully demonstrated the opportunities good search brings to users and companies alike. It's now up to you to leverage the ideas we examined in this chapter to make your applications richer. Specifically, you should know the basics of indexing and searching content, how to set up and use Apache Solr, and also some of the issues involved in making search (and specifically Solr) perform in real-world applications. From this launching pad, we'll next examine techniques for working with text in situations where the results aren't always cut and dried, or as we call it, *fuzzy string matching.*

## 3.10 Resources

Baeza-Yates, Ricardo and Ribiero-Neto, Berthier. 2011 *Modern Information Retrieval: The Concepts and Technology Behind Search, Second Edition.* Addison-Wesley.

Brin, Sergey, and Lawrence Page. 1998. "The Anatomy of a Large-Scale Hypertextual Web Search Engine." http://infolab.stanford.edu/~backrub/google.html.

Grossman, David A. and Frieder, Ophir. 1998. *Information Retrieval: Algorithms and Heuristics.* Springer.

Nie, Jian-yun; Gao, Jiangfeng; Zhang, Jian; Zhou, Ming. 2000. "On the Use of Words and N-grams for Chinese Information Retrieval." Fifth International Workshop on Information Retrieval with Asian Languages, IRAL2000, Hong Kong, pp 141-148.

Salton, G; Wong, A; Yang, C. S. 1975. "A Vector Space Model for Automatic Indexing." *Communications of the ACM*, Vol 18, Number 11. Cornell University. http://www.cs.uiuc.edu/class/fa05/cs511/Spring05/other_papers/p613-salton.pdf.

"Vector space model." Wikipedia. http://en.wikipedia.org/wiki/Vector_space_model.

Witten, Ian; Moffatt, Alistair; Bell, Timothy. 1999. *Managing Gigabytes: Compressing and Indexing Documents and Images*, Morgan Kaufmann, New York.

# *Fuzzy string matching*

One of the most difficult aspects of dealing with text is the approximate nature of many of the tasks you'd like to perform. Whether this is the relevance of search results or the clustering of similar items, what exactly is meant by relevance or similarity is difficult to specify in a way that's both intuitive and specific. In language, we encounter this phenomenon all the time, typically with little consideration. For example, you'll hear a new band described as, "They're like Radiohead, only different." Typically you just nod, taking whatever interpretation that comes to mind, not considering the vast range of other potential and valid interpretations.

We distinctly remember when the Did You Mean feature (see figure 4.1—since replaced by Google with Showing Results For when Google has high confidence of a misspelling) arrived on Google search. Though the target audience of such a feature was likely people whose queries had typos, for others who are (shall we say?)

*challenged* by spelling, this was a boon to productivity. Not only did it mean that you could improve search productivity, but it also provided access to a means to look up words that are either not found in dictionaries or for which an attempted spelling wasn't close enough to generate a reasonable suggestion. Today, you can quickly write about the "joie de vivre of coding late into the evening" rather than just saying that "coding is something to do" because the effort to look up a correct spelling of that borrowed French phrase is now trivial.

A feature like Did You Mean, or as it's sometimes called, *query spell-checking*, requires fuzzy matching. Specifically you need to generate multiple possible suggestions for the query that was entered, rank these suggestions, and determine whether you're even going to show the suggestion to the user. *Fuzzy string matching* (which is like regular string matching, only different), or just *fuzzy matching*, is the process of finding strings that are similar, but not necessarily exactly alike. In contrast, *string matching* is concerned with exact matches. Similarity is usually defined by a distance, score, or a likelihood of similarity. For instance, using the edit distance (Levenshtein distance), which we'll describe later, the words *there* and *here* have an edit distance of one. Though you can probably guess at the meaning of that particular score, we'll leave it for now knowing that we'll return to it further into the chapter.

Spell-checking is just one example of fuzzy string matching. Another common use case occurs regularly when companies merge and must combine customer lists, or governments and airlines check flight manifests for potential criminals. In these cases, often called either *record linkage* or *entity resolution*, you must compare one list of names against another list and try to determine whether two similarly spelled names actually are the same people. Simply matching names doesn't completely answer the question, but it does help immensely. To explore these use cases, this chapter will describe various approaches to fuzzy string matching, as well as look at several open source implementations of these approaches. You'll learn how to take words, short phrases, and names and compare them to one another in such a way as to identify other words and phrases that are close matches and rank the closeness of those matches. We'll also look at how to apply these techniques to specific applications and leverage Solr and

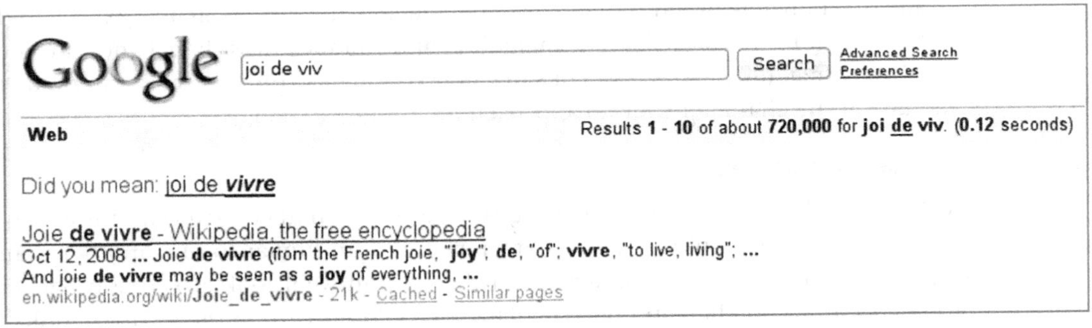

**Figure 4.1   Example of a Did You Mean suggestion from Google search. Image captured 2/1/2009.**

relatively small amounts of custom Java code to build these applications. Finally, we'll combine some of the techniques you've learned to build some common fuzzy string matching applications.

## 4.1 Approaches to fuzzy string matching

How strings are compared is something that, as programmers, you rarely have to think about. Most programming languages provide a means to compare strings for you. Even when you do consider this question, it's relatively straightforward to imagine an implementation of a string comparison function that considers each letter of the two strings and returns true only if each letter matches.

Fuzzy string matching immediately opens up a number of questions for which the answers aren't so clear. For instance:

- How many characters need to match?
- What if the letters are the same but not in the same order?
- What if there are extra letters?
- Are some letters more important than others?

Different approaches to fuzzy matching answer these questions differently. Some approaches focus on character overlap as their primary means of looking at string similarity. Other approaches model the order in which the characters occur more directly, whereas still others look at multiple letters simultaneously. We'll break these approaches down into three sections. In the first, titled "Character overlap measures," we'll look at the Jaccard measure and some of its variations, as well as the Jaro-Winkler distance as a way of addressing the character overlap approaches. Our next section, titled "Edit distance measures," will look at the character order approach and some of its variations. Finally, we'll consider the simultaneous approach in the section titled "*N*-gram edit distance."

Before we begin to consider these differences, you must first come to terms with the notion that, unlike in regular string matching, the output of a fuzzy matching algorithm is almost never a Boolean value. Instead, these algorithms return a value representing the degree to which strings match. A typical convention is to return a real-valued number between 0 and 1, where 1 means the strings match exactly and would be equal in traditional string matching, and numbers less than 1 indicate the level of fuzzy matching. Let's now consider how you might compute such values, first by looking at the character overlap approach mentioned earlier.

### 4.1.1 Character overlap measures

One way to look at fuzzy string matching is in terms of character overlap. Intuitively, strings that share many of the same characters are more similar to one another than strings that share few or no characters. In this section we'll look at two approaches that rely primarily on character overlap. The first is the Jaccard measure. We'll look at it and some of its variations and then examine the Jaro-Winkler distance.

## JACCARD MEASURE

The *Jaccard measure,* or *similarity coefficient,* is one approach to capturing the intuition that strings which share more of the same characters are more similar. In the context of string comparisons, it's computed as the percentage of unique characters that two strings share when compared to the total number of unique characters in both strings. More formally, where $A$ is the set of characters in the first string, and $B$ is the set of characters in the second string, this can be expressed as follows:

$$\frac{|A \cap B|}{|A \cup B|}$$

The Jaccard measure treats all letters equally; it doesn't discount letters that may overlap because they're common or promote uncommon letters that match. The code to calculate the Jaccard measure is shown next.

**Listing 4.1  Computing the Jaccard measure**

```java
public float jaccard(char[] s, char[] t) {
  int intersection = 0;
  int union = s.length+t.length;
  boolean[] sdup = new boolean[s.length];       // Find duplicates and
  union -= findDuplicates(s,sdup);               // subtract from union.
  boolean[] tdup = new boolean[t.length];
  union -= findDuplicates(t,tdup);
  for (int si=0;si<s.length;si++) {
    if (!sdup[si]) {                             // Skip duplicates.
      for (int ti=0;ti<t.length;ti++) {
        if (!tdup[ti]) {
          if (s[si] == t[ti]) {                  // Find intersection.
            intersection++;
            break;
          }
        }
      }
    }
  }
  union-=intersection;                           // Return
  return (float) intersection/union;             // Jaccard
}                                                // distance.

private int findDuplicates(char[] s, boolean[] sdup) {
  int ndup =0;
  for (int si=0;si<s.length;si++) {
    if (sdup[si]) {
      ndup++;
    }
    else {
      for (int si2=si+1;si2<s.length;si2++) {
        if (!sdup[si2]) {
          sdup[si2] = s[si] == s[si2];
        }
      }
    }
```

```
    }
  }
  return ndup;
}
```

In the implementation code in listing 4.1, you first calculate the union part (the denominator) of the equation by subtracting the number of duplicate characters in the two strings from a counter keeping track of the union count. Next, you calculate the number of items in common between the two (the numerator). Finally, you finish it off by returning the score.

A common extension to the Jaccard measure is to weight characters based on frequency, such as the TF-IDF measure you saw in chapter 3. Using this weighting approach, the cosine similarity measure is a natural choice for computing the similarity between two strings due to its similarity to search, but it returns a value in the range of -1 to 1. To normalize this measure to return between 0 and 1, you can modify the measure slightly as shown here:

$$\frac{A \cdot B}{\|A\|^2 + \|B\|^2 - A \cdot B}$$

The resulting measure, known as the *Tanimoto coefficient*, is identical to the Jaccard coefficient when every character is weighted identically.

Since Solr uses cosine-based scoring for its retrieval, which provides similar scoring results as Tanimoto, the easiest way to implement this type of scoring is to index your dictionary or other set of terms, treating each term as a document and each character as its own token in Solr. This can be done by specifying a pattern tokenizer as follows:

```
<fieldType name="characterDelimited" class="solr.TextField">
  <analyzer>
   <tokenizer class="solr.PatternTokenizerFactory" pattern="."
                                                  group="0" />
  </analyzer>
</fieldType>
```

You can then query this field with a term and Solr will provide a cosine-based ranking of terms based on the frequency of characters in the dictionary words. If you want to try a quick version of indexing terms this way, see com.tamingtext.fuzzy.Overlap-Measures and its cosine method. In practice, this will produce reasonable results, but it may be difficult to choose between results with similar scores. This approach also disregards character position in scoring, which can help you better choose suggestions. To address this concern, let's look at a different measure that can account for position.

**JARO-WINKLER DISTANCE**
One disadvantage of character overlap approaches is that they don't model character order. For example, in the previous measures we've discussed, a character in the beginning of a string can match a character at the end of a string and this match isn't

treated differently from a match in a similar area of the string. The extreme version of this scenario is that if a word is reversed, its score is identical to a string that matches exactly. The Jaro-Winkler distance tries to heuristically address this in three distinct ways. The first is that it limits matching to a window of characters in the second string based on the length of the larger of the strings. The second is that it also factors in the number of transpositions or matching letters that don't occur in the same order. Finally, it adds a bonus based on the length of the largest common prefix of both words. Many discussions of this approach are available on the internet which may be of interest, and for those interested in using this distance measure, an efficient implementation is built into Lucene in the `org.apache.lucene.search.spell.Jaro-WinklerDistance` class.

The primary disadvantage of character overlap approaches is that they don't model character order well. In the next section, we'll look at an approach known as *edit distance* that models character order more formally. Modeling character order typically comes at a higher computational cost than measures that only use character overlap. We'll also look at ways to efficiently compute these measures.

### 4.1.2 *Edit distance measures*

Another approach to determining how similar one string is to another is by *edit distance*. The edit distance between two strings is the number of edit operations required to turn one string into the other string. Edit distances comes in a variety of forms, but typically include insertion, deletion, and substitution operations:

- An insertion adds a character to the source string to make it more similar to the target string.
- A deletion removes a character.
- A substitution replaces one character in the source string with another from the target string.

The edit distance is the sum of the number of insertions, deletions, and substitutions required to transform one string into another. For example, to turn the string *tamming test* into *taming text* would require one deletion of an *m* and one substitution of an *s* with an *x*, resulting in an edit distance of 2. This simple form of edit distance where the edit operations of insertions, deletions, and substitutions are allowed and each given an equal weight of 1 is known as the *Levenshtein distance.*

#### COMPUTING EDIT DISTANCE

Though there are multiple sequences of operations that will transform one string into another, you typically want the edit distance for two strings with the minimal number of operations to do so. Computing the minimum sequence of operations needed to transform one string into another may initially appear to be computationally expensive, but it can be done by performing $n \times m$ comparisons where $n$ is the length of one of the strings and $m$ is the length of the other. The algorithm to perform this task is a classic example of dynamic programming where the problem is decomposed into determining the optimal edit action given two offsets into each of the strings being compared. The code in listing 4.2 is the reduction of this process to Java. Note that we've chosen to show the straightforward approach to implementing Levenshtein distance; there are more efficient implementations that use less memory. We'll leave it as an exercise for the reader to explore this more.

**Listing 4.2   Computing edit distance**

```java
public int levenshteinDistance(char s[], char t[]) {
  int m = s.length;
  int n = t.length;
  int d[][] = new int[m+1][n+1];            ← Allocate
                                              distance
                                              matrix.
  for (int i=0;i<=m;i++)                     ← Initialize
    d[i][0] = i;                               upper bound
  for (int j=0;j<=n;j++)                       on distance.
    d[0][j] = j;
  for (int j=1;j<=n;j++) {
    for (int i=1;i<=m;i++) {
      if (s[i-1] == t[j-1]) {                 ← Cost is same
        d[i][j] = d[i-1][j-1];                  as previous
      } else {                                  match.
        d[i][j] = Math.min(Math.min(
                d[i-1][j] + 1,                ← Cost is 1 for an
                d[i][j-1] + 1),                 insertion, deletion,
                d[i-1][j-1] + 1);               or substitution.
      }
    }
  }
  return d[m][n];
}
```

Table 4.1 shows what this distance matrix looks like for our two sample strings: *taming text* and *tamming test*. Each cell contains the minimum cost of editing one string to arrive at the other string. For instance, you can see the cost of the deletion of the *m* in row 3 column 4, and the cost of the substitution in row 10 column 11. The minimal edit distance is always found in the lower-right corner of the distance matrix.

**Table 4.1   Matrix for computing edit distance**

|   |   | t | a | m | m | i | n | g |   | t | e | s | t |
|---|---|---|---|---|---|---|---|---|---|---|---|---|---|
|   | 0 | 1 | 2 | 3 | 4 | 5 | 6 | 7 | 8 | 9 | 10 | 11 | 12 |
| t | 1 | 0 | 1 | 2 | 3 | 4 | 5 | 6 | 7 | 7 | 8 | 9 | 10 |
| a | 2 | 1 | 0 | 1 | 2 | 3 | 4 | 5 | 6 | 7 | 8 | 9 | 10 |
| m | 3 | 2 | 1 | 0 | 1 | 2 | 3 | 4 | 5 | 6 | 7 | 8 | 9 |
| i | 4 | 3 | 2 | 1 | 1 | 1 | 2 | 3 | 4 | 5 | 6 | 7 | 8 |
| n | 5 | 4 | 3 | 2 | 2 | 2 | 1 | 2 | 3 | 4 | 5 | 6 | 7 |
| g | 6 | 5 | 4 | 3 | 3 | 3 | 2 | 1 | 2 | 3 | 4 | 5 | 6 |
|   | 7 | 6 | 5 | 4 | 4 | 4 | 3 | 2 | 1 | 2 | 3 | 4 | 5 |

**Table 4.1  Matrix for computing edit distance (continued)**

|   |    | t | a | m | m | i | n | g |   | t | e | s | t |
|---|----|---|---|---|---|---|---|---|---|---|---|---|---|
| t | 8  | 6 | 6 | 5 | 5 | 5 | 4 | 3 | 2 | 1 | 2 | 3 | 4 |
| e | 9  | 7 | 7 | 6 | 6 | 6 | 5 | 4 | 3 | 2 | 1 | 2 | 3 |
| x | 10 | 8 | 8 | 7 | 7 | 7 | 6 | 5 | 4 | 3 | 2 | 2 | 3 |
| t | 11 | 8 | 9 | 8 | 8 | 8 | 7 | 6 | 5 | 3 | 3 | 3 | 2 |

Now that you can compute the edit distance, we'll look at how to use it.

NORMALIZING EDIT DISTANCE

In most applications using edit distance, you'll want to set a threshold for edit distances to exclude corrections that are too different or, said another way, involve too many edits. In performing this calculation you quickly run into the following issue. Intuitively, an edit distance of 2 for a string of length 4 is a much larger edit than the same edit distance for a string of length 10. Additionally, you need to rank many possible corrections to a string based on edit distance. Keep in mind these correction strings may be of different lengths. In order to compare the edit distances with strings of multiple sizes, it's helpful to normalize the edit distance based on the size of the strings.

To normalize this distance into a number between 0 and 1, you subtract it from the length of the larger of the two strings and divide by the same length. In the preceding case this would be the length of *tamming test*, 12 minus 2, divided by 12, or 0.833. If you're correcting a short string such as editing *tammin* to produce *taming*, the result is 6 minus 2, divided by 6, or 0.666. This normalization helps capture the intuition that the two edits in the second example constitute a bigger change than the two edits in the first example. This process also makes it easier to assign thresholds for these distances, because edit distances can be compared across strings of many different lengths.

WEIGHTING EDITS

For different applications, the edit operations used to determine the edit distance can be weighted. In such cases the edit distance is the sum of the weights for each operation used in the transformation of one string into another. As you saw previously with Levenshtein distance, the simplest weighting assigns each of these operations a weight of one. Using different weights for different operations can be useful in cases where different types of operations aren't equally likely. For example, in spelling correction, the replacement of one vowel with another may be more likely than the replacement of a consonant with another. Weighting different operations or different operations based on their operands can help better capture these distinctions.

A common variation on Levenshtein distance is *Damerau-Levenshtein distance*. This measure allows the additional operation of transpositions of adjacent letters. This can be thought of as an alternative weighting scheme where transpositions of adjacent letters are given a weight of one instead of the standard weighting of two edits for the corresponding deletion and insertion operation that would be required without this operation.

Many discussions of Levenshtein distance are available on the internet, including more formal analysis of the algorithm presented and proofs of its correctness. For those interested in using this distance measure, there's also an optimized implementation built into Lucene in the org.apache.lucene.search.spell.Levenshtein-Distance class. This version of the code only allocates two rows of the distance matrix, noting that only the previous row is needed in the computation of the subsequent row. It also performs length normalization as described previously.

### 4.1.3  N-gram edit distance

In the variations of edit distance we've looked at so far, the operations have only involved single characters. One way to extend the notion of edit distance is to allow it to capture multiple characters at a time, or what's known as *n-gram edit distance*. *N*-gram edit distance takes the idea of Levenshtein distance and treats each *n*-gram as a character. Looking at the example we considered before using *n*-grams of size 2 (bigrams), the distance matrix is computed in table 4.2.

**Table 4.2  Matrix for computing *n*-gram edit distance**

|     |     | ta | am | mm | mi | in | ng | g_ | _t | te | es | st |
| --- | --- | -- | -- | -- | -- | -- | -- | -- | -- | -- | -- | -- |
|     | 0   | 1  | 2  | 3  | 4  | 5  | 6  | 7  | 8  | 9  | 10 | 11 |
| ta  | 1   | 0  | 1  | 2  | 3  | 4  | 5  | 6  | 7  | 8  | 9  | 9  |
| am  | 2   | 1  | 0  | 1  | 2  | 3  | 4  | 5  | 6  | 7  | 8  | 9  |
| mi  | 3   | 2  | 1  | 1  | 1  | 2  | 3  | 4  | 5  | 6  | 7  | 8  |
| in  | 4   | 3  | 2  | 2  | 2  | 1  | 2  | 3  | 4  | 5  | 6  | 7  |
| ng  | 5   | 4  | 3  | 3  | 3  | 2  | 1  | 2  | 3  | 4  | 5  | 6  |
| g_  | 6   | 5  | 4  | 4  | 4  | 3  | 2  | 1  | 2  | 3  | 4  | 5  |
| _t  | 7   | 6  | 5  | 5  | 5  | 4  | 3  | 2  | 1  | 2  | 3  | 4  |
| te  | 8   | 7  | 6  | 6  | 6  | 5  | 4  | 3  | 2  | 1  | 2  | 3  |
| ex  | 9   | 8  | 7  | 7  | 7  | 6  | 5  | 4  | 3  | 2  | 2  | 2  |
| xt  | 10  | 9  | 8  | 8  | 8  | 7  | 6  | 5  | 4  | 3  | 2  | 3  |

The impact of this *n*-gram approach is that insertions and deletions which don't involve double letters are more heavily penalized using *n*-gram methods than unigram methods, whereas substitutions are equally penalized.

#### ENHANCEMENTS TO *N*-GRAM EDIT DISTANCE

Several enhancements are typically applied to the *n*-gram approach. The first is the result of noticing that the initial character only participates in a single *n*-gram, whereas intermediate characters often participate in all *n*-grams. In many applications, these initial characters are more important to match than intermediate characters. An approach to take advantage of this is called *affixing*. Affixing involves prepending *n-1* characters (for whatever value of *n* is being used) to the beginning of the string. The result is that the first character participates in the same number of *n*-grams as an intermediate character. Also, words that don't begin with the same *n-1* characters receive a penalty for not matching the prefix. The same process could also be applied to the end of the string, in cases where matching the end of the string is deemed important.

A second enhancement is to allow some level of partial credit for *n*-grams that share common characters. You could use the Levenshtein distance to determine the edit distance between two *n*-grams and normalize this by dividing by the size of the *n*-gram so that the partial credit remains in the range between 0 and 1. A simple positional matching approach will also work well instead of the Levenshtein distance. In this approach, you count the number of characters that match in value and position for the two *n*-grams. This is faster to compute for *n*-grams larger than 2. In the bigram case, it's equivalent to the Levenshtein distance. In table 4.3, we present a distance matrix that includes affixing and partial credit for partial matches.

**Table 4.3    Matrix for computing *n*-gram edit distance with enhancements**

| | | Ot | ta | am | mm | mi | in | ng | g_ | _t | te | es | st |
|----|----|----|----|----|----|----|----|----|----|----|----|----|----|
| | 0 | 1 | 2 | 3 | 4 | 5 | 6 | 7 | 8 | 9 | 10 | 11 | 12 |
| Ot | 1 | 0 | 1 | 2 | 3 | 4 | 5 | 6 | 7 | 8 | 9 | 10 | 11 |
| ta | 2 | 1 | 0 | 1 | 2 | 4 | 5 | 6 | 7 | 8 | 8.5 | 9.5 | 10.5 |
| am | 3 | 2 | 1 | 0 | 1.5 | 3 | 4 | 5 | 6 | 7 | 8 | 9 | 10 |
| mi | 4 | 3 | 2 | 1 | 0.5 | 1.5 | 2.5 | 3.5 | 4.5 | 5.5 | 6.5 | 7.5 | 8 |
| in | 5 | 4 | 3 | 2 | 1.5 | 1.5 | 1.5 | 2.5 | 3.5 | 4.5 | 5.5 | 6.5 | 7 |
| ng | 6 | 5 | 4 | 3 | 2.5 | 2.5 | 2.5 | 1.5 | 2.5 | 3.5 | 4.5 | 5.5 | 6 |
| g_ | 7 | 6 | 5 | 4 | 3.5 | 3.5 | 3.5 | 2.5 | 1.5 | 2.5 | 3.5 | 4.5 | 5 |
| _t | 8 | 6.5 | 6 | 5 | 4.5 | 4.5 | 4.5 | 3.5 | 2.5 | 1.5 | 2.5 | 3.5 | 4 |
| te | 9 | 7.5 | 6.5 | 6 | 5.5 | 5.5 | 5.5 | 4.5 | 3.5 | 2.5 | 1.5 | 2.5 | 3 |
| ex | 10 | 8.5 | 7.5 | 7 | 6.5 | 6.5 | 6.5 | 5.5 | 4.5 | 3.5 | 2.5 | 2 | 3 |
| xt | 11 | 9.0 | 8.5 | 8 | 7.5 | 7.5 | 7.5 | 6.5 | 5.5 | 4.5 | 3.5 | 3 | 2.5 |

Lucene contains an implementation of the *n*-gram edit distance that uses affixing and length normalization. The implementation is in the `org.apache.lucene.search` `.spell.NgramDistance` class.

In this section, we examined various approaches to determine how similar two strings are to one another based on the distance measure between two strings. We examined string overlap measures such as the Jaccard measure and extensions to it using frequency as a means to weight letters. We also discussed the Jaro-Winkler measure, which uses overlap measures in a moving window across the string. We then considered edit distance and looked at a simple form of this measure, Levenshtein distance. We discussed enhancements such as length normalization and customizing the weighting for different edit operations, and finally extended this measure to look at multiple letters. Up until now we've assumed you have the two strings you want to compare and have focused on how to perform the comparison. In the next section, we'll look at how to find good candidate string matches for a given input string without having to compare the input string against all possible candidates.

## 4.2 Finding fuzzy string matches

Being able to compute some measure of similarity between two strings is useful, but only if you already have both strings. In many applications that use string matching, you only have one of the strings that you'd like to use as input for one of the string similarity functions outlined in the previous section. For example, in spelling correction you typically have a word that isn't found in a dictionary and that you suspect is misspelled. If you had a list of suggestions, you could use one of the previous functions to rank that list, and present the user with some of the top-ranked alternatives. Theoretically, you could compute the similarity between the word for which you'd like to generate a suggestion and all the words in the dictionary. Unfortunately, this is computationally expensive (also known as slow) and most of the strings you're comparing have low similarity and few characters in common. In practice, you need a fast way to determine a small list of likely candidates on which you can perform one of the more computationally expensive comparisons. In this section we'll describe two approaches to determine such a list—prefix matching and *n*-gram matching—as well as efficient implementations for them.

### 4.2.1 Using prefixes for matching with Solr

One approach to quickly determining a set of strings that are similar to another string is *prefix matching*. Prefix matching returns the set of strings that share a common prefix with the string you're looking for. For example, if you want to correct the word *tamming*, then considering words with the prefix *tam* reduces a dictionary of about 100,000 words to about 35 entries which are all forms of the following seven words: tam, tamale, tamarind, tambourine, tame, tamp, tampon. From a computational perspective, this is a significant reduction, and since the strings share a common prefix, you're guaranteed that they'll have this much in common.

One way to perform prefix matching is with Solr. When documents are being put into a Solr index, you can compute all the prefixes of a given length and store these as terms which Solr will match against. At query time, the same operation can be performed on the query and a list of terms that contain some level of prefix matching will be returned. Since this is a fairly common task, Solr includes an implementation called the `EdgeNGramTokenFilter` (the full class name is `org.apache.lucene.analysis.ngram.EdgeNGramTokenFilter`). The result is that when a term such as *taming* is indexed, the terms *ta*, *tam*, *tami*, and *tamin* are indexed as well. As you saw in chapter 3, this can be done by specifying the field type that's applied to document fields at index and query time in the schema.xml file. This can be seen in the following listing.

**Listing 4.3  Specifying a field type for prefix matching in Solr**

```
<fieldtype name="qprefix" stored="false" indexed="true"
           class="solr.TextField">
  <analyzer>
    <tokenizer class="solr.WhitespaceTokenizerFactory"/>
    <filter class="solr.LowerCaseFilterFactory"/>
    <filter class="solr.EdgeNGramFilterFactory"
        side="front" minGramSize="2" maxGramSize="3"/>
  </analyzer>
</fieldtype>
```

In the example, we use Solr's built-in `EdgeNGramFilterFactory` class in combination with a whitespace tokenizer and a lowercase token filter to produce the prefixes.

This filter is used at both indexing and query time. At query time it generates the prefixes that match against the ones generated at index time. One of the common use cases for this functionality is in implementing query type-ahead, also known as *auto-suggest*. Prefix matching is useful in this case because it has well-understood semantics and a user presented with a list of words that match the prefix of the query they're typing understands why these items are in the list, and how typing another character will change the list's contents. We'll explore type-ahead matching later in this chapter, and in the next section we'll consider data structures for storing prefixes efficiently in memory, which may be required by some applications.

### 4.2.2  Using a trie for prefix matching

Though Solr can be leveraged to perform prefix matching, in some cases it may not be practical to make a connection to a Solr instance for every prefix you want to look up. In such cases it's desirable to be able to perform prefix queries on an in-memory data structure. A data structure well suited for this task is a *trie* (pronounced "tree" by some, "try" by others).

#### WHAT'S A TRIE?

A trie, or *prefix tree*, is a data structure that stores strings by decomposing them into characters. The characters form a path through a tree until such time as a child node of the tree represents a string uniquely or all characters of the string have been used. In the trie in figure 4.2, you can see that most words are represented by nodes which represent only a fraction of their characters because they're the sole word in the trie with a specific prefix. But the word *tamp* is a prefix to another word in the trie, *tampon*, and as such contains a node in the trie for each character.

#### IMPLEMENTING A TRIE

A simple implementation of a trie is much like implementing any tree structure. In a trie, the number of children for each node is typically equal to the size of the alphabet being represented by the trie. In the next listing, you can see an implementation for strings consisting solely of the lowercase letters, a-z.

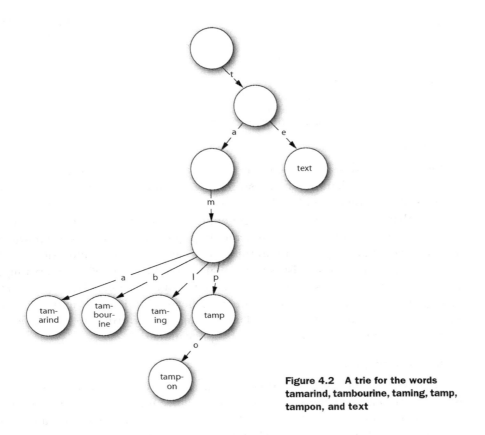

**Figure 4.2   A trie for the words tamarind, tambourine, taming, tamp, tampon, and text**

---

**Listing 4.4   Constructing the node of a trie**

```
private boolean isWord;                          ⟵——— Does this prefix make a word?
private TrieNode[] children;
private String suffix;                           ⟵——— Rest of word if prefix is unique.

public TrieNode(boolean word, String suffix) {
  this.isWord = word;
  if (suffix == null) children = new TrieNode[26];   ⟵┐ Initialize children
  this.suffix = suffix;                                │ for each letter.
}
```

The trie needs to support adding and retrieving words based on a common prefix. Since a trie is a tree structure, it's common to use a recursive approach of removing the first character, and then descending the structure using the remaining characters. For performance reasons, the splitting of the string isn't explicitly performed, and instead the split point is represented as an integer. Though there are several cases to consider, the recursive nature of the code makes it relatively short; see the following listing.

### Listing 4.5 Adding words to a trie

```
public boolean addWord(String word) {
  return addWord(word.toLowerCase(),0);
}

private boolean addWord(String word, int index) {        Check if end
  if (index == word.length()) {                          of word.
    if (isWord) {
      return false;                                      Existing word; return false.
    }
    else {                                               Mark prefix
      isWord = true;                                     as word.
      return true;
    }
  }
  if (suffix != null) {                                  Check if this node
    if (suffix.equals(word.substring(index))) {          has a suffix.
      return false;                                      Existing word;
    }                                                    return false.
    String tmp = suffix;
    this.suffix = null;
    children = new TrieNode[26];
    addWord(tmp,0);                                      Split up suffix.
  }
  int ci = word.charAt(index)-(int)'a';
  TrieNode child = children[ci];
  if (child == null) {
    if (word.length() == index -1) {                     Prefix creates
      children[ci] = new TrieNode(true,null);            new word.
    }
    else {
      children[ci] = new TrieNode(false,word.substring(index+1));
    }
    return true;                                         Recurse
  }                                                      on next
  return child.addWord(word, index+1);                   character.
}
```

Prefix and suffix create new word. → `children[ci] = new TrieNode(false,word.substring(index+1));`

Retrieving words is done by traversing the tree structure to the node that represents the prefix being queried. This is done by looking at each character of the prefix and then accessing the child node for the character. When the prefix node has been found, a depth-first search is performed to collect all words with the common prefix. In cases where the prefix node doesn't exist, at most one word will be returned depending on whether the word represented by that node matches the prefix being queried. An implementation of this approach is shown next.

### Listing 4.6 Retrieving words from a trie

```
public String[] getWords(String prefix, int numWords) {        Traverse tree
  List<String> words = new ArrayList<String>(numWords);        until prefix is
  TrieNode prefixRoot = this;                                   consumed.
  for (int i=0;i<prefix.length();i++) {
```

```
    if (prefixRoot.suffix == null) {
      int ci = prefix.charAt(i)-(int)'a';
      prefixRoot = prefixRoot.children[ci];
      if (prefixRoot == null) {
        break;
      }
    }
    else {
      if (prefixRoot.suffix.startsWith(prefix.substring(i))) {
        words.add(prefix.substring(0,i)+prefixRoot.suffix);
      }
      prefixRoot = null;
      break;
    }
  }
  if (prefixRoot != null) {
    prefixRoot.collectWords(words,numWords,prefix);
  }
  return words.toArray(new String[words.size()]);
}

private void collectWords(List<String> words,
                          int numWords, String prefix) {
  if (this.isWord()) {
    words.add(prefix);
    if (words.size() == numWords) return;
  }
  if (suffix != null) {
    words.add(prefix+suffix);
    return;
  }
  for (int ci=0;ci<children.length;ci++) {
    String nextPrefix = prefix+(char)(ci+(int)'a');
    if (children[ci] != null) {
      children[ci].collectWords(words, numWords, nextPrefix);
      if (words.size() == numWords) return;
    }
  }
}
```

> Handle case where prefix hasn't been split.

> Collect all words that are children of prefix node.

This implementation of a trie is efficient for adding and retrieving words, but its representation requires that an array the size of the alphabet be used. This array is constructed for each node that doesn't contain a suffix. Though this makes the lookup of characters efficient, often only a small fraction of the possible next letters actually occur. Other implementations of tries, such as the double-array trie, reduce the memory required for storing transitions but incur addition costs during an insertion. Many of the uses of tries such as dictionary lookup are computed on relatively static content, making this approach beneficial since the additional work required to add words is a one-time cost. A discussion of this approach can be found in "An efficient digital search algorithm by using a double-array structure" (Aoe 1989).

**TRIES IN SOLR**

Solr 3.4 supports a trie-inspired implementation of numeric fields that greatly improves the performance of range queries on these fields. This can be used by specifying that the field type be implemented as a trie field as shown in the following listing.

**Listing 4.7  Using the Solr `TrieField` type**

```
<fieldType name="tint" class="solr.TrieField" type="integer"
  omitNorms="true" positionIncrementGap="0" indexed="true"
          stored="false" />
```

Unlike the trie implementation shown previously, the Solr version is implemented in a fashion similar to the prefix token approach taken earlier. Though trie fields are used for numeric types in Solr, to understand how this works, let's consider an example using strings first. If you wanted to perform a range query on spanning the string *tami* to the string *tamp*, you could use their common prefix, *tam*, to limit your search, and then check each returned document field for inclusion in the range. As you saw in the case of prefixes, this significantly reduces the number of documents you need to consider as potential matches for a range query. You could further refine your search by introducing the notion of an increment to your prefixes such as *tamj, tamk, taml...* *tamp* and then search for documents matching these prefixes. Note that any document matching one of the incremented prefixes before *tamp* will only include documents that match the range query.

To determine which documents match, you'd only have to consider documents that match the edge prefixes and compare those against the actual range terms. The size of the increment relative to the number of documents which match that prefix determines how many comparisons are needed to compute which documents match the range query. Here we're using an increment of one character applied to the four characters of the string, but a variety of other increments are possible. You can imaging searching an integer range such as [314 TO 345] by searching for numbers with the prefixes 31, 32, 33, and 34. The `solr.TrieField` uses a similar approach to compute numerical ranges for integers and floats using binary representations as opposed to base-10 representations in this example.

In this section we looked at trie representations which are an efficient way to insert and retrieve prefixes. We've provided a simple implementation and discussed how Solr uses similar approaches to improve performance for range queries. In the next section we'll move beyond prefix matching and look at more robust matching approaches that incorporate characters beyond the beginning of a word.

### 4.2.3  Using n-grams for matching

Though prefix matching is powerful, it does have limitations. One of these limitations is that any similar term suggested using prefix matching must contain some common prefix. For a word or term where the initial character is incorrect, prefix matching will never be able to make a suggestion with this type of correction. Though such cases may be rare, they're not unheard of. Let's look at another technique that's more robust in these cases.

You saw in the previous section that prefixes can be used to limit the set of strings considered for matching against a string that has been provided by a user. You also saw how a larger prefix provides a greater reduction in the number of suggestions that need to be considered, but that a larger prefix also increases the risk that the best term to suggest will be excluded because a correction is required in a character contained in the prefix. An extension of the idea of using prefixes is suggested when you consider that a prefix of size *n* is the first *n*-gram of a string. By also considering the second, third, and remaining *n*-grams, you can generalize the notion of prefixes to apply to all positions in a string.

*N*-gram matching works by limiting potential matches to those that share one or more *n*-grams with a query string. Using our previous example, *tamming*, you could consider strings that contain the prefix *tam* as well as all the other trigrams for this word: *amm, mmi, min, ing*. Applied to our 100,000-word dictionary, only about a tenth of the words match one of these trigrams. Though this is as significant a reduction as the prefix alone, you're now able to deal with a larger range of possible errors in your original text, including the initial character being incorrect. The *n*-gram approach also provides a straightforward means of ranking your various matches, as some words match multiple *n*-grams, and more matches typically means a better suggestion. In the preceding cases, 19 words match 4 of the 5 *n*-grams and 74 words (including the 19) match 3 of the 4 *n*-grams. By ranking the *n*-gram matches, you can consider the approach of only considering a fixed number of suggestions with reasonable certainty that the word with the lowest edit distance will be among the top-ranked matches.

### N-GRAM MATCHING IN SOLR

As with prefix matching, Solr comes with *n*-gram analysis capabilities by way of the `org.apache.lucene.analysis.ngram.NGramTokenFilter` and the associated factory class, `org.apache.solr.analysis.NGramFilterFactory`.

The piece of information that *n*-gram matching doesn't capture is positional information. No distinction is given to an *n*-gram that's found at the beginning of a string but matches at the end of another string. One way to overcome this limitation is to use string affixing to capture this positional information at the beginning or end of strings. You saw this technique used previously in section 4.1.3.

In this section, we've covered techniques for quickly finding fuzzy string matches. Combining these tools with the previous techniques for computing edit distances allows you to find and rank fuzzy string matches. We can now look at how these tools can be combined to build applications that use them. In the next section, we'll explore three such applications that use these techniques.

## 4.3  *Building fuzzy string matching applications*

Building on the tools we've described so far, this section will look at three uses of fuzzy string matching in real applications. Specifically, we'll explore type-ahead functionality in search, query spell-checking, and record matching. *Type-ahead functionality*, which is also often called *auto-complete* or *auto-suggest*, provides users examples of terms that occur in the index so as to save keystrokes by selecting the word instead of finishing typing. It also has the benefit that the user knows the word is spelled correctly, thus resulting in a better search experience. Spell-checking the query, often shown on a site like Google via the Did You Mean section of the page, is a simple way to guide users to an alternate spelling of a word that should produce better results. Note, we say *alternate*, as it doesn't necessarily have to be a correctly spelled word. In some cases, the majority of occurrences in the index are spelled incorrectly (for instance, in online forums) and would thus yield better results to a user by showing the incorrectly spelled word. Finally, *record matching*, sometimes called *record linkage* or *entity resolution*, is the process of determining when two distinct records actually are the same thing. For instance, when merging two user databases, record matching tries to determine whether the Bob Smith in one record is the same Bob Smith in another record. We'll focus on these three examples since they're common usages of fuzzy string matching in many of today's text-based applications.

### 4.3.1 Adding type-ahead to search

A common feature of many applications is automatic completion of text entry. For instance, many integrated development environments (IDEs) will auto-complete variable names for you as you use them while programming. In search applications, type-ahead is often used as the user begins entering their query in the search box, and likely completions of it are suggested as the user types. Though this feature saves the user time from typing in the entire query, it also guides the refinement of the search process by only suggesting queries that will match some document in the search index. Type-ahead allows the user to quickly refine their search to a phrase that will provide good results on the index being searched and improves a user's overall experience. Providing suggestions based on what the user is typing can be thought of as a prefix query. Specifically, you want to return results that have the same prefix as the query that the user is typing. As with our previous example, you can use Solr to return the results of such queries.

#### INDEXING PREFIXES IN SOLR

The first step is to allow Solr to create prefix queries. For partial queries that are incomplete, you can once again use the EdgeNGramFilterFactory to compute prefixes and add them to the set of tokens generated. A field type using it can be specified in your schema.xml file similar to before and then assigned to a field to store prefixes, as in listing 4.8. Note that in this case, you have a maximum *n*-gram size to account for more variations as the user types. This will increase the size of the underlying data structures, but they'll still be manageable.

**Listing 4.8   Specifying a field type for type-ahead matching in Solr**

```
<fieldtype name="prefix" stored="false" indexed="true"
           class="solr.TextField">
  <analyzer type="index">                                      Specify analyzers
    <tokenizer class="solr.WhitespaceTokenizerFactory"/>       for indexing.
    <filter class="solr.LowerCaseFilterFactory"/>
    <filter class="solr.EdgeNGramFilterFactory"                Use edge-bounded
    minGramSize="2" maxGramSize="10"/>                         n-grams (prefixes).
  </analyzer>
  <analyzer type="query">
    <tokenizer class="solr.WhitespaceTokenizerFactory"/>       Remove edge
    <filter class="solr.LowerCaseFilterFactory"/>             n-gram filter;
  </analyzer>                                                  queries are
</fieldtype>                                                   already prefixes.
```

This field type handles multiword queries and allows matches to begin at word boundaries. Note that the EdgeNGramFilterFactory need not be applied to the query as it's already a prefix. In order to apply this field type, you need to specify a field that uses this type and index documents which populate that field. For this example, let's assume you're indexing dictionary entries in the field word. You'd then add a new field using this field type in your schema.xml file, as in the following example:

```
<fields>
  <!-- other fields -->
  <field name="wordPrefix" type="prefix" />
</fields>
<!-- other schema attributes -->
<copyField source="word" dest="wordPrefix"/>
```

Documents with a word field will now have their prefixes stored in the wordPrefix field during indexing. With these prefixes indexed, you can now turn to querying these prefixes.

### RETRIEVING PREFIX MATCHES FROM SOLR

Using this field and field type, you can now query with prefixes from Solr and return a list of words. This can be done with the following query:

```
http://localhost:8983/solr/select?q=wordPrefix:tam&fl=word
```

In order to have this work from a search input field from a browser, you'd also need to write JavaScript to perform the queries as the user typed and display the top-ranked results. The JavaScript for this involves handling keypress events typed in the search field, periodically sending requests to a server that responds with a list of query expansions, and displaying those results. Fortunately, this is a common enough activity that there are many JavaScript libraries which will perform these actions for you. One of the more popular of these libraries is script.aculo.us. (JQuery also has support for this functionality.) It requires that you be able to specify the prefix query and return the query expansions as an unordered HTML list. Though you could easily write a servlet to interact with Solr and format the result appropriately, we can use this as an opportunity to demonstrate Solr's ability to customize the request format and response output.

Customizing the response format requires writing a `QueryResponseWriter` as well as specifying that it should be used to render the response to type-ahead queries. Writing a custom response writer is straightforward and several are included with Solr on which to model your code. For our simple case the code is shown next.

**Listing 4.9   A Solr response writer for formatting type-ahead results**

```
public class TypeAheadResponseWriter implements QueryResponseWriter {

  private Set<String> fields;

  @Override
  public String getContentType(SolrQueryRequest req,
                              SolrQueryResponse solrQueryResponse) {
    return "text/html;charset=UTF-8";
  }

  public void init(NamedList n) {                            Specify field
    fields = new HashSet<String>();                          displayed by
    fields.add("word");                                  <─┘ response writer.
  }

  @Override
  public void write(Writer w, SolrQueryRequest req,
                    SolrQueryResponse rsp) throws IOException {
    SolrIndexSearcher searcher = req.getSearcher();
    NamedList nl = rsp.getValues();
    int sz = nl.size();
    for (int li = 0; li < sz; li++) {                        Find
      Object val = nl.getVal(li);                            document
      if (val instanceof DocList) {                       <─┘ list.
        DocList dl = (DocList) val;
        DocIterator iterator = dl.iterator();
        w.append("<ul>n");
        while (iterator.hasNext()) {                         Retrieve
          int id = iterator.nextDoc();                       document with
          Document doc = searcher.doc(id, fields);        <─┘ specified field.
          String name = doc.get("word");
          w.append("<li>" + name + "</li>n");
        }
        w.append("</ul>n");
      }
    }
  }
}
```

A JAR containing this class would need to be placed in Solr's library directory, typically solr/lib, so that Solr could resolve this class. You also need to tell Solr about your response writer and create an endpoint that will use it by default. This is done in the solrconfig.xml file, as shown next.

**Listing 4.10    Specifying the response writer and request handler in Solr**

```
<queryResponseWriter name="tah"                                    Specify custom
                                                                   response writer.
  class="com.tamingtext.fuzzy.TypeAheadResponseWriter"/>
<requestHandler name="/type-
    ahead" class="solr.SearchHandler">        <—— Specify request handler as URL path.
  <lst name="defaults">
    <str name="wt">tah</str>                  <—— Specify default response writer.

    <str name="defType">dismax</str>
    <str name="qf"> wordPrefix^1.0 </str>     <—— Specify search field.

  </lst>
</requestHandler>
```

This new request handler will allow you to query for prefixes and format them appropriately for script.aculo.us. Specifically, you can now use the following Solr query and no longer need to specify the response type or search field as query parameters.

**Listing 4.11    A Solr URL for accessing a prefix using a query response handler**

```
http://localhost:8983/solr/type-ahead?q=tam
```

**DYNAMICALLY POPULATING THE SEARCH BOX**

Now you can build a type-ahead search box, as shown next.

**Listing 4.12    HTML and JavaScript for performing search type-ahead**

```
<html>
  <head>
    <script src="./prototype.js" type="text/javascript">
    </script>
    <script src="./scriptaculous.js?load=effects,controls"
      type="text/javascript">
    </script>                                  <—— Import script.aculo.us.

    <link rel="stylesheet" type="text/css"
      href="autocomplete.css" />
  </head>
  <body>
    <input type="text" id="search"            <—— Specify input field.

      name="autocomplete_parameter"/>
    <div id="update" class="autocomplete"/>   <—— Specify div for type-ahead result.

    <script type="text/javascript">
      new Ajax.Autocompleter('search','update',   <—— Create type-ahead object.
                         '/solr/type-ahead',
                      {paramName: "q",method:"get"});
    </script>
  </body>
</html>
```

The results of the JavaScript rendered in a browser are shown in figure 4.3.

In this example, you saw how you could use prefix matching to allow type-ahead functionality to be added to a search application. You were able to add a field and field type in Solr to store the prefixes and use its token filters to generate prefixes of a particular size. The flexibility of Solr also allowed you to customize the processing of the request as well as the response to make integrating with popular JavaScript libraries like script.aculo.us easy. In our next example, we'll continue using the fuzzy matching tools introduced in the previous sections to build additional applications.

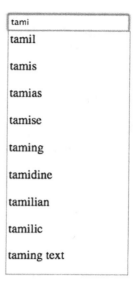

Figure 4.3  Suggested type-ahead completions for the prefix *taml*

### 4.3.2   Query spell-checking for search

Adding query spell-checking, or Did You Mean, functionality for a website can help a user identify the difference between a misspelled query and one that doesn't return any results. This can make the user's experience of refining their query much more productive and satisfying. In this section, we'll look at how to rank spellings and their corrections from a probabilistic perspective and then show how you can use the tools and techniques discussed earlier in the chapter to implement an approximation of those probabilities. This can be done easily using Solr, SolrJ, and libraries provided with Lucene. Though the resulting spell-checker may not be ready for prime time, it provides a basis on which you can make improvements to customize it or the spell-checker provided in Lucene. Finally, we'll describe how to use the spelling correction component provided with Solr and how the component architecture in Solr makes it easy to integrate a custom spelling component.

#### OUTLINING YOUR APPROACH

The task of picking the best correction for a misspelled word is typically formalized as the task of maximizing the probability of a spelling and a correction. This is based on the product of two probabilities, $p(s|w)$ x $p(w)$, where $s$ is a spelling and $w$ is a word. The first probability is the probability of seeing a word spelled a particular way given the word, and the second is the probability of the word itself. Since it's difficult to estimate $p(s|w)$ without a lot of corrected data that has been human-checked, a reasonable approximation is to use edit distance. The normalized edit distance for a spelling $s$, and a word $w$, can be seen as an estimate of $p(s|w)$. The probability of the word being suggested ($p(w)$) is typically easier to estimate than the probability of a particular spelling. In many cases, reasonable results can be achieved by estimating this probability crudely or ignoring it all together. This is what most spell-checkers do, opting to let the user choose from a list. One way to explain this is that the vast majority of spelling errors, 80-95%, are single-letter mistakes. Edit distance can provide a reasonable ranking of suggestions.

Cases where such an approach breaks down include where the spelling that needs to be corrected is itself another word, where the number of reasonable suggestions is very large, and when only a single suggestion can be made. In these cases, being able to influence the rank of a suggestion based on its likelihood can greatly improve performance. This can be based on query logs or the indexed text with a basic notion of word frequency. For multiword phrases, *n*-gram models can be used to estimate sequences of words, but a discussion of *n*-gram models is beyond the scope of this book.

Now that you have a theoretical basis for how to approach spelling corrections, let's look at how to implement spelling correction. Our fuzzy matching approach to spelling correction is as follows:

- Construct a set of candidate corrections.
- Score each of those candidates.
- Apply a threshold for showing a suggestion.

As you saw earlier, *n*-gram matching is a good way to construct a set of candidate matches. Looking at the terms that contain the most *n*-gram matches with the spelling you're trying to correct will provide a good list of candidates. You can then apply an edit distance metric to each of these terms and rerank them based on the edit distance. Finally, you need to apply a threshold for the edit distance metric so that in cases where there's no appropriate suggestion, one isn't made. The exact threshold value used for this typically requires some experimentation.

### IMPLEMENTING DID YOU MEAN WITH SOLR

You can implement the previous approach using Solr and SolrJ. You first need to define a field type, a field, and its source of data in your schema.xml file for storing the *n*-grams, as in the following example.

#### Listing 4.13  Schema changes to support *n*-gram matching in Solr

```
<fieldtype name="ngram" stored="false" indexed="true"
           class="solr.TextField">
  <analyzer>
    <tokenizer class="solr.KeywordTokenizerFactory"/>
    <filter class="solr.LowerCaseFilterFactory"/>
    <filter class="solr.NGramFilterFactory"
      minGramSize="2" maxGramSize="10"/>
  </analyzer>
</fieldtype>
<!-- other types -->
<field name="wordNGram" type="ngram" />
<!-- other fields -->
<copyField source="word" dest="wordNGram"/>
```

Next you need to query that field and compute the edit distance between the results and a particular spelling, as in the following listing.

**Listing 4.14   Java code to get possible corrections from Solr and rank them**

```java
public class SpellCorrector {

  private SolrServer solr;
  private SolrQuery query;
  private StringDistance sd;
  private float threshold;

  public SpellCorrector(StringDistance sd, float threshold)
    throws MalformedURLException {
    solr = new CommonsHttpSolrServer(
            new URL("http://localhost:8983/solr"));
    query = new SolrQuery();
    query.setFields("word");
    query.setRows(50);                       //  Number of n-gram matches to consider.
    this.sd = sd;
    this.threshold = threshold;
  }

  public String topSuggestion(String spelling)
        throws SolrServerException {
    query.setQuery("wordNGram:"+spelling);   //  Query field that contains n-gram.
    QueryResponse response = solr.query(query);
    SolrDocumentList dl = response.getResults();
    Iterator<SolrDocument> di = dl.iterator();
    float maxDistance = 0;
    String suggestion = null;
    while (di.hasNext()) {
      SolrDocument doc = di.next();                            //  Compute
      String word = (String) doc.getFieldValue("word");       //  edit
      float distance = sd.getDistance(word, spelling);        //  distance.
      if (distance > maxDistance) {
        maxDistance = distance;
        suggestion = word;                   //  Keep best suggestion.
      }
    }
    if (maxDistance > threshold) {           //  Check threshold; otherwise return no suggestion.
      return suggestion;
    }
    return null;
  }
}
```

The object passed to the `SpellCorrector` constructor that implements the `org .apache.lucene.search.spell.StringDistance` interface returns a 1 if the strings are identical and a 0 (zero) if they're maximally different. Several implementations of this interface are included with Lucene, including Levenshtein distance, Jaro-Winkler distance, and an *n*-gram distance implementation.

The approach we've outlined so far is equivalent to ignoring (or treating as constant) the word probability term of our previous model. Estimating the word probability can be done by counting the number of times a word occurs in your document collection or query logs, divided by the number of words. This term can then be used in ranking along with edit distance. If you want this probability to influence the suggestions returned by Solr, you can do this with document boosting.

A *document boost* is a multiplicative factor for increasing the relevancy of a document; it's set at index time and is typically above 1. A document boost of 2 indicates that this document is inherently twice as relevant as a document with no boost. Since each of your possible spelling suggestions are modeled as documents in Solr and because the probability of a word is independent of the spellings, you can model $p(w)$ as the inherent relevancy of a document. Determining the boosting values that are most appropriate to your domain requires some experimentation. When boost values have been determined, they'll impact the order in which results are returned from the $n$-gram query used previously to determine candidate suggestions.

#### USING SOLR'S SPELL-CHECK COMPONENT

Now that you have an understanding of an implementation of spelling correction using Solr, let's take a look at the mechanisms for spelling correction that are built into Solr. A spell-checking implementation is provided in Lucene and integrated into Solr. Its approach is similar to the one outlined here. It can be invoked in Solr as a search component and added to a request handler. The search component for spelling can be defined as follows.

**Listing 4.15  Defining a spell-checker as a search component in Solr**

```
<searchComponent name="spell_component"
  class="org.apache.solr.handler.component.SpellCheckComponent">
  <lst name="spellchecker">
    <str name="name">default</str>                      Possible suggestions
    <str name="field">word</str>                        stored here.
    <str name="distanceMeasure">                        Distance
      org.apache.lucene.search.spell.LevensteinDistance measure
    </str>                                               to use.
    <str name="spellcheckIndexDir">./spell</str>
    <str name="accuracy">0.5</str>                       Threshold
  </lst>                                                  for making
</searchComponent>                                       suggestion.
```

It can be added to a request handler by placing it as an argument after the defined defaults for the handler.

**Listing 4.16  Adding the spell-checker search component to your request handler in Solr**

```
<requestHandler ...
  <lst name="defaults">
  ...
  </lst>
  <arr name="last-components">
    <str>spell_component</str>
  </arr>
</requestHandler>
```

Queries to the spell-checker are made along with regular queries and suggestions returned with regular search results. This has the benefit of allowing a suggestion to be made and a result retrieved with a single request to Solr. In cases where the spelling correction requires a different tokenization than the request handler, such as with a dismax handler, then the spelling query can be placed in an alternate parameter, spellcheck.q.

As we mentioned previously, the spell-checking component provided with Solr and found in Lucene uses a similar approach to the one we implemented with SolrJ. Some of the differences include additional boosting for matching the prefix of a correction, and functionality to only suggest words whose frequency is higher than the query term. You can also build a customized spell-checking component and integrate it into your build of Solr. This is done by extending the abstract class org.apache .solr.spelling.SolrSpellChecker and implementing the getSuggestions method, as well as methods for building and reloading the component. As you saw earlier, this class needs to be included in a JAR that's made available to Solr in its solr/lib directory. After this is done, the component can be specified in the configuration, as was done with the SpellCheckComponent class.

In this section, you've seen how to combine techniques for finding fuzzy matches with *n*-gram with techniques for computing edit distances to perform spelling correction. Next, we'll use these techniques and others to perform fuzzy matches across a wider range of fields in a record matching task.

### 4.3.3 *Record matching*

Our final fuzzy string matching application isn't as prominently featured as our previous examples, but is the basis for many interesting applications. At its core, record matching is the application of the mashup. If you have two data sources that contain entries for the same entity in the world, and you can match the entries of those records, then you can mash up the distinct information contained in each data source. This combination of information can often provide a distinct perspective that neither of the individual data sources can provide on their own. In some cases this is straightforward, but in many cases it requires some fuzzy matching.

#### OUTLINING THE APPROACH

Our fuzzy matching approach to record matching is as follows:

- Find candidate matches.
- Rank, or score, the candidate matches.
- Evaluate the results and pick a candidate.

This is similar to the approach taken for spelling correction, where we determined candidate matches with *n*-gram matching, scored matches with an edit distance metric, and applied a threshold. The main addition is the criteria that only a single match that exceeds the threshold be found. This prevents matches from being asserted in cases where there are multiple candidates and the algorithm hasn't clearly ranked them.

Our example domain is theatrically released movies. This is a domain where a number of different sources of information contain references to this common space. This could include data sources such as the Internet Movie Database (IMDb), NetFlix, TV and On-Demand listings, iTunes and Amazon Rentals, or DVDs. In this example, you'll match up entries for movies between IMDb and Tribune Media Service (TMS). TMS provides TV listings data to Tivo and online at http://tvlistings.zap2it.com.

### FINDING CANDIDATE MATCHES WITH SOLR

Your first task is to find a means to identify a candidate set of matches for which you'd like to perform more advanced matching. As with spelling corrections, you can do this using *n*-gram matching in Solr. Here you apply *n*-gram matching to the field that you think is most likely to match and which is the most informative. For a movie, this would be the title. Unlike the spelling correction case where you had an obvious choice about which dataset to apply the *n*-grams to (the corrections), in this case you could construct *n*-gram tokens from either data source. Though there may be application-specific reasons why one data source is preferable to another, it's typically favorable to apply *n*-grams to the data source with the most entries. This is because you may run your matching algorithm over the entries several times and the *n*-gram construction is less likely to change. As you improve your algorithm, it's quicker to iterate over the smaller set of entries. Additionally, indexing time is often faster than record matching.

For your dataset, an XML document has been constructed for each movie in our IMDb database. Typically entries look as follows.

**Listing 4.17   Examples of entries in our IMDb dataset**

```
<doc>
  <field name="id">34369</field>
  <field name="imdb">tt0083658</field>
  <field name="title">Blade Runner</field>
  <field name="year">1982</field>
  <field name="cast">Harrison Ford</field>
  <field name="cast">Sean Young</field>
  <!-- Many other actors -->
</doc>
```

The relevant portions of the schema.xml entries for these fields are shown next.

**Listing 4.18   Additions to the Solr schema for record matching**

```
<field name="title" type="ngram"                          N-gram field used
  indexed="true" stored="true"/>                          earlier for spelling
<field name="year" type="integer                          correction.
  indexed="true" stored="true"/>
<field name="imdb" type="string"
  indexed="false" stored="true"/>
<field name="cast" type="string" indexed="true"           Multivalued cast field.

        multiValued="true" stored="true"/>
```

Candidates can be queried and retrieved with SolrJ as follows.

**Listing 4.19  Retrieving candidate matches from Solr for record matching**

```
private SolrServer solr;
private SolrQuery query;

public Iterator<SolrDocument> getCandidates(String title)
    throws SolrServerException {
    String etitle = escape(title);                    ◁── Escaped title.
    query.setQuery("title:""+etitle+""");             ◁─┐ Title in quotes
    QueryResponse response = solr.query(query);          │ to prevent
    SolrDocumentList dl = response.getResults();         │ tokenization.
    return dl.iterator();
}
```

The title needs to be escaped to prevent special characters such as AND, +, or ! from being interpreted as query functions when used as a query.

### RANKING CANDIDATE MATCHES

After you have a set of candidate matches, the question becomes how to score these matches. In the spelling case, you used edit distance. This may be a good candidate for the title, but you'll achieve the best matching by leveraging data from several fields. Let's consider the following fields as things you'd like to match as well as how you might score each component and the entire record match.

- *Title*—Edit distance is probably the most appropriate measure here. Since titles are more like names, you'll use the Jaro-Winkler distance measure rather than Levenshtein distance or *n*-gram distance.

- *Actors*—Though you could use edit distance for actors' names, since actors' names are really their brand, they tend to have standard spellings. (No one refers to the actor *Thomas Cruise*.) As such, exact match with some normalization will work in almost all cases. Your measure for actor overlap will be the percentage of actors who match exactly. Since there are often differences in the number of cast members listed between data sources, using the smaller number of cast members as the denominator is typically acceptable.

- *Release date*—The release date is also useful to distinguish between items with the same title. Minor differences in these numbers occur depending on whether the date is when the project started, its theatrical release, or DVD release year. The difference between the year listed in each feature provides a good measure that can be normalized by taking a reciprocal rank, so items with the same year receive a score of 1 and those that differ by 2 receive a score of 1/2. Differences could also be degraded linearly if a cutoff can be establish for when the score should become 0 or another constant.

You then need to combine each of these terms. This can be done by weighting each of the preceding terms and adding them together. Since each of your terms is normalized such that it returns a value between 0 and 1, if weights are chosen such that they sum to 1, then the resulting sum of weighted terms will also be between 0 and 1. For the task at hand, you'll a priori assign half of the weight to the title portion and divide the remaining weight between the other two terms. This is implemented in listing 4.20. You could also use a collection of already matched records to determine these weights empirically. Matching proceeds by querying Solr with the title of the record being matched and then scoring each of those candidates.

**Listing 4.20   Retrieving candidate matches from Solr for record matching**

```
private StringDistance sd = new JaroWinklerDistance();

private float score(String title1, int year1, Set<String> cast1,
        String title2, int year2, Set<String> cast2) {
    float titleScore = sd.getDistance(title1.toLowerCase(),
        title2.toLowerCase());

    float yearScore = (float) 1/(Math.abs(year1-year2)+1);

    float castScore = (float) intersectionSize(cast1,cast2)/
                Math.min(cast1.size(),cast2.size());
    return (titleScore*.5f)+
        (yearScore*0.2f)+
        (castScore*0.3f);
}

private int intersectionSize(Set<String> cast1,
                            Set<String> cast2) {
    int size = 0;
    for (String actor : cast1)
        if (cast2.contains(actor)) size++;
    return size;
}
```

- Use Jaro-Winkler on titles.
- Use reciprocal on years.
- Use cast overlap percentage.
- Combine scores into single score.
- Compute intersection using exact string matching.

**EVALUATING THE RESULTS**

Let's look at some examples using this approach. An example where you can see the benefits of combining multiple sets of data for matching is shown in tables 4.4 and 4.5.

**Table 4.4   Example of importance of combining multiple sets of data**

| ID | Title | Year | Cast |
|---|---|---|---|
| MV000000170000 | Nighthawks | 1981 | Sylvester Stallone, Billy Dee Williams, ... |

**Table 4.5   Second example of importance of combining multiple sets of data**

| Score | Title term + year term + cast term | ID | Title | Year | Cast |
|---|---|---|---|---|---|
| 0.55 | (0.5*1.00) + (0.2*0.25) + (0.3*0.00) | tt0077993 | Nighthawks | 1978 | Ken Robertson, Tony Westrope, ... |
| 0.24 | (0.5*0.43) + (0.2*0.12) + (0.3*0.00) | tt0097487 | Hawks | 1988 | Timothy Dalton, Anthony Edwards, ... |
| 0.96 | (0.5*0.98) + (0.2*1.00) + (0.3*0.88) | tt0082817 | Night Hawks | 1981 | Sylvester Stallone, Billy Dee Williams, ... |

The candidates are listed as returned by Solr based on title matches alone. You see that combination of data allows you not only to rank the correct entry higher than the other candidates, but also to exclude the other candidates such that you're confident that the best-scoring match is correct. In general, using an *n*-gram approach to retrieving candidates and the Jaro-Winkler edit distance allows this approach to deal with a number of variations in the data such as punctuation, numbers, subtitles, and even misspellings. Some examples of these titles are shown next:

- *Willy Wonka and the Chocolate Factory* and *Willy Wonka & the Chocolate Factory*
- *Return of the Secaucus 7* and *Return of the Secaucus Seven*
- *Godspell* and *Godspell: A Musical Based on the Gospel According to St. Matthew*
- *Desert Trail* and *The Desert Trail*

Evaluating this approach on 1,000 movies in TMS, we're able to match 884 of them to IMDb. These are all correctly matched, giving a precision of 100% and a recall of 88.4%, assuming that all movies can be matched. This also suggests that if you were tuning your algorithm, you might want to allow for looser matches, since you're not currently making any mistakes using your current algorithm and weights. Though the goal of this example isn't to optimize movie matching, looking at some of the cases where the algorithm failed to find a match is useful in that it exposes other factors you might consider when constructing record matching algorithms in other domains. Some of the matches that were missed are analyzed in table 4.6.

**Table 4.6  Analysis of missed matches**

| TMS title/year | IMDb title/year | Description |
|---|---|---|
| *M\*A\*S\*H* (1970) | *MASH* (1970) | This is a case where the *n*-gram matching will fail because all the *n*-grams in one of the titles will contain asterisks and none of the *n*-grams in the other title will contain that character. |
| *9 to 5* (1980) | *Nine to Five* (1980) | Here's a case where numeric normalization would be required to match the titles. |
| *The Day the World Ended* (1956) | *Day the World Ended* (1955) | In this case, the algorithm is unable to compensate for the mismatches in the leading determiner due to other mismatches between fields such as the date. Removing leading *Thes Ans* and *As* from titles would help alleviate this problem. |
| *Quest for Fire* (1981) | *La guerre du feu* (1981) | In some cases no amount of normalization will help. This case needs either to be handled editorially or for alternative titles to be leveraged. |

**Table 4.6  Analysis of missed matches** *(continued)*

| TMS title/year | IMDb title/year | Description |
|---|---|---|
| Smokey and the Bandit (1977) | Smokey and the Bandit (1977) | In this case, though the best match was the correct match, the score for the match between this movie and its sequel, Smokey and the Bandit II also scored above the threshold and so the match was canceled. |
| The Voyage of the Yes (1972) | The Voyage of the Yes (1972) | Here's a case where one data source, TMS, classifies this as a movie and another as a TV show. As such it wasn't a candidate for matching. |

These cases demonstrate that even using the best techniques, data normalization is important to successful matching. The algorithm would benefit from a number of normalization steps for numerics, determiners, and alternative titles. In order to produce highly effective algorithms, you must spend a fair amount of effort making sure that what gets to your matching code is the data you want.

In this section, you've seen how various string matching techniques can be used to power a number of applications. For supporting type-ahead, we used prefix matching in Solr. We showed how a combination of *n*-gram matching and edit distance can be used to suggest alternative spellings. Finally, we used *n*-gram matching, edit distance, and exact matching to perform record matching for movies.

## 4.4  Summary

The chapter began with the question of what it means for strings to be similar—how fuzzy is fuzzy matching? It then introduced several approaches to fuzzy string matching to provide a formal notion of how similar two strings are to one another. These included measures that use just the characters, such as the Jaccard measure; the character's order, such as edit distance; and windows of characters, such as Jaro-Winkler measure and *n*-gram edit distance. We also showed how prefix and *n*-gram matching can be used to efficiently produce candidate matches for the more computationally expensive edit distance computations. Finally, we built applications that leverage these techniques and also leverage Solr as a platform to make building these applications easy. In the next chapter, we'll move from comparing strings to one another to finding information inside strings and documents.

## 4.5  Resources

Aoe, Jun-ichi. 1989. "An efficient digital search algorithm by using a double-array structure." IEEE Transactions on Software Engineering, 15, no.9:1066–1077.

# Identifying people, places, and things

People, places, and things—nouns—play a crucial role in language, conveying the sentence's subject and often its object. Due to their importance, it's often useful when processing text to try to identify nouns and use them in applications. This task, often called either *entity identification* or *named-entity recognition (NER)* is often handled by a parser or chunker, as you saw in chapter 2. Though using a parser is nice for understanding a sentence, text applications often will find it more useful to focus on a subset of nouns that identify specific instances of an object such as proper nouns, also often called *named entities*. Furthermore, fully parsing a sentence is a process-intensive task, whereas finding proper nouns need not be so intensive.

In many situations, it's also useful to go beyond names of people and places and include temporal and numeric concepts like July 2007 or $50.35. From a text-based application perspective, proper nouns are everywhere and, at the same time, specific instances of a proper noun may be exceedingly rare. For example, consider any recently occurring news event (especially those not involving a celebrity or high-ranking government officials). How many proper nouns are in the story? How many are people you've never heard of before? How many of those people will still be in the news in six months? Where and when did the events take place?

Obviously, the context of the article informs you that a particular sequence of words is a proper noun and there are probably other clues like capitalization, or titles such as Mr. or Mrs., but how can you codify this so a text processing application can learn to recognize these entities? In this chapter, we'll first spend some time understanding the background behind named-entity identification, and then we'll look into Apache OpenNLP to enable you to learn how to recognize named entities. We'll also examine performance considerations and look at customizing a model to your domain, but let's start here by looking at what you can do with named entities.

Identifying people, organization, places, and other named entities allows you to capture what an article is about in an actionable way. For instance, with this information you can provide more information about these entities, suggest other content which also features them or is related to them, and ultimately increase engagement in your site. In many large companies or organizations, this work of identifying named entities is often done editorially. The result can be a site where people get lost reading part of one article, seeing another interesting link and wandering off to another article, only to look up at the clock not realizing that they spent the last hour on the site. For example, in figure 5.1, Yahoo! has highlighted the named-entity *Sarah Palin* and then added a pop-up that highlights other content about the 2008 vice presidential candidate. They're even showing ads based on the named entity at the bottom of the pop-ups in the hopes of capturing more revenue. This kind of engagement is invaluable for a site (especially one monetized by ad impressions), and fostering that engagement provides an experience that has users returning to the site time and again. As you can imagine, doing this editorially is labor intensive and companies are often looking for ways to automate, or at least partially automate, the process of identifying named entities.

Furthermore, unlike with keywords, tags, or other meaning-based representations of an article's content, the notion of a related article based on the presence or absence of an entity is a clear relationship (assuming you've done proper record matching to make sure they're the same entities, as described in chapter 4!) and makes intuitive sense to a user.

In this chapter, we'll look at how to perform the task of identifying names in text automatically. We'll examine the accuracy of a popular open source tool for performing named-entity recognition as well as its runtime performance characteristics in order to assist you in choosing where and when to employ this technology. We'll also

**Figure 5.1**   **Snippet of article on Yahoo! News and entity page click. Sarah Palin is marked as a Y! News Shortcut. Image captured 9/21/2008.**

examine how to customize its models to perform better on your data. Even if you don't want to expose named-entity information directly to users, it may be useful in constructing data to engage users such as a site zeitgeist or the top 10 most popular people mentioned on a site. With all these possible uses, let's dig into the details.

## 5.1   Approaches to named-entity recognition

In undertaking named-entity recognition (NER), we're interested in identifying some or all mentions of people, places, organizations, time, and numbers (not all are technically proper nouns, but we'll classify them all as such for brevity). NER boils down to answering the questions of where, when, who, and how often or how much. For example, given the sentence

> The Minnesota Twins won the 1991 World Series,

an NER system may recognize *Minnesota Twins, 1991,* and *World Series* as named entities (or possibly, *1991 World Series* as a single named entity). In practice, not all systems have the same requirements for extracting named entities. For example, marketers might be looking for names of their products so they can understand who's talking about them; whereas a historian responsible for constructing a chronology of events from hundreds of eyewitness accounts will be interested in not only the people taking part in the event, but also the exact times and locations where each person witnessed the event.

### 5.1.1   Using rules to identify names

One approach to performing NER is to use a combination of lists and regular expressions to identify named entities. With this approach, you need only codify some basic rules about capitalization and numbers and then combine that with lists of things like common first and last names and popular locations (not to mention the days of the week, names of months, and so on) and then throw it at a bunch of text. This approach was popular in early research on named-entity recognition systems but has become less popular because such a system is difficult to maintain for the following reasons:

- Maintaining the lists is labor intensive and inflexible.
- Moving to other languages or domains may involve repeating much of the work.
- Many proper nouns are also valid in other roles (such as Will or Hope). Said another way: dealing with ambiguity is hard.
- Many names are conjunctions of other names, such as the *Scottish Exhibition and Conference Center* where it's not always clear where the name ends.
- Names of people and places are often the same—Washington (state, D.C., or George) or Cicero (the ancient philosopher, the town in New York, or some other place).
- It's difficult to model dependencies between names across a document using rules based on regular expressions.

It should be noted that rule-based approaches can perform nicely within specific well-understood domains, and shouldn't be discarded completely. For a domain such as capturing length measurements, where the items themselves are typically rare and the number of units of length bounded, this approach is probably applicable. Many useful resources are available publicly to help in bootstrapping such a process for a number of entity types. Basic rules and some general resources are available at the CIA World Fact Book (https://www.cia.gov/library/publications/the-world-factbook/index.html) and Wikipedia (http://www.wikipedia.org). Also available are dictionaries of proper nouns (many available online), along with domain-specific resources like the Internet Movie Database or domain-specific knowledge that can be effectively utilized to achieve reasonable performance, while minimizing the work required.

### 5.1.2  *Using statistical classifiers to identify names*

A less brittle approach that's easy to extend to other domains and languages and that doesn't require creating large lists (gazetteers) to be maintained is much more desirable. This approach is to use a statistical classifier to identify named entities. Typically the classifier looks at each word in a sentence and decides whether it's the start of a named entity, the continuation of an already started entity, or not part of a name at all. By combining these predictions, you can use a classifier to identify a sequence of words that make up a name.

Though the tagging approach is fairly common to most classifier-based approaches to identifying names, variation exists in how different entity types are identified. One approach is to use the tagging approach or even a regular expression–based approach to simply identify text that contains a name of any type and, in a second pass, distinguish between the different types of names or entity types. Another approach is to simultaneously distinguish between different entity types by predicting the entity type along with the name start or continuation. Yet another approach is to build a separate classifier for each name type, and to combine the results for each sentence. This is the approach taken by the software we'll work with later in this chapter. Also, later in this chapter, we'll examine some of these variations in approach in more detail and discuss their trade-offs.

Regardless of which of the various classification approaches is used, a classifier needs to be trained on a collection of human-annotated text to learn how to identify names. Some of the advantages of such an approach include these:

- Lists can be incorporated as features and as such are only one source of information.
- Moving to other languages or domains may only involve minimal code changes.
- It's easier to model the context within a sentence and in a document.
- The classifier can be retrained to incorporate additional text or other features.

The main disadvantage of such approaches is the need for human-annotated data. Whereas a programmer can write a set of rules and see them being applied to a collection of text immediately, the classifier will typically need to be trained on approximately 30,000 words to perform moderately well. Though annotation is tedious, it doesn't require the set of specialized skills needed for rule crafting and is a resource that can be extended and reused. With sufficient amounts of training data, the performance can be near to human quality, even if people are less than perfect at the task of identifying names. Good NER systems are usually capable of properly recognizing entities better than 90% of the time in evaluation experiments. In the real world, with real data, expectations must be lowered, but most systems should still provide decent quality that's usable. Furthermore, a good system should be easy to set up and, if needed, trained to learn proper nouns. Ideally, the system would also support incremental updates when new examples or counterexamples are available. With these requirements in mind, the next section takes a look at how the OpenNLP project provides named-entity identification capabilities.

## 5.2  *Basic entity identification with OpenNLP*

The OpenNLP project, as mentioned in chapter 2 and currently available for download at http://opennlp.apache.org, maintains a suite of tools for doing many common NLP tasks such as part of speech tagging, parsing, and, most useful to us in this chapter, named-entity recognition. These tools are licensed under the Apache Software License (ASL) and were originally developed by Thomas Morton and others, but are now an Apache Software Foundation project much like Solr and maintained by a community of users and contributors. Though several tools will perform named-entity recognition, the majority of these either aren't open source or are research projects, many of which are distributed with research-only licenses or under the GPL, which isn't always viewed as usable in many companies. OpenNLP is distributed with a collection of models that perform well for some common entity types, and is actively maintained and supported. For these reasons and due to our familiarity with the software itself, we'll focus on it for providing named-entity capabilities.

OpenNLP is distributed with prebuilt models that allow you to identify proper nouns and numeric amounts and to semantically tag them into seven distinct categories. The categories and examples of text which fall into them are provided next:

- *People*—Bill Clinton, Mr. Clinton, President Clinton
- *Locations*—Alabama, Montgomery, Guam
- *Organizations*—Microsoft Corp., Internal Revenue Service, IRS, Congress
- *Dates*—Sept. 3, Saturday, Easter
- *Times*—6 minutes 20 seconds, 4:04 a.m., afternoon
- *Percentages*—10 percent, 45.5 percent, 37.5%
- *Money*—$90,000, $35 billion, one euro, 36 pesos

Users can select any subset of these categories depending on the requirements of their particular project.

In the remainder of this section, you'll learn how to use OpenNLP to identify the previously mentioned categories in text, and then we'll look at some provided tools that help you understand what was extracted. Finally, we'll finish up the section by looking at how to leverage OpenNLP's scores to understand the likelihood that an extraction (or multiple extractions) is correct.

### 5.2.1 Finding names with OpenNLP

Let's get started by looking at an example of how to use OpenNLP to identify people by writing a few lines of Java code.

**Listing 5.1   Identifying names with OpenNLP**

```
String[] sentences = {
  "Former first lady Nancy Reagan was taken to a " +
      "suburban Los Angeles " +
  "hospital "as a precaution" Sunday after a " +
      "fall at her home, an " +
  "aide said. ",



  "The 86-year-old Reagan will remain overnight for " +
  "observation at a hospital in Santa Monica, California, " +
      "said Joanne " +
  "Drake, chief of staff for the Reagan Foundation."};

NameFinderME finder = new NameFinderME(
  new TokenNameFinderModel(new FileInputStream(getPersonModel()))
);


Tokenizer tokenizer = SimpleTokenizer.INSTANCE;
```

Initialize new model for identifying people names based on the binary compressed model in the file en-ner-person.bin.

Initialize tokenizer to split sentence into individual words and symbols.

Identify names in sentence and return token-based offsets to these names.

```
for (int si = 0; si < sentences.length; si++) {
    String[] tokens = tokenizer.tokenize(sentences[si]);
    Span[] names = finder.find(tokens);
    displayNames(names, tokens);
}

finder.clearAdaptiveData();
```

Split sentence into array of tokens.

Clear data structures that store which words have been seen previously in the document and whether these words were considered part of a person's name.

In the example, you first create a document of two sentences and then initialize the `NameFinderME` class and a tokenizer to be used with it. The `NameFinderME` class is given a model for identifying a particular type of named entity you want to find (people, in this case), and is based on the person model file distributed with OpenNLP. Each sentence is then tokenized and the names contained within it are identified and then displayed to the user. Finally, after all sentences in a document are processed, a call is made to the `clearAdaptiveData()` method. This tells the `NameFinderME` to clear any document-level data that has been stored based on the processing thus far. By default, OpenNLP's `NameFinderME` class keeps track of whether a word has been identified as part of a name previously; this is a good indication as to whether subsequent mentions should also be considered as parts of a name. The call to `clearAdaptiveData()` clears this cache.

The example shows that the `NameFinderME` processes a single sentence at a time. Though not explicitly required, this prevents names from being erroneously found that cross sentence boundaries. In general, it's beneficial to have the name finder process the smallest units of text that won't split the occurrence of a name. This is because the OpenNLP implementation is actually considering up to three alternative sets of names for every unit of text processed. If you process a document, you get three alternatives for the entire document, but if you process a sentence, you get three alternatives for each sentence.

The input to the `NameFinderME.find()` method is a sequence of tokens. This means that each sentence that will be processed will also need to be tokenized. Here you use a tokenizer provided by OpenNLP that splits tokens based on character classes. Because tokenization affects how the `find()` method sees the sentence, it's important to use the same tokenization procedure for finding new names as was used in training the name finding model. In section 5.5, we'll discuss training new named-entity identification models with alternative tokenizations.

### 5.2.2 *Interpreting names identified by OpenNLP*

The `NameFinderME.find()` method returns an array of spans that specify the location of any name identified in the input sentence. The OpenNLP span data type stores the index of the first token of a name (accessible via the `getStart()` method), and the index of the token immediately following the last token of a name (accessible via the `getEnd()` method). In this case, spans are used to represent token offsets, but

OpenNLP also uses this data type to represent character offsets. The following code sequence prints each name on a line as a sequence of tokens.

**Listing 5.2    Displaying names with OpenNLP**

```
private void displayNames(Span[] names, String[] tokens) {
  for (int si = 0; si < names.length; si++) {                    ⟵┐ Iterate over
    StringBuilder cb = new StringBuilder();                          each name.
    for (int ti = names[si].getStart();
                  ti < names[si].getEnd(); ti++) {    ⟵┐ Iterate over each
      cb.append(tokens[ti]).append(" ");                  token in name.
    }
    System.out.println(cb.substring(0, cb.length() - 1));    ⟵┐ Remove extra
    System.out.println("ttype: " + names[si].getType());         space at end of
  }                                                              name and print.
}
```

OpenNLP also provides a utility to convert a span into the string representing the name, as is done in listing 5.3, using the `Span.spansToStrings()` method.

If you want to see the name in its untokenized form, you can map the name onto its character offsets as shown next. In this case, you ask the tokenizer to return the character offset spans for the tokens using the `tokenizePos()` method rather than the String representation of the tokens. This allows you to determine where in the original sentence a name occurred.

**Listing 5.3    Displaying names using spans**

```
                    for (int si = 0; si < sentences.length; si++) {         ⟵┐ Iterate over
                      Span[] tokenSpans = tokenizer.tokenizePos(sentences[si]);   each sentence.
Split into tokens;  ⊳ String[] tokens = Span.spansToStrings(tokenSpans, sentences[si]);
return character       Span[] names = finder.find(tokens);                  ⟵
offsets (spans).
                                                                            Convert spans
                                                                            to strings.
Compute start       ⊳ for (int ni = 0; ni < names.length; ni++) {
character index       Span startSpan = tokenSpans[names[ni].getStart()];   Identify names;
of name.              int nameStart  = startSpan.getStart();               return token-
                                                                           based offsets.

Compute end         ⊳ Span endSpan    = tokenSpans[names[ni].getEnd() - 1];
character index       int nameEnd      = endSpan.getEnd();
(last character +1).

Compute string      ⊳ String name = sentences[si].substring(nameStart, nameEnd);
that represents       System.out.println(name);
name.               }
                  }
```

### 5.2.3    *Filtering names based on probability*

OpenNLP uses a probabilistic model that makes it possible to determine the probability associated with a particular name that has been identified. This can be particularly useful in cases where you want to filter out some of the names returned by the name finder, which may be mistakes. Though there's no way to automatically determine which names have been identified erroneously, in general, names that the model has assigned lower probabilities are less likely to be accurate. To determine the probability associated with a particular name, you can call the `NameFinderME.getProbs()` method after each sentence has been processed, as shown in the following listing. The returned array of values correspond by index to the names identified by the spans given as input.

**Listing 5.4　Determining name probabilities**

```
for (int si = 0; si < sentences.length; si++) {
    String[] tokens = tokenizer.tokenize(sentences[si]);
    Span[] names = finder.find(tokens);
    double[] spanProbs = finder.probs(names);
}
```

Split sentence into array tokens. ⟶

Iterate over each sentence. ⟵

Identify names; return token-based offsets. ⟵

Return probability associated with each name. ⟶

Filtering names would then consist of determining a threshold probability below which a name would be excluded based on the needs of your application.

In this section, you've seen how to identify a single name type using OpenNLP, interpret the data structures used by OpenNLP to designate the location of names, and determine which names are more likely to be accurate. In the next section, we'll look at identifying multiple names and get into the details of how OpenNLP actually determines the presence or absence of a name in text.

## 5.3　*In-depth entity identification with OpenNLP*

Now that you've seen the basics, let's look into some more advanced cases that will likely come up when building a real system using these tools. As you saw in section 5.1, there are multiple approaches to identifying a named entity. The primary limitation of the examples you've seen so far is that they involve only a single type of named entity. In this section, you'll see how OpenNLP can be used to identify multiple named-entity types in the same sentence as well as examine what information it uses to identify individual name types.

### 5.3.1　*Identifying multiple entity types with OpenNLP*

In OpenNLP, each name type uses its own independent model to identify a single name type. This has the advantages that you only need to employ the subset of models that your particular application needs, and that you can add your own models for other name types to the existing ones. It also implies that different models can identify names from overlapping sections of text, as shown next:

```
<person> Michael Vick </person>, the former <organization> <location>
 Atlanta </location> Falcons </organization> quarterback, is serving a 23-
month sentence at maximum-security prison in <location> Leavenworth </
location>, <location> Kansas </location>.
```

Here you see that *Atlanta* is marked as a location as well as part of an organization.

The disadvantage of such an approach is that you need to combine the results of each model. In this section, you'll look at some approaches to overcome this problem. Having each name type use its own model also has implications on performance and training. We'll talk more about these implications in sections 5.4 and 5.5.

Since each model is independent of the others, using multiple models is a simple matter of processing a sentence with each of the models, followed by the less simple matter of combining the results. In listing 5.5, we collect the names from three models. To facilitate this, we've created a helper class, Annotation, to hold the name spans along with their probability and type.

**Listing 5.5   Running multiple name models on the same text**

**Initialize new model for identifying people, locations, and dates based on the binary compressed model in the files en-ner-person.bin, en-ner-location.bin, en-ner-date.bin.**

**Obtain reference to a tokenizer to split sentence into individual words and symbols.**

**Split sentence into array of tokens.**

**Iterate over each name finder (person, location, date).**

**Get probabilities with associated matches.**

**Iterate over each sentence.**

**Identify names in sentence and return token-based offsets.**

**Collect each identified name from name finders.**

**Resolve overlapping names in favor of more probable names.**

```java
String[] sentences = {
  "Former first lady Nancy Reagan was taken to a " +
      "suburban Los Angeles " +
  "hospital "as a precaution" Sunday after a fall at " +
      "her home, an " +
  "aide said. ",
  "The 86-year-old Reagan will remain overnight for " +
  "observation at a hospital in Santa Monica, California, " +
      "said Joanne " +
  "Drake, chief of staff for the Reagan Foundation."};
NameFinderME[] finders = new NameFinderME[3];
String[] names = {"person", "location", "date"};
for (int mi = 0; mi < names.length; mi++) {
  finders[mi] = new NameFinderME(new TokenNameFinderModel(
    new FileInputStream(
        new File(modelDir, "en-ner-" + names[mi] + ".bin")
    ))));
}

Tokenizer tokenizer = SimpleTokenizer.INSTANCE;
for (int si = 0; si < sentences.length; si++) {
  List<Annotation> allAnnotations = new ArrayList<Annotation>();
  String[] tokens = tokenizer.tokenize(sentences[si]);
  for (int fi = 0; fi < finders.length; fi++) {
    Span[] spans = finders[fi].find(tokens);
    double[] probs = finders[fi].probs(spans);
    for (int ni = 0; ni < spans.length; ni++) {
      allAnnotations.add(
          new Annotation(names[fi], spans[ni], probs[ni])
      );
    }
  }
  removeConflicts(allAnnotations);
}
```

Combining the output of the three models is only problematic when the names overlap. Depending on the application, the criteria for when names overlap may be different. In order to combine the results, a series of things should be considered:

- Is it OK for the same span of text to be identified as a name by different models? Typically, no.
- Is it OK for a name that's smaller to be found within a larger name? Typically, yes.
- Can names overlap but also each contain distinct text? Typically, no.
- If names collide, what criteria should be used to adjudicate? Typically, the probability.

The following is an implementation that follows these default criteria: names must have distinct spans and can overlap, but if they do so, one name must completely contain the other.

**Listing 5.6  Resolving conflicting names**

```java
private void removeConflicts(List<Annotation> allAnnotations) {
    java.util.Collections.sort(allAnnotations);
    List<Annotation> stack = new ArrayList<Annotation>();
    stack.add(allAnnotations.get(0));
    for (int ai = 1; ai < allAnnotations.size(); ai++) {
        Annotation curr = (Annotation) allAnnotations.get(ai);
        boolean deleteCurr = false;
        for (int ki = stack.size() - 1; ki >= 0; ki--) {
            Annotation prev = (Annotation) stack.get(ki);
            if (prev.getSpan().equals(curr.getSpan())) {
                if (prev.getProb() > curr.getProb()) {
                    deleteCurr = true;
                    break;
                } else {
                    allAnnotations.remove(stack.remove(ki));
                    ai--;
                }
            } else if (prev.getSpan().intersects(curr.getSpan())) {
                if (prev.getProb() > curr.getProb()) {
                    deleteCurr = true;
                    break;
                } else {
                    allAnnotations.remove(stack.remove(ki));
                    ai--;
                }
            } else if (prev.getSpan().contains(curr.getSpan())) {
                break;
            } else {
                stack.remove(ki);
            }
        }
    }
```

Annotations for listing 5.6:

- **Initialize stack to track previous names.**
- **Iterate over each name.**
- **Sort names based on their span's start index ascending, then end index descending.**
- **Iterate over each item in stack.**
- **Test if name span is identical to another name span, and if so remove the less probable one.**
- **Update index of name after deletion to negate ai++ at end of for loop.**
- **Test if name span is overlapping another name span, and if so remove the less probable one.**
- **Update index of name after deletion to negate ai++ at end of for loop.**
- **Test if name span is subsumed by another name span, and if so exit loop.**
- **Test if name span is subsumed by another name span, and if so exit loop.**

```
        if (deleteCurr) {
          allAnnotations.remove(ai);
          ai--;                                  ⟵   Test if name span is past
                                                     another name span, and
          deleteCurr = false;                        if so remove previous
        } else {                                     name from the stack.
          stack.add(curr);
        }
      }
    }
  }
```

This approach to merging is linear in time complexity with respect to the length of the sentence, but because you're allowing names to occur within other names, you use a second loop to process the stack that holds nested names. This stack size can never exceed the number of name types being used, so the time taken by the second loop can be treated as a constant. Now that we've discussed some of the background and seen an example of using multiple models, let's take a look at the engineering details that go into how names are identified in OpenNLP.

### 5.3.2   *Under the hood: how OpenNLP identifies names*

If we asked a non-engineer, "How does a TV work?" he might answer, "Well, you point the remote at it, and push this red button..." Thus far we've described how to use the named-entity identification software in OpenNLP and provide this kind of answer. In this section, we'll look at how that software actually performs the task of identifying names. This information will prove valuable in sections 5.4 and 5.5 when we consider the topics of performance and customization.

OpenNLP treats identifying names as a tagging task, similar to what will be discussed in chapter 7. The process is one of labeling each token with one of three tags:

- *Start*—Begin a new name starting at this token.
- *Continue*—Append an existing name onto this token.
- *Other*—This token is not part of a name.

For a typical sentence, this tagging looks like table 5.1.

**Table 5.1   Sentence tagged for named-entity identification**

| 0 | 1 | 2 | 3 | 4 | 5 | 6 | 7 | 8 | 9 | 10 | 11 |
|---|---|---|---|---|---|---|---|---|---|----|----|
| " | It | is | a | familiar | story | , | " | Jason | Willaford | said | . |
| other | other | other | other | other | other | other | other | start | continue | other | other |

By connecting start tags with any number of continue tags, the example sequence of classifications can be turned into a set of Spans. The statistical modeling package used by OpenNLP builds a model to determine when it should be predicting each of the three tags. This model uses a set of *features*, specified in the code, to predict which outcome is most likely. These features are designed to distinguish proper names, different types of numeric strings, and the surrounding context of words and tagging decisions. The features used by OpenNLP for named-entity identification are as follows:

1 The token being tagged
2 The token 1 place to the left
3 The token 2 places to the left
4 The token 1 place to the right
5 The token 2 places to the right
6 The token class for the token being tagged
7 The token class for the token 1 place to the left
8 The token class for the token 2 places to the left
9 The token class for the token 1 place to the right
10 The token class for the token 2 places to the right
11 The token and token class for the token being tagged
12 The token and token class for the token 1 place to the left
13 The token and token class for the token 2 places to the left
14 The token and token class for the token 1 place to the right
15 The token and token class for the token 2 places to the right
16 The predicted outcome for the token 1 place to the left or null
17 The predicted outcome for the token 2 places to the left or null
18 The token and the token 1 place to the left
19 The token and the token 1 place to the right
20 The token class and the token class 1 place to the left
21 The token class and the token class 1 place to the right
22 The outcome previously assigned to this token string or null

Many of these features are based on the token being tagged and its adjacent neighbors, but some of these features are based on the token class. A token's class is based upon basic characteristics of the token, such as whether it consists solely of lowercase characters.

These features model the decision about what tokens constitute an entity and its type based on the words used, a set of classes for those words, and the decisions made previously in this document or sentence. The words themselves are important and take the place of lists in a rule-based approach. If the training data contains a word that's annotated as an entity enough times, then the classifier using feature 1 can simply memorize that word. Feature 6, like feature 1, focuses on the word being tagged, but instead of using the word itself, it uses the token class.

The token classes used for named-entity identification are as follows:

1 Token is lowercase alphabetic
2 Token is two digits
3 Token is four digits

4  Token contains a number and a letter
5  Token contains a number and a hyphen
6  Token contains a number and a backslash
7  Token contains a number and a comma
8  Token contains a number and a period
9  Token contains a number
10 Token is all caps, single letter
11 Token is all caps, multiple letters
12 Token's initial letters are caps
13 Other

The token classes outlined here are designed to help predict certain entity types. For instance, token class 3 is indicative of year dates such as 1984. Token classes 5 and 6 are also typical of dates, whereas token classes 7 and 8 are more typical of monetary amounts. Features 2–15 allow the context that the word occurs in to be taken into account so that an ambiguous word such as *Washington* might be more likely to be identified as a location in the context "in Washington" and a person in the context "Washington said." Features 16 and 17 allow the model to capture that continue tags follow start tags, and feature 18 allows the model to capture that if a word was previously tagged as part of a person entity, then a subsequent mention of the same word might also be part of a person entity. Though none of the features by themselves are entirely predictive, an empirically weighted combination of them usually captures the name types used in OpenNLP.

The features are targeted to capture the types of information needed to identify the named-entity types that OpenNLP identifies. It may be the case that, for your application, the entities that OpenNLP identifies will suffice. Since automated techniques for identifying names will never be perfect (and neither will manual approaches), the question for your application is, are they good enough? In the next section, we'll look at how well the models distributed with OpenNLP perform at identifying these entities, as well as the runtime performance of the software. These characteristics will help you determine whether you can use this software out of the box and in what types of applications it can be applied. You may also need to identify additional entity types for your application. In this case, the features shown here may not capture the kind of information needed to model these new kinds of entities.

## 5.4  *Performance of OpenNLP*

We'll consider three areas of performance as it relates to named-entity identification. The first is the quality of the linguistic annotations, or specifically the names found by the OpenNLP components. As we described before, linguistic analysis is never perfect, but that shouldn't stop you from looking at how closely a system matches human performance. Using this information, you can access whether the models provided are likely to be accurate enough for your application or whether additional training materials or customization will be necessary.

The second area of performance we'll consider is the speed at which we can perform the tasks. We'll discuss some of the optimizations OpenNLP performs to improve runtime efficiency and evaluate the speed at which various numbers of models can be applied to text. Finally, we'll look at the amount of memory required to run the name finder. As we mentioned before, the named-entity identification models are treated separately so that you only need to use the ones you want. This is in part due to the large amount of memory required by the named-entity models. We'll look at exactly how much memory is required as well as an approach to significantly reduce the amount of memory required to load a subsequent model. This information can be used to identify where this technology will be applicable to your applications and specifically whether named-entity technology can be incorporated in an online fashion or as an offline batch process.

## 5.4.1 Quality of results

The linguistic quality of the named-entity identification system is dependent on the data that it's trained on. OpenNLP trains its named-entity models on data designed for the MUC-7 (http://www-nlpir.nist.gov/related_projects/muc/proceedings/muc_7_toc.html) task. This dataset is used commonly for research into systems for identifying names. This task has specific criteria for what's considered a person, an organization, a location, or some other entity type. Though these may seem like clear categories, a number of cases occur in real text that aren't obvious and require guidelines to resolve. For example, most artifacts that have names, such as Space Shuttle Discovery, aren't classified, but according to the guidelines, airports are considered locations. What's important in learning to identify these categories is not so much the exact set of choices that are made about particular edge cases, but that these cases are annotated consistently so that the models can learn them.

We evaluated the models distributed with OpenNLP using the training and test sets for the MUC-7 task. OpenNLP isn't trained on the data in the test set, so it also provides a reasonable measure of its performance on unseen text. Results of this evaluation are shown in table 5.2.

*Precision* is a measure of how often, when the system identifies a name, that name is correct. *Recall* is a measure of how many of the total number of actual names have been identified. The *F-measure* is the weighted harmonic mean of precision and recall. In this case, the F-measure is computed by equally weighting precision and recall. You can see from these results that the system is able to identify at least 75% of the entities and is only mistaken about 10% of the time.

**Table 5.2** Evaluation of quality of annotations produced by OpenNLP

| Dataset | Precision | Recall | F-measure |
|---------|-----------|--------|-----------|
| train muc7 | 87 | 90 | 88.61 |
| test muc7 | 94 | 75 | 83.481 |

### 5.4.2    *Runtime performance*

The second area of performance that we'll consider is runtime performance. As we discussed in section 5.1.2, the model identifies names by tagging each word in a sentence with a start, continue, or other tag. This means that for each type of name that needs to be detected, the model must make a decision for each token. This is potentially multiplied by a factor of three, as up to three alternative sets of names are considered for any unit of text processed. As models are added to a system, this cost can become prohibitive.

OpenNLP mitigates the cost of this processing in two ways. First, caching is performed on the outcome probabilities so that when the features that are generated to predict an outcome are identical for any of the three alternative name sets, that probability distribution is computed once and the result cached. Second, caching is performed on the feature generation itself. Since the same features are used across all models, and the sentences are processed one at a time, sentence-level features that aren't dependent on previous decisions made by the model are computed once and the results cached. The result of this is that, though using fewer models is obviously faster than using more, there's not a strict linear cost in adding models. The performance graph in figure 5.2 demonstrates that as the number of models increases, the runtime performance isn't reduced in a strictly linear fashion.

In section 5.5, we'll describe an alternative model that gives up some flexibility, but performs comparably to a single model while detecting all entity types.

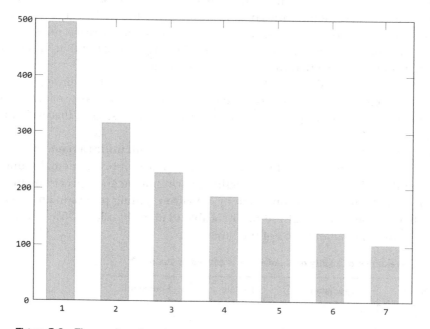

**Figure 5.2    The number of sentences per second processed by the name finder against the number of model types being identified**

### 5.4.3 *Memory usage in OpenNLP*

In this section, we'll examine the memory requirements of OpenNLP's named-entity identification system. As you saw in the previous section, maintaining separate models comes with some cost. The memory that a process consumes when using the person model is approximately 68M. Some of this space is taken up by code and the JVM, but approximately 54M of that memory is taken up by the model. A model consists of features, outcomes, and parameter values, but much of this space is taken up by storing the names of the features. This is because we use lexical features, so every word in our training data that occurs more than a certain number of times will be stored in our model as a feature. As lexical features are potentially combined with other lexical and nonlexical features, the total number of features that the model needs to store can be large. To load all models into memory requires approximately 400M of memory.

We noted in the previous section that each of the named-entity models uses the same feature set. If they're trained on the same data, then they'll contain the same features and only their parameter values for those features will be different, as different factors will be important to different types of named entities. Even if the models aren't trained on the same data, there will be significant overlap in features, as two pieces of text will typically contain many of the same words. If you could somehow share the memory allocated to these features, you'd expect a significant amount of memory reduction when using more than one model. One mechanism for doing this is Java's `String.intern()` method. This method returns a canonical representation of the string that it's applied to by implementing a string pool. Using this method, you can ensure that all references to a particular string reference the same object in memory.

The *Taming Text* source code includes a model reader which uses the `String.intern()` method to achieve this effect. The following example revisits the previous example that uses multiple name models to see how to use this model reader.

**Listing 5.7  Using string pooling to reduce memory size in named-entity identification**

```
String[] names = {"person","location","date"};
NameFinderME[] finders = new NameFinderME[names.length];
for (int mi = 0; mi < names.length; mi++) {
  finders[mi] = new NameFinderME(
    new PooledTokenNameFinderModel(
      new FileInputStream(
        new File(modelDir, "en-ner-"
          + names[mi] + ".bin")))));
}
```

Initialize name finders for identifying people, locations, and dates.

Use string pooling model to reduce footprint.

Using this approach, all seven models can be loaded into memory using approximately 225M, saving you about 175M. Because the mapping of features to a common representation is performed at model load time, there's no impact on the runtime performance of applying the model to text.

Now that you understand the basics of OpenNLP quality, speed, and memory usage, let's take things up another level and look at how you can customize OpenNLP for your domain. In the next section, we'll take a look at what it takes to train your own model and other customizations you might need for deployment in your application.

## 5.5 Customizing OpenNLP entity identification for a new domain

In many cases, the models provided with OpenNLP will be sufficient for your application or domain. But there may be cases when you want to train your own model. In this section, we'll cover how to train models with OpenNLP and how to change the features used to predict the names, and describe an alternative way to use OpenNLP to identify names, which has certain advantages in some cases.

### 5.5.1 The whys and hows of training a model

There are many reasons to train your own model. For instance, you may need to identify a new type of entity, such as a vehicle. Alternatively, you may need to detect people or some other type of entity supported by OpenNLP, but your domain is sufficiently different that the models provided with OpenNLP aren't performing well. Or perhaps you have a special case where you need a different definition of people than the one used in the OpenNLP model. In addition, if you're detecting a different entity type or working in another domain, you may have new features that you'd like the model to use. Finally, the tokenization used by OpenNLP may not be appropriate to the domain or to subsequent processing, in which case you'd want to train a model using a different tokenizer.

The biggest difficulty in training a new model with OpenNLP is finding or creating training data in sufficient amounts that are practical for statistical modeling. Though some datasets are available publicly, if you're building models for a new entity type, then you'll almost certainly need to annotate some text of your own. Though annotation is time consuming, it doesn't typically require someone with a specialized skill set, and is often less expensive than having a programmer construct a set of rules. An annotated dataset can also be reused with different types of models, so that as the modeling improves (perhaps with the identification of more predictive features), you can improve the performance of the named-entity identification system without additional annotation costs. Typical datasets for named-entity identification consist of at least 10K–15K words for training. You'll also need to set some of the annotated data aside to evaluate progress and to ensure that changes to a system are improving overall performance.

If you're looking to improve the performance of a model distributed with OpenNLP on a new domain, then there are more options. Though OpenNLP distributes a set of models, it doesn't distribute the training data used to build these models due to licensing restrictions. Three common solutions to this problem are these:

- *Only use data from the domain*—With enough data, this is likely to produce the most accurate model as it's targeted to the domain.
- *Build a separate model and combine the results*—This is similar to the approach you saw earlier in this section, where we also combined different types of annotations,

only in this case, both classifiers are predicting the same class. If both classifiers are high-precision, then combining them should help improve recall.

■ *Use the output of the OpenNLP model for training data*—This is a method to bootstrap the amount of training data available to use. It works best if combined with some human correction. The OpenNLP models are trained on newswire text, so best results will come from applying them to similar text.

No matter the case for customizing OpenNLP, the contents of the following sections will help you understand how to undertake the process.

### 5.5.2 Training an OpenNLP model

Now that you're clear about when and why you'd want to train a new named-entity identification model, and you have some annotated data, let's look at how to do the training. OpenNLP provides code for training in `NameFinderME.main()`, which supports options such as specifying the character encoding and a few other features. In the next listing, we'll look at a stripped-down version of that code that has been slightly rearranged.

**Listing 5.8   Training a named-entity model with OpenNLP**

```
File inFile = new File(baseDir,"person.train");
NameSampleDataStream nss = new NameSampleDataStream(       ⟵┐ Create stream of
  new PlainTextByLineStream(                                 │ name samples based
    new java.io.FileReader(inFile)));                        │ on annotated data.

int iterations = 100;
int cutoff = 5;
TokenNameFinderModel model = NameFinderME.train(           ⟵── Train model.
  "en", // language
  "person", // type
  nss,
  (AdaptiveFeatureGenerator) null,
  Collections.<String,Object>emptyMap(),
  iterations,
  cutoff);

File outFile = new File(destDir, "person-custom.bin");
FileOutputStream outFileStream = new FileOutputStream(outFile);
model.serialize(outFileStream);                          ⟵── Save model to file.
```

The first two lines of the code specify the file containing the training data and create a `NameSampleStream`. `NameSampleStream` is a simple interface that allows you to iterate through a series of `NameSamples`, where a `NameSample` is a simple data structure for holding named-entity spans and tokens. `NameSampleDataStream` implements that interface and parses one sentence per line. Each line consists of space-delimited tokens where names are marked with space-delimited <START> and <END> tags:

```
"It is a familiar story " , <START> Jason Willaford <END> said .
```

Though support for this format is provided, other formats can easily be supported by writing a class to parse them that implements the NameSampleStream interface.

The training routine takes a number of parameters. The first two indicate the language and type of model you're producing. The next is the NameSampleDataStream that will be used to generate NameSamples, which are turned into a stream of events used to train the model. As you saw in section 5.1.2, OpenNLP sees each name as a series of start/continue/other decisions based on a set of contextual features.

The next parameter to the train method is an object containing training parameters created by the ModelUtil.createTrainingParameters method. This encapsulates the number of iterations and the feature cutoff that are used in model creation. The iterations parameter can largely be ignored, but as the model trains, it'll output for each step of these 100 iterations. The feature cutoff parameter provides the lower bound for the number of times a feature must occur to be included in the model. The default setting says that any feature which occurs less than five times won't be included in the model. This is necessary in order to control the size of the model as well as the amount of potential noise, since the model will also not be very accurate at estimating parameter values for features that only occur a few times. Setting this value too low will lead to models that perform poorly on unseen data. But for small datasets, this cutoff value means that the model may improperly classify an example that it has seen in the training data if the words of that example occur fewer than five times and the context of the example isn't very predictive.

The next parameters to the train method are placeholders. Providing a null for the AdaptiveFeatureGenerator parameter will cause NameFinderME to use the default set of feature generators that are effective for named-entity detection. An empty map is used for the resources argument because you have no additional resources to add to the generated model.

The last few lines of code write the model to disk. The filename indicates that the model should be written in the binary format and compressed. Though the opennlp.maxent package supports other formats, this is the one expected by the code that applies the model to new text.

### 5.5.3   *Altering modeling inputs*

So far, we've discussed several reasons why you might train your own model and shown you the basics of training a model. As mentioned earlier, two of the reasons involve changing the inputs to the modeling procedure, in addition to acquiring or building your own set of annotated data. The first change we'll look at involves the tokenization process.

Changing the tokenization process involves a couple of steps. First, in the training procedure, the training and test text must be converted from whatever format it's in to one that contains space-delimited tokens similar to the Jason Willaford example shown in the previous section. Though this conversion can be done as you see fit, we suggest using the same code base as used in the second step of the process: applying the model to unseen text. For applying the model to unseen text, it's a matter of identifying the new tokens and passing them to the `NameFinderME.find` method. This step involves writing your own implementation of the OpenNLP `Tokenizer` class, similar to the `opennlp.tools.tokenize.SimpleTokenizer` we used in section 5.2. Since extending this class only involves splitting up a String and returning an array of Strings, we'll forgo showing an example here and instead move on to looking at altering the features used.

The other change to the input of the training and testing routine we'll consider is changing the features used by the model to predict the name. Like tokenization, changing the features used to identify a name is also straightforward, as the `Name-FinderME` class is configured to accept an `AggregatedFeatureGenerator`, which can be configured to contain a collection of feature generators, as shown next.

**Listing 5.9   Generating custom features for named-entity identification with OpenNLP**

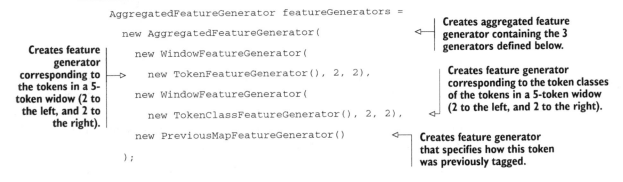

OpenNLP contains a large number of different implementations of `AdaptiveFeature-Generators` to choose from, or you can easily implement your own. Here are some of the available classes and what they do:

- `CharacterNgramFeatureGenerator`—Uses character *n*-grams to generate features about each token.
- `DictionaryFeatureGenerator`—Generates features if the tokens are contained in the dictionary.
- `PreviousMapFeatureGenerator`—Generates features indicating the outcome associated with a previously occurring word.
- `TokenFeatureGenerator`—Generates a feature that contains the token itself.
- `TokenClassFeatureGenerator`—Generates features reflecting various token aspects: character class (digit/alpha/punctuation), token length, and upper-/lowercasing.
- `TokenPatternFeatureGenerator`—Partitions tokens into subtokens based on character classes and generates class features for each of the subtokens and combinations of those subtokens.

- WindowFeatureGenerator—Generates features for a given `AdaptiveFeature-Generator` across a window of tokens (such as 1 to the left, 1 to the right).

In the training routine, you need to modify the call to the `NameFinderEventStream` class to also include a custom `NameContextGenerator` class constructor, as shown here.

**Listing 5.10  Training a named-entity model with custom features in OpenNLP**

```
File inFile = new File(baseDir,"person.train");
NameSampleDataStream nss = new NameSampleDataStream(      Create
    new PlainTextByLineStream(                            sample
    new java.io.FileReader(inFile)));                     stream.

int iterations = 100;
int cutoff = 5;
TokenNameFinderModel model = NameFinderME.train(          Train model with
    "en", // language                                    custom feature
    "person", // type                                    generator.
    nss,
    featureGenerators,
    Collections.<String,Object>emptyMap(),
    iterations,
    cutoff);

File outFile = new File(destDir,"person-custom2.bin");    Save
FileOutputStream outFileStream = new FileOutputStream(outFile);  model
model.serialize(outFileStream);                           to file.
```

Likewise, for testing, you modify the call to the `NameFinderME` class to also include the `NameContextGenerator` class constructor, as shown next.

**Listing 5.11  Using a named-entity model with custom features in OpenNLP**

```
NameFinderME finder = new NameFinderME(
    new TokenNameFinderModel(
        new FileInputStream(
            new File(destDir, "person-custom2.bin")
        )), featureGenerators, NameFinderME.DEFAULT_BEAM_SIZE);
```

Having explored how to change the inputs to OpenNLP's training mechanism, you can now model new types of names and capture new types of information about the named entities you detect. This will allow you to extend the software to a wide variety of other name types and text domains. Even armed with this information, in some cases, the trade-off made by OpenNLP to allow it to be flexible with respect to how it models different entity types comes at too great a cost in terms of memory and runtime performance. In the next section, we'll explore some ways to further customize OpenNLP's named-entity software to realize improved performance.

### 5.5.4  *A new way to model names*

We've discussed previously that OpenNLP creates a separate model for each name type to allow users to flexibly choose which models they want to use. In this section, we'll look at an alternative way to model names which isn't as flexible, but has other advantages. Earlier you saw that names are modeled by predicting one of three outcomes (start, continue, other) for each token. Here we consider a model where the outcomes also include the type of entity being identified. Using this approach you'd predict outcomes such as person-start, person-continue, date-start, date-continue, other, and so on, depending on the types you want your model to predict. Table 5.3 shows the predictions assigned to a sentence.

**Table 5.3   Sentence tagged under alternate model for named-entity identification**

| 0 | 1 | 2 | 3 | 4 | 5 | 6 | 7 | 8 | 9 |
|---|---|---|---|---|---|---|---|---|---|
| Britney | Spears | was | reunited | briefly | with | her | sons | Saturday | . |
| person-start | person-continue | other | other | other | other | other | other | date-start | other |

This approach provides several distinct advantages over the approach of using a separate model for each name type, but also comes with some limitations and disadvantages.

The advantages are

- *Potential runtime gains*—Since only a single model is used, features need only be computed once for all categories. Likewise, only one set of predictions needs to be computed for this model. The number of alternative sets examined when processing a sentence may need to be increased as a larger number of outcomes are possible, but it's unlikely that you need three for each name type being computed.
- *Potential memory savings*—Only one set of features needs to be loaded into memory with the model. Also, there are fewer parameters, as the *other* tag is shared across name types in this model.
- *Entity merging*—With only one model, no entity merge process is necessary.

The disadvantages are

- *Non-overlapping entities*—Since only a single tag is assigned to each token, nested named entities can't be tagged. This is usually addressed by only tagging the named entity with the largest span in training data.
- *Potential memory/runtime losses*—Because there's only a single model, you can't choose to only use the parts of the model that are needed. This may incur memory or runtime penalties, especially in cases where only one or two categories is needed.
- *Training data*—You can't leverage training data that hasn't been annotated for all the categories. The addition of a new category to this model would require the annotation of all training data.

As with any set of trade-offs, whether this approach is preferable will depend on the application requirements. It may be that a combination of these two models is what works best for the application. The methods described in section 5.3.1 for combining individual models also apply to combining these types of models to single name type models that might be developed.

To build a model of this type, a couple of changes need to be made. The first is that the training data needs to reflect all annotations instead of a single annotation type. This can be done by altering the training data to use a format that supports multiple tag types. One example of this is as follows:

```
<START:person> Britney Spears <END> was reunited with her sons <START:date>
    Saturday <END>.
```

With training data in this form, you can use the NameSampleDataStream provided by OpenNLP in the same way as was done in section 5.5.2. The code in the next listing demonstrates how such a model is produced.

**Listing 5.12   Training a model with different name types**

```
String taggedSent =
  "<START:person> Britney Spears <END> was reunited " +
  "with her sons <START:date> Saturday <END> ";
ObjectStream<NameSample> nss = new NameSampleDataStream(
    new PlainTextByLineStream(new StringReader(taggedSent)));
TokenNameFinderModel model = NameFinderME.train(
    "en",
    "default" ,
    nss,
    (AdaptiveFeatureGenerator) null,
    Collections.<String,Object>emptyMap(),
    70 , 1 );

File outFile = new File(destDir,"multi-custom.bin");
FileOutputStream outFileStream = new FileOutputStream(outFile);
model.serialize(outFileStream);

NameFinderME nameFinder = new NameFinderME(model);

String[] tokens =
    (" Britney Spears was reunited with her sons Saturday .")
    .split("\s+");
Span[] names = nameFinder.find(tokens);
displayNames(names, tokens);
```

This model maps start and continue outcomes onto names of a given type. The type of name is prepended to the tag's name in the outcomes. Sequences of person-start and person-continue tags produce spans of tokens that specify people, and likewise date-start and date-continue tags specify dates. The name type is accessed via the get-Type() method in each span produced when input is processed using the model.

## 5.6   *Summary*

Identifying and classifying proper names in text can be a rich source of information for applications that involve text processing. We've discussed how to use OpenNLP to identify names and also provided metrics on the performance of the quality of the names, the quantity of memory required, and the quickness of the processing. We've also looked at how to train your own models and explored the reasons you might want to do so. Finally we described how OpenNLP performs this task and examined how to customize models, going so far as to consider an alternative way to model names. These topics will allow you to leverage high-performance named-entity identification in text processing applications. Additionally, they give a sense of how classification systems are used in text processing. We'll revisit these themes in greater detail later in the book when we look into classification and categorization. Next, we'll look into how to group similar items such as whole documents and search results automatically using a technique called *clustering*. Unlike classification, clustering is typically an unsupervised task, meaning it doesn't involve training a model but instead automatically groups items based on some measure of similarity.

## 5.7 *Further reading*

Mikheev, Andrei; Moens, Marc; Glover, Claire. 1999. "Named Entity Recognition without Gazetteers." Proceedings of EACL '99. HCRC Language Technology Group, University of Edinburgh. http://acl.ldc.upenn.edu/E/E99/E99-1001.pdf.

Wakao, Takahiro; Gaizauskas, Robert; Wilks, Yorick. 1996. "Evaluation of an algorithm for the recognition and classification of proper names." Department of Computer Science, University of Sheffield. http://acl.ldc.upenn.edu/C/C96/C96-1071.pdf.

Zhou, GuoDong; Su, Jian. 2002. "Named Entity Recognition using an HMM-based Chunk Tagger." Proceedings of the Association for Computational Linguistics (ACL), Philadelphia, July 2002. Laboratories for Information Technology, Singapore. http://acl.ldc.upenn.edu/acl2002/MAIN/pdfs/Main036.pdf.

# Clustering text

How often have you browsed through content online and clicked through on an article that had an interesting title, but the underlying story was basically the same as the one you just finished? Or perhaps you're tasked with briefing your boss on the day's news but don't have the time to wade through all the content involved when all you need is a summary and a few key points. Alternatively, maybe your users routinely enter ambiguous or generic query terms or your data covers a lot of different topics and you want to group search results in order to save users from wading through unrelated results. Having a text processing tool that can automatically group similar items and present the results with summarizing labels is a good way to wade through large amounts of text or search results without having to read all, or even most, of the content.

In this chapter, we'll take a closer look at how to solve problems like these using a machine learning approach called *clustering*. Clustering is an unsupervised task (no human intervention, such as annotating training text, required) that can automatically put related content into buckets, helping you better organize your content or reduce the amount of content that you must manually process. In some cases, it also can assign labels to these buckets and even give summaries of what's in each bucket.

After looking at the concepts of clustering in the first section, we'll delve into how to cluster search results using a project called Carrot[2]. Next up, we'll look at how Apache Mahout can be used to cluster large collections of documents into buckets. In fact, both Carrot[2] and Mahout come with several different approaches to clustering, each with their own merits and demerits. We'll also look at how clustering can be applied at the word level to identify topics in documents (sometimes called *topic modeling*) by using a technique called *Latent Dirichlet Allocation*, which also happens to be in Apache Mahout. Throughout the examples, we'll show how this can all be built on the work you did earlier with Apache Solr, making it easy to access cluster information alongside all of your other access pathways, enabling richer access to information. Finally, we'll finish the chapter with a section on performance, with an eye toward both quantity (how fast?) and quality (how good?). First, let's look at an example application that many of you are probably already familiar with but may not have known that it was an implementation of clustering: Google News.

## 6.1    *Google News document clustering*

In the age of the 24-hour news cycle with countless news outlets hawking their version of events, Google News enables readers to quickly see most of the stories published in a particular time period on a topic by grouping similar articles together. For instance, in figure 6.1, the headline "Vikings Begin Favre era on the road in Cleveland" shows there are 2,181 other similar stories to the main story. Though it's not clear what clustering algorithms Google is using to implement this feature, Google's documentation clearly states they're using clustering (Google News 2011):

> Our grouping technology takes into account many factors, such as titles, text, and publication time. We then use various clustering algorithms to identify stories we think are closely related. These stories displayed on Google News present news articles, videos, images and other information.

The power of being able to do this kind of grouping at a large scale should be obvious to anyone with an internet connection. And though there's more to the problem of grouping news content on a near-real-time basis than running a clustering algorithm over the content, having clustering implementations designed to scale like those in Apache Mahout are vital to getting off the ground.

In a task like news clustering, an application needs to be able to quickly cluster large numbers of documents, determine representative documents or labels for display, and deal with new, incoming documents. There's more to the issue than just having a good clustering algorithm, but for our purposes we'll focus on how clustering can help solve these and other unsupervised tasks that aide in the discovery and processing of information.

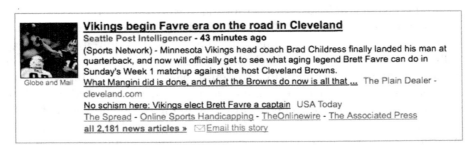

**Vikings begin Favre era on the road in Cleveland**
Seattle Post Intelligencer - 43 minutes ago
(Sports Network) - Minnesota Vikings head coach Brad Childress finally landed his man at quarterback, and now will officially get to see what aging legend Brett Favre can do in Sunday's Week 1 matchup against the host Cleveland Browns.
Globe and Mail   What Mangini did is done, and what the Browns do now is all that ...   The Plain Dealer - cleveland.com
No schism here: Vikings elect Brett Favre a captain   USA Today
The Spread - Online Sports Handicapping - TheOnlinewire - The Associated Press
all 2,181 news articles »   ⊠Email this story

**Figure 6.1   Example of clustering news documents on Google News. Captured on 09/13/2009.**

## 6.2   *Clustering foundations*

Clustering boils down to grouping similar unlabeled documents together based on some similarity measure. The goal is to divide all documents in the collection that are similar into the same cluster as each other while ensuring that dissimilar documents are in different clusters. Before we begin looking into the foundations of clustering, it's important to set expectations about clustering in general. Though clustering is often useful, it's not a cure-all. The quality of the clustering experience often comes down to setting expectations for your users. If your users expect perfection, they'll be disappointed. If they expect something that will, for the most part, help them wade through large volumes of data quickly while still dealing with false positives, they'll likely be happier. From an application designer standpoint, a fair amount of testing may be required to find the right settings for striking a balance between speed of execution and quality of results. Ultimately, remember your goal is to encourage discovery and serendipitous interaction with your content, not necessarily perfectly similar items.

With the basic definition and admonitions out of the way, the remaining foundational sections below will examine

- Different types of text clustering can be applied to
- How to choose a clustering algorithm
- Ways to determine similarity
- Approaches to identifying labels
- How to evaluate clustering results

### 6.2.1   *Three types of text to cluster*

Clustering can be applied to many different aspects of text, including the words in a document, the documents themselves, or the results from doing searches. Clustering is also useful for many other things besides text, like grouping users or data from a series of sensors, but those are outside the scope of this book. For now, we'll focus on three types of clustering: document, search result, and word/topic.

In document clustering, the focus is on grouping documents as a whole together, as in the Google News example given earlier. Document clustering is typically done as an offline batch processing job and the output is typically a list of documents and a centroid vector. Since document clustering is usually a batch processing task, it's often worthwhile to spend the extra time (within reason) to get better results. Descriptions of the clusters are often generated by looking at the most important terms (determined by some weighting mechanism such as TF-IDF) in documents closest to the centroid. Some preprocessing is usually required to remove stopwords and to stem words, but neither of these are necessarily a given for all algorithms. Other common text techniques such as identifying phrases or using *n*-grams may also be worth experimenting with when testing approaches. To read more on document clustering, see *An Introduction to Information Retrieval* (Manning 2008) for starters.

For search result clustering, the clustering task, given a user query, is to do a search and group the results of the search into clusters. Search result clustering can be quite effective when users enter generic or ambiguous terms (such as *apple*) or when the dataset contains a disparate set of categories. Search result clustering is often characterized by several factors:

- Clustering on short snippets of text (title, maybe a small section of the body where the query terms matched).
- Algorithms designed to work on small sets of results and to return as fast as possible.
- Labels take on more significance, since users will likely treat them like facets to make decisions about how to further navigate the result set.

Preprocessing is often done just as in document clustering, but since labels are usually more significant, it may make sense to spend the extra time to identify frequently occurring phrases. For an overview of search result clustering, see "A Survey of Web Clustering Engines" (Carpineto 2009).

Clustering words into topics, otherwise called *topic modeling*, is an effective way to quickly find the topics that are covered in a large set of documents. The approach is based on the assumption that documents often cover several different topics and that words related to a given topic are often found near each other. By clustering the words, you can quickly see which words appear near each other and then also what documents are attached to those words. (In a sense, the approach also does document clustering.) For instance, the output from running a topic modeling algorithm (see section 6.6) yields the clustered words in table 6.1 (formatted for display from the original).

**Table 6.1   Example topics and words**

| Topic 0 | Topic 1 |
|---|---|
| win saturday time game know nation u more after two take over back has from texa first day man offici 2 high one sinc some sunday | yesterday game work new last over more most year than two from state after been would us polic peopl team run were open five american |

In this example, the first thing to notice is that the topics themselves lack names. Naming the topic is the job of the person generating the topics. Next, you don't even know what documents contain which topic. So why bother? Generating the topics for a collection is one more way to aid users in browsing a collection and discovering interesting information about the collection without having to read the whole collection. Additionally, there has been some more recent work on better characterizing the topics through phrases (see Blei [2009]).

To learn more on topic modeling, start with the references at the end of this chapter and also http://en.wikipedia.org/wiki/Latent_Dirichlet_allocation, which will lead you to the primary academic papers written on the topic.

Now that you have some groundwork for the types of text you want to cluster, let's take a look at the factors that play into the selection of a clustering algorithm.

### 6.2.2   *Choosing a clustering algorithm*

Many different algorithms are available for clustering, and covering them all is beyond the scope of this book. For instance, as of this writing, Apache Mahout contains implementations of K-Means (demonstrated later), Fuzzy K-Means, Mean-Shift, Dirichlet, Canopy, Spectral, and Latent Dirichlet Allocation, and there will no doubt be more by the time this book is published. Instead of digging too much into how each is implemented, let's look at some of the more common features of clustering algorithms in order to better understand what criteria are helpful in picking a clustering algorithm.

In discussing clustering algorithms, there are many aspects to examine to determine what's going to work best for an application. Traditionally, one of the main deciding factors has been whether the algorithm is hierarchical in nature or flat. As the name implies, *hierarchical* approaches work either top-down or bottom-up, building a hierarchy of related documents that can be broken down into smaller and smaller sets. Flat approaches are usually much faster since they don't have to relate the clusters to other clusters. Also keep in mind that some flat algorithms can be modified to be hierarchical.

Moving beyond hierarchical versus flat, table 6.2 provides details on many other factors that play out when choosing a clustering approach.

**Table 6.2   Clustering algorithm choices**

| Characteristic | Description |
|---|---|
| Cluster membership (soft/hard) | Hard—Documents belong to one and only one cluster. |
| | Soft—Documents can be in more than one cluster and often have an associated probability of membership. |
| Updateable | Can the clusters be updated when new documents are added or does the entire calculation need to be re-executed? |
| Probabilistic approach | Understanding the underpinnings of an approach will help you know the benefits and failings of such an approach. |

**Table 6.2  Clustering algorithm choices** *(continued)*

| Characteristic | Description |
|---|---|
| Speed | The runtime of most flat clustering approaches is linear in the number of documents, whereas many hierarchical approaches are nonlinear. |
| Quality | Hierarchical approaches are often more accurate than flat ones, at the cost of execution time. More on evaluation in section 6.2.5. |
| Handles feedback | Can the algorithm adjust/improve based on user feedback? For instance, if a user marked a document as not appropriate for a cluster, can the algorithm exclude that document? Does it change other clusters? |
| Number of clusters | Some algorithms require an application to decide on the number of clusters up front; others pick the appropriate number as part of the algorithm. If the algorithm requires this to be specified, expect to experiment with this value to obtain good results. |

Individual algorithms also have their own quirks that need to be considered when evaluating what approach to take, but table 6.2 should provide some overall guidance on choosing an algorithm. From here, expect to spend some time evaluating the various approaches to determine which works best for your data.

### 6.2.3  *Determining similarity*

Many clustering algorithms contain a notion of similarity that's used to determine whether a document belongs to a cluster. Similarity, in many clustering algorithms, is implemented as a measure of the distance between two documents. In order for these distance measures to work, most systems represent documents as vectors (almost always sparse—meaning most entries are zero) where each cell in the vector is the weight of that particular term for that particular document. The weight can be any value the application wants, but is typically some variation on TF-IDF. If this all sounds vaguely familiar to you, it should, as the approaches for weighting documents for clustering are similar to those used for searching. To remind yourself of these concepts, see section 3.2.3.

In practice, document vectors are almost always normalized first using a *p*-norm ($p >= 0$) so that really short and really long documents don't affect the results in a negative way. Normalizing by a *p*-norm just means dividing each vector by its length, thereby scaling all the vectors onto the unit shape (for example, the 2-norm's is a unit circle). The most common norms used, and the ones most readers will be familiar with, are the 1-norm (Manhattan distance) and 2-norm (Euclidean distance). You'll notice that the examples later in the chapter use the Euclidean distance for normalizing our vectors. For more information on *p*-norms, see http://en.wikipedia.org/wiki/Norm_(mathematics).

After the vectors are created, it's then reasonable to measure the distance between two documents as the distance between two vectors. There are many different distance measures available, so we'll focus on the few most common ones:

- *Euclidean distance*—The tried and true "as the crow flies" distance between any two points. Variations include the squared Euclidean distance (saving a square root calculation) and one that can weight parts of the vector.
- *Manhattan distance*—Otherwise known as the *taxicab distance*, as it represents the distance traveled if one were driving a taxicab in a city laid out on a grid, as in Manhattan in New York City. Sometimes the parts of the calculation may be weighted.
- *Cosine distance*—Takes the cosine of the angle formed by putting the tails of two vectors together; so two similar documents (angle == 0) have a cosine equal to 1. See section 3.2.3.

As you'll see in the Apache Mahout section later, the distance measure is often a parameter that can be passed in, allowing experimentation with different measures. As to which distance measure to use, you should use one that corresponds to the normalization applied to the vector. For instance, if you used the 2-norm, then the Euclidean or Cosine distances would be most appropriate. That being said, though theoretically incorrect, some approaches will work without such an alignment.

For probabilistic approaches, the question of similarity is really a question of the probability that a given document is in a cluster. They often have a more sophisticated model of how documents are related based on statistical distributions and other properties. Also, some of the distance-based approaches (K-Means) can be shown to be probabilistic.

### 6.2.4 *Labeling the results*

Because clustering is often used in discovery tools with real users, picking good labels and/or good representative documents is often as important to a clustering-based application as determining the clusters themselves. Without good labels and representative documents, users will be discouraged from interacting with the clusters to find and discover useful documents.

Picking representative documents from a cluster can be done in several ways. At the most basic, documents can be selected randomly, giving users a wider mix of results, and potentially lead to new discoveries, but also, if the documents are far from the center, failing to capture what the cluster is about. To remedy this, documents can be picked based on their proximity to the cluster's centroid or their likelihood of membership. In this way, documents are likely good indicators of what the cluster is about, but may lose some of the serendipity associated with random selection. This leads to a dual approach where some documents are picked randomly and some are picked based on proximity/probability.

Picking good labels, or topics, is more difficult than picking representative documents, and there are many approaches, each with their pros and cons. In some applications, simple techniques akin to faceting (see chapter 3) can be used to effectively showcase the frequency of tags common to a cluster, but most applications are better served by finding and displaying important terms and phrases in the cluster. Of course, what's deemed important is a subject of ongoing research. One simple approach is to leverage the weights in the vector (say, using our friend TF-IDF; see section 3.2.3) and return a list of the terms sorted by weight. Using $n$-grams, this can be extended to return a list of phrases (technically they're phrases, but they may not be of high quality) based on their weights in the collection/cluster. Another common approach is to do some conceptual/topic modeling through techniques that utilize singular value decomposition, such as latent semantic analysis (see Deerwester [1990]) or Latent Dirichlet Allocation (see Blei [2003], demonstrated later in the chapter). Another useful approach is to use the log-likelihood ratio (LLR; see Dunning [1993]) of terms that are in the cluster versus those outside of the cluster. The underlying math for the approaches other than TF-IDF (which we've already discussed) is beyond the scope of this book. But in using this chapter's tools (Carrot[2] and Apache Mahout), you'll see demonstrations of all of these approaches either implicitly as part of the algorithm itself or explicitly via a specific tool. Regardless of how you get labels, the results will be useful in understanding the quality of your clusters, which is the subject of the next section.

### 6.2.5 *How to evaluate clustering results*

As with any text processing tool, experimenting and evaluating clustering results should be as much a part of building the application as designing the architecture or figuring out how to deploy it. Just as in search, named entity recognition, and the other concepts in this book, clustering can be evaluated in a number of ways.

The first approach most people use is the *laugh test*, otherwise known as the *smell test*. Do these clusters look reasonable when viewed by a person with some knowledge of what a good result should be? Though you should never read too much into the smell test, it's nevertheless an invaluable part of the process and one that usually catches "dumb" mistakes like bad or missing input parameters. The downsides are that it's impossible to replicate a person's reaction on demand and in a repeatable manner, not to mention it's only one person's opinion. It's also, for better or worse, dependent on the label generation process, which may not capture the clusters accurately.

Taking a few people and having them rate the results is often the next step up testing-wise. Whether it's a quality assurance team or a group of target users, correlating the reactions of a small group of people can provide valuable feedback. The cost is the time and expense involved in arranging these tests, not to mention the human error and lack of on-demand repeatability. But if done several times, a gold standard can be derived, which is the next approach.

A gold standard is a set of clusters created by one or more people that are interpreted as the ideal set of results for the clustering task. Once constructed, this set can then be compared against clustering results from various experiments. Creating a gold standard is often impractical, brittle (dealing with updates, new documents, and so on), or prohibitively expensive for large datasets. If you know your collection isn't going to change much and if you have the time, creating a gold standard, perhaps on a subset of the total, may be worthwhile. One semi-automated approach is to run one or more of the clustering algorithms and then have one or more people adjust the clusters manually to arrive at the final result. When the judgments are in place, a number of formulas (purity, normalized mutual information, Rand index, and F-measure) can be used to sum up the results into a single metric that indicates the quality of the clustering. Rather than lay out their formulas here, we'll refer the interested reader to section 16.3 of *An Introduction to Information Retrieval* (Manning 2008), where proper treatment is given these measures.

Finally, some mathematical tools are available that can help evaluate clusters. These tools are all heuristics for evaluating clustering and don't require human input. They shouldn't be used in isolation, but instead as helpful indicators of clustering quality. The first measure is calculated by randomly removing some subset of the input data and then running the clustering. After the clustering is complete, calculate the percentage of documents in each cluster out of the total number of points and set it aside. Next, add back in the random data, rerun the clustering, and recalculate the percentage. Given that the held back data was randomly distributed, you'd expect it to roughly conform to the distribution from the first set. If cluster A had 50% of the documents in the first set, it's reasonable to expect it (but not guaranteed) to still hold 50% of the documents in the larger set.

From information theory (see http://en.wikipedia.org/wiki/Information_theory for starters) come several other useful measures that may help assess clustering quality. The first is the notion of *entropy*. Entropy is a measure of the uncertainty of a random variable. In practical terms, it's a measure of the information contained in a cluster. For text-based clustering, you can build on the entropy and calculate the perplexity, which measures how well cluster membership predicts what words are used.

There's plenty more to learn about clustering. For those interested in learning more about the concepts behind clustering, a good starting point is *An Introduction to Information Retrieval* (Manning 2008). In particular, chapters 16 and 17 focus at a deeper level on the concepts discussed here. Cutting et al. also provide good information on how to utilize clustering in discovery in their paper "Scatter/Gather: A Cluster-based Approach to Browsing Large Document Collections" (Cutting 1992). For now, we'll continue on and look at how to run several clustering implementations, including one for search results and another for document collections.

## 6.3    *Setting up a simple clustering application*

For the discussions in the following sections on clustering, we'll demonstrate the concepts using the content from several news websites via their RSS/Atom feeds. To that end, we've set up a simple Solr Home (schema, config, and so forth), located under the solr-clustering directory, that ingests the feeds from several newspapers and news organizations. This instance will rely on Solr's Data Import Handler to automatically ingest and index the feeds into the schema. From these feeds, we can then demonstrate the various clustering libraries discussed in the following sections.

Building on the search knowledge gained in chapter 3, the three primary Solr pieces of interest for our new clustering application are schema.xml, rss-data-config.xml, and the addition of the Data Import Handler to solrconfig.xml. For the schema and the RSS configuration, we examined the content from the various feeds and mapped that into a few common fields, which were then indexed. We also stored term vectors, for reasons shown later in section 6.5.1.

The details of the Data Import Handler (DIH) configuration can be found on Solr's wiki at http://wiki.apache.org/solr/DataImportHandler. To run Solr with the clustering setup from the *Taming Text* source, execute the following commands in the source distribution root directory:

- `cd apache-solr/example`
- `./bin/start-solr.sh solr-clustering`
- Invoke the Data Import Handler import command: http://localhost:8983/solr/dataimport?command=full-import
- Check the status of the import: http://localhost:8983/solr/dataimport?command=status

With this basic setup, we can now begin to demonstrate clustering in action using the data indexed from the feeds we just described. We'll start with Carrot[2] for search results and then look into document collection clustering using Apache Mahout.

## 6.4    *Clustering search results using Carrot[2]*

Carrot[2] is an open source search results clustering library released under a BSD-like license and found at http://project.carrot2.org/. It's specifically designed for delivering high-performance results on typical search results (say, a title and small snippet of text). The library comes with support for working with a number of different search APIs, including Google, Yahoo!, Lucene, and Solr (as a client) as well as the ability to cluster documents in XML or those created programmatically. Additionally, the Solr project has integrated Carrot[2] into the server side, which we'll demonstrate later.

Carrot[2] comes with two clustering implementations: STC (suffix tree clustering) and Lingo.

STC was first introduced for web search result clustering by Zamir and Etzioni in "Web document clustering: a feasibility demonstration" (Zamir 1998). The algorithm is based on the suffix tree data structure, which can be used to efficiently (linear time) identify common substrings. Efficiently finding common substrings is one of the keys to quickly finding labels for clusters. To read more on suffix trees, start with http:// en.wikipedia.org/wiki/Suffix_tree.

The Lingo algorithm was created by Stanisław Osiński and Dawid Weiss (the creators of the Carrot[2] project). At a high level, Lingo uses singular value decomposition (SVD; see http://en.wikipedia.org/wiki/Singular_value_decomposition to learn more) to find good clusters and phrase discovery to identify good labels for those clusters.

Carrot[2] also comes with a user interface that can be used for experimenting with your own data, and a server implementation supporting REST that makes it easy to interact with Carrot[2] via other programming languages. Finally, if so inclined, an application may add its own clustering algorithm into the framework via a well-defined API. To explore Carrot[2] in greater depth, refer to the manual at http:// download.carrot2.org/head/manual/.

For the remainder of this section, we'll focus on showing how to use the API to cluster a data source and then look at how Carrot[2] is integrated into Solr. We'll finish the section with a look at performance both in terms of quality and speed for both of the algorithms.

### 6.4.1   *Using the Carrot[2] API*

Carrot[2] architecture is implemented as a pipeline. Content is ingested from a document source and then handed off to one or more components that modify and cluster the sources, outputting the clusters at the other end. In terms of actual classes, at its most basic, the pipeline consists of one or more `IProcessingComponents` that are controlled by the `IController` implementation. The controller handles initializing the components and invoking the components in the correct order and with the appropriate inputs. Examples of `IProcessingComponent` implementations include the various document sources (`GoogleDocumentSource`, `YahooDocumentSource`, `Lucene-DocumentSource`) as well as the clustering implementations themselves: `STC-ClusteringAlgorithm` and `LingoClusteringAlgorithm`.

Naturally, a bunch of other pieces get used by the implementation to do things like tokenize and stem the text. As for the controller, there are two implementations: `SimpleController` and `CachingController`. The `SimpleController` is designed for easy setup and one-time use, whereas the `CachingController` is designed for use in production environments where it can take advantage of the fact that queries are often repeated and therefore cache the results.

To see Carrot[2] in action, let's look at some sample code that clusters some simple documents. The first step is to create some documents. For Carrot[2], documents contain three elements: a title, a summary/snippet, and a URL. Given a set of documents with these characteristics, it's straightforward to cluster them, as is demonstrated in the next listing.

> **Listing 6.1  Simple Carrot² example**

```
//... setup some documents elsewhere
final Controller controller =
        ControllerFactory.createSimple();          <--- Create IController.
documents = new ArrayList<Document>();
for (int i = 0; i < titles.length; i++) {
  Document doc = new Document(titles[i], snippets[i],
        "file://foo_" + i + ".txt");
  documents.add(doc);
}
final ProcessingResult result = controller.process(documents,
        "red fox",
        LingoClusteringAlgorithm.class);           <--- Cluster documents.
displayResults(result);                    <--- Print out clusters.
```

Running listing 6.1 yields the following results:

```
Cluster: Lamb
     Mary Loses Little Lamb.  Wolf At Large.
     March Comes in like a Lamb
Cluster: Lazy Brown Dogs
     Red Fox jumps over Lazy Brown Dogs
     Lazy Brown Dogs Promise Revenge on Red Fox
```

Though the documents of the example are obviously made up (see Carrot2ExampleTest.java in the source for their construction), the code effectively demonstrates the simplicity of using the Carrot² APIs. Moving beyond the simple case, many applications will want to use the CachingController for performance reasons. As the name implies, the CachingController caches as much of the results as possible in order to improve performance. Applications may also want to use other data sources (such as Google or Yahoo!) or implement their own IDataSource to represent their content. Additionally, many of the components come with a variety of attributes that can be set to tune/alter both the speed and quality of results, which we'll discuss in section 6.7.2.

Now that you have an idea of how to implement some of the basics of clustering with Carrot², we can take a look at how it integrates with Solr.

### 6.4.2  Clustering Solr search results using Carrot²

As of version 1.4, Apache Solr adds full support for search result clustering using Carrot², including the ability to configure, via the solrconfig.xml file, all of the component attributes and the algorithms used for clustering. Naturally, Carrot² uses the Solr search results to cluster on, allowing the application to define which fields are used to represent the title, snippet, and URL. In fact, this has already been set up and configured in the *Taming Text* source distribution under the solr-clustering directory.

There are three parts to configuring Solr to use the Carrot² clustering component. First, the component is implemented as a SearchComponent, which means it can be plugged into a Solr RequestHandler. The XML to configure this component looks like this:

```
<searchComponent
  class="org.apache.solr.handler.clustering.ClusteringComponent"
  name="cluster">
    <lst name="engine">
      <str name="name">default</str>
      <str name="carrot.algorithm"><lineArrow/>
      org.carrot2.clustering.lingo.LingoClusteringAlgorithm</str>
    </lst>
    <lst name="engine">
      <str name="name">stc</str>
      <str name="carrot.algorithm"><lineArrow/>
      org.carrot2.clustering.stc.STCClusteringAlgorithm</str>
    </lst>
</searchComponent>
```

In the `<searchComponent>` declaration, you set up the `ClusteringComponent` and then tell it which Carrot$^2$ clustering algorithms to use. In this case, we set up both the Lingo and the STC clustering algorithms. The next step is to hook the Search-Component into a `RequestHandler`, like this:

```
<requestHandler name="standard"
  class="solr.StandardRequestHandler" default="true">
    <!-- default values for query parameters -->
    <!-- ... -->
    <arr name="last-components">
      <str>cluster</str>
    </arr>
</requestHandler>
```

Finally, it's often useful in Solr to set up some intelligent defaults so that all of the various parameters need not be passed in on the command line. In our example, we used this:

```
<requestHandler name="standard"
  class="solr.StandardRequestHandler" default="true">
    <!-- default values for query parameters -->
    <lst name="defaults">
    <!-- ... -->
      <!-- Clustering -->
      <!--<bool name="clustering">true</bool>-->
      <str name="clustering.engine">default</str>
      <bool name="clustering.results">true</bool>
      <!-- The title field -->
      <str name="carrot.title">title</str>
      <!-- The field to cluster on -->
      <str name="carrot.snippet">desc</str>
      <str name="carrot.url">link</str>
      <!-- produce summaries -->
      <bool name="carrot.produceSummary">false</bool>
      <!-- produce sub clusters -->
      <bool name="carrot.outputSubClusters">false</bool>
    </lst>
</requestHandler>
```

In the configuration of the default parameters, we declared that Solr should use the default clustering engine (Lingo) and that Carrot$^2$ should use the Solr title field as the

Carrot² title, the Solr description field as the Carrot² snippet field, and the Solr link field as the Carrot² URL field. Lastly, we told Carrot² to produce summaries but to skip outputting subclusters. (For the record, subclusters are created by clustering within a single cluster.)

That's all the setup needed! Assuming Solr was started as outlined in listing 6.3, asking Solr for search result clusters is as simple as adding the `&clustering=true` parameter to the URL, as in http://localhost:8983/solr/select/?q=*:*&clustering =true&rows=100. Executing that command will result in Solr retrieving 100 documents from the index and clustering them. A screenshot of some of the results of running this clustering query appears in figure 6.2.

At the bottom of figure 6.2, we purposefully left in a junk result of *R Reuters sportsNews 4* to demonstrate the need for proper tuning of Carrot² via the various

```
- <lst>
  - <arr name="labels">
      <str>Overtime</str>
      <str>Minnesota Vikings</str>
      <str>Bears Beat Vikings</str>
    </arr>
  + <arr name="docs"></arr>
  </lst>
- <lst>
  - <arr name="labels">
      <str>Texas Tech Suspends</str>
      <str>Player after a Concussion</str>
      <str>Tech Suspended Mike Leach</str>
    </arr>
  - <arr name="docs">
    - <str>
        http://www.nytimes.com/aponline/2009/12/28/sports/AP-FBC-T25-Texas-Tech-Leach-Suspended.html
      </str>
      <str>761b5a908469a491fb58782175c4b19b</str>
      <str>a5a74692f6bd858a630324aebccc47de</str>
    </arr>
  </lst>
- <lst>
  - <arr name="labels">
      <str>PORTLAND</str>
      <str>Sixers</str>
      <str>Trail Blazers</str>
    </arr>
  - <arr name="docs">
      <str>00493468085a22165e409053d3b2c87f</str>
      <str>439a216eb8832b259b8203318b623d33</str>
      <str>6c677f6d6cd2fa744c76cb12daad1723</str>
      <str>d7c18a049c230eeb428c99f19699fd5a</str>
      <str>0dfd31d031f5eba2f6153acc9afee5d1</str>
    </arr>
  </lst>
- <lst>
  - <arr name="labels">
      <str>R Reuters sportsNews 4</str>
```

**Figure 6.2   A screenshot of running a Solr clustering command**

attributes available, which will be discussed in section 6.7.2. See http://wiki.apache.org/solr/ClusteringComponent for a full accounting of the options available for tuning the clustering component in Solr.

Now that you have an understanding of how to cluster search results, let's move on and take a look at how to cluster whole document collections using Apache Mahout. We'll revisit Carrot[2] later in the chapter when we look at performance.

## 6.5    *Clustering document collections with Apache Mahout*

Apache Mahout is an Apache Software Foundation project with the goal of developing a suite of machine learning libraries designed from the ground up to be scalable to large numbers of input items. As of this writing, it contains algorithms for classification, clustering, collaborative filtering, evolutionary programming, and more, as well as useful utilities for solving machine learning problems such as manipulating matrices and storing Java primitives (Maps, Lists, and Sets for storing ints, doubles, and so on). In many cases, Mahout relies on the Apache Hadoop (http://hadoop.apache.org) framework (via the MapReduce programming model and a distributed filesystem called *HDFS*) for developing algorithms designed to scale. And though much of this chapter focuses on clustering with Mahout, chapter 7 covers classification with Mahout. The other parts of Mahout can be discovered on its website at http://mahout.apache.org/ and in *Mahout in Action* (see http://manning.com/owen/). To get started for this section, you'll need to download Mahout 0.6 from http://archive.apache.org/dist/mahout/0.6/mahout-distribution-0.6.tar.gz and unpack it into a directory, which we'll call $MAHOUT_HOME from here on out. After you download it and unpack it, change into the $MAHOUT_HOME directory and run `mvn install -DskipTests` (you can run the tests, but they take a long time!).

Without further ado, the next three sections examine how to prepare your data and then cluster it using Apache Mahout's implementation of the K-Means algorithm.

### Apache Hadoop—The yellow elephant with big computing power

Hadoop is an implementation of ideas put forth by Google (see Dean [2004]), first implemented in the Lucene project Nutch, and since spun out to be its own project at the Apache Software Foundation. The basic idea is to pair a distributed filesystem (called *GFS* by Google and *HDFS* by Hadoop) with a programming model (MapReduce) that makes it easy for engineers with little-to-no background in parallel and distributed systems to write programs that are both scalable and fault tolerant to run on very large clusters of computers.

Though not all applications can be written in the MapReduce model, many text-based applications are well suited for the approach.

For more information on Apache Hadoop, see *Hadoop: The Definitive Guide* (http://oreilly.com/catalog/9780596521981) by Tom White or *Hadoop in Action* (http://manning.com/lam/) by Chuck Lam.

### 6.5.1 Preparing the data for clustering

For clustering, Mahout relies on data to be in an `org.apache.mahout.matrix.Vector` format. A `Vector` in Mahout is simply a tuple of floats, as in <0.5, 1.9, 100.5>. More generally speaking, a vector, often called a *feature vector,* is a common data structure used in machine learning to represent the properties of a document or other piece of data to the system. Depending on the data, vectors are often either densely populated or sparse. For text applications, vectors are often sparse due to the large number of terms in the overall collection, but the relatively few terms in any particular document. Thankfully, sparseness often has its advantages when computing common machine learning tasks. Naturally, Mahout comes with several implementations that extend `Vector` in order to represent both sparse and dense vectors. These implementations are named `org.apache.mahout.matrix.SparseVector` and `org.apache.mahout.matrix.DenseVector`. When running your application, you should sample your data to determine whether it's spare or dense and then choose the appropriate representation. You can always try both on subsets of your data to determine which performs best.

Mahout comes with several different ways to create `Vectors` for clustering:

- *Programmatic*—Erite code that instantiates the `Vector` and then saves it to an appropriate place.
- *Apache Lucene index*—Transforms an Apache Lucene index into a set of `Vectors`.
- *Weka's ARFF format*—Weka is a machine learning project from the University of Waikato (New Zealand) that defines the ARFF format. See http://cwiki.apache.org/MAHOUT/creating-vectors-from-wekas-arff-format.html for more information. For more information on Weka, see *Data Mining: Practical Machine Learning Tools and Techniques (Third Edition)* (http://www.cs.waikato.ac.nz/~ml/weka/book.html) by Witten and Frank.

Since we're not using Weka in this book, we'll forgo coverage of the ARFF format here and focus on the first two means of producing `Vectors` for Mahout.

#### PROGRAMMATIC VECTOR CREATION

Creating `Vectors` programmatically is straightforward and best shown by a simple example, as shown here.

**Listing 6.2   Vector creation using Mahout**

Create SparseVector with a label of my-sparse and a cardinality of 3000.

Set values to first 3 items in sparse vectors.

```
double[] vals = new double[]{0.3, 1.8, 200.228};
Vector dense = new DenseVector(vals);
assertTrue(dense.size() == 3);
Vector sparseSame = new SequentialAccessSparseVector(3);
Vector sparse = new SequentialAccessSparseVector(3000);
for (int i = 0; i < vals.length; i++) {
    sparseSame.set(i, vals[i]);
```

Create DenseVector with label of my-dense and 3 values. The cardinality of this vector is 3.

Create SparseVector with a label of my-sparse-same that has cardinality of 3.

```
                    sparse.set(i, vals[i]);
```

**The dense and sparse Vectors aren't equal because they have different cardinality.**

```
                }
                assertFalse(dense.equals(sparse));

                assertEquals(dense, sparseSame);

                assertFalse(sparse.equals(sparseSame));
```

**The dense and sparse Vectors are equal because they have the same values and cardinality.**

Vectors are often created programmatically when reading data from a database or some other source that's not supported by Mahout. When a Vector is constructed, it needs to be written to a format that Mahout understands. All of the clustering algorithms in Mahout expect one or more files in Hadoop's SequenceFile format. Mahout provides the org.apache.mahout.utils.vectors.io.SequenceFileVectorWriter to assist in serializing Vectors to the proper format. This is demonstrated in the following listing.

**Listing 6.3   Serializing vectors to a SequenceFile**

**Create Hadoop SequenceFile. Writer to handle the job of physically writing out the vectors to a file in HDFS.**

**A VectorWriter processes the Vectors and invokes the underlying write methods on SequenceFile.Writer.**

```
File tmpDir = new File(System.getProperty("java.io.tmpdir"));
File tmpLoc = new File(tmpDir, "sfvwt");
tmpLoc.mkdirs();
File tmpFile = File.createTempFile("sfvwt", ".dat", tmpLoc);

Path path = new Path(tmpFile.getAbsolutePath());
Configuration conf = new Configuration();
FileSystem fs = FileSystem.get(conf);
SequenceFile.Writer seqWriter = SequenceFile.createWriter(fs, conf,
        path, LongWritable.class, VectorWritable.class);
VectorWriter vecWriter = new SequenceFileVectorWriter(seqWriter);
List<Vector> vectors = new ArrayList<Vector>();
vectors.add(sparse);
vectors.add(sparseSame);
vecWriter.write(vectors);
vecWriter.close();
```

**Create Configuration for Hadoop.**

**◁——— Do work of writing out files.**

Mahout can also write out Vectors to JSON, but doing so is purely for human-readability needs as they're slower to serialize and deserialize at runtime, and slow down the clustering algorithms significantly. Since we're using Solr, which uses Apache Lucene under the hood, the next section on creating vectors from a Lucene index is much more interesting.

### CREATING VECTORS FROM AN APACHE LUCENE INDEX

One or more Lucene indexes are a great source for creating Vectors, assuming the field to be used for Vector creation was created with the termVector="true" option set in the schema, as in this code:

```
<field name="description" type="text"
          indexed="true" stored="true"
          termVector="true"/>
```

Given an index, we can use Mahout's Lucene utilities to convert the index to a SequenceFile containing Vectors. This conversion can be handled on the command line by running the `org.apache.mahout.utils.vector.lucene.Driver` program. Though the `Driver` program has many options, table 6.3 outlines the more commonly used ones.

**Table 6.3   Lucene index conversion options**

| Argument | Description | Required |
|---|---|---|
| `--dir <Path>` | Specifies the location of the Lucene index. | Yes |
| `--output <Path>` | The path to output the `SequenceFile` to on the filesystem. | Yes |
| `--field <String>` | The name of the Lucene `Field` to use as the source. | Yes |
| `--idField <String>` | The name of the Lucene `Field` containing the unique ID of the document. Can be used to label the vector. | No |
| `--weight [tf\|tfidf]` | The type of weight to be used for representing the terms in the field. TF is term frequency only; TF-IDF uses both term frequency and inverse document frequency. | No |
| `--dictOut <Path>` | The location to output the mapping between terms and their position in the vector. | Yes |
| `--norm [INF\|-1\|A double >= 0]` | Indicates how to normalize the vector. See http://en.wikipedia.org/wiki/Lp_norm. | No |

To put this in action in the context of our Solr instance, we can point the driver at the directory containing the Lucene index and specify the appropriate input parameters, and the driver will do the rest of the work. For demonstration purposes, we'll assume Solr's index is stored in <Solr Home>/data/index and that it has been created as shown earlier in the chapter. You might generate your `Vectors` by running the driver as in the next listing.

**Listing 6.4   Sample `Vector` creation from a Lucene index**

```
<MAHOUT_HOME>/bin/mahout lucene.vector

    --dir <PATH>/solr-clustering/data/index

    --output /tmp/solr-clust-n2/part-out.vec --field description

    --idField id --dictOut /tmp/solr-clust-n2/dictionary.txt --norm 2
```

In the example in listing 6.4, the driver program ingests the Lucene index, grabs the necessary document information from the index, and writes it out to the part-out.dat (the *part* is important for Mahout/Hadoop) file. The dictionary.txt file that's also created will contain a mapping between the terms in the index and the position in the vectors created. This is important for re-creating the vectors later for display purposes.

Finally, we chose the 2-norm here, so that we can cluster using the `CosineDistance-Measure` included in Mahout. Now that we have some vectors, let's do some clustering using Mahout's K-Means implementation.

### 6.5.2   *K-Means clustering*

There are many different approaches to clustering, both in the broader machine learning community and within Mahout. For instance, Mahout alone, as of this writing, has clustering implementations called

- Canopy
- Mean-Shift
- Dirichlet
- Spectral
- K-Means and Fuzzy K-Means

Of these choices, K-Means is easily the most widely known. K-Means is a simple and straightforward approach to clustering that often yields good results relatively quickly. It operates by iteratively adding documents to one of $k$ clusters based on the distance, as determined by a user-supplied distance measure, between the document and the centroid of that cluster. At the end of each iteration, the centroid may be recalculated. The process stops after there's little-to-no change in the centroids or some maximum number of iterations have passed, since otherwise K-Means isn't guaranteed to converge. The algorithm is kicked off by either seeding it with some initial centroids or by randomly choosing centroids from the set of vectors in the input dataset. K-Means does have some downsides. First and foremost, you must pick $k$ and naturally you'll get different results for different values of $k$. Furthermore, the initial choice for the centroids can greatly affect the outcome, so you should be sure to try different values as part of several runs. In the end, as with most techniques, it's wise to run several iterations with various parameters to determine what works best for your data.

Running the K-Means clustering algorithm in Mahout is as simple as executing the `org.apache.mahout.clustering.kmeans.KMeansDriver` class with the appropriate input parameters. Thanks to the power of Hadoop, you can execute this in either standalone mode or distributed mode (on a Hadoop cluster). For the purposes of this book, we'll use standalone mode, but there isn't much difference for distributed mode.

Instead of looking at the options that `KMeansDriver` takes first, let's go straight to an example using the `Vector` dump we created earlier. The next listing shows an example command line for running the `KMeansDriver`.

**Listing 6.5   Example of using the `KMeansDriver` command-line utility**

```
<$MAHOUT_HOME>/bin/mahout kmeans \
    --input /tmp/solr-clust-n2/part-out.vec \
    --clusters /tmp/solr-clust-n2/out/clusters -k 10 \
    --output /tmp/solr-clust-n2/out/ --distanceMeasure \
```

```
org.apache.mahout.common.distance.CosineDistanceMeasure \
--convergenceDelta 0.001 --overwrite --maxIter 50 --clustering
```

Most of the parameters should be self-explanatory, so we'll focus on the six main inputs that drive K-Means:

- `--k`—The *k* in K-Means. Specifies the number of clusters to be returned.
- `--distanceMeasure`—Specifies the distance measure to be used for comparing documents to the centroid. In this case, we used the Cosine distance measure (similar to how Lucene/Solr works, if you recall). Mahout comes with several that are located in the `org.apache.mahout.common.distance` package.
- `--convergenceDelta`—Defines the threshold below which clusters are considered to be converged and the algorithm can exit. Default is 0.5. Our choice of 0.001 was purely arbitrary. Users should experiment with this value to determine the appropriate time-quality trade-offs.
- `--clusters`—The path containing the "seed" centroids to cluster around. If `--k` isn't explicitly specified, this path must contain a file with *k* Vectors (serialized as described in listing 6.3). If `--k` is specified, then *k* random vectors will be chosen from the input.
- `--maxIter`—Specifies the maximum number of iterations to run if the algorithm doesn't converge before then.
- `--clustering`—Take the extra time to output the members of each cluster. If left off, only the centroids of the clusters are determined.

When running the command in listing 6.5, you should see a bunch of logging messages go by and (hopefully) no errors or exceptions. Upon completion, the output directory should contain several subdirectories containing the output from each iteration (named clusters-*X*, where *X* is the iteration number) as well as the input clusters (in our case, they were randomly generated) and the points that map to the final iteration's cluster output.

Since Hadoop sequence files themselves are the output, they're not human-readable in their raw form. But Mahout comes with a few utilities for viewing the results from a clustering run. The most useful of these tools is the `org.apache.mahout.utils.clustering.ClusterDumper`, but the `org.apache.mahout.utils.ClusterLabels`, `org.apache.mahout.utils.SequenceFileDumper`, and `org.apache.mahout.utils.vectors.VectorDumper` can also be useful. We'll focus on the `ClusterDumper` here. As you can probably guess from the name, the `Cluster-Dumper` is designed to dump out the clusters created to the console window or a file in a human-readable format. For example, to view the results of running the `KMeans-Driver` command given earlier, try this:

```
<MAHOUT_HOME>/bin/mahout clusterdump \
  --seqFileDir /tmp/solr-clust-n2/out/clusters-2 \
  --dictionary /tmp/solr-clust-n2/dictionary.txt --substring 100 \
  --pointsDir /tmp/solr-clust-n2/out/points/
```

In this representative example, we told the program where the directory containing the clusters (--seqFileDir), the dictionary (--dictionary), and the original points (--pointsDir) were. We also told it to truncate the printing of the cluster vector center to 100 characters (--substring) so that the result is more legible. The output from running this on an index created based on July 5, 2010, news yields is shown in the following code:

```
:C-129069: [0:0.002, 00:0.000, 000:0.002, 001:0.000, 0011:0.000, \
  002:0.000, 0022:0.000, 003:0.000, 00
    Top Terms:
            time                            =>0.027667414950403202
            a                               => 0.02749764550779345
            second                          => 0.01952658941437323
            cup                             =>0.018764212101531803
            world                           =>0.018431212697043415
            won                             =>0.017260178342226474
            his                             => 0.01582891691616071
            team                            =>0.015548434499094444
            first                           =>0.014986381107308856
            final                           =>0.014441638909228182
:C-129183: [0:0.001, 00:0.000, 000:0.003, 00000000235:0.000, \
  001:0.000, 002:0.000, 01:0.000, 010:0.00
    Top Terms:
            a                               => 0.05480601091954865
            year                            =>0.029166628670521253
            after                           =>0.027443270009727756
            his                             =>0.027223628226736487
            polic                           => 0.02445617250281346
            he                              =>0.023918227316575336
            old                             => 0.02345876269515748
            yearold                         =>0.020744182153039508
            man                             =>0.018830109266458044
            said                            =>0.018101838778995336
. . .
```

In this example output, the ClusterDumper outputs the ID of the cluster's centroid vector along with some of the common terms in the cluster based on term frequency. Close examination of the top terms reveals that though there are many good terms, there are also some bad ones, such as a few stopwords (a, his, said, and so on). We'll gloss over this for now and revisit it later in section 6.7.

Though simply dumping out the clusters is often useful, many applications need succinct labels that summarize the contents of the clusters, as discussed earlier in section 6.2.4. Mahout's ClusterLabels class is a tool for generating labels from a Lucene (Solr) index and can be used to provide a list of words that best describe the clusters. To run the ClusterLabels program on the output from our earlier clustering run, execute the following on the command line in the same directory the other commands were run:

```
<MAHOUT_HOME>/bin/mahout \
org.apache.mahout.utils.vectors.lucene.ClusterLabels \
--dir /Volumes/Content/grantingersoll/data/solr-clustering/data/index/\
```

```
--field desc-clustering --idField id \
--seqFileDir /tmp/solr-clust-n2/out/clusters-2  \
--pointsDir /tmp/solr-clust-n2/out/clusteredPoints/ \
--minClusterSize 5 --maxLabels 10
```

In this example, we told the program many of the same things we did to extract the content from the index, such as the location of the index and the fields to use. We also added information about where the clusters and points live. The `minClusterSize` parameter sets a threshold for how many documents must be in a cluster in order to calculate the labels. This will come in handy for clustering really large collections with large clusters, as the application may want to ignore smaller clusters by treating them as outliers. The `maxLabels` parameter indicates the maximum number of labels to get for the cluster. Running this on our sample of data created earlier in the chapter yields (shortened for brevity) this:

```
Top labels for Cluster 129069 containing 15306 vectors
Term            LLR               In-ClusterDF         Out-ClusterDF
team            8060.366745727311          3611            2768
cup             6755.711004478377          2193            645
world           4056.4488459853746         2323            2553
reuter          3615.368447394372          1589            1058
season          3225.423844734556          2112            2768
olymp           2999.597569386533          1382            1004
championship    1953.5632186210423         963             781
player          1881.6121935029223         1289            1735
coach           1868.9364836380992         1441            2238
u               1545.0658127206843         35              7101

Top labels for Cluster 129183 containing 12789 vectors
Term            LLR               In-ClusterDF         Out-ClusterDF
polic           13440.84178933248          3379            550
yearold         9383.680822917435          2435            427
old             8992.130047334154          2798            1145
man             6717.213290851054          2315            1251
kill            5406.968016825078          1921            1098
year            4424.897345832258          4020            10379
charg           3423.4684087312926         1479            1289
arrest          2924.1845144664694         1015            512
murder          2706.5352747719735         735             138
death           2507.451017449319          1016            755
...
```

In the output, the columns are

- *Term*—The label.
- *LLR (log-likelihood ratio)*—The LLR is used to score how good the term is based on various statistics in the Lucene index. For more on LLR, see http://en.wikipedia .org/wiki/Likelihood-ratio_test.
- *In-ClusterDF*—The number of documents the term occurs in that are in the cluster. Both this and the Out-ClusterDF are used in calculating the LLR.
- *Out-ClusterDF*—The number of documents the term occurs in that are not in the cluster.

As in the case of the `ClusterDumper` top terms, closer inspection reveals some good terms (ignoring the fact that they're stemmed) and some terms of little use. It should be noted that most of the terms do a good job of painting a picture of what the overall set of documents in the cluster are about. As mentioned earlier, we'll examine how to improve things in section 6.7. For now, let's look at how we can use some of Mahout's clustering capabilities to identify topics based on clustering the words in the documents.

## 6.6   *Topic modeling using Apache Mahout*

Just as Mahout has tools for clustering documents, it also has an implementation for topic modeling, which can be thought of, when applied to text, as clustering at the word level. Mahout's only topic modeling implementation is of the Latent Dirichlet Allocation (LDA) algorithm. LDA (Deerwester 1990) is a

> ...generative probabilistic model for collections of discrete data such as text corpora. LDA is a three-level hierarchical Bayesian model, in which each item of a collection is modeled as a finite mixture over an underlying set of topics. Each topic is, in turn, modeled as an infinite mixture over an underlying set of topic probabilities.

In laymen's terms, LDA is an algorithm that converts clusters of words into topics based on the assumption that the underlying documents are on a number of different topics, but you're not sure which document is about which topic, nor are you sure what the topic is actually labeled. Though on the surface this may sound less than useful, there's value in having the topic words associated with your collection. For instance, they could be used in conjunction with Solr to build more discovery capabilities into the search application. Alternatively, they can be used to succinctly summarize a large document collection. The topic terms may also be used for other tasks like classification and collaborative filtering (see Deerwester [1990] for more on these applications). For now, let's take a look at how to run Mahout's LDA implementation.

To get started using LDA in Mahout, you need some vectors. As outlined earlier after listing 6.3, you can create vectors from a Lucene index. But for LDA you need to make one minor change to use just term frequencies (TF) for weight instead of the default TF-IDF, due to the way the algorithm calculates its internal statistics. This might look like this:

```
<MAHOUT_HOME>/bin/mahout lucene.vector \
--dir <PATH TO INDEX>/solr-clustering/data/index/ \
--output /tmp/lda-solr-clust/part-out.vec \
--field desc-clustering --idField id \
--dictOut /tmp/lda-solr-clust/dictionary.txt \
--norm 2 --weight TF
```

This example is nearly identical to the one generated earlier, with the exception of the different output paths and the use of the TF value for the `--weight` input parameter.

With vectors in hand, the next step is to run the LDA algorithm, like this:

```
<MAHOUT_HOME>/bin/mahout lda --input /tmp/lda-solr-clust/part-out.vec \
--output /tmp/lda-solr-clust/output --numTopics 30 --numWords 61812
```

Though most of the parameters should be obvious, a few things are worth calling out. First, we gave the application some extra memory. LDA is a fairly memory-intensive application, so you may need to give it more memory. Next, we asked the LDADriver to identify 30 topics (--numTopics) in the vectors. Similar to K-Means, LDA requires you to specify how many items you want created. For better or worse, this means you'll need to do some trial and error to determine the appropriate number of topics for your application. We chose 30 rather unscientifically after looking at the results for 10 and 20. Last, the --numWords parameter is the number of words in all the vectors. When using the vector creation methods outlined here, the number of words can easily be retrieved from the first line of the dictionary.txt file. After running LDA, the output directory will contain a bunch of directories named *state-\**, as in state-1, state-2, and so on. The number of directories will depend on the input and the other parameters. The highest-numbered directory represents the final result.

Naturally, after running LDA, you'll want to see the results. LDA doesn't, by default, print out these results. But Mahout comes with a handy tool for printing out the topics, appropriately named LDAPrintTopics. It takes three required input parameters and one optional parameter:

- --input—The state directory containing the output from the LDA run. This can be any state directory, not necessarily the last one created. Required.
- --output—The directory to write the results. Required.
- --dict—The dictionary of terms used in creating the vectors. Required.
- --words—The number of words to print per topic. Optional.

For the example run of LDA shown earlier, LDAPrintTopics was run as

```
java -cp "*" \
        org.apache.mahout.clustering.lda.LDAPrintTopics \
        --input ./lda-solr-clust/output/state-118/  \
        --output lda-solr-clust/topics \
        --dict lda-solr-clust/dictionary.txt --words 20
```

In this case, we wanted the top 20 words in the state-118 directory (which happens to be the final one). Running this command fills the topics output directory with 30 files, one for each topic. Topic 22, for example, looks like this:

```
Topic 22
===========
yearold
old
cowboy
texa
14
second
year
manag
```

```
3414
quarter
opera
girl
philadelphia
eagl
arlington
which
dalla
34
counti
five
differ
1996
tri
wide
toni
regul
straight
stadium
romo
twitter
```

In looking at the top words in this category, the topic is likely about the fact that the Dallas Cowboys beat the Philadelphia Eagles in the NFL playoffs on the day before we ran the example. And, though some of the words seem like outliers (opera, girl), for the most part you get the idea of the topic. Searching in the index for some of these terms reveals there are in fact articles about just this event, including one about the use of Twitter by Eagles receiver DeSean Jackson to predict the Eagles would beat the Cowboys (don't these athletes ever learn?) That's all you need to know about running LDA in Apache Mahout. Next up, let's take a look at clustering performance across Carrot$^2$ and Mahout.

## 6.7    *Examining clustering performance*

As with any real-world application, when the programmer has a basic understanding of how to run the application, their mind quickly turns to how to use the application in production. To answer that question, we need to look at both qualitative and quantitative measures of performance. We'll start by looking at feature selection and reduction to improve quality and then look at algorithm selection and input parameters for both Carrot$^2$ and Apache Mahout. We'll finish by doing some benchmarking on Amazon's (http://aws.amazon.com) compute-on-demand capability called *EC2*. For the Amazon benchmarking, we've enlisted the help of two contributors, Timothy Potter and Szymon Chojnacki, and set out to process a fairly large collection of email content and see how Mahout performs across a number of machines.

### 6.7.1    *Feature selection and reduction*

Feature selection and feature reduction are techniques designed to either improve the quality of results or reduce the amount of content to be processed. Feature selection focuses on choosing good features up front, either as part of preprocessing or algorithm input, whereas feature reduction focuses on removing features that contribute little value as part of an automated process. Both techniques are often beneficial for a number of reasons, including those listed here:

- Reducing the size of the problem to something more tractable both in terms of computation and storage
- Improving quality by reducing the amount of noise, such as stopwords, in the data
- Visualization and post-processing—too many features can clog up user interfaces and downstream processing techniques

In many respects, you're already familiar with feature reduction thanks to our work in chapter 3. In that chapter, we employed several analysis techniques such as stopword removal and stemming to reduce the number of terms to be searched. These techniques are also helpful for improving results for clustering. Moreover, in clustering, it's often beneficial to be even more aggressive in feature selection, since you're often processing very large sets of documents, and reductions up front can make for large savings.

For instance, for the examples in this chapter, we used a different stopword file than the one used in the chapter on search, with the difference being that the clustering stopwords (see stopwords-clustering.txt in the source) are a superset of the original. To build the stopwords-clustering.txt, we examined the list of the most frequently occurring terms in the index and also ran several iterations of clustering to determine what words we thought were worth removing.

Unfortunately, this approach is ad hoc in nature and can require a fair amount of work to produce. It also isn't portable across languages or necessarily even different corpora. To make it more portable, applications generally try to focus on removing terms based on term weights (using TF-IDF or other approaches) and then iteratively looking at some measure to determine whether the clusters improved. For example, see the References section (Dash [2000], Dash [2002], and Liu [2003]) for a variety of approaches and discussions. You can also use an approach based on singular value decomposition (SVD), which is integrated into Mahout, to significantly reduce the size of the input. Note, also, that Carrot[2]'s Lingo algorithm is built on SVD out of the box, so there's nothing you need to do for Carrot[2].

Singular value decomposition is a general feature reduction technique (meaning it isn't limited to just clustering) designed to reduce the dimensionality (typically in text clustering, each unique word represents a cell in an $n$-dimensional vector) of the original dataset by keeping the "important" features (words) and throwing out the unimportant features. This reduction is a lossy process, so it's not without risk, but generally speaking it can make for a significant savings in storage and CPU costs. As for the notion of importance, the algorithm is often likened to extracting the concepts in a corpus, but that isn't guaranteed. For those mathematically inclined, SVD is the factorization of the matrix (our documents, for clustering, are represented as a matrix) into its eigenvectors and other components. We'll leave the details of the

math to others; readers can refer to https://cwiki.apache.org/confluence/display/
MAHOUT/Dimensional+Reduction for more details on Mahout's implementation as
well as links to several tutorials and explanations of SVD.

To get started with Mahout's singular value decomposition, we can again rely on
the bin/mahout command-line utility to run the algorithm. Running SVD in Mahout is
a two-step process. The first step decomposes the matrix and the second step does
some cleanup calculations. The first step of running SVD on our clustering matrix
(created earlier) might look like this:

```
<MAHOUT_HOME>/bin/mahout svd --input /tmp/solr-clust-n2/part-out.vec \
--tempDir /tmp/solr-clust-n2/svdTemp \
--output /tmp/solr-clust-n2/svdOut \
--rank 200 --numCols 65458 --numRows  130103
```

In this example, we have the usual kinds of inputs, like the location of the input
vectors (`--Dmapred.input.dir`) and a temporary location to be used by the system
(`--tempDir`), as well as some SVD-specific items:

- `--rank`—Specifies the rank of the output matrix.
- `--numCols`—This is the total number of columns in the vector. In this case, it's
  the number of unique terms in the corpus, which can be found at the top of the
  /tmp/solr-clust-n2/dictionary.txt file.
- `--numRows`—The total number of vectors in the file. This is used for sizing data
  structures appropriately.

Of these options, rank is the one that determines what the outcome will look like, and
is also the hardest to pick a good value for. Generally speaking, some trial and error is
needed, starting with a small number (say, 50) and then increasing. According to Jake
Mannix (Mannix 2010, July), Mahout committer and the original author of Mahout's
SVD code, a rank in the range of 200-400 is good for text problems. Obviously, several
trial runs will need to be run to determine which rank value yields the best results.

After the main SVD algorithm has been run, a single cleanup task must also be run
to produce the final output, as shown here:

```
<MAHOUT_HOME>/bin/mahout cleansvd \
--eigenInput /tmp/solr-clust-n2/svdOut \
--corpusInput /tmp/solr-clust-n2/part-out.vec \
--output /tmp/solr-clust-n2/svdFinal --maxError 0.1 \
--minEigenvalue 10.0
```

The keys to this step are picking the error threshold (`--maxError`) and the minimum
eigenvalue (`--minEigenValue`) items. For the minimum eigenvalue, it's always safe to
choose 0, but you may wish to choose a higher value. For the maximum error value,
trial and error along with use of the output in the clustering algorithm will lead to
insight into how well it performs (see Mannix [2010, August] for more details).

As you can see, there are many ways to select features or reduce the size of the
problem. As with most things of this nature, experimentation is required to determine

what will work best in your situation. Finally, if you want to use the results of the SVD in clustering (that's the whole point, right?), there's one final step. You need to do a multiplication of the transpose of the original matrix with the transpose of the SVD output. These can all be done using the `bin/mahout` command, making sure to get the input arguments correct. We'll leave it as an exercise to the reader to verify this. For now, we'll move on and look at some of the quantitative performance aspects of both Carrot[2] and Apache Mahout.

### 6.7.2   *Carrot[2] performance and quality*

When it comes to performance and quality of results, Carrot[2] provides a myriad of tuning options, not to mention several considerations for which algorithm to pick in the first place. We'll take a brief look at algorithm performance here, but leave an in-depth discussion of all the parameter options to the Carrot[2] manual.

PICKING A CARROT[2] ALGORITHM

First and foremost, both the STC and the Lingo algorithms have one thing in common: documents may belong to more than one cluster. Beyond that, the two algorithms take different approaches under the hood in order to arrive at their results. Generally speaking, Lingo produces better labels than STC, but at the cost of being much slower, as can be seen in figure 6.3.

As you can see in the figure, Lingo is a lot slower than STC, but for smaller result sizes, the quality of the labels may be worth the longer running time. Also, keep in

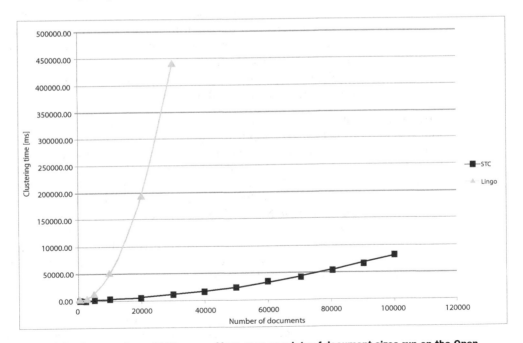

**Figure 6.3   A comparison of STC versus Lingo over a variety of document sizes run on the Open Directory Project Data (http://www.dmoz.org)**

mind Carrot[2] can link with some native code matrix libraries to help speed up the Lingo matrix decomposition. For applications where performance is more important, we recommend starting with STC. If quality is more important, then start with Lingo. In either case, take the time to flesh out which attributes help the most on your data. See http://download.carrot2.org/head/manual/index.html#chapter.components for a full accounting of the Carrot[2] attributes.

### 6.7.3  *Mahout clustering benchmarks*

One of Mahout's strongest attributes is the ability to distribute its computation across a grid of computers thanks to its use of Apache Hadoop. To demonstrate this, we ran K-Means and other clustering algorithms on Amazon's Elastic MapReduce (http://aws.amazon.com/elasticmapreduce/) and EC2 instances using an increasing number of instances (machines) to benchmark Mahout's scalability.

#### PREPARATION

As discussed in section 6.5.1, the mail archives must be transformed into Mahout vectors. The preparation steps can be done on your local workstation and don't require a Hadoop cluster. The prep_asf_mail_archives.sh script (in the utils/bin directory) in the Mahout distribution does the following:

- Download the files from s3://asf-mail-archives/ and extract using `tar`.
- Convert extracted directories containing gzipped mail archives into Hadoop SequenceFiles using a custom utility based on Mahout's `seqdirectory` utility. (See `org.apache.mahout.text.SequenceFilesFromMailArchives` in the Mahout source.) Each file contains multiple mail messages; we split the messages and extract the subject and body text using regular expressions. All other mail headers are skipped, as they provide little value for clustering. Each message is appended to a block-compressed SequenceFile, resulting in 6,094,444 key-value pairs in 283 files taking around 5.7 GB of disk.

**HADOOP SETUP**   We performed all benchmarking work described in this section with Mahout 0.4 on Hadoop 0.20.2 using Amazon EC2. Specifically, we used EC2 `xlarge` instances deployed using the contrib/ec2 scripts provided in the Hadoop distribution. We allocated three reducers per node (mapred.reduce.tasks = n*3) with 4 GB max. heap per child process (mapred.child.java.opts = -Xmx4096M). The Hadoop contrib/ec2 scripts allocate an extra node for the NameNode, which we don't include in our cluster sizes—a 4-node cluster actually has five running EC2 instances. Detailed instructions on how to set up a Hadoop cluster to run Mahout are available on the Mahout Wiki at https://cwiki.apache.org/confluence/display/MAHOUT/Use+an+Existing+Hadoop+AMI.

#### VECTORIZING CONTENT

The SequenceFiles need to be converted into sparse vectors using Mahout's `seq2sparse` MapReduce job. We chose sparse vectors because most mail messages are short and we have many unique terms across all messages. Using the default seq2sparse configuration produces vectors with several million dimensions, as each unique term in the corpus represents a cell in an *n*-dimensional vector. Clustering vectors of this magnitude isn't feasible and is unlikely to produce useful results given the long tail of unique terms within the mail archives.

To reduce the number of unique terms, we developed a custom Lucene analyzer that's more aggressive than the default StandardAnalyzer. Specifically, the MailArchivesClusteringAnalyzer uses a broader set of stopwords, excludes non-alphanumeric tokens, and applies porter stemming. We also leveraged several feature reduction options provided by seq2sparse. The following command shows how we launched the vectorization job:

```
bin/mahout seq2sparse \ --input
s3n://ACCESS_KEY:SECRET_KEY@asf-mail-archives/mahout-0.4/sequence-files
/ \
--output /asf-mail-archives/mahout-0.4/vectors/ \
--weight tfidf \ --minSupport 500 \ --maxDFPercent 70 \
--norm 2 \ --numReducers 12 \ --maxNGramSize 1 \
--analyzerName org.apache.mahout.text.MailArchivesClusteringAnalyzer
```

For input, we used Hadoop's S3 Native protocol (s3n) to read the SequenceFiles directly from S3. Note that you must include your Amazon Access and Secret Key values in the URI so that Hadoop can access the asf-mail-archives bucket. If you're unsure about these values, please see the EC2 page on the Mahout Wiki.

**AUTHOR'S NOTE** The asf-mail-archives bucket no longer exists due to potential abuse by malicious users. We're keeping the commands here for historical accuracy given that's what was used to generate the performance metrics based on Mahout 0.4, and due to the fact that we're out of credits on Amazon and these benchmarks are an expensive undertaking! In order for you to produce similar results, you can use Amazon's public dataset containing a newer version of the ASF public mail Archives. These archives are located at http://aws.amazon.com/datasets/7791434387204566.

Most of the parameters have already been discussed, so we'll concentrate on the ones that we found to be important for clustering:

- --minSupport 500—Excludes terms that don't occur at least 500 times across all documents. For smaller corpora, 500 may be too high and may exclude important terms.
- --maxDFPercent 70—Excludes terms that occur in 70% or more documents, which helps remove any mail-related terms that were missed during text analysis.
- --norm 2—The vectors are normalized using the 2-norm, as we'll be using Cosine distance as our similarity measure during clustering.
- --maxNGramSize 1—Only consider single terms.

With these parameters, seq2sparse created 6,077,604 vectors with 20,444 dimensions in about 40 minutes on a 4-node cluster. The number of vectors differs from the number of input documents because empty vectors are excluded from the seq2sparse output. After running the job, the resulting vectors and dictionary files are copied to a public S3 bucket so that we don't need to re-create them each time we run the clustering job.

We also experimented with generating bigrams (`--maxNGramSize=2`). Unfortunately, this made the vectors too large with roughly ~380K dimensions. In addition, creating collocations between terms greatly impacts the performance of the seq2sparse job; the job takes roughly 2 hours and 10 minutes to create bigrams, with at least half the time spent calculating collocations.

### K-MEANS CLUSTERING BENCHMARKS

To begin clustering, we need to copy the vectors from S3 into HDFS using Hadoop's distcp job; as before, we use Hadoop's S3 Native protocol (s3n) to read from S3:

```
hadoop distcp -Dmapred.task.timeout=1800000 \
        s3n://ACCESS_KEY:SECRET_KEY@BUCKET/asf-mail-archives/mahout-0

.4/sparse-1-gram-stem/tfidf-vectors \
        /asf-mail-archives/mahout-0.4/tfidf-vectors
```

This should only take a few minutes depending on the size of your cluster and doesn't incur data transfer fees if you launched your EC2 cluster in the default us-east-1 region. After the data is copied to HDFS, launch Mahout's K-Means job using the following command:

```
bin/mahout kmeans \ -i /asf-mail-archives/mahout-0.4/tfidf-vectors/ \
        -c /asf-mail-archives/mahout-0.4/initial-clusters/ \
        -o /asf-mail-archives/mahout-0.4/kmeans-clusters \
        --numClusters 60 --maxIter 10 \
        --distanceMeasure org.apache.mahout.common.distance.CosineD

 istanceMeasure \
        --convergenceDelta 0.01
```

This job begins by creating 60 random centroids using Mahout's RandomSeedGenerator, which takes about 9 minutes to run on the master server only (it's not a distributed MapReduce job). After the job completes, we copy the initial clusters to S3 to avoid having to re-create them for each run of the benchmarking job, which works as long as $k$ stays the same. Our selection of 0.01 for the convergenceDelta was chosen to ensure the K-Means job completes at least 10 iterations for benchmarking purposes; at the end of 10 iterations, 59 of 60 clusters converged. As was discussed in section 6.5.2, we use Mahout's clusterdump utility to see the top terms in each cluster.

To determine the scalability of Mahout's K-Means MapReduce implementation, we ran the K-Means clustering job in clusters of 2, 4, 8, and 16 nodes, with three reducers per node. During execution, the load average stays healthy ($< 4$) and the nodes don't swap. The graph in figure 6.4 demonstrates that the results are nearly linear, as we hoped they'd be.

Each time we double the number of the nodes, we can see an almost two-fold reduction in the processing time. But the curve flattens slightly as the number of nodes

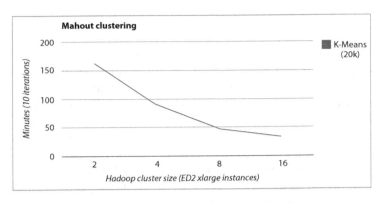

**Figure 6.4  A graph of Mahout's K-Means performance on Amazon EC2 over 2 to 16 nodes**

increases. This convex shape occurs because some nodes receive more demanding samples of data and others have to wait for them to finish. Hence, some resources are underutilized and the more nodes we have, the more likely this is to occur. Moreover, the differences among samples of documents are envisioned when two conditions are met. First, the vectors are represented with sparse structures. Second, the dataset possesses the long tail feature, which leads to an appearance of computationally demanding large vectors. Both conditions are fulfilled in our setting. We also attempted the same job on a 4-node cluster of EC2 large instances with two reducers per node. With this configuration, we expected the job to finish in about 120 minutes, but it took 137 minutes and the system load average was consistently over 3.

### BENCHMARKING MAHOUT'S OTHER CLUSTERING ALGORITHMS

We also experimented with Mahout's other clustering algorithms, including Fuzzy K-Means, Canopy, and Dirichlet. Overall, we were unable to produce any conclusive results with the current dataset. For example, one iteration of the Fuzzy K-Means algorithm runs on average 10 times slower than one iteration of K-Means. But Fuzzy K-Means is believed to converge faster than K-Means, in which case you may require fewer iterations. A comparison of running times of Fuzzy K-Means and two variants of K-Means is depicted in figure 6.5.

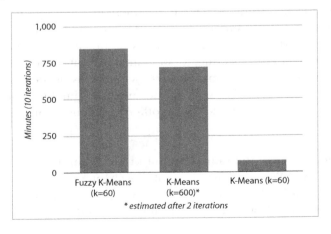

**Figure 6.5  Comparison of running times with different clustering algorithms**

We used four extra-large instances during experiments. It took over 14 hours (848 minutes) to complete all 10 iterations of Fuzzy K-Means with 60 clusters and the smoothing parameter $m$ set to 3. It's approximately 10 times longer than with the K-Means algorithm, which took only 91 minutes. We've observed that the first iteration of both clustering algorithms is always much faster than the subsequent ones. Moreover, the second, third, and later iterations require comparable amounts of time. Therefore, we utilized the feedback from the second iteration to estimate an overall 10-iterations time consumption for various levels of $k$. When the number of clusters $k$ is increased 10 times, we can expect proportional slowdown. Precisely, we've estimated the running time with k=600 to be 725 minutes. It's a bit below 10 x 91 because increasing $k$ lets us better utilize an overhead of the fixed-cost processing. The difference between the first and the second iteration can be attributed to the fact that in the first iteration, random vectors are used as centroids. In the following iterations, centroids are much denser and require longer computations.

Mahout's Canopy algorithm is potentially useful as a preprocessing step to identify the number of clusters in a large dataset. With Canopy, a user has to define only two thresholds, which impact the distances between created clusters. We've found that Canopy outputs a nontrivial set of clusters when T1=0.15 and T2=0.9. But the time required to find these values doesn't seem to pay back in speeding up other algorithms. Keep in mind, also, that Mahout is still in a pre-1.0 release at the time of this writing, so speedups are likely to occur as more people use the code.

We also encountered problems with Dirichlet, but with some assistance from the Mahout community, we were able to complete a single iteration using alpha0 = 50 and modelDist = L1ModelDistribution. Using a larger value for alpha0 helps increase the probability of choosing a new cluster during the first iteration, which helps distribute the workload in subsequent iterations. Unfortunately, subsequent iterations still failed to complete in a timely fashion because too many data points were assigned to a small set of clusters in previous iterations.

### BENCHMARKING SUMMARY AND NEXT STEPS

At the outset of this benchmarking process, we hoped to compare the performance of Mahout's various clustering algorithms on a large document set and to produce a recipe for large-scale clustering using Amazon EC2. We found that Mahout's K-Means implementation scales linearly for clustering millions of documents with roughly 20,000 features. For other types of clustering, we were unable to produce comparable results, and our only conclusion is that more experimentation is needed, as well as more tuning of the Mahout code. That said, we documented our EC2 and Elastic MapReduce setup notes in the Mahout wiki so that others can build upon our work.

## 6.8    *Acknowledgments*

The authors wish to acknowledge the valuable input of Ted Dunning, Jake Mannix, Stanisław Osiński, and Dawid Weiss in the writing of this chapter. The benchmarking of Mahout on Amazon Elastic MapReduce and EC2 was possible thanks to credits from the Amazon Web Services Apache Projects Testing Program.

## 6.9    Summary

Whether it's reducing the amount of news you have to wade through, quickly summarizing ambiguous search terms, or identifying topics in large collections, clustering can be an effective way to provide valuable discovery capabilities to your application. In this chapter, we discussed many of the concepts behind clustering, including some of the factors that go into choosing and evaluating a clustering approach. We then focused in on real-world examples by demonstrating how to use Carrot[2] and Apache Mahout to cluster search results, documents, and words into topics. We finished off the chapter by looking at techniques for improving performance, including using Mahout's singular value decomposition code.

## 6.10    References

Blei, David; Lafferty, John. 2009. "Visualizing Topics with Multi-Word Expressions." http://arxiv.org/abs/0907.1013v1.

Blei, David; Ng, Andrew; Jordan, Michael. 2003. "Latent Dirichlet allocation." *Journal of Machine Learning Research*, 3:993–1022, January.

Carpineto, Claudio; Osiński, Stanisław; Romano, Giovanni; Weiss, Dawid. 2009. "A Survey of Web Clustering Engines." *ACM Computing Surveys*.

Crabtree, Daniel; Gao, Xiaoying; Andreae, Peter. 2005. "Standardized Evaluation Method for Web Clustering Results." The 2005 IEEE/WIC/ACM International Conference on Web Intelligence (WI'05).

Cutting, Douglass; Karger, David; Pedersen, Jan; Tukey, John W. 1992. "Scatter/Gather: A Cluster-based Approach to Browsing Large Document Collections." Proceedings of the 15th Annual International ACM/SIGIR Conference.

Dash, Manoranjan; Choi, Kiseok; Scheuermann, Peter; Liu, Huan. 2002. "Feature Selection for Clustering - a filter solution." Second IEEE International Conference on Data Mining (ICDM'02).

Dash, Manoranjan, and Liu, Huan. 2000. "Feature Selection for Clustering." Proceedings of Fourth Pacific-Asia Conference on Knowledge Discovery and Data Mining.

Dean, Jeffrey; Ghemawat, Sanjay. 2004. "MapReduce: Simplified Data Processing on Large Clusters." OSDI'04: 6th Symposium on Operating Systems Design and Implementation. http://static.usenix.org/event/osdi04/tech/full_papers/dean/dean.pdf.

Deerwester, Scott; Dumais, Susan; Landauer, Thomas; Furnas, George; Harshman, Richard. 1990. "Indexing by latent semantic analysis." *Journal of the American Society of Information Science*, 41(6):391–407.

Dunning, Ted. 1993. "Accurate methods for the statistics of surprise and coincidence." *Computational Linguistics*, 19(1).

Google News. 2011. http://www.google.com/support/news/bin/answer.py?answer=40235&topic=8851.

Liu, Tao; Liu, Shengping; Chen, Zheng; Ma, Wei-Ying. 2003. "An evaluation on feature selection for text clustering." Proceedings of the Twentieth International Conference on Machine Learning (ICML-2003).

Manning, Christopher; Raghavan, Prabhakar; Schütze, Hinrich. 2008. *An Introduction to Information Retrieval.* Cambridge University Press.

Mannix, Jake. 2010, July. "SVD Memory Reqs." http://mail-archives.apache.org/mod_mbox/mahout-user/201007.mbox/%3CAANLkTik-uHrN2d838dHfYwOhxHDQ3bhHkvCQvEIQCLT@mail.gmail.com%3E.

Mannix, Jake. 2010, August. "Understanding SVD CLI inputs." http://mail-archives.apache.org/mod_mbox/mahout-user/201008.mbox/%3CAANLkTi=ErpLuaWK7Z-2an786v5AsX3u5=adU2WJM5Ex7@mail.gmail.com%3E.

Steyvers, Mark, and Griffiths, Tom. 2007. "Probabilistic Topic Models." *Handbook of Latent Semantic Analysis.* http://citeseerx.ist.psu.edu/viewdoc/download?doi -0.=10.1.1.80.9625&rep=rep1&type=pdf.

Zamir, Oren, and Etzioni, Oren. 1998. "Web document clustering: a feasibility demonstration." Association of Computing Machinery Special Interest Group in Information Retrieval (SIGIR).

# Classification, categorization, and tagging

## In this chapter

- Learn the basic concepts behind classification, categorization, and tagging
- Discover how categorization is used in text applications
- Build, train, and evaluate classifiers using open source tools
- Integrate categorization into a search application
- Build a tag recommendation engine trained using tagged data

Chances are you've encountered keyword tags somewhere among the websites you've visited. Photos, videos, music, news or blog articles, and tweets are frequently accompanied by words and phrases that provide a quick description of the content you're viewing and a link to related items. You've possibly seen tag clouds: displays of different-sized words displaying someone's favorite discussion topics, movie genres, or musical styles. Tags are everywhere on the web and are used as navigation devices or to organize everything from news to bookmarks (see figure 7.1).

**Figure 7.1   Tags used in a twitter post. Hashtags starting with the #
character are words used to identify key words in a tweet, whereas
tags referencing other users start with the @ character.**

Tags are data about data, otherwise referred to as *metadata*. They can be applied to any sort of content and come in unstructured forms, from a simple list of relevant keywords or usernames to highly structured properties such as height, weight, and eye color.

How are these tags created? Some are generated as part of an editorial process. An author or curator assigns descriptive terms, possibly the first words that come to mind or carefully selected from a set of approved words and phrases. In other cases, tags are assigned by users of a site. Each individual tags items, choosing the terms that make sense based on their own point of view. Be it a book or a song, a piece of content comes to be defined by the way it's viewed by hundreds or thousands of individuals, and the wisdom or lunacy of crowds prevails.

Machine learning allows you to automatically or semiautomatically generate tags from content. Algorithms are used to observe how things are tagged and suggest alternatives to existing tags or tags for new, untagged content. This form of automated tagging is a specialization of classification.

The challenge of classification is simply this: given an object, how do you assign it to one or more predefined categories? To solve this challenge you must consider the object's properties. What about it is like other objects? How do you group objects that share properties and exclude those that are different?

Classification algorithms learn by example using data that has been organized into classes manually or through some other automated process. Through the training process, the classification algorithm determines which properties (or features) indicate that an item belongs to a given class of objects. When trained, classification algorithms can classify previously unlabeled data.

In chapter 6, we covered another class of learning algorithms known as *clustering algorithms*. Classification and clustering are different sides of the same coin. Both of these types of algorithms seek to assign labels to objects using the features of those objects to determine the appropriate assignments. Classification is different from clustering in that classification uses a predefined set of labels and learns how best to fit objects into this scheme. This approach is referred to as *supervised learning*, where the labels assigned by the classification algorithm are based on external input such as a human-defined set of categories. Clustering is a type of unsupervised learning that doesn't use a predefined set of labels. Clustering forms groups of objects based on common characteristics. Despite this difference, both classification and clustering algorithms are used to perform document categorization.

Document categorization is the act of assigning a category- or subject related-tag to a document. It's one application of classification algorithms. In categorization, you begin with a set of training example documents, each assigned to one or more categories or subject areas. A categorization algorithm builds a model of how individual terms and other document features such as length or structure are related to subjects. When finished, the model can then be used to assign subject areas—in other words, categorize a new document.

In this chapter, we'll begin with an overview of classification and categorization and discuss the process of training a classifier for use in a production system. From there we'll examine a few different classification algorithms and learn how they're used to automatically categorize and tag text documents. Some of these algorithms, such as the naive Bayes and maximum entropy classifiers, are based upon statistical models, whereas other techniques such as the k-nearest neighbor and TF-IDF categorizers employ the vector space model used for information retrieval, as presented in chapter 3.

These algorithms will be presented through a number of hands-on examples using command-line tools and code from open source projects such as OpenNLP, Apache Lucene, Solr, and Mahout. In each case, we'll take you through every step in the process of creating a classifier. We'll explore different approaches to obtaining and preparing training data, train classifiers using each of the algorithms, and see how to evaluate the quality of their output. Finally, we'll demonstrate ways in which classifiers are integrated into a production system. Throughout each of these demonstrations we'll take you through the commands and code necessary for you to follow along. By the end of the chapter you'll be able to customize each of these examples to meet your own goals and create an automatic categorizer and tag recommender for your own applications.

## 7.1  Introduction to classification and categorization

Classification, in a computational sense, seeks to assign labels to data. Given a set of features for an object, a classifier attempts to assign a label to that object. The classifier does this by drawing upon knowledge derived from examples of how other objects have been labeled. These examples, referred to as *training data,* serve as a source of prior knowledge that the classifier uses to make decisions about previously unseen objects.

Categorization is a specialization of classification. It deals with assigning a category to an object. Other classification algorithms may simply make a yes/no decision based upon inputs, such as a fraud detector that indicates whether a credit card transaction is fraudulent. Categorization algorithms place an object in one of a small set of categories, such as categorizing cars as coupes, sedans, SUVs, or vans. Many of the concepts we discuss in this chapter pertain to classification as a whole, whereas others are more closely related to categorization. You'll see some terms used interchangeably.

Document categorization in the sense that we'll discuss in this chapter is the process of assigning a category to text documents. In the examples here, we'll assign subject-based categories to documents, but a number of other applications of document categorization such as sentiment analysis are used to determine the positivity or negativity of product reviews, or the emotion behind an email message or customer support request.

To understand how automatic classification is performed, think about what makes a helicopter different from an airplane. Chances are no one explicitly told you that "blades that spin horizontally" or "lack of fixed wings" are the features that distinguish helicopters from airplanes. After seeing examples of each type of flying machine, you were able to distinguish between which was an airplane and which was a helicopter. Unconsciously you were able to extract the features of the thing named *helicopter*, and use those features to identify other helicopters and determine that the things with jet engines attached to wings weren't helicopters. Upon seeing a flying machine with a horizontal rotor, you can immediately recognize it as a helicopter. Classification algorithms work in a similar way.

This example also touches on the importance in feature selection of determining the differences between classes of objects. Both helicopters and airplanes fly and both transport people. Neither of these features are useful in distinguishing between a helicopter and an airplane, so it'd be useless to train a classifier to use these features. In the example from the previous paragraph, suppose that the helicopter were yellow and the airplane were blue. If these were the only examples of each type of vehicle you'd seen, you might consider that all airplanes are blue and all helicopters are yellow. Your own world experience makes it clear that color isn't something you can use to determine the difference between an airplane and a helicopter. Without this knowledge, a classification algorithm that takes colors into account in its decision process would be incorrect. This highlights the importance of training an algorithm on a wide variety of training data that covers as many feature possibilities and combinations as possible.

Classification algorithms learn by example, using training data that has been organized into classes manually or through some automated process. By observing the relationship between features and classes, the algorithm learns which features are important in determining the proper label and which features provide little or misleading information about the appropriate label for the object in question. The result of the training process is a model that's used later to classify previously unlabeled objects. The classifier inspects the features of the objects to classify and uses its model to determine the best label for each object. Depending upon the classification algorithm used, the classifier may emit a single label or it may emit multiple labels, each accompanied by a score or probability that ranks the label against other possible labels for the object in question.

There are many different types of classification algorithms. One distinguishing feature is the output they produce. There are binary algorithms that produce two discrete outcomes, such as a yes/no answer. Other algorithms support multiple outcomes, producing a result from a discrete set of categories or a continuous value, such as a floating-point score or probability.

Binary classifiers produce an indication whether the object being evaluated is a member of a class. The simplest example of this sort of classifier would be a spam filter. A spam filter analyzes the features present in an email message and determines whether it's spam or not spam. The Bayes classification algorithms we explore in section 7.4, which happen to be used frequently for spam detection, develop a statistical model in order to determine whether an object is a member of a class. *Support vector machines (SVM)* is also a binary classification algorithm, which attempts to find a line or *n*-dimensional plane known as a *hyperplane* that will divide the feature space between examples within a class and outside of a class.

Binary classifiers are sometimes combined in order to perform multiclass classification. Multiple binary classifiers are each assigned a class, and input is evaluated against each class to determine which it falls into. Depending upon the algorithm, the output will be a single class that the input is most likely to fall into or a number of classes that the input is a member of, each weighted in some way to describe the relative likelihood that an object is a member of a given class. The Mahout Bayes classifier we'll explore later in this chapter is an example of training many binary classifiers in order to assign categories from a multiclass classification scheme.

Multiple binary classifiers are sometimes organized in tree-like structures. In such a case, a document that falls into class A, which has child classes B and C, will be evaluated against the classifiers trained for each class, B and C. If it matches B, it'd be evaluated by B's children, E and F. In cases where a document fails to be assigned to either E or F, it'd be considered to be in B; otherwise the document is assigned to the lowest-level leaf category it matches. This approach is useful where the classes are naturally hierarchical in nature such as in a topic taxonomy. Variants of this hierarchical approach have been used to great effect in approaches such as hierarchical binary decision trees and random forests.

The maximum entropy document categorizer we'll explore in section 7.5 is an example of a multiclass classification algorithm. This categorizer uses the words found in documents as features and subject areas as categories. The training process constructs a model of the relationship between words and subjects. For an uncategorized document, the model is used to determine feature weights that are ultimately used to produce an outcome that describes the subject area of the document.

In section 7.3, we'll explore document categorization algorithms that take advantage of the properties of the vector space model discussed in chapter 3. In these approaches, the distance in vector space between all documents that have been classified is compared to a document that hasn't been classified, and the result is used to determine the appropriate classification for the document. In this context, the uncategorized document becomes a query that's used to retrieve documents that are classified or documents that represent the contents of each category. We'll explore this approach in this chapter as well as in an example that uses Lucene as a mechanism for indexing training data and returning matching documents for a given query.

There are numerous classification algorithms and many work well for document categorization or tagging. This chapter presents a few algorithms that are easy to implement using code from open source projects. The examples here will serve as a launching point for further explorations in classification techniques. Much of what's covered here is relevant to performing classification and other supervised learning tasks regardless of the approach taken or algorithm used. We'll explore these cross-cutting concerns, such as collecting training data, identifying feature sets, and evaluating classification quality throughout this chapter by way of a series of examples. Each presents a different approach toward categorization or tagging, but builds on what's been explored in prior examples, both within this chapter and in other sections of this book.

## 7.2    *The classification process*

Developing an automatic classifier follows the same general process regardless of the algorithm used. This process, shown in figure 7.2, consists of multiple phases: preparation, training, testing, and production. Often you iterate through this process, repeating each phase a number of times, either automatically or manually, in order to fine-tune the behavior of the classifier and produce the best results. The feedback from each phase helps determine the ways in which the preparation and training phases should be modified to produce better results. Tuning represents taking the results from the testing phase and using these to improve the training process. After a classifier has been put into production, it's often necessary to extend it to cover additional cases not covered in the training data.

The *preparation phase* involves getting the data ready for the training process. Here you choose the set of labels the classifier will be trained to identify, the manner in which the features you're using for training will be identified, and the items in the dataset that will be held back for testing. When these decisions have been made, the data must be transformed into the format used by the training algorithm.

After the data has been prepared, you enter the *training phase*, where the training algorithm processes each labeled example and identifies how features of each relate to its label. Each feature is associated with the label assigned to the document and the training algorithm models the relationship between features and class labels. There are numerous algorithmic approaches toward training classification models, but, in the end, the training algorithm identifies those features that are important for

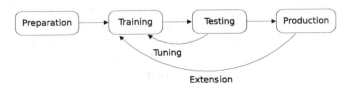

**Figure 7.2    Phases of the process used to develop an automatic classifier: preparation of data, training the model, testing the model, and deploying the classifier into production. Tuning adjusts training in response to test results. Extension extends a classifier to cover new cases that arise after deployment.**

distinguishing one class of data from another and those that provide little differentiation between classes. Frequently a classification algorithm will accept parameters that control the way models are built. In many cases, an educated guess is made as to the best values for these parameters and they're refined through an iterative process.

In the *testing phase*, the classification algorithm is evaluated using additional example data known as *test data*. The evaluation process compares the class each example belongs to with the class assigned by the classifier. A number of correct and incorrect class assignments are used to determine the accuracy of the training algorithm. Some algorithms also produce output from the training phase that helps you understand how they're interpreting the training data. This output is then used as feedback in adjusting the parameters and techniques used in the preparation and training phases.

Throughout its lifetime, a classifier may be trained multiple times. When performing the initial development of the classifier, it's common to repeat the training and testing phases, tuning the training process with each repetition in order to produce (hopefully) better results. Modifications may involve tweaking training material by adding or removing examples, changing the way in which features are extracted from the data, modifying the classes to identify, or modifying parameters that control the behavior of the learning algorithm. Many classification algorithms, such as the maximum entropy algorithm we'll explore in section 7.5, are designed to automatically iterate through the training process a number of times in order to converge upon the best answer. With other classification approaches, iteration is a manual process. In some cases iterative training is parallelized and multiple variants of a classifier are trained at the same time. The classifier that produces the best results is chosen and placed into production.

After a classifier is put into production, often it will later need to be retrained to extend its knowledge of the domain it operates within. This is commonly the case when new vocabulary emerges over time that plays a key role in differentiating between one class and another. Take, for example, a classifier that organizes product reviews by topic area. As new products are released, it'll need to see examples of tagged documents containing product names; otherwise it won't be able to determine that the term *android* most likely refers to a smartphone or *ipad* is a mobile computing device.

Now that you have a working knowledge of the steps in the classification process, we'll discuss some of the issues you must consider in each phase in greater detail.

### 7.2.1 Choosing a classification scheme

Classification algorithms learn by example using data that has been organized into classes manually or through some other automated process. The classes or categories you assign to objects have a name and meaning separate from the object being classified. Each class exists within a context of other classes, a system known as a *classification* or *categorization scheme*. Some classification schemes may be rigid, allowing each object to fall into only one class within the scheme. Other classification schemes are more flexible and acknowledge that in the real world things often have different aspects or facets. Some classification schemes, such as the Linnaean taxonomy for the classification of biological organisms, may have a strict hierarchy of meaning. Others may not have a particular structure other than that connoted by linguistic relationships, such as simple keyword tags found on Flickr or Technorati. Classification schemes may vary greatly in their scope. They may cover a broad subject area, like the Dewey Decimal System used in libraries does, or narrow, domain-specific schemes like the scheme used to describe technical aids for people with disabilities.

In many contexts, the classification scheme is organic and evolving. In cases such as social-tagging website delicious.com, tags are defined by how they're used to classify web pages. Users choose words that describe a web page and this action is multiplied millions of times a day. The vocabulary used in the categorization scheme constantly evolves, and meaning has potential to change continuously based on how the tags are used. The classification scheme emerges and changes over time from the bottom up, as opposed to top-down methods to classification where a predefined, possibly hierarchical set of subjects are made available to the user to choose from.

Deciding upon a classification scheme for your application is a matter of evaluating the trade-offs. Bottom-up tag-based schemes trade precision for simplicity, but can run afoul of language usage issues when tags have multiple meanings or multiple words describe the same concept, or even simpler issues such as when one user uses a plural to annotate a resource but another searches for a singular form. Top-down taxonomy-based schemes may not share some of these issues and provide an authoritative representation of a space of classes, but have difficulty adapting to new vocabularies or meanings.

### 7.2.2    *Identifying features for text categorization*

In chapter 2 we discussed different approaches to preprocessing text to extract words that are used for later processing schemes. The words extracted from text are thought of as *features* of that text. These words as features are used in classification algorithms to determine which class or category documents containing these words appear in.

The simplest approach, known as the *bag-of-words approach*, treats a document as a set of words. Each word appearing in a document is considered a feature and these features are weighted according to their frequency of occurrence. The TF-IDF weighting scheme presented in chapter 3 is used to generate weights for each word, in order to assign importance to words in a document based on how frequently each word occurs in a training corpus. Depending upon the size of the corpus, it may be necessary to use a subset of the terms in the corpus as the set of features to build a classifier upon. Eliminating words that occur frequently or that have a low IDF allows you to train a classifier on the most important words in the corpus: the words that have the greatest strength in discriminating between different categories. Chapter 3 also presented a number of alternate weighting schemes that are used to weight words for the purpose of choosing a set of features for making class determinations.

Word combinations often make useful document features. Instead of treating every word as it appears in a document as a feature, *n*-grams are used to capture important word combinations. A category usually contains word combinations that are unique to that category, such as *title insurance, junk bond,* or *hard disk.* Choosing all word combinations in a corpus may result in an explosion of features, but algorithms can identify statistically relevant word combinations known as *collocations,* and eliminate word combinations that provide little value.

Aside from content, other document features may be useful when building classifiers. The documents that make up a corpus may have properties that can improve the quality of the categorization algorithm. Document metadata such as authors and sources are often useful. The fact that a document is published in a Japanese newspaper may suggest that a document is more likely to be a member of the Asian Business category. Certain authors may commonly write about sports, whereas others write about technology. Document length may also be a factor in determining the difference between an academic paper, email message, or tweet.

Additional resources may be brought to bear to derive features from a document. A lexical resource such as WordNet may be used to perform term expansion by adding synonyms or hypernyms for key document terms as features. Names are often extracted by algorithms such as those described in chapter 5 and added, so *Camden Yards* or *Baltimore Orioles* become individual features that are used to determine that an article fits into the Sports category. Furthermore, the output of clustering algorithms or other classifiers may be used as features fed into a classifier that can also be used to make category determinations.

With all of these options, where's the best place to start? You can get far with the bag-of-words approach combined with TF-IDF weighting using the standard vector space model. In our examples in this chapter, we'll begin with these and identify alternate approaches towards feature selection as we proceed. Algorithms play an important role in the accuracy of an automatic categorization system, but feature selection can make or break the results regardless of the algorithms chosen.

### 7.2.3 *The importance of training data*

A classifier's accuracy is determined by the features it's trained on and the quality and quantity of examples available for training. Without a sufficient number of examples, a classifier will be unable to determine how features relate to categories. The training process will make incorrect assumptions about these relationships if insufficient data is available. It may not be able to differentiate between two categories, or incomplete data may suggest that a feature is related to one specific category when it's not. For example, you intuitively know that color isn't a distinguishing characteristic when determining whether something is a helicopter or an airplane, but if your classification algorithm only saw examples of yellow airplanes and saw no yellow helicopters, it might believe that all yellow flying vehicles are airplanes. A comprehensive and balanced training set that includes as many relevant features as possible, along with a uniform number of training examples, is important to produce an accurate model.

But where does training data come from? One approach is to manually assign classes to data. News organizations such as Reuters have invested considerable time and effort in manually tagging stories that flow through their organizations. The manual tagging efforts of millions of delicious.com users may be leveraged as a source of annotated web pages.

It's also possible to derive training data using automated processes. In the Mahout Bayes example in section 7.4, we'll explore how keyword search is used to collect a number of documents that are related to a subject area. One or more keywords are associated with a class and a search is used to retrieve the documents containing those keywords. The features contained in the documents retrieved for each class determine the nature of the category associated with the keyword search. This process, known as *bootstrapping*, is able to produce classifiers that generate reasonably accurate results.

There's a wealth of useful data on the internet when training a classifier. Projects such as Wikipedia and its relatives, such as Freebase, make bulk data dumps available[1] that can provide a tremendous corpus of documents where many have been assigned categories, tags, or other information useful for training a classifier.

In conjunction with machine learning research, a number of test collections are made available. These are useful when attempting to reproduce the results of the research or in comparing the performance of alternate approaches. Many of these are restricted to noncommercial use and require citation, but they're a great way to hit the ground running, exploring different aspects of classification and providing a benchmark to let you know you're headed in the right direction.

One of the most well-known research test collections is the RCV1-v2/LYRL2004 text categorization test collection (see Lewis [2004]), which contains more than 800,000 manually categorized stories from the Reuters news wire. The paper that accompanies this test collection describes the collection in depth and presents the training methodology and results for several well-known text classification approaches. Prior to the release of RCV2, another Reuters test collection was made available, know as Reuters-21578, which is also widely used. Though this collection contains a significantly smaller number of files, it's still useful as a benchmark collection of news wire content due to the amount of research based upon it that has been published. Another test collection, referred to as the 20 Newsgroups collection (available at http://people .csail.mit.edu/jrennie/20Newsgroups/), contains approximately 11,000 articles from 20 separate internet newsgroups that cover subjects from computing to sports, cars, politics, and religion, and is useful as a small, well-organized training and test corpus.

Stack Exchange, the parent company of Stack Overflow (http://www.stackoverflow .com) and many other social question answering sites, makes a data dump available under the Creative Commons license (found at http://blog.stackoverflow.com/ category/cc-wiki-dump/). Each of the questions on Stack Overflow has been tagged with keywords by the user community. The data dump contains these tags and serves as

---

[1] Wikipedia makes bulk dumps available at http://en.wikipedia.org/wiki/Wikipedia:Database_download; Freebase dumps are available from http://wiki.freebase.com/wiki/Data_dumps.

an excellent source of training data. In section 7.6.1 we'll use a subset of this data to build our own tag recommender.

If the data you need isn't available in bulk-dump form but is available on the internet, it's not uncommon to develop a targeted web crawler that will retrieve the data needed to train a classifier. Some large sites such as Amazon even provide a web services API that allows you to collect content from their site. Open source crawling frameworks such as Nutch and Bixo both provide excellent starting points for collecting training data from the internet. When doing so, pay careful attention to each site's copyright and terms of service to be sure that the data you collect may be used for your purpose. Be kind to websites, restricting your crawl to a handful of pages every few seconds, and act as if you're paying for the bandwidth to pull the data. Take what you need, nothing more, and don't place such a burden on any given site as to impose a cost on its owners or deny the service to regular users. Be a good citizen, and when in doubt contact the site's owners. There may be opportunities to obtain data available to you that's not advertised to the general public.

If all else fails and you find yourself having to annotate your collection of objects by hand, don't despair. Aside from recruiting your friends, family, bridge club members, and random passersby on the street to hand-tag a collection of Twitter messages for you, you can turn to Amazon Mechanical Turk. Mechanical Turk is a mechanism by which you, an enterprising machine learning developer, can funnel tasks that require human intelligence (*HITs* or *human intelligence tasks* in Amazon MT parlance) to other people around the globe for a small fee per task. The Amazon Mechanical Turk website contains a wealth of information on the setup and execution of such tasks.

Most classification algorithms support additional parameters that are used to influence the calculations performed

### Using human judgments as training data

People have been used to provide feedback in evaluating or training computer algorithms in many ways. It's common to use human judges to assess the relevancy of documents in an information retrieval context, where people will determine whether a search result is relevant to the initial query and score the quality of the search algorithm based on that judgment. A significant amount of research is available describing the issues related to using human judges in depth; some of these papers are cited at the end of this chapter.

Keep in mind, we humans are less than perfect. When embarking on collecting large-scale human judgments, it's important to validate that the people you're about to use understand the meaning of your categories or labels, are capable of making consistent judgments, and don't change significantly over time. You can check a human judge's reliability and the clarity of your categorization scheme by comparing one person's judgments against documents that have already been classified either by other people or a machine. Consistency is determined by having the user repeat judgments over time.

as a part of the training or classification process. Algorithms such as naive Bayes have few parameters, whereas others such as support vector machines (SVMs) have a number of modifiable parameters. Often training a classifier is a process involving many iterations: training with a starting value for each parameter, performing an evaluation, and then adjusting the values slightly in order to identify the best classification performance.

### 7.2.4   *Evaluating classifier performance*

Trained classifiers are evaluated by classifying documents that are already labeled and comparing these labels to the results produced by the classifier. The quality of a classifier is measured in terms of its ability to produce a result identical to the label previously assigned to the data. The percentage of cases where the assigned class correctly matches the pre-assigned labels is known as the classifier's *accuracy*. This provides an overall sense of the classifier's performance, but it's necessary to delve deeper to determine the nature of the errors encountered.

Variations of the precision and recall metrics introduced in chapter 3 are adapted to generate more detailed metrics for classifiers. These metrics are based on the types of errors encountered.

When you consider the output of a binary classifier, there are four basic outcomes, as shown in table 7.1. Two of these outcomes indicate a correct response and two indicate an incorrect response. The two correct outcomes include cases where both the label and the classifier indicate a positive result and cases where both the label and the classifier indicate a negative result. These are known as *true positive* and *true negative*. The second pair of outcomes indicate an error, where there's a disagreement between the classifier and existing label.

The first is *false positive*, where the classifier indicates an object belongs to a class when it indeed doesn't. The second is known as *false negative*, where the classifier indicates that an object doesn't belong to a class when it actually does. In statistics these are known as *Type I* and *Type II* errors respectively.

In the context of classification, precision is calculated as the number of true positives divided by the sum of the number of true and false positives. Recall is the number of true positives divided by the sum of the number of true positives and false negatives. A third measure, known as *specificity* or *true negative rate*, is measured as the number of true negatives divided by the sum of the number of true negatives and false positives.

**Table 7.1   Classification outcomes**

|  | In class | Not in class |
| --- | --- | --- |
| Assigned to class | True positive | False positive (Type I error) |
| Not assigned to class | False negative (Type II error) | True negative |

Depending upon your application, you may be more sensitive to one kind of error more than another. In spam detection, false positives come with a high cost because it'll cause a customer to miss a nonspam email; false negatives may be more acceptable because seeing spam in your inbox, though frustrating, is easily remedied with the Delete key. As your application demands, you may focus on overall accuracy, precision, recall, or specificity.

In the case of multiclass classifiers, it's common to produce each of these metrics for each individual class that the classifier may assign. They're then aggregated to produce an average accuracy, precision, and/or recall for the entire classifier.

Often it's more useful to understand the interaction between two classes in addition to the number of true or false positives. A representation of results known as a *confusion matrix* describes the nature of error cases by displaying how the documents with each label were assigned to classes. In the cases where errors are made, the confusion matrix displays the category the document was assigned to in error. In some cases the majority of the mistakes may involve assigning documents to one other class. They may identify issues with the training data used or the feature selection strategy.

In order to calculate these metrics it's necessary to hold some labeled data out from the training process. If you have 200 news stories related to the category Soccer, you might choose to train on 180 of them and hold 20 back so that you're sure that your classifier can accurately identify documents about soccer. It's important to never train upon your test data; otherwise your tests will be skewed and produce deceptively accurate results. If you ever encounter a case where your results appear to be too good to be true, check to be certain you're not training on your test data.

There are a number of different ways to split your training data into training and test sets. Choosing a random selection of documents is a good starting point. If the documents have a temporal dimension such as publication date, it may be useful to sort them by date and hold back the most recent documents as test data. This would validate that new documents that arrive are accurately classified based on the features found in older documents.

It's sometimes useful to go beyond a single split of training and test data when performing classifier evaluation. Our set of 200 news stories from before may be separated into 10 groups of 20 documents each. A number of classifiers will be trained using different combinations of groups as training and test data. For example, one classifier might be trained using groups 1 to 9 and tested using group 10, another trained using groups 2 to 10 and tested using group 1, another trained on groups 1 and 3 to 10 and tested using group 2, and so on. The resulting accuracy of each test is averaged to produce a final accuracy that evaluates the performance of the classifier. This approach is known as *k-fold cross validation* where *k* refers to the number of groups the data is split into, and is commonly used for statistically rooted classification approaches.

Aside from these, other evaluation methodologies can be used to judge classifier performance. A metric known as *area under curve* or *AUC* is useful in cases where there's an unbalanced set of training documents across the categories of the corpus. A metric named the *log-likelihood ratio* (or sometimes just log-likelihood) is often used when evaluating statistical models to compare results of multiple training runs.

### 7.2.5   *Deploying a classifier into production*

When you have a classifier trained and producing results of sufficient quality, it's necessary to consider the following issues:

1  Deploying the classifier into production as a part of a larger application
2  Updating the classifier while it's in production
3  Evaluating the accuracy of the classifier model over time

Each of the classifiers examined in this chapter may be deployed as a component of a larger service. A common deployment model is one where the classifier is deployed as a part of a long-running process. At startup the model is loaded into memory and the service receives requests for classification, either as individual requests or as a batch of documents. The OpenNLP MaxEnt classifier operates in such a manner, loading its models into memory at startup and then reusing them throughout its lifecycle. Large models that can't fit into working memory must have portions stored on disk. Apache Lucene uses a hybrid disk/memory scheme for storing document indexes, so it also works well here for supporting large models. The Mahout Bayes classifier supports multiple mechanisms for storing data, using both an in-memory store and storage based on the distributed database HBase. It also provides an API to extend to implement a data store appropriate for your deployment model.

After the classifier is deployed, it must be possible to update the model it uses as new information becomes available. Some models may be updated online, whereas others require building a replacement model offline and swapping it in to use. A classifier that's able to be updated online may be dynamically extended to handle new vocabularies. Lucene's index structure makes it simple to add or replace documents without taking the index offline for queries. In other cases, such as when the model is stored in memory, the application using the classifier must be developed in such a way that a second model may be loaded into memory while the original model remains active. When the load of the second model is complete, it replaces the original model and the original is dropped from memory.

Evaluation of a classifier's performance over time involves collecting additional data to use in order to evaluate the classifier's performance. This may involve preserving some of the input the classifier has seen in production and manually choosing the appropriate category. Keeping an eye out for cases where your classifier falls down on the job is useful, but it's important to collect a broad sample of data for evaluation, not simply the cases where classification does poorly. Keep an eye out for new subject areas or terms or topics of discussion. Regardless of the data, the process of evaluating a classifier in production doesn't differ from evaluating a classifier as a part of the development process. You must still have labeled test documents that you can classify and then compare the results of classification with the labels.

Often it's necessary to modify the categorization scheme to accommodate new data. When designing your application, consider how this may impact you. If you store categorized documents, the categories assigned may become obsolete as your categorization scheme changes. Depending upon your application, you may need to recategorize documents to match a new scheme and it'll be necessary to have access to their original contents in order to do so. An alternative may be to develop a mapping scheme from old to new categories, but as categories merge and split, this frequently becomes untenable.

Now that we've examined the issues surrounding the training and deployment process, let's get our hands dirty by training and testing some categorization algorithms. In the following sections we'll explore variations on three classification and categorization algorithms and develop a tag recommendation engine. Throughout each of these examples, we'll explore important aspects of the preparation, training, testing, and deployment process.

## 7.3    *Building document categorizers using Apache Lucene*

Some classification algorithms are called *spatial techniques*. These algorithms use the vector space model introduced in chapter 3 to represent a document's content as a *feature vector*, a point within vector space. These algorithms determine the proper category for a document by measuring the distance or angle between the term vector of the document to be labeled and other vectors that represent either documents or categories.

In this section, we cover two spatial classification algorithms: k-nearest neighbor and TF-IDF. Each algorithm treats the document to be categorized as a query and performs searches against a Lucene index to retrieve matching documents. The categories of the retrieved documents are used to determine the category of the query document. The k-nearest neighbor algorithm searches an index of categorized documents, whereas the TF-IDF approach searches an index where each document represents one of the categories we will assign. Each algorithm has advantages in terms of ease of implementation and performance.

The vector space model is at the heart of Lucene. Lucene is optimized for making the kind of distance calculations required for both of these algorithms quickly, providing an excellent base upon which to build this functionality.

In this section, you'll build document categorizers that use Apache Lucene and the k-nearest neighbor and TF-IDF algorithms to assign documents to subject areas. You'll train these categorizers using a freely available test corpus and learn how to evaluate the quality of results produced by the categorizers. This being our first example, we'll keep things simple, but the concepts introduced here will be carried through to the other examples in this chapter. You'll also notice that each of the sections in this example parallel the classification process laid out in section 7.2.

### 7.3.1    *Categorizing text with Lucene*

Lucene is highly efficient when it comes to performing distance calculations. Given a query document, similar documents are returned in subsecond response times even with an index populated with millions of documents. The score returned by Lucene is the inverse of the distance between two documents: the higher the score for a match in Lucene, the closer the document is in vector space. Within each algorithm the documents that are closest to the query will be used to make a category assignment.

In the k-nearest neighbor (k-NN) algorithm, a category is assigned to a document based on the categories of the document's neighbors in vector space. The *k* in k-nearest neighbor refers to one of the tunable parameters of the algorithm: the number of neighbors that are inspected when making the determination of which category is most appropriate. If *k* is set to 10, for example, a document's 10 closest neighbors are evaluated when choosing a category to assign to the query document.

In the TF-IDF algorithm, you create a single document for each category you seek to assign. In the example in this section, each category document is a simple concatenation of all of the documents in the given category. An alternate approach is to choose representative documents by hand. This approach is referred to as the *TF-IDF* approach because the term frequency-inverse document frequency weight of each word in a category is used as the basis for making categorization decisions. A term's relative importance is based upon the number of categories in which it appears. Furthermore, this drives query term selection and distance calculations between the query document and the categories in the index. The differences between the k-nearest neighbor and TF-IDF aproaches can be seen in figure 7.3.

The implementations of the k-nearest neighbor and TF-IDF algorithms share a significant amount of code. Each implementation builds a Lucene index from the training data. From the perspective of the Lucene API, this means creating an `IndexWriter`, configuring how it analyzes text, and creating `Document` objects to index. The content of each `Document` object will vary based upon the classification

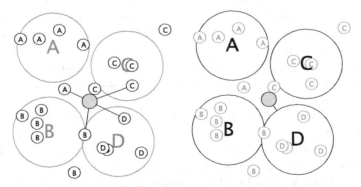

**Figure 7.3  Comparing the k-nearest neighbor (k-NN) and TF-IDF categorization algorithms. On the left, the document being categorized (in grey) is linked to its 5 nearest neighbors (k=5). Two neighbors are in category C, whereas one neighbor each is in A, B, and D. As a result, the document is assigned to category C. The large circles represent the category documents used in the TF-IDF algorithm which are a concatenation of each of the original documents in a given category. The result of the TF-IDF algorithm, shown on the right, demonstrates that the document being categorized is closest to category D and is assigned a label of D instead of C.**

algorithm. At a minimum each document will have a category `Field` object and a content `Field`. The category field holds category labels whereas the document text is stored in the content field. The code used to read and parse training data, add documents to the index, classify documents, and evaluate the performance of each algorithm is shared between each implementation.

An important aspect of this process is the conversion of the document you're seeking to classify into a Lucene query. One simple approach would be to take each unique term in the document and add it to the query. For short documents, this may be sufficient, but you'd quickly encounter difficulty processing long documents. Many words in such documents may not be useful to determine the appropriate category. Removing stopwords would reduce the size of document-based queries, but it's helpful to consider the contents of the index being searched. It'd be useless to search for a term that's not in the index, and searching upon a term that appears in every document in the index would provide no value but would significantly impact query time.

In order to determine the best words to use for categorization, you can use metrics such as term frequency (TF) and document frequency (DF) that you already calculated as a part of the index building process. Inverse document frequency is used to filter out those words with little importance. You end up with a list of query terms extracted from the document to be categorized chosen based upon their relative importance in the document index. This way you don't waste any time executing a query for a term that serves little purpose in determining whether a document belongs in category A, B, or C.

Luckily for us, the Lucene developers have made choosing terms for these sorts of queries extremely easy. Lucene includes a query type, the `MoreLikeThisQuery`, that performs index-based term selection from query documents. For the categorizers you'll build in this section, you'll use `MoreLikeThisQuery` to generate Lucene `Query` objects from your input data.

Throughout this section, we'll discuss a categorization implementation that uses the Lucene API to tokenize a document, generate a `MoreLikeThis` query, and execute that query against a Lucene index in order to obtain categories for the input document. The Lucene index is built from individual training documents in the case of the k-nearest neighbor algorithm, or categories documents in the case of the TF-IDF algorithm. Since the two algorithms share a significant amount of code, they'll be packaged as separate options within a single implementation we'll refer to as the `MoreLikeThis` categorizer. The code for this implementation is available in the `com.tamingtext.classifier.mlt` package in the source code that accompanies this book.

### 7.3.2 Preparing the training data for the MoreLikeThis categorizer

For this example, you'll train the `MoreLikeThis` categorizer to assign articles to the correct subject categories using the 20 Newsgroups test corpus. This data consists of articles posted to 20 different internet newsgroups and is split into a training and test set. The newsgroups cover a variety of subject areas, with some such as `talk.politics`

`.mideast` and `rec.autos` being clearly separate subjects, and others such as `comp.sys.ibm.pc.hardware` and `com.sys.mac.hardware` being potentially quite similar. The training data contains roughly 600 articles for each newsgroup, whereas the test data has close to 400 articles for each newsgroup. This set makes a nice sample set because it contains a uniform number of training and test examples per target category. As the name of the archive file suggests, the training/test split has been performed by date, with the training data made up of files that appear chronologically prior to the files in the test set.

The 20 Newsgroups test corpus you'll use for these examples can be downloaded from http://people.csail.mit.edu/jrennie/20Newsgroups/20news-bydate.tar.gz.

After you've downloaded and extracted the archive, you'll have two directories, 20news-bydate-train and 20news-bydate-test. Each of these directories contains one subdirectory for each newsgroup. Each of the newsgroup subdirectories contains a single file for each newsgroup posting. In order to train and test your classifier, you must take these files and transform them into the appropriate format. For simplicity, you use the same input format used by Mahout in all of the examples in this chapter. The `PrepareTwentyNewsgroups` utility from Mahout is used to create your test input. Run the following commands to convert the training and test data into the format you'll use:

```
$MAHOUT_HOME/bin/mahout \
  org.apache.mahout.classifier.bayes.PrepareTwentyNewsgroups \
  -p 20news-bydate-train \
  -o 20news-training-data \
  -a org.apache.lucene.analysis.WhitespaceAnalyzer \
  -c UTF-8

$MAHOUT_HOME/bin/mahout \
  org.apache.mahout.classifier.bayes.PrepareTwentyNewsgroups \
  -p 20news-bydate-test \
  -o 20news-test-data \
  -a org.apache.lucene.analysis.WhitespaceAnalyzer \
  -c UTF-8
```

**NOTE** Throughout the examples in this chapter, you'll see references to the environment variables $MAHOUT_HOME and $TT_HOME. MAHOUT_HOME should point to the base directory of a Mahout 0.6 installation, which contains a directory named bin that in turn contains a script named mahout. TT_HOME should point to the root directory containing the book's source code. This directory contains a directory named bin that in turn contains a script named tt. Each of these scripts is a wrapper for the Java command that sets up the appropriate environment in which to execute Java classes included in their respective distributions. Using environment variables like these allows you to set up your own working directory, which keeps the data generated by these examples separate from your copies of Mahout and the *Taming Text* code.

By the time this book is published, Mahout 0.7 will be released. This release includes significant changes to the Bayes classifiers, so be sure you're using the Mahout 0.6 releases with the examples in the book. Keep an eye on the book's author forums for updates to the sample code related to Mahout 0.7 and future releases.

As you see from the command, you use the `WhitespaceAnalyzer` to perform simple tokenization of the input data. The data will have stemming performed and stopwords removed using Lucene's `EnglishAnalyzer` later as a part of the training and test process, so there's no need to perform anything other than whitespace tokenization at this point. Other classifiers such as Mahout's Bayes classifier benefit from performing stemming and stopword removal as a part of the data preparation phase.

The preparation commands create a series of files containing training and test data. There's one file per category and each file has multiple lines, each line split into two columns delimited by a tab character. The first column contains the newsgroup name; the second contains a string, the contents of a training document with newlines and tabs removed. The following is an excerpt of some of the files in the training set. Each line contains the headers of the message followed by the message contents:

```
alt.atheism     ... Alt.Atheism FAQ: Atheist Resources Summary: Books,
...
alt.atheism     ... Re: There must be a creator! (Maybe) ...
alt.atheism     ... Re: Americans and Evolution  ...
...
comp.graphics    ... CALL FOR PRESENTATIONS ...
comp.graphics    ... Re: Text Recognition ...
comp.graphics    ... Re: 16 million vs 65 ...
...
comp.os.ms-windows.misc   ... CALL FOR PRESENTATIONS ...
comp.os.ms-windows.misc   ... Re:color or Monochrome? ...
comp.os.ms-windows.misc   ... Re: document of .RTF Organization: ...
```

Now that your training and test data has been prepared, you can train the More-LikeThis classifier.

### 7.3.3 *Training the MoreLikeThis categorizer*

The training process for the `MoreLikeThis` classifier is executed from a command prompt using code included in the examples provided with this book. The following command generates a model using the k-NN algorithm discussed in section 7.3.1:

```
$TT_HOME/bin/tt trainMlt \
  -i 20news-training-data \
  -o knn-index \
  -ng 1 \
  -type knn
```

This command builds a Lucene index using the training data you prepared in the previous section. Building an index that's used for the TF-IDF algorithm is as simple as changing the `-type` argument to `tfidf`.

We'll start by looking at the code behind each of these commands. Listing 7.1 presents the code required to create an index and set up the text processing pipeline in order to index your training data.

**Listing 7.1    Creating a Lucene index**

```
Directory directory                                    ← ❶ Create index directory.
  = FSDirectory.open(new File(pathname));
Analyzer analyzer                                      ← ❷ Set up analyzer.
  = new EnglishAnalyzer(Version.LUCENE_36);

if (nGramSize > 1) {                                   ← ❸ Set up shingle filter.
  ShingleAnalyzerWrapper sw
    = new ShingleAnalyzerWrapper(analyzer,
        nGramSize, // min shingle size
        nGramSize, // max shingle size
        "-",       // token separator
        true,      // output unigrams
        true);     // output unigrams if no shingles
  analyzer = sw;
}

IndexWriterConfig config                               ← ❹ Create IndexWriter.
  = new IndexWriterConfig(Version.LUCENE_36, analyzer);
config.setOpenMode(OpenMode.CREATE);
IndexWriter writer =  new IndexWriter(directory, config);
```

At ❶ you get started by creating a Lucene `Directory` object that represents the location on disk where the index is stored. Here the `Directory` is created by calling the `FSDirectory.open()` method with the full path to the directory in which the index should be created. At ❷ you instantiate the analyzer that's used to generate tokens from text input.

Lucene's `EnglishAnalyzer` is a good starting point that provides reasonable stemming and stopword removal. Alternate analyzer implementations are available in Lucene or as external libraries. You should experiment with the different options available in order to obtain the tokens that are most useful for your application. For example, you may want to choose an analyzer that can handle languages other than English, or use a filter that eliminates alphanumeric terms or normalizes mixed-representation words like *Wi-Fi*. A number of examples of various analyzers and combinations are present in the standard configuration shipped with Solr, as discussed in chapter 3.

In this example, you augment the output of Lucene's `EnglishAnalyzer` using *n*-grams. The code at ❸ shows how the Lucene `ShingleAnalyzerWrapper` is used to produce *n*-grams in addition to individual words if the `nGramSize` parameter is greater than 1.

**THE SHINGLEANALYZER AND WORD *N*-GRAMS**    When we encountered *n*-grams previously in chapter 4, we were exploring character-based *n*-grams. The *n*-grams produced by Lucene's shingle analyzer are word-based *n*-grams.

When the text *now is the time* is processed and the nGramSize is set to 2, the shingle analyzer will produce tokens such as *now-is, is-the,* and *the-time* (assuming that stopwords aren't removed). Each of these tokens will be used as features that may be useful in determining the difference between one category of text and another. In this specific case, the ShingleFilter operates on output of the EnglishAnalyzer. If the input *now is the time* has the stopwords *is* and *the* removed, and the *n*-grams *now-_* and *_-time* are produced. The underscores capture the position of the removed stopword to prevent capturing word pairs that didn't appear in the original text.

The command to run the trainer shown at the beginning of this section uses the default setting of 1 for the nGramSize parameter. This is changed by adding the -ng parameter followed by a number to the command, such as -ng 2.

When the EnglishAnalyzer has been created and potentially wrapped with the ShingleAnalyzerWrapper, it's ready to be used to create the Lucene index. At ❹ you create the IndexConfig and IndexWriter you'll use to build the index of training data.

Now you read the training data from the files on disk and transform them into Lucene Documents that are then added to the index. You must begin by creating the Field objects that will be used to hold the information that's stored in each document.

You have three fields in this case: the document's ID (a unique identifier), the document's category, and the document's content, which contains the tokens produced by the analyzer that will be used as features for training. The following listing shows how each of the fields are created.

##### Listing 7.2   Setting up document fields

```
Field id = new Field("id", "", Field.Store.YES,
    Field.Index.NOT_ANALYZED, Field.TermVector.NO);
Field categoryField = new Field("category", "", Field.Store.YES,
    Field.Index.NOT_ANALYZED, Field.TermVector.NO);
Field contentField = new Field("content", "", Field.Store.NO,
    Field.Index.ANALYZED, Field.TermVector.WITH_POSITIONS_OFFSETS);
```

You don't need to analyze or create term vectors for either the ID or the category field. Each of these is stored in the index for later retrieval. The content field is analyzed using the analyzer you created in listing 7.1, and the term vectors you create for this field include full-term positions and offsets in order to record the order in which terms appeared in the original document.

The trainer code loops over each document in the input file and indexes documents using different techniques based upon the categorization algorithm. The next listing shows how documents are built for the k-nearest neighbor algorithm in which each training example exists as a single document in the index.

**Listing 7.3   Indexing training documents for k-NN categorization**

```
while ((line = in.readLine()) != null) {
  String[] parts = line.split("t");
  if (parts.length != 2) continue;
  category = parts[0];
  categories.add(category);

  Document d = new Document();
  id.setValue(category + "-" + lineCount++);
  categoryField.setValue(category);
  contentField.setValue(parts[1]);
  d.add(id);
  d.add(categoryField);
  d.add(contentField);

  writer.addDocument(d);
}
```

◄──❶ **Collect content.**

◄──❷ **Build document.**

◄──❸ **Index document.**

In the implementation of the k-NN algorithm, the trainer first reads each document in a category at ❶, and ❷ produces documents which are added to the Lucene index at ❸. With this approach, the index size is proportional to the number of documents in the training set.

The following listing shows how training data is indexed for use by the TF-IDF algorithm.

**Listing 7.4   Indexing training documents for TF-IDF categorization**

```
StringBuilder content = new StringBuilder();
String category = null;
while ((line = in.readLine()) != null) {
  String[] parts = line.split("t");
  if (parts.length != 2) continue;
  category = parts[0];
  categories.add(category);
  content.append(parts[1]).append(" ");
  lineCount++;
}

in.close();

Document d = new Document();
id.setValue(category + "-" + lineCount);
categoryField.setValue(category);
contentField.setValue(content.toString());
d.add(id);
d.add(categoryField);
d.add(contentField);

writer.addDocument(d);
```

◄──❶ **Collect content.**

◄──❷ **Build document.**

◄──❸ **Index document.**

In the implementation of the TF-IDF algorithm, the trainer reads each document in a category at ❶ and concatenates the content into a single string. After all of the documents for a single category have been read, at ❷ a Lucene document is created and is added into the index at ❸. If you have a large amount of text for each category, this algorithm will consume more memory than the k-NN algorithm because a buffer containing the text of all documents in the category is built in memory before passing the result to Lucene.

Now that you've built indexes containing your training data, you can implement and test your categorization algorithms.

### 7.3.4 Categorizing documents with the MoreLikeThis categorizer

The first step to categorizing documents is to open the Lucene index and set up the analyzers used to parse the text that you want to categorize. It's important that the analyzers created here are the same as those used for training, configured in the same manner so that the terms that make up the query are formed the same way as the terms stored in the index. This means using the same stopword list, stemming algorithm, and *n*-gram settings. When the index and analyzers are ready, you create and configure an instance of the MoreLikeThis class. The next listing demonstrates how this is done.

**Listing 7.5  MoreLikeThis categorizer setup**

```
Directory directory = FSDirectory.open(new File(modelPath));

IndexReader indexReader = IndexReader.open(directory);        ①  Open index.
IndexSearcher indexSearcher = new IndexSearcher(indexReader);

Analyzer analyzer                                             ②  Set up analyzer.
  = new EnglishAnalyzer(Version.LUCENE_36);

if (nGramSize > 1) {                                          ③  Set up n-grams.
  analyzer = new ShingleAnalyzerWrapper(analyzer, nGramSize,
        nGramSize);
}

MoreLikeThis moreLikeThis  = new MoreLikeThis(indexReader);   ④  Create
moreLikeThis.setAnalyzer(analyzer);                              MoreLikeThis.
moreLikeThis.setFieldNames(new String[] {
  "content"
});
```

At ① you create the Directory instance and open both an IndexReader and IndexSearcher. The reader will be used to retrieve terms to build the query and also later, after queries have been executed, to retrieve document content. At ② and ③ you create the EnglishAnalyzer and optionally wrap it in a ShingleAnalyzer in order to produce *n*-grams if that setting is enabled. At ④, you create the MoreLikeThis class, passing it an instance of the IndexReader, setting the analyzer, and configuring it to use information about terms in the content field to choose which terms to use in its query. When building queries, MoreLikeThis will look at the frequencies of terms in the query document and in the index to determine which terms to use. Terms that fall below the specified frequencies in the query or index, or those that appear too frequently in the index, will be dropped as candidates for query terms because they'd add little in terms of discriminatory power to the query.

Now that you've created the objects you'll need to build and execute queries against the index, you can start performing searches and retrieving categories for documents. The next listing dives into the method you use to retrieve documents in order to demonstrate how categorization is performed.

**Listing 7.6  Categorizing text with `MoreLikeThis`**

```
Reader reader = new FileReader(inputPath);                    ◄─❶ Create query.
Query query = moreLikeThis.like(reader);

TopDocs results
    = indexSearcher.search(query, maxResults);                ◄─❷ Perform search.

HashMap<String, CategoryHits> categoryHash
    = new HashMap<String, CategoryHits>();

for (ScoreDoc sd: results.scoreDocs) {                        ◄─❸ Collect results.
  Document d = indexReader.document(sd.doc);
  Fieldable f = d.getFieldable(categoryFieldName);
  String cat = f.stringValue();
  CategoryHits ch = categoryHash.get(cat);
  if (ch == null) {
    ch = new CategoryHits();
    ch.setLabel(cat);
    categoryHash.put(cat, ch);
  }
  ch.incrementScore(sd.score);
}
                                                             ❹ Rank
SortedSet<CategoryHits> sortedCats                      ◄─┘    categories.
    = new TreeSet<CategoryHits>(CategoryHits.byScoreComparator());
sortedCats.addAll(categoryHash.values());

for (CategoryHits c: sortedCats) {                           ◄─❺ Display categories.
  System.out.println(
      c.getLabel() + "t" + c.getScore());
}
```

At ❶ you create a `Reader` to read the contents of the document you want to categorize. This gets passed to the `MoreLikeThis.like()` method, which performs the task of producing a Lucene query based on the key terms in the document. Now that you have a query, you perform the search at ❷, obtaining the standard Lucene response, a `TopDocs` object containing the matching documents. At ❸, you loop over each document returned, retrieve its category, and then collect the category name and score into a `CategoryHits` object. When you've iterated over all of the results, you rank them at ❹, where you sort the set of `CategoryHits` objects, and then print them for display at ❺. The highest-ranking category is the category assigned to the document. This scoring and ranking algorithm is primitive but can produce reasonable results. We encourage you to explore different approaches toward scoring categories and through the evaluation process determine what works best for you.

Categories are chosen the same way regardless of whether the index was built using the k-NN or TF-IDF algorithm. In the case of k-NN, there may be one or more documents in the result set for each category; for TF-IDF there will only be one document per category. The final score for each document is based upon the scores of the document or documents that match the query.

Integrating the `MoreLikeThis` categorizer into a production system is as simple as performing the setup once within the application lifetime, and then for each document to be categorized, formulating the `MoreLikeThis` query and retrieving and ranking the categories returned as a part of a search.

Each of these tasks has been integrated into a class named the `MoreLikeThis-Categorizer` in the sample code that accompanies the book. This class may be used as a starting point for a production categorizer deployment. In this class you'll see that the code described in example 7.6, though present, is organized slightly differently and performs the same operations of setup and categorization. We'll use this class in the next section in order to evaluate the categorizer's accuracy.

### 7.3.5  *Testing the MoreLikeThis categorizer*

Test the `MoreLikeThis` classifier using the following command:

```
$TT_HOME/bin/tt testMlt \\
   -i category-mult-test-data \\
   -m knn-index \\
   -type knn \\
   -contf content -catf category
```

When this command completes execution, you'll be presented with two metrics that describe the quality of the results produced by the categorizer. The first is a count and percentage of the correctly and incorrectly classified test document instances. This represents the accuracy of the categorizer as discussed in section 7.2.4. The second metric is a table called a *confusion matrix* that describes successful and failed test document categorizations. Each column and row of the matrix represents one of the categories the algorithm can assign to a piece of input. Rows represent the labels pre-assigned to the test documents; columns represent the categories assigned to the test documents by the categorizer. Each cell of the matrix contains a count of the number of test documents that were pre-assigned the corresponding label (corresponding to the row) and how that test document was categorized (according to the column). A document has been categorized correctly when both the row and column are the same category. The confusion matrix presented next is an excerpt of the full confusion matrix you might see when running the `testMlt` command:

```
=========================================================
Summary
---------------------------------------------------------
Correctly Classified Instances          :     5381   71.4418%
Incorrectly Classified Instances        :     2151   28.5582%
Total Classified Instances              :     7532

=========================================================
Confusion Matrix
---------------------------------------------------------
```

```
a      b      c      d      e      f     ...  <--Classified as
315    3      4      5      0      20    ...  |  393    a    = rec.motorcycles
0      308    0      1      0      2     ...  |  390    b    = comp.windows.x
0      0      320    4      1      0     ...  |  372    c    = talk.politics.mideast
2      3      13     271    9      0     ...  |  361    d    = talk.politics.guns
1      0      10     19     129    0     ...  |  246    e    = talk.religion.misc
18     3      2      6      2      293   ...  |  394    f    = rec.autos
...
Default Category: unknown: 20
```

Confusion matrices are used in the evaluation of any kind of binary or multiclass classifier. In the case of binary classifiers, they'll be a 2 x 2 matrix with four cells, similar to table 7.1. They're always $N$ x $N$ squares, where $N$ is the number of classes the classifier has been trained to produce.

In this example, we've limited the matrix to show only the results for the first six categories in the 20 Newsgroups corpus. Each row represents one of the categories in the corpus and each column contains a count of the number of test documents that were assigned to that category. In the example, category a is rec.motorcycles. Of the 393 test documents in this category, the categorizer correctly assigned the category of rec.motorcycles to 315 of them. The counts in the rest of the columns in this row show how many of the test documents belonging to rec.motorcycles were assigned to other categories. This matrix shows that 20 of them were assigned to the rec.autos category. Not surprising considering the potential similarity between subject areas and terminology used for those newsgroups.

You'll notice that this classifier tends to assign the correct categories to the test documents in each of the categories by observing that the largest numbers appear on the diagonal where the category rows and columns intersect. You can also identify areas where the classifier is running into issues; for example where 20 documents about motorcycles were classified as being about autos and 18 documents about autos were classified as having to do with motorcycles. There also appears to be some confusion between the various talk categories, with only 129 of 246 training examples for talk.religion.misc being correctly classified, and 19 of them being classified as talk.religion.guns. In cases where documents aren't correctly assigned, the confusion matrix indicates the classes that were assigned and indicates cases where your training data contains ambiguity.

Listing 7.7 demonstrates how we test a trained MoreLikeThis classifier by reading a number of files from training data. Each document is classified and we compare the result to the category previously assigned to that document. We use the class Result-Analyzer from Apache Mahout to collect these judgments and present the metrics described in the previous paragraphs.

**Listing 7.7  Evaluating results from the `MoreLikeThisCategorizer`**

```
final ClassifierResult UNKNOWN = new ClassifierResult("unknown",
    1.0);

ResultAnalyzer resultAnalyzer =                      ←① Create ResultAnalyzer.
  new ResultAnalyzer(categorizer.getCategories(),
    UNKNOWN.getLabel());

for (File ff: inputFiles) {                          ←② Read test data.
  BufferedReader in =
     new BufferedReader(
         new InputStreamReader(
            new FileInputStream(ff),
            "UTF-8"));
  while ((line = in.readLine()) != null) {
    String[] parts = line.split("t");
    if (parts.length != 2) {
      continue;
    }
                                                         ③ Categorize.
    CategoryHits[] hits                             ←┘
      = categorizer.categorize(new StringReader(parts[1]));
    ClassifierResult result = hits.length > 0 ? hits[0] : UNKNOWN;
    resultAnalyzer.addInstance(parts[0], result);   ←┐  Collect
  }                                                  ④ results.

  in.close();
}
System.out.println(resultAnalyzer.toString());   ←⑤ Display results.
```

You begin by creating a `ResultAnalyzer` at ① using the list of categories the categorizer produces and provide the default `UNKNOWN` category that will be used in cases where you're unable to categorize a document. At ② you read test data from an input file into an array of parts. `parts[0]` contains the category label; `parts[1]` contains the training document text. Documents are categorized at ③, where you obtain a ranked list of categories for the document you're categorizing. You take the highest-ranked category assigned to the document and add it to the `resultAnalyzer` at ④. If you have no results from the categorizer, you use the `UNKNOWN` class. After you've processed all of the training data, at ⑤ you display the percentage of the correct categorizations and confusion matrix.

### 7.3.6  MoreLikeThis in production

We've explored the basic building blocks of a Lucene-based document categorizer. We covered the interactions with the Lucene API required to train a categorizer by building a Lucene index of categorized documents, how to categorize documents by transforming them into Lucene queries, and how to evaluate the quality of the categorizer. We covered some of the basics as to how these algorithms may be used in a production environment. We'll expand on one deployment scenario in section 7.4.7. The scenario covered there is easily adapted to deploy the `MoreLikeThis` classifier into a production environment. The Lucene query API is highly flexible and makes it easy to integrate these sorts of classifiers in many other contexts as well.

Lucene's indexing API makes it easy to modify the model used for classification. For k-NN classification, enhancing the model is as simple as adding more categorized documents to the index. Training can occur incrementally and is limited chiefly by index size. For the TF-IDF model, it's as simple as replacing an existing category document by adding updated content for a category as a new document and deleting the old one. The ability to add new training data to the classifier in an incremental manner such as this is known as *online learning* and is often a desirable property of classification algorithms. Offline learning algorithms—classifiers that can't be extended in this way—must be retrained from scratch each time an improvement must be made, which may be expensive in terms of time and CPU cycles.

Now that you're familiar with the process of building a categorizer using Lucene to implement a distance-based classification method, we'll repeat this process in section 7.4 and train a naive Bayes text categorizer using Apache Mahout. In addition to exploring a statistical categorization algorithm, we'll investigate how existing data, such as the results of a web crawl, can be adapted to be used as training data.

## 7.4    *Training a naive Bayes classifier using Apache Mahout*

In chapter 6, you saw how Apache Mahout could be used to group documents into clusters of similar subject areas. Mahout also includes a number of classification algorithms that are used to assign category labels to text documents. One algorithm that Mahout provides is the naive Bayes algorithm. This algorithm is used for a wide variety of classification problems and is an excellent introduction into probabilistic classification. In order to perform class assignments, the algorithms that employ probabilistic classification techniques build a model based upon the probability that document features appear for a given class.

In this section, you'll use the Mahout implementation of the naive Bayes algorithm to build a document categorizer. In the first example in this chapter, we demonstrated how we could use the 20 Newsgroups test corpus to train a classifier based on Lucene. In this example, you'll develop your own test corpus from data we collected from the internet and use it to train the classifier. You'll use the content collected as part of the clustering chapter to build training and test sets. From there we'll demonstrate how training a classifier is an iterative process and present strategies for reorganizing training data in order to improve categorization accuracy. Finally, we'll demonstrate how the document categorizer is integrated into Solr so that documents are automatically assigned to categories as they're indexed. Let's begin by discussing the theoretical underpinnings of the naive Bayes classification algorithm.

### 7.4.1    *Categorizing text using naive Bayes classification*

The naive Bayes algorithm is a probabilistic classification algorithm. It makes its decisions about which class to assign to an input document using probabilities derived from training data. The training process analyzes the relationships between words in the training documents and categories, and the relationships between categories and the entire training set. The available facts are collected using calculations based on Bayes' Theorem to produce the probability that a collection of words (a document) belongs to a certain class.

What makes the algorithm naive is the assumption it makes about the independence of words appearing in a given class. Intuitively we know that words don't occur independently in text documents within a given subject area. Words like *fish* are more likely to occur in documents containing the word *water* than the word *space*. As a result, the probabilities that are produced by the naive Bayes algorithm aren't true probabilities. They're nevertheless useful as relative measures. These probabilities may not predict the absolute probability that a document belongs to a certain class, but they're used to determine that a document containing *fish* is more likely about oceanography than space travel by comparing the probabilities assigned to the term *fish* for each category.

When training, the naive Bayes algorithm counts the number of times each word appears in a document in the class and divides that by the number of words appearing in that class. This is referred to as a *conditional probability*, in this case the probability that a word will appear in a particular category. This is commonly written as *P(Word | Category)*. Imagine you have a small training set that contains three documents for the category Geometry, and the word *angle* appears in one of the documents. There's a probability of 0.33 or 33% that any document labeled *geometry* would contain the word *angle*.

You can take individual word probabilities and multiply them together to determine the probability of a document given a class. This isn't strictly useful on its own, but Bayes' Theorem provides a way for you to turn these calculations around to provide the probability of a category given a document, the essence of the classification problem.

Bayes' Theorem states that the probability of a category given a document is equal to the probability of a document given the category multiplied by the probability of the category divided by the probability of a document. This is expressed as follows:

```
P(Category | Document) = P(Document | Category) x P(Category) / P(Document)
```

We've shown how to calculate the probability of a document given a category. The probability of a category is the number of training documents for a category divided by the total number of training documents. The probability of a document isn't needed in this case because it serves as a scaling factor. If you set the P(Document) = 1, the results produced by this function will be comparable across different categories. You can determine which category a document most likely belongs to by performing this calculation for each class you're attempting to assign to a document; the relationship between these results will have the same relative ranking as long as the P(Document) is larger than zero for each calculation.

This explanation is a useful starting point but it only provides part of the picture. The Mahout implementation of the naive Bayes classification algorithm includes numerous enhancements to account for some unique cases where this algorithm falls down in the face of text data, such as the problem described earlier with dependent terms. A description of these enhancements is found on the Mahout wiki and in the paper "Tackling the Poor Assumptions of naive Bayes Text Classifiers" by Rennie et al. (see Rennie [2003]).

### 7.4.2    Preparing the training data

A classifier performs only as well as its input. The amount of training data, the way it's organized, and the features chosen as input to the training process all play a vital role in the classifier's ability to accurately categorize new documents.

This section describes how training data must be prepared for use with the Mahout Bayes classifier. We'll demonstrate the process of extracting data from a Lucene index and present the process of bootstrapping to produce a training set using attributes of the existing data. By the end of this example you'll understand how different bootstrapping approaches have an effect on the overall quality of the classifier.

In chapter 6, we described how to set up a simple clustering application using Solr. This application imported content from a number of RSS feeds and stored them in a Lucene index. You'll use the data from this index to build a training set. If you haven't already collected data using the Clustering Solr instance, follow the instructions in section 6.3 now and run the Data Import Handler a number of times over a period of a few days to build up a reasonable corpus of training documents. After you've collected some data, you can inspect the index to determine what can be used for training.

Now that you have some data in a Lucene index, you need to review what's there and determine how to use it to train a classifier. There are a number of ways to view data stored in a Lucene index, but by far the easiest to use is Luke. We'll look at the data to determine which fields in the documents may be used as a source of categories you'll base your categorization scheme upon. We'll determine a set of categories whose contents you'll use for training, and then extract documents and write them in the training data format used as input to Mahout. The Bayes classifier training process will analyze the words that appear in documents assigned to a particular category and will produce a model that's used to determine the most likely category for a document based upon the words it contains.

You can download the latest release of Luke from http://code.google.com/p/luke/; the file lukeall-version.jar, where version is the current version of Luke, is the one you want. After you've downloaded the JAR file, running the command java -jar lukeall-version.jar will start Luke.

Upon startup you'll be greeted with a dialog window that will allow you to browse your filesystem in order to select the index you wish to open. Choose the directory containing your Lucene index and click OK to open the index (the other default options should be fine).

As you browse through the index with Luke, you'll notice that many sources provide categories for their documents. These categories vary from highly general labels such as Sports to the more specific Baseball or even New York Yankees. You'll use these entries as a basis for organizing the training data. The goal here is to build a list of terms that you can use to group articles into coarse-grained categories that you'll use to train your classifier. The following list displays the top 12 categories found in the field named `categoryFacet` of the index we put together, each accompanied by the number of documents found in that category:

```
2081  Nation & World
923   Sports
398   Politics
356   Entertainment
295   sportsNews
158   MLB
128   Baseball
127   NFL
115   Movies
94    Sounders FC Blog
84    Medicine and Health
84    Golf
```

You'll notice right away that 2,081 appear in the Nation & World category and that the number of documents per category drops off quickly, with only 84 articles appearing in Golf, the 12th-ranked category. You'll also notice overlapping subject areas like Sports, Baseball, and MLB, or different representations of the same subject such as Sports and sportsNews. It's your job to clean up this data in such a way that you can use it effectively for training. It's important to take care in the preparation of training data because it can have a significant effect on the classifier's accuracy. To demonstrate this, we'll begin with a simple strategy for identifying training documents, follow up with a more complex strategy, and observe the difference in results.

From the list of categories found in the index, you can see that some useful terms appear at the top of the list. You'll add some other interesting categories from the list of categories found in the index by exploring it with Luke:

```
Nation
Sports
Politics
Entertainment
Movies
Internet
Music
Television
Arts
Business
Computer
Technology
```

Enter this into your favorite text editor and save it to a file named `training-categories.txt`. Now that you have a list of categories you're interested in, run the `extractTrainingData` utility using the category list and Lucene index as input:

```
$TT_HOME/bin/tt extractTrainingData \
  --dir index \
  --categories training-categories.txt \
  --output category-bayes-data \
  --category-fields categoryFacet,source \
  --text-fields title,description \
  --use-term-vectors
```

This command will read documents from the Lucene index and search for matching categories in the category and source fields. When one of the categories listed in training-categories.txt is found in one of these documents, the terms will be extracted from term vectors stored in the title and description fields. These terms will be written to a file in the category-bayes-data directory. There will be a single file for each category. Each is a plain text file that may be viewed with any text editor or display utility.

If you choose to inspect these files, you may notice that each line corresponds to a single document in the Lucene index. Each line has two columns delimited by a tab character. The category name appears in the first column; each of the terms that appear in the document is contained in the second column. The Mahout Bayes classifiers expect the input fields to be stemmed, so you'll see this reflected in the test data. The --use-term-vectors argument to the extractTrainingData command causes the stemmed terms from each document's term vector to be used:

```
arts    6 a across design feast nut store world a browser can chosen ...
arts    choic dealer it master old a a art auction current dealer ...
arts    alan career comic dig his lay moor rest unearth up a a ...

business    app bank citigroup data i iphon phone say store account ...
business    1 1500 500 cut job more plan tech unit 1 1500 2011 500 ...
business    caus glee home new newhom sale up a against analyst ...

computer    bug market sale what access address almost ani bug call ...
computer    end forget mean web age crisi digit eras existenti face ...
computer    mean medium onlin platon what 20 ad attract billion ...
```

When the ExtractTrainingData class has completed its run, it'll output a count of documents found in each category, similar to the following list:

```
5417    sports
2162    nation
1777    politics
1735    technology
778     entertainment
611     business
241     arts
147     music
115     movies
80      computer
60      television
32      internet
```

Note that more documents appear in some categories than others. This may affect the accuracy of the classifier. Some classification algorithms like naive Bayes tend to be sensitive to unbalanced training data because the probabilities on the features in the categories with a larger number of examples will be more accurate that those on categories with few training documents.

**BOOTSTRAPPING**    This process of assembling a set of training documents using simple rules is known as *bootstrapping*. In this example, you're bootstrapping your classifier using keywords to match existing category names assigned to the documents. Bootstrapping is often required because properly labeled data is often difficult to obtain. In many cases there isn't enough data to train an accurate classifier. In other cases the data comes from a number of different sources with inconsistent categorization schemes. This keyword bootstrapping approach allows you to group documents based upon the presence of common words in the description of the document. Not all documents in a given category may conform to this particular rule, but it allows you to generate a sufficient number of examples to train a classifier properly. Countless bootstrapping techniques exist. Some involve producing short documents as category seeds or using output from other algorithms, such as the clustering algorithms we used in the last chapter or even other types of classifiers. Bootstrapping techniques are often combined to further enhance training sets with additional data.

### 7.4.3    *Withholding test data*

Now you need to reserve some of the training data you've produced for testing. After you've trained the classifier, you'll use the model to classify the test data and verify that the categories produced by the classifier are identical to those that are already known for the document. In the code accompanying this book, we include a utility for executing a simple split called `SplitBayesInput`. We'll point `SplitBayesInput` at the directory the extraction task wrote to and `SplitBayesInput` will produce two additional directories: one containing the training date and the other containing the test data. `SplitBayesInput` is run using the following command:

```
$TT_HOME/bin/tt splitInput \
  -i category-bayes-data \
 -tr category-training-data \
 -te category-test-data \
 -sp 10 -c UTF-8
```

In this case, we're taking 10% of the documents in each category and writing them to the test directory; the rest of the documents are written to the training data directory. The `SplitBayesInput` class offers a number of different methods for selecting a variety of training/test splits.

### 7.4.4    *Training the classifier*

After the training data has been prepped using `SplitBayesInput`, it's time to roll up your sleeves and train your first classifier. If you're running on a Hadoop cluster, copy the training and test data up to the Hadoop distributed filesystem and execute the following command to build the classifier model. If you're not running on a Hadoop cluster, data will be read from your current working directory despite the `-source hdfs` argument:

```
$MAHOUT_HOME/bin/mahout trainclassifier \
  -i category-training-data \
  -o category-bayes-model \
  -type bayes -ng 1 -source hdfs
```

Training time will vary depending on the amount of data you're training on and whether you're executing the training process locally or in distributed mode on a Hadoop cluster.

   When training has completed successfully, a model is written to the output directory specified in the command. The model directory contains a number of files in Hadoop SequenceFile format. Hadoop SequenceFiles contain key/value pairs and are usually the output of a process run using Hadoop's MapReduce framework. The keys and values may be primitive types or Java objects serialized by Hadoop. Apache Mahout ships with utilities that are used to inspect the contents of these files:

```
$MAHOUT_HOME/bin/mahout seqdumper \
  -s category-bayes-model/trainer-tfIdf/trainer-tfIdf/part-00000 | less
```

The files in the trainer-tfIdf directory contain a list of all of the features the naive Bayes algorithm will use to perform classification. When dumped they'll produce output like the following:

```
no HADOOP_CONF_DIR or HADOOP_HOME set, running locally
Input Path: category-bayes-model/trainer-tfIdf/trainer-tfIdf/part-00000
Key class: class org.apache.mahout.common.StringTuple
Value Class: class org.apache.hadoop.io.DoubleWritable
Key: [__WT, arts, 000]: Value: 0.9278920383255315
Key: [__WT, arts, 1]: Value: 2.4908377174081773
. . .
Key: [__WT, arts, 97]: Value: 0.8524586871132804
Key: [__WT, arts, a]: Value: 9.251850977219403
Key: [__WT, arts, about]: Value: 4.324291341340667
. . .
Key: [__WT, business, beef]: Value: 0.5541230386115379
Key: [__WT, business, been]: Value: 7.833436391647611
Key: [__WT, business, beer]: Value: 0.6470763007419856
. . .
Key: [__WT, computer, design]: Value: 0.9422458820512981
Key: [__WT, computer, desktop]: Value: 1.1081452859525993
Key: [__WT, computer, destruct]: Value: 0.48045301391820133
Key: [__WT, computer, develop]: Value: 1.1518455320100698
. . .
```

It's often useful to inspect this file to determine whether the features you're training on truly relate to those being extracted. Inspecting this output may inform you that you're not properly filtering out stopwords, there's something wrong with your stemmer, or you're not producing *n*-grams when you expect to. It's also useful to inspect the number of features you're training on, as the size of the feature set will impact the Mahout Bayes classifier in terms of memory usage.

### 7.4.5 *Testing the classifier*

After the classifier has been trained, you can evaluate its performance using the test data that you held back earlier. The following command will load the model produced by the training phase into memory and classify each of the documents in the test set. The label assigned to each document by the classifier will be compared to the label assigned to the document manually and results for all of the documents will be tallied:

```
$MAHOUT_HOME/bin/mahout testclassifier \
  -d category-test-data \
  -m category-bayes-model \
  -type bayes -source hdfs -ng 1 -method sequential
```

When the testing process is complete, you'll be presented with two evaluation aids: classification accuracy percentages and the confusion matrix. These are introduced in section 7.3.5:

```
=====================================================Summary
-------------------------------------------------------
Correctly Classified Instances          :      906      73.6585%
Incorrectly Classified Instances        :      324      26.3415%
Total Classified Instances              :     1230

=======================================================
Confusion Matrix
-------------------------------------------------------
a    b    c    d    e    f    g    h    i    j    k    l    <--Classified as
0    0    0    0    5    0    0    0    1    0    3    2   |  11   a  = movies
0    0    0    0    0    0    0    0    1    0    1    4   |   6   b  = computer
0    0    0    0    0    0    0    0    0    0    1    2   |   3   c  = internet
0    0    0    4    0    0    0    5    4    0    4   42   |  59   d  = business
0    0    0    1   26    0    0    6   10    0   18   10   |  71   e  = enter...

0    0    0    0    2    0    0    0    1    0    3    0   |   6   f  = television

0    0    0    0    7    0    1    0    0    2    4    0   |  14   g  = music
0    0    0    0    0    0    0  103   43    0   10   10   | 166   h  = politics

0    0    0    0    1    0    0   25  145  0   16   10   | 197   i  = nation
0    0    0    0    8    0    0    3    7    1    3    1   |  23   j  = arts
1    0    0    0    1    0    0    1    7    0  493    4   | 507   k  = sports
0    0    0    0    0    0    0   15   12    0    7  133   | 167   l  = technology
Default Category: unknown: 12
```

In this case, you can use the confusion matrix to tune your bootstrapping process. The matrix shows you that the classifier did an excellent job classifying sports documents as belonging to the Sports category; 493 of 507 instances of sports-related documents were assigned to this class. Technology did well also with 133 of 167 documents being assigned to this class. Movies didn't do very well: out of 11 documents labeled with the movies class, none of them were properly assigned. The largest single number of movie-labeled documents was assigned to the Entertainment category. This makes sense, considering that movies are a form of entertainment and you had significantly more entertainment documents (778) than movie documents (115) in the training set. This demonstrates the effects of an unbalanced training set and overlapping examples. Entertainment clearly overpowers movies due to the significantly larger number of training documents available for that class, whereas you also see misclassification of entertainment content as related to the nation, sports, and technology as a result of the larger amount of training data in those categories. This instance suggests that you can obtain better accuracy with better subject separation and a more balanced training set.

### 7.4.6    *Improving the bootstrapping process*

In the previous example, you used a single term to define each class of documents. `ExtractTrainingData` built groups of documents for each class by finding all documents that contained that class's term in their source or category fields. This produced a classifier that confused several classes due to topic similarity and imbalance in training sets assigned to each category. To address this issue you'll use a group of related terms to define each class of documents. This allows you to collapse all of the sports-related categories into a single sports category and all of the entertainment-related categories into another. In addition to combining similar categories, this approach also allows you to reach further into the pool of documents in your Lucene index and retrieve additional training samples.

Create a file named training-categories-mult.txt containing the following labels:

```
Sports MLB NFL MBA Golf Football Basketball Baseball
Politics
Entertainment Movies Music Television
Arts Theater Books
Business
Technology Internet Computer Science
Health
Travel
```

In this file, the first word on each line becomes the name of the category. Each word on a line is used when searching for documents. If any word on the line matches a term in the document's category or source field, that document is written to the training data file for that category. For example, any document containing the string *MLB* in its category field will be considered part of the Sports category; documents possessing a category field containing the term *music* will be a part of the Entertainment category; and those with category fields containing *Computer* will be part of the Technology category.

Rerun `ExtractTrainingData` using the following command:

```
$TT_HOME/bin/tt extractTrainingData \
  --dir index \
  --categories training-categories-mult.txt \
  --output category-mult-bayes-data \
  --category-fields categoryFacet,source \
  --text-fields title,description \
  --use-term-vectors
```

Output will be written to the categories-mult-bayes-data directory and the following document counts will be displayed in your terminal:

```
Category document counts:
5139 sports
1757 technology
1676 politics
988  entertainment
591  business
300  arts
173  health
12   travel
```

It's likely that you'll be unable to train the classifier to accurately assign documents to the Travel category based on the number of training examples, so you might consider collecting additional training documents or discarding the Travel category entirely at this point, but we'll leave it there for now to demonstrate the outcome.

Once again, perform the split, training, and testing steps:

```
$TT_HOME/bin/tt splitInput \
  -i category-mult-bayes-data \
 -tr category-mult-training-data \
 -te category-mult-test-data \
 -sp 10 -c UTF-8

$MAHOUT_HOME/bin/mahout trainclassifier \
  -i category-mult-training-data \
  -o category-mult-bayes-model \
  -type bayes -source hdfs -ng 1

$MAHOUT_HOME/bin/mahout testclassifier \
  -d category-mult-test-data \
  -m category-mult-bayes-model \
  -type bayes -source hdfs -ng 1 \
  -method sequential
```

The output of the testing phase shows that you've produced an improved classifier that can correctly assign categories 79.5% of the time:

```
Summary
-------------------------------------------------------
Correctly Classified Instances      :      846   79.5113%
Incorrectly Classified Instances    :      218   20.4887%
Total Classified Instances          :     1064

=======================================================
```

```
Confusion Matrix
-------------------------------------------------------------
a    b    c    d    e    f    g    h    <--Classified as
0    0    0    0    0    0    1    0    |   1    a   = travel
0    3    0    0    8    0    5    43   |   59   b   = business
0    0    2    1    7    1    2    4    |   17   c   = health
0    1    0    57   12   1    19   9    |   99   d   = entertainment
0    0    0    0    142  0    14   12   |   168  e   = politics
0    0    0    17   3    3    4    3    |   30   f   = arts
0    1    0    3    9    0    495  6    |   514  g   = sports
0    1    0    1    23   0    7    144  |   176  h   = technology
Default Category: unknown: 8
```

From the output you'll see that your classifier output has improved 6%, a reasonable amount. Although you're heading in the right direction, from the confusion matrix it's clear that other issues need to be addressed.

Fortunately for the goals of this example, you have a significant amount of flexibility in terms of obtaining training data and choosing a categorization scheme. First and foremost, it's clear that you don't have enough training data for the Travel category because the majority of the documents you do have aren't being categorized at all. The Health and Arts categories suffer from the same problems, with the majority of their documents being miscategorized. The fact that the majority of arts documents were assigned to the Entertainment category suggests that it may be worth combining these classes.

### 7.4.7    *Integrating the Mahout Bayes classifier with Solr*

After a classifier has been trained, it must be deployed into production. This section will demonstrate how the Mahout Bayes classifier can be integrated into the Solr search engine indexing process as a document categorizer. As Solr loads data into a Lucene index, you also run it through your document categorizer and produce a value for a category field that's used as an additional search term or for faceted display of results.

This is done by creating a custom Solr UpdateRequestProcessor that's called when an index update is received. When it's initialized, this update processor will load the model you've trained for Mahout's Bayes classifier, and as each document is processed, its content will be analyzed and classified. The UpdateProcessor adds the category label as a Field in the SolrDocument that gets added to the Lucene index.

You begin by adding a custom update request processor chain (see org.apache .solr.update.processor.UpdateRequestProcessorChain) to Solr by defining one in solrconfig.xml. This chain defines a number of factories that are used to create the object that will be used to process updates. The BayesUpdateRequestProcessor-Factory will produce the class that's used to process each update and assign a category, while the RunUpdateProcessorFactory will process the update and add it to the Lucene index built by Solr, and the LogUpdateProcessorFactory tracks update statistics and writes them to the Solr logs, as shown in the next listing.

**Listing 7.8  Update request processor chain configuration in solrconfig.xml**

```
<updateRequestProcessorChain key="mahout" default="true">
  <processor class=
      "com.tamingtext.classifier.BayesUpdateRequestProcessorFactory">
    <str name="inputField">details</str>
    <str name="outputField">subject</str>
    <str name="model">src/test/resources/classifier/bayes-model</str>
  </processor>
  <processor class="solr.RunUpdateProcessorFactory"/>
  <processor class="solr.LogUpdateProcessorFactory"/>
</updateRequestProcessorChain>
```

You configure the `BayesUpdateRequestProcessorFactory` using the `inputField` parameter to provide the name of a field that contains the text to classify, the `output-Field` parameter to provide a name of the field to write the class label, and the `model` parameter to define the path to the model to use for classification. The `default-Category` parameter is optional and, if specified, defines the category that will be added to a document in the event the classifier is unable to make a determination of the correct category label. This commonly happens when the input document contains no features that are present in the model. The factory is created when Solr starts up and initializes its plugins. At this time, the parameters are validated and the model is loaded through the initialization of a Mahout `Datastore` object. The classification algorithm is created and a `ClassifierContext` is initialized using each of these elements.

The following listing shows how the classifier model is loaded into an `InMemory-BayesDatastore`.

**Listing 7.9  Setting up the Mahout `ClassifierContext`**

```
BayesParameters p = new BayesParameters();
p.set("basePath", modelDir.getCanonicalPath());
Datastore ds = new InMemoryBayesDatastore(p);
Algorithm a  = new BayesAlgorithm();
ClassifierContext ctx = new ClassifierContext(a,ds);
ctx.initialize();
```

This approach is fine for smaller models trained with a modest amount of features, but isn't practical for models that can't fit into memory. Mahout provides an alternative datastore that pulls data from HBase. It's straightforward enough to implement alternative datastores as well.

After the `ClassifierContext` is initialized, it's stored as a member variable in `BayesUpdateRequestProcessorFactory` and injected into each new `BayesUpdate-RequestProcessor` instantiated when an update request is received by Solr. Each update request arrives in the form of one or more `SolrInputDocuments`. The Solr API makes it trivial to extract a field from a document, and from there it's easy to preprocess and classify the document using the classifier context you initialized earlier. Listing 7.10 shows how preprocessing is achieved using the Solr analyzer, which performs the appropriate preprocessing steps based upon the input field's configuration in the Solr schema, and the result is written into a `String[]` array which Mahout's classifier context accepts as input. The Solr analyzer follows the Lucene `Analyzer` API, so the tokenization code presented here is used in any context that makes use of the Lucene analyzers.

**Listing 7.10  Tokenizing a `SolrInputDocument` using the Solr analyzer**

```
String input = (String) field.getValue();

ArrayList<String> tokenList = new ArrayList<String>();
TokenStream ts = analyzer.tokenStream(inputField,
        new StringReader(input));
while (ts.incrementToken()) {
  tokenList.add(ts.getAttribute(CharTermAttribute.class).toString());
}
String[] tokens = tokenList.toArray(new String[tokenList.size()]);
```

When you have tokens upon which the classifier can operate, obtaining the result is as simple as calling the `classifyDocument` method on the Mahout `ClassifierContext`. Listing 7.11 shows how this operation returns a `ClassifierResult` object containing the label of the document's assigned class. The `classify` method also takes a default category which is assigned in the event that no category is defined, such as the case where the input document and the model have no words in common. After the label is obtained, it's assigned to the `SolrInputDocument` as a new field as long as the `ClassifierResult` isn't null or equal to the default value for the `defaultCategory` parameter, represented by the constant NO_LABEL.

**Listing 7.11  Classifying a `SolrInputDocument` using the `ClassifierContext`**

```
SolrInputField field = doc.getField(inputField);
String[] tokens = tokenizeField(inputField, field);
ClassifierResult result = ctx.classifyDocument(tokens,
        defaultCategory);
if (result != null && result.getLabel() != NO_LABEL) {
  doc.addField(outputField, result.getLabel());
}
```

A drawback to this approach, depending upon the type of documents being indexed, is the need to hold the results of tokenization in memory in order to provide them to the classifier. In the future perhaps Mahout will be extended to take a token stream as input directly. A second drawback to this approach is the need to effectively tokenize a document's field twice at indexing time. Tokenization is performed once in the process at classification time and a second time, later on in the processing stream, in order to add the tokens to the Lucene index.

These issues aside, this is an effective mechanism for classifying documents as they're added to a Solr index and demonstrates how to use the Mahout Bayes classifier's API to classify documents programmatically. Either or both of these mechanisms may be used in your own projects as a way of tagging documents as they're indexed or automatically classifying documents using the Mahout classifier.

In this section, we explored the naive Bayes algorithm, a statistical classification algorithm that determines the probability of a set of words given a category based on observations taken from a set of training data. The algorithm then uses Bayes' Theorem to invert this conditional probability in order to determine the probability of a category, given a set of words from a document. In the following section we present another statistical classification algorithm that also models the probability of a category given a set of words, without first having to determine the inverse relationship.

We also investigated techniques for making use of training data collected from the web. We examined the process of bootstrapping, experimented with different approaches toward grouping training documents, and demonstrated how the amount of available training data has an impact on classifier accuracy. We'll continue this exploration in section 7.5, where we'll introduce the use of named entities as a way of enhancing training data in order to improve your results.

## 7.5　*Categorizing documents with OpenNLP*

The naive Bayes classification algorithm we explored in section 7.4 is a probabilistic algorithm that builds a model based on relationships between features and categories in training data in order to perform text categorization. In this section we'll use another statistical algorithm, OpenNLP's maximum entropy algorithm, to perform text categorization. The maximum entropy algorithm constructs a model based on the same information as the Bayes algorithm, but uses a different approach toward building the model. The MaxEnt algorithm uses a regression algorithm to determine how document features relate to categories. Its training process iteratively analyzes the training corpus in order to find weights for each feature and generates a mathematical formula that will produce output that's most similar to the outcomes observed in the training data. In this section we'll provide a basic overview of regression models in order to explain how this works and relate those concepts back to our core task of categorizing text.

Another useful part of OpenNLP we'll cover in this section is the name finder API. This API was presented in chapter 5 where we described how it could be used to identify named entities: people, places, and things. In this section we'll use these entities to improve the performance of the MaxEnt document classifier. In addition to treating each individual word in the training data as a feature, combinations of words that OpenNLP determines to be named entities, such as *New York City*, will be used as features.

The OpenNLP name finder is also a classifier. It's trained to detect words that appear to be named entities based on a variety of different features. OpenNLP ships with models that can be used to extract a variety of named-entity types, so in order to take advantage of the API you don't need to train your own name detector, although the option is available if necessary.

So, in addition to using OpenNLP to categorize your documents, you'll use a separate aspect of OpenNLP to generate features upon which those categorization decisions are based. This is an example of the process of *piggybacking*, where one classifier, the document categorizer, is trained using the output of another classifier, the named-entity detector. This is a common practice. You might also encounter cases where a classifier is used to determine sentence boundaries, word boundaries, or parts of speech in order to generate features for categorization. You must be sensitive to the fact that the performance of the classifier receiving the data is tied to the performance of the classifier producing the features.

At the end of this section, you'll have an understanding of how the maximum entropy classifier works, as well as understand the terminology used in its code and how it relates to document categorization. The example we present demonstrates how OpenNLP's document categorization API and name finder API work, and takes you through the process of building a categorizer from training to performing evaluation of its quality.

### 7.5.1 *Regression models and maximum entropy document categorization*

The multinomial logistic regression model used in OpenNLP's MaxEnt classifier is one of many styles of *regression models*. In general, regression models are concerned with determining the relationship between a dependent variable and a number of independent variables. Each regression model is a mathematical function with a weight for each feature. When these weights are combined with values for each feature and the weighted features are then combined, the result represents the model's prediction or outcome. The regression algorithm is concerned with determining the appropriate weights for each feature based upon the outcomes observed in the training data.

Figure 7.4 shows a trivial regression model used to predict the speed of a computer program. This model relates the number of CPUs in a computer with the amount of time it takes the program to run. This model has a single independent variable, or feature, which is the number of CPUs. The dependent variable is processing time. Each point on the graph represents an element of our training dataset, where we've measured the running time of the program on computers with certain numbers of CPUs. We have a total of five training samples ranging from 1000ms for 1 CPU to about 100ms for 8 CPUs.

The regression algorithm attempts to create a function that will allow you to predict the amount of time it'll take your program to compete running on computers with a number of CPUs that you don't have measurements for. The curved line on the graph represents the output of the function determined by the regression algorithm. This output shows that it's likely to take roughly 450ms to run the program with 3 CPUs or 110ms to run the program with 7 CPUs. The formula produced by the regression algorithm for this case appears below the graph. In this formula you raise the

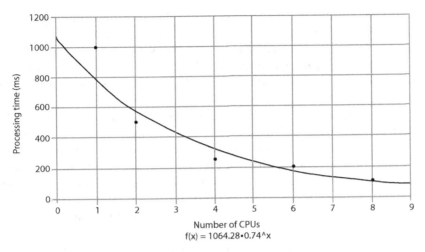

**Figure 7.4  A simple two-dimensional regression model. Each dot represents a point of observed data. The line, drawn by the regression function below the graph, allows you to extrapolate a value for instances you haven't observed. The same principle may be used for categorizing text, where each word represents a separate dimension.**

value 0.74 to the power of the number of CPUs and multiply the result by 1064.28. The value used to weight the independent variable whose value is 0.74 is called a *parameter*; the other variable whose value is 1064.28 is referred to as the *correction constant*.

In a regression model, each feature is accompanied by a parameter that's used to weight it and there's a single correction constant for the entire formula. The regression algorithm determines the best value for both the correction constant and each parameter that will produce a curve that deviates the least from the training data. In this trivial example we have only a single independent variable, but the typical cases where regression models are used are where there are a large number of independent variables, each with a parameter that must be determined.

There are many different forms of regression models that combine independent variables, parameters, and correction constants in various ways. In the preceding exponential model, each parameter is raised to the power of the value of its independent variable, and the result of each is multiplied with the correction constant. In the linear model, each parameter is multiplied with its independent variable and the results are summed with the correction constant. Each regression formula produces a different-shaped result: possibly a line, curve, or more complex shape.

Aside from the basic structure of the formula, regression algorithms vary based on how they arrive at values for their parameters. This is where you'll run into names of techniques such as *gradient descent* and *iterative scaling*: each adopts different approaches for finding the best weights for each feature value in order to produce the expected outcomes.

Regression algorithms also vary based on the output they produce. Some algorithms produce continuous output such as the one in our software performance example, whereas others produce binary results that provide a simple yes/no answer. Multinomial logistical regression as employed by the maximum entropy classifier produces a result reflecting a series of discrete outcomes, for example, a set of categories. The result returned by the maximum entropy algorithm associates a probability with each of the possible outcomes; the highest-ranked outcome is assigned as the label for the input being classified.

Regression models are used for predicting everything from the chance of a heart attack given a variety of health factors to real estate prices given such inputs as location, square footage, and number of bedrooms. As we've described, the model itself is nothing more than parameters that get plugged into the regression function. Building the regression model is a matter of fitting the observed features to the outcomes stated in the training data, whereas using the model to produce an outcome is a matter of filling in values for the features and generating a result using the weights stored in the model.

How does this all relate to the concepts we've been using to discuss text categorization? The output of the regression model (the dependent variable) corresponds to the output of a classifier: the category label produced by a categorizer. The input into the regression model, the independent variables, are known as features—aspects of the text such as terms—in the classification context. Regression models used for text categorization are large because each unique word in a corpus is treated as an independent variable. Training is further complicated by the sparsity of text; each training sample has information regarding a relatively small sample of all of the independent variables that make up the regression function. You can imagine that determining the appropriate feature weights for many independent variables is difficult enough in itself without having to worry about cases where a complete set of data isn't available.

The terminology used within the OpenNLP API and source code to describe classification is more general than the language we've used in this chapter to describe text classification. To understand document categorization with OpenNLP, you must first explore the relationship between these domains. In the nomenclature of the OpenNLP classifier, the features you train on are known as *predicates*. Predicates appear within contexts, with any given predicate possibly appearing in multiple contexts. In document categorization, the predicates are words or other document features. *Contexts* are documents. The training corpus consists of a number of contexts. Each context is associated with an *outcome*. The outcomes are equivalent to the category labels that the categorizer assigns to documents. These concepts can also be mapped into the language of regression models. Each predicate (feature or term) is an independent variable. Each independent variable is used to predict the value of the dependent variable—the outcome or category label. The corpus of training data consists of contexts that map predicates to outcomes. These mappings are the observations you train and test on. As you train your model, you compare the observed results with the results of the model to determine how the model is improving.

The training process compares each of the unique terms (predicates) found in a corpus to the outcomes they produce, and performs a series of iterations in order to find the best weight for each predicate in order to produce the desired outcome. Each iteration improves the ability of the regression equation to produce the results indicated by the training data.

### 7.5.2 Preparing training data for the maximum entropy document categorizer

For the examples in this chapter we'll reuse the training data you collected for the Mahout Bayes example in section 7.4, but you could also use the 20 Newsgroups data used in section 7.3.

Unlike the Mahout Bayes classifier, the MaxEnt categorizer will perform its own stemming on the text you're processing. As a result, you'll extract training data from the Lucene index using a slightly different command. Instead of extracting stemmed terms from Lucene term vectors, the following command will extract the raw text stored for each field in the index:

```
$TT_HOME/bin/tt extractTrainingData \
  --dir index \
  --categories training-categories.txt \
  --output category-maxent-data \
  --category-fields category,source \
  --text-fields title,description
```

If you take a look at the training data, you'll see that terms aren't stemmed and words are still in mixed case. Case is important because it's one of the clues used by the Max-Ent classifier to find named entities:

```
arts      6 Stores Across the World Are a Feast for Design Nuts A few ...

arts      For Old Masters, It's Dealers' Choice While auction houses ...

arts      Alan Moore Digs Up 'Unearthing' and Lays His Comics Career ...

...
business      Citigroup says iPhone banking app stored data Citigroup ...

business      United Tech plans 1,500 more job cuts HARTFORD, Conn. - ...

business      New-home sales up, but no cause for glee New-home sales ...

...
computer          What's for Sale on the Bug Market? Almost any ...
computer          The Web Means the End of Forgetting The digital age ...

computer          The Medium: What 'Platonic' Means Online Craigslist ...
```

Next you use `splitInput` to divide your data into separate training and test sets:

```
$TT_HOME/bin/tt splitInput \
  -i category-maxent-data \
  -tr category-maxent-training-data \
  -te category-maxent-test-data \
  -sp 10 -c UTF-8
```

Now that you've prepared the training and test data, let's train the maximum entropy document categorizer.

### 7.5.3   *Training the maximum entropy document categorizer*

The OpenNLP project supplies a document categorizer as a part of its distribution, but a fair amount of programming is required to be able to used it. The following section describes the code required to train and test a categorizer built using OpenNLP's `DocumentCategorizer` class.

The classes `TrainMaxent` and `TestMaxent` implement a categorizer based on OpenNLP that's run from the command prompt. The `trainMaxent` command is used to train the categorizer. The input directory specified by the `-i` argument must contain training data in the format we've used for the preceding examples: one file per category, each file containing one document per line. The MaxEnt document categorizer expects to receive whitespace-delimited text with no prior stemming or case normalization, as it requires case to perform named-entity detection. The `-o` parameter is used to specify the filename the MaxEnt model will be written to:

```
$TT_HOME/bin/tt trainMaxent \
        -i category-maxent-training-data \
        -o maxent-model
```

Let's take a deeper look into the code used to train an OpenNLP document categorizer model and the aspects of the training process you can customize to meet your goals.

In order to train the MaxEnt model, you must set up the input directory and output files, create the raw data source and feature generators that will convert your training data into features, and pass these to the trainer that will build a statistical model of your training set. The following listing demonstrates this process.

**Listing 7.12   Training the `DocumentCategorizer`**

```
File[] inputFiles = FileUtil.buildFileList(new File(source));
File modelFile = new File(destination);

Tokenizer tokenizer = SimpleTokenizer.INSTANCE;          ◄──❶ Create data stream.
CategoryDataStream ds =
    new CategoryDataStream(inputFiles, tokenizer);

int cutoff = 5;
int iterations = 100;
NameFinderFeatureGenerator nffg                          ◄──❷ Set up feature generators.
  = new NameFinderFeatureGenerator();
BagOfWordsFeatureGenerator bowfg
  = new BagOfWordsFeatureGenerator();

DoccatModel model = DocumentCategorizerME.train("en",
    ds, cutoff, iterations, nffg, bowfg);               ◄──❸ Train categorizer.
model.serialize(new FileOutputStream(modelFile));
```

At ❶ you set up the `SimpleTokenizer` and `CategoryDataStream` to extract category labels and tokens from the training data files.

At ❷ you create the `NameFinderFeatureGenerator` and `BagOfWordsFeature-Generator` classes, which are used to produce features that include the raw terms in the document and the named entities identified by OpenNLP's name finder.

After the data stream and feature generators are created, you train the categorizer model using `DocumentCategorizerME`. At ❸ you first pass the data stream, feature generators, and training parameters to the `train()` method and then serialize the trained model to disk.

It's worth taking a closer look at the tokenization and feature generation process in order to understand how training data is transformed into the events used to train the categorizer. The next listing shows how `CategoryDatastream` is used to generate `DocumentSamples` from training data.

**Listing 7.13  Producing `DocumentSamples` from training data**

```
public DocumentSample read() {
  if (line == null && !hasNext()) {                          ⟵─❶ Read line training data.
    return null;
  }
  int split = line.indexOf('t');                             ⟵─❷ Extract category.
  if (split < 0)
    throw new RuntimeException("Invalid line in "
        + inputFiles[inputFilesIndex]);
  String category = line.substring(0,split);
  String document = line.substring(split+1);
  line = null; // mark line as consumed                      ❸ Tokenize
  String[] tokens = tokenizer.tokenize(document);   ⟵┘  content.   ❹ Create
  return new DocumentSample(category, tokens);               ⟵┘           sample.
}
```

At ❶ `CategoryDataStream`'s `read()` method obtains lines from the input data by calling the `hasNext()` method. `hasNext()` implicitly reads new lines of training data and makes them available in the `line` variable, setting `line` to null when the end of the training data is reached. As each line of training data is read, the code at ❷ extracts category and document data. The document data is then tokenized at ❸ to produce a collection of terms that will be used as features in the training process. Finally, at ❹ a `DocumentSample` object is created using category labels and tokens found in the training sample.

Within `DocumentCategorizerME`, the collection of `DocumentSamples` is passed to the feature generators by the `DocumentCategorizerEventStream`. This produces the events upon which the model will be trained. These events consist of outcomes and contexts. Outcomes are category labels; the contexts are the collections of words produced by tokenizing document content.

The `DocumentSample` event objects created by the `CategoryDataStream` are processed into features by the `NameFinderFeatureGenerator` and the `BagOfWords-FeatureGenerator`. The latter, provided as a part of the OpenNLP API, returns the

tokens in the document examples as a collection of features. The NameFinder-
FeatureGenerator uses the OpenNLP NameFinder API to find named entities within
the tokens and returns these as features. You encapsulate the setup of the OpenNLP
NameFinder and loading of the various models used to find named entities within the
NameFinderFactory, which is in charge of finding and loading the various models
used to identify named objects. The following listing shows how NameFinderEngine
finds and loads the models used for identifying named entities.

**Listing 7.14   Loading name finder models**

```
File modelFile;

File[] models                                              ←—❶ Find models.
  = findNameFinderModels(language, modelDirectory);
modelNames = new String[models.length];
finders = new NameFinderME[models.length];

for (int fi = 0; fi < models.length; fi++) {               ┌─❷ Determine
  modelFile = models[fi];                                  │    model
  modelNames[fi] = modelNameFromFile(language, modelFile); ←┘    name.

  log.info("Loading model {}", modelFile);
  InputStream modelStream = new FileInputStream(modelFile);
  TokenNameFinderModel model =                             ←┐  Read
      new PooledTokenNameFinderModel(modelStream);          ❸ model.
  finders[fi] = new NameFinderME(model);

}
```

At ❶ the findNameFinderModels() method scans the model directory for model files
to load. Each model file is then loaded into an array maintained by the NameFinder-
Factory. As each model is loaded, modelNameFromFile() is used at ❷ to convert the
model file name into a model name by stripping any leading path and trailing suffix.
At ❸ the PooledTokenNameFinderModel does the heavy lifting related to reading and
uncompressing the model and writing the results into memory. As each model is
loaded, instances of the NameFinderME class are created using the loaded model. Each
of these models is stored in an array returned by the NameFinderFactory.getName-
Finders() method.

   Now that you've loaded the instances of the NameFinder class you'll use to identify
named entities in your input, the code in the next listing from the class NameFinder-
FeatureGenerator is used to perform the named-entity extraction upon the
DocumentSamples returned by the CategoryDataStream.

**Listing 7.15   Using NameFinderFeatureGenerator to generate features**

```
public Collection extractFeatures(String[] text) {
  NameFinderME[] finders = factory.getNameFinders();      ←—❶ Get name finders.
  String[] modelNames    = factory.getModelNames();

  Collection<String> features = new ArrayList<String>();
  StringBuilder builder = new StringBuilder();
```

```
for (int i=0; i < finders.length; i++) {
  Span[] spans = finders[i].find(text);        ◄── ❷ Find names.
  String model = modelNames[i];

  for (int j=0; j < spans.length; j++) {
    int start = spans[j].getStart();            ◄── ❸ Extract names.
    int end   = spans[j].getEnd();

    builder.setLength(0);
    builder.append(model).append("=");
    for (int k = start; k < end; k++ ) {
      builder.append(text[k]).append('_');
    }
    builder.setLength(builder.length()-1);
    features.add(builder.toString());           ◄── ❹ Collect names.
  }
}
return features;
}
```

You obtain references to the `NameFinderME` and model names loaded by the `NameFinder` factory at ❶. The `NameFinderFactory` has stored the finders and their corresponding model names in parallel arrays. Each model will be used to identify a different named-entity type such as locations, people, times, and dates.

At ❷ you process the input tokens with each `NameFinderME` loaded by the engine by calling the `find` method. Each `Span` in the array returned by this method call references the points at which one or more tokens that represent a named entity appear in the original text using a start and end offset. At ❸ you use these offsets to generate the strings you'll store as features. In each case, the model name is prepended to each string which results in features like `location=New_York_City`.

All of the features you generate are collected into a list, which is returned to the document categorizer in ❹.

As training is run, you'll see output similar to the following:

```
Indexing events using cutoff of 5

Computing event counts...  done. 10526 events
Indexing...
done.
Sorting and merging events... done. Reduced 10523 events to 9616.
Done indexing.
Incorporating indexed data for training...
done.
Number of Event Tokens: 9616
  Number of Outcomes: 12
  Number of Predicates: 11233
...done.
Computing model parameters...
Performing 100 iterations.
   1:  .. loglikelihood=-26148.6726757207    0.0024707782951629764
   2:  .. loglikelihood=-24970.114236056226  0.6394564287750641
   3:  .. loglikelihood=-23914.53191047887   0.6485793024802813
 ...
```

```
 99:   .. loglikelihood=-7724.766531988901    0.8826380309797586
100:   .. loglikelihood=-7683.407561473442    0.8833982704551934
```

Before training, the document categorizer must organize the features it'll use for training in an index where they're accessed quickly throughout the training process. The first few lines of output describe the results of this process. Each labeled training document produces an event, and in the indexing phase duplicate events are counted and certain documents may be dropped if they don't contain useful features.

The cutoff referred to in the trainer output is a minimum term frequency cutoff. Any terms that appear fewer than five times in the entire training corpus are ignored. Any document that consists of only terms that fall below the cutoff is also dropped. Predicates represent the terms used for training, and here you see that a total of 11,233 unique predicates are in the corpus. These include the single word tokens produced by the OpenNLP BagOfWordsFeatureGenerator, and the named entities produced by the NameFinderFeatureGenerator. In the regression model, each predicate is an independent variable.

The output also indicates that when the indexing process is complete, you have a total of 12 outcomes and a total number of 9,616 training samples after deduping.

When the indexing is complete, you begin to see output from the training process. The process itself consists of 100 iterations; each iteration represents a pass through the entire set of training data in order to adjust the model parameters and determine the regression function's output. For each iteration, the log-likelihood ratio is calculated that compares the output of the model with the observed output.

Log likelihood is a measure of the similarity between two models. You don't use the value as an absolute measure; rather, it serves as a relative measure of how much the model is changing across each iteration. You should expect the log likelihood to move closer to zero with each iteration. This indicates that the model is producing results closer to the outcomes observed in the training data with each step. If the log likelihood moves further away from zero, it indicates that the model is getting worse and there's potentially a problem with the training data. You'll also notice that the log likelihood will change more significantly in the first few training steps than it will as the iterations increase. If you notice that the log likelihood continues to change significantly after you reach the 100th iteration, it may be worth experimenting with a training process that uses more iterations.

When you reach the 100th iteration, the trainer will write the model to disk and you now have a model you can use for document categorization. The next section demonstrates the API calls necessary to use the model for categorization as a part of the testing process.

### 7.5.4 *Testing the maximum entropy document classifier*

We'll use the same approach to test the maximum entropy document classifier that we used in sections 7.3.5 and 7.4.5: categorizing a number of labeled documents and comparing the assigned categories with the original labels. The TestMaxent class that does this is invoked using the following command:

```
$TT_HOME/bin/tt testMaxent \
        -i category-maxent-test-data \
        -m maxent-model
```

Here you're using the test data produced by the extractTrainingData utility along with the model produced by the trainMaxent command. When the test has completed, you'll be greeted with the familiar percentage correct and confusion matrix.

The TestMaxent class demonstrates how a trained model is loaded into memory and used to classify documents. The code in listing 7.16 loads the model from disk and prepares the tokenization pipeline for document processing. You'll notice that much of the code is similar to the code used for training the categorizer in listing 7.12.

**Listing 7.16   Preparing the DocumentCategorizer**

```
NameFinderFeatureGenerator nffg                          ◄───┐  Set up feature
    = new NameFinderFeatureGenerator();                     ❶  generators.
BagOfWordsFeatureGenerator bowfg
    = new BagOfWordsFeatureGenerator();

InputStream modelStream =                                 ◄──❷  Load model.
    new FileInputStream(modelFile);
DoccatModel model = new DoccatModel(modelStream);
DocumentCategorizer categorizer                           ◄──❸  Create categorizer.
    = new DocumentCategorizerME(model, nffg, bowfg);
Tokenizer tokenizer = SimpleTokenizer.INSTANCE;

int catCount = categorizer.getNumberOfCategories();
Collection<String> categories
    = new ArrayList<String>(catCount);
for (int i=0; i < catCount; i++) {                            ❹  Prepare
    categories.add(categorizer.getCategory(i));                  result
}                                                                analyzer.
ResultAnalyzer resultAnalyzer =
    new ResultAnalyzer(categories, "unknown");
runTest(inputFiles, categorizer, tokenizer, resultAnalyzer);
```

Execute
test.  ❺

You begin again by setting up the feature generators at ❶, and then move on to loading the model from disk ❷ using the DoccatModel class. This model is then used to create an instance of the DocumentCategorizer class at ❸. Finally, at ❹ you initialize the ResultAnalyzer using the list of categories obtained from the categorizer via the model, and at ❺ you run the test.

In the next section, we'll look at the code used to integrate the maximum entropy document categorizer into a production context.

### 7.5.5   *Maximum entropy document categorization in production*

Now that you've loaded the model and set up the tokenizer, feature generators, categorizer, and results evaluator, you're ready to categorize some documents. Listing 7.17 shows how documents read from a file are processed, categorized, and then delivered to the ResultAnalyzer class you also used to evaluate the MoreLikeThis and Bayes classifiers in sections 7.3.5 and 7.4.5.

**Listing 7.17   Categorizing text with `DocumentCategorizer`**

```
for (File ff: inputFiles) {
  BufferedReader in = new BufferedReader(new FileReader(ff));
  while ((line = in.readLine()) != null) {
    String[] parts = line.split("t");
    if (parts.length != 2) continue;

    String docText   = parts[1];                                ◄── ❶ Preprocess text.
    String[] tokens  = tokenizer.tokenize(docText);

    double[] probs   = categorizer.categorize(tokens);          ◄── ❷ Categorize.
    String label     = categorizer.getBestCategory(probs);
    int     bestIndex = categorizer.getIndex(label);
    double score     = probs[bestIndex];

    ClassifierResult result                                     ◄── ❸ Analyze results.
      = new ClassifierResult(label, score);
    resultAnalyzer.addInstance(parts[0], result);
  }
  in.close();
}

System.err.println(resultAnalyzer.toString());                 ◄── ❹ Present results.
```

As you recall, each test document appears in the second column of a single line in the input file. You begin by extracting the text from each training document and then using the `SimpleTokenizer` to produce a set of tokens ❶. The tokens are then delivered to the categorizer at ❷. The categorize method generates features using the `BagOfWords-FeatureGenerator` and `NameFinderFeatureGenerator` set up in listing 7.16, and then combines these features with the model to produce a list of possible outcomes, each accompanied by a probability derived from the model computation. Each outcome present corresponds to a specific document category, and the highest-ranked category is ultimately assigned to the document. At ❸ you create a `ClassifierResult` to feed into the `ResultAnalyzer`. After you've processed all of the documents in this manner, you print the summary of the result at ❹.

The code required to integrate the OpenNLP `DocumentCategorizer` into a production system doesn't differ significantly from the code described in this section. A production system would need to perform a one-time setup of the tokenizers, feature generators, and categorizer in a manner similar to that demonstrated in listing 7.16 and categorize documents using code like that found in listing 7.17. Consider how you might adapt the example in section 7.4.7, where you integrated the Mahout Bayes classifier into Solr to use the OpenNLP document classifier instead.

Now that we've presented a collection of algorithms used to categorize documents based on their content, we'll explore one application of these algorithms—content tagging—and how a variation of the algorithms we've presented here is used to organize content by presenting a mechanism for browsing a large collection of documents based on subject area or an additional subject facet on search results.

## 7.6     *Building a tag recommender using Apache Solr*

Before we begin our implementation of an automatic content tagger, let's discuss the background of how tagging emerged as a popular mechanism for locating content and why it's important.

In the early days of the internet, two primary modes of finding content emerged. Search engines indexed the web and presented simple search interfaces where keywords could be entered to locate content. Other sites classified web pages into enormous taxonomies, trees of subject-based categories. Each of these approaches addressed a different sort of information seeking behavior; each had its advantages and drawbacks.

The indexes and user interfaces maintained by search engines met the needs of many, but end users suffered when they had no idea how to describe their information need in keywords. Keyword search was further complicated by the fact that many concepts could be described using a number of different terms, so important content could be missed based upon the disconnect between the terms used in a search and the vocabulary present in a document. As a result, keyword searching often consisted partially of guessing the proper terms and partially of exploration of the search results to uncover additional query terms.

Other sites developed large organizational schemes and assigned web pages to categories within these schemes. Categories were frequently organized in trees, where each level past the root would become more specific in meaning. Low-level, broad categories like Arts or Travel would give way to highly specific categories such as Kabuki or Tourism in Tokyo. These schemes, known as *taxonomies*, were managed by a single entity and often grew to the point they couldn't be easily understood by the end user. Which branch would you navigate to locate pages about Japanese cuisine? The explosive rate of growth on the web made it impossible to keep up. Each new website would have to be categorized by hand by individuals who knew the taxonomy inside and out. Information seekers wanted to be able to quickly find what they were looking for instead of having to drill down through a complex taxonomy of indeterminate depth.

Social tagging emerged as an alternative to the large, centrally managed taxonomy. Instead of forcing content into a single scheme of hierarchical categories, tagging gives the power of organizing content to the users. For example, when a user wants to remember a web page, they assign words—tags—to that page that make sense to them. Twitter users embed hashtags in their posts by prepending a hash mark (#) to keywords so that others interested in the same subject can locate their tweets.

In both cases, the tags used are public and, as a result, content is findable by anyone who has an interest in the same tag. As this behavior is repeated by tens to thousands of users, a categorization scheme emerges based on the common usage of terms. The definition of each tag emerges from the way it's used. Instead of forcing content into a strictly controlled taxonomy of categories, social content tagging leverages the perspective of a large number of people to define the context of content.

This organically emerging organization scheme is often referred to as a *folksonomy,* a social, collaboratively generated variation of a taxonomy. A folksonomy is a way of organizing or classifying objects that has naturally emerged from the way a large group of people organize things over time. With this organization scheme, content doesn't need to fit into a rigid taxonomy of categories but is represented by a group of terms, each of which is considered a sort of category in its own right.

The act of tagging content on the web is simple enough. You create or find something interesting on the web, click a button in your browser, and associate some words to it that will help you find it later. As you tag more content, interesting things emerge when looking at the tags in aggregate. Take a look at the tag cloud in figure 7.5 that displays a summary of all of the tags a user has assigned to web pages on delicious .com. Can't you quickly determine what they're interested in?

Social tagging, as demonstrated on sites like Delicious and Twitter, harnesses the power of millions of people tagging content. Some people have tagged the same content our user has, choosing different words meaningful to them. Other people use the same tags as our user to tag different pieces of content. Though someone may use their own tags to navigate their content collection, they can use others' tags to find web pages that might be related or interesting to them in some way. Tags take on different meanings based upon how people use them.

In figure 7.6, you'll notice the recommended tags. Where do these come from? How are they determined? A simple tag recommendation algorithm may inspect a user's existing tags and the tags assigned to the web page by other users and generate a list based on these metrics. Other algorithms may recommend tags based on the content of the page being tagged. Analyzing the text of the web page being tagged and comparing this with a statistical model based on the tags of other pages with similar content can produce a highly accurate set of tag suggestions.

You can build upon each of these examples to create a tag recommendation engine using Lucene. In the distance-based approaches introduced in section 7.3, each document or category vector is labeled with a single category, and you chose the single most relevant category from a number of matching candidates. In the Bayes example, you witnessed that there are often many good categories for each document, and often these range from general to specific or describe different facets of meaning.

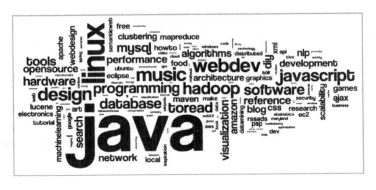

**Figure 7.5   Delicious.com tag cloud generated by wordle.net. This size of each word relates to the frequency of a tag in a collection of documents.**

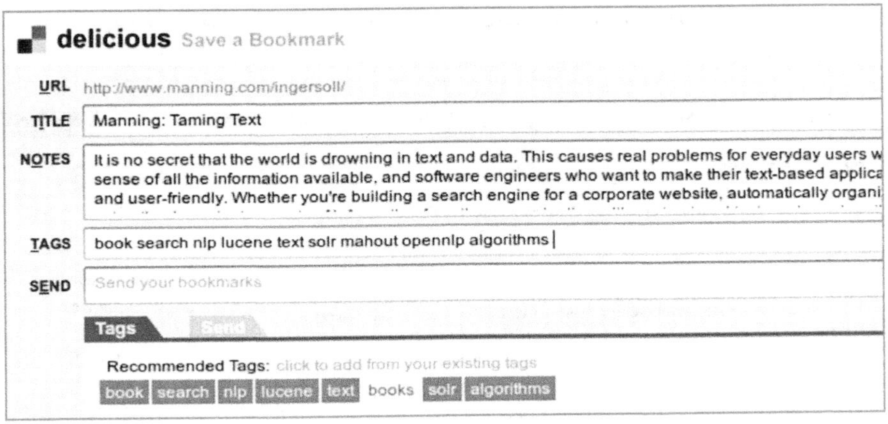

**Figure 7.6  Tagging a web page on delicious.com: users assign a number of keyword tags to describe the web page so that they can easily find it later by searching on any of these tags. The tags capture facets of what the page is about.**

Instead of creating a constrained set of categories, how can you take advantage of the existing tags in a collection of documents to generate tags for other documents?

In this section you'll do just that. We'll demonstrate how you can use the k-nearest neighbor categorization algorithm coupled with a set of pretagged documents to build a tag recommender using Apache Solr. Like the k-nearest neighbor implementation in section 7.3, you'll build an index that contains your training data and use the `MoreLikeThis` query to match a document to those in the index. The tags you recommend will be harvested from the results of each query.

### 7.6.1  Collecting training data for tag recommendations

To build your tag recommender, you'll use a collection of data from the question answering website Stack Overflow (http://www.stackoverflow.com). Stack Overflow is a "collaboratively edited question answering site for professional and enthusiast programmers." It's operated by Stack Exchange, a company that runs similar question answering sites focused on a number of different subject areas. People visit each site to participate in the process of posting questions, composing new answers, or rating existing answers from the user community. Each question is assigned a series of keyword tags by the person asking the question. As of January 2011, the Stack Overflow data dump contained more than 4 million posts. Of these, approximately a million posts are questions accompanied by tags. Questions vary in length, but the majority of these posts provide text and tags that are useful for training a tag suggestion engine such as the one you'll build in this example.

In addition to being an excellent source of training data, Stack Overflow and its sister sites present an excellent use case for tags on a content-oriented site. Figure 7.7 shows the page describing the *java* tag. The page presents the most popular questions that are tagged with the term *java*. It also presents some statistics regarding the tag,

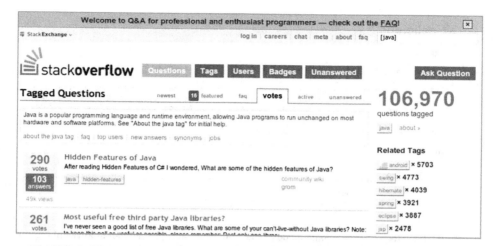

**Figure 7.7   A page from stackoverflow.com that presents information about the questions tagged with the word java. This demonstrates one way in which tags are used to navigate information and also presents a useful source of training data.**

such as the number of questions tagged with java and related tags and counts. It's particularly useful that a definition of the tag is presented as well. This prevents users from misusing the tag on questions about Indonesia or beverages.

You'll start small by identifying a training set of 10,000 posts and a test set of 1,000 posts. The criteria for judging whether a recommended tag is appropriate will be relatively lax at first. Each question may have more than one tag, so you'll use the text of each question as training data for each associated tag. If a given question includes the tags *php*, *javascript*, and *ajax*, you'll use the question as a training sample for each of those categories.

When you evaluate the quality of the tagging engine with regard to the test data, you'll look at the tags assigned to an item by the engine and compare these with the user-assigned tags. If you see one or more matching tags, you'll consider there to be a match.

Like the first examples we explored in this chapter, your tag recommender will be trained by indexing training documents with Lucene. You'll take advantage of Solr as a platform to quickly load and index the Stack Overflow data using the Data Import Handler and expose the results of your tag recommender as a web service.

### Classification and recommendation

The terms *classification* and *recommendation* each formally describe related families of machine learning algorithms. The difference between the two is that classification offers a small number of possible choices from a controlled list of choices, whereas recommendation offers a larger subset of options for a nearly infinite set of options such as a product catalog or a database of scholarly articles.

In addition to or instead of content-based decisions, many recommenders analyze user behavior to determine what to recommend, for example, tracking your likes and dislikes or watching what you choose or purchase, and comparing those to the behavior of others in order to recommend items to you that you may also like. Companies like Amazon or Netflix use this sort of recommendation algorithm in order to suggest books for you to purchase or movies for you to watch.

This example recommends tags using solely the content of an input article and the content of articles already present on the system. In this way it's more like the classification and categorization algorithms that we've explored so far as opposed to behavior-based recommenders. It'd be interesting to combine the two approaches.

If you're interested in learning more about recommenders, check out *Mahout in Action* by Owen, Anil, Dunning, and Friedman, also published by Manning (Owen 2010).

## 7.6.2 *Preparing the training data*

To get started with this example, you can download the subset of the Stack Overflow training and test data we've made available at http://www.tamingtext.com or you can download the full dump directly from Stack Overflow by following the instructions at http://blog.stackoverflow.com/category/cc-wiki-dump/. From this page you can download a torrent that will allow you to download the data with your favorite BitTorrent client. The data dump torrent includes files for all of the Stack Exchange site, so use your BitTorrent client to choose only the Stack Overflow data dump, in Content\Stack Overflow 11-2010.7z, which is an archive in 7-Zip format.

After you unpack the archive you'll have files such as badges.xml, comments.xml, posthistory.xml, and posts.xml. You'll use posts.xml as your source of training data. That file contains a series of row elements nested within a posts element containing the data you're looking for. We'll briefly describe how to generate the splits we're interested in and then discuss the format of the file itself.

You can use the following command to split it into training and test sets:

```
$TT_HOME/bin/tt extractStackOverflow \
        -i posts.xml \
        -te stackoverflow-test-posts.xml \
        -tr stackoverflow-training-posts.xml
```

By default `extractStackOverflow` will extract the first 100,000 questions it finds as training documents and the first 10,000 questions it finds as test data. You should feel free to experiment with extracting more or less data and observe how the amount of data affects training time and quality.

In the posts.xml file, there are a number of XML elements with the name `row`. We're interested in finding those rows that are questions that have tags. Each question appears in a row, but not every row in the Stack Overflow data is a question. The `extractStackOverflow` utility will take care of filtering out nonquestion rows by looking at each row's `PostTypeId` attribute. Those with a value of 1 are questions and will be kept; others will be rejected. The other attributes we're interested in are the `Title`, `Tags`, and `Body`. We'll use these as the raw training data. Some of the other attributes might come in handy as well, so we'll preserve them too.

The tags for a question may be found in the `tags` attribute of each row, where multiple tags are demarcated with < and > marks. The entire attribute value might look like `<javascript><c++><multithreaded programming>` for a post that's been tagged with three separate tags: *javascript, c++,* and *multithreaded programming.* You'll need to parse this format when training and testing with this data.

### 7.6.3  *Training the Solr tag recommender*

You'll train the Solr tag recommender using the Stack Overflow data with Solr's data import handler. Provided with the code examples is a Solr instance that's configured to read the training data file, extract the necessary fields from the XML, and convert the tags into discrete values stored in the index. The relevant portion of the configuration is the following listing.

**Listing 7.18  Excerpt from dih-stackoverflow-config.xml**

```
<entity name="post"
        processor="XPathEntityProcessor"
        forEach="/posts/row"
        url="../stackoverflow-corpus/training-data.xml"
        transformer="DateFormatTransformer,HTMLStripTransformer,
            com.tamingtext.tagrecommender.StackOverflowTagTransformer">
    <field column="id"    xpath="/posts/row/@Id"/>
    <field column="title" xpath="/posts/row/@Title"/>
    <field column="body"  xpath="/posts/row/@Body"
                                   stripHTML="true"/>
    <field column="tags"  xpath="/posts/row/@Tags"/>
```

The data import handler will use the `XPathEntity` processor to break the training data into individual Lucene documents for each occurrence of the <row> tag within the enclosing <posts> tag. The various attributes within the row tag will be used to populate the ID, title, body, and tags fields in the index. The contents of the body attribute will have HTML code stripped.

The `StackOverflowTagTransformer` is a simple custom transformer that explicitly searches for the `tags` attribute and processes any content found there in the manner just described. This produces separate instances of the tag field for each document in the solr index. The following listing shows the class in its entirety.

**Listing 7.19  Transforming data in Solr's data import handler instances**

```
public class StackOverflowTagTransformer {
  public Object transformRow(Map<String,Object> row) {
    List<String> tags = (List<String>) row.get("tags");
    if (tags != null) {
      Collection<String> outputTags =
```

```
                StackOverflowStream.parseTags(tags);
    row.put("tags", outputTags);
  }
  return row;
  }
}
```

The data import handler passes one row of data at a time to the `transformRow` method, and the transformer is free to modify the columns of this row in many ways. In this case the row's columns are replaced with a new collection of tags parsed from the original format. You know that you can treat the value of the `row.get("tags")` call as a `List` because the `tags` field is defined as multivalued within the Solr schema for this instance.

As you'll notice if you inspect the entire dih-stackoverflow-config.xml file, the data import handler configuration also adds a number of other fields from the Stack Overflow data.

Now that you have a feel for how the indexing process works, you can get it started by running the Solr instance and loading the documents into it. Start the Solr server by running the following:

```
$TT_HOME/bin/start-solr.sh solr-tagging
```

Solr will start and emit a large amount of logging information to your terminal as it loads each of its components and configuration items. It should finish start up within a couple seconds, when you see the following message:

```
Started SocketConnector@0.0.0.0:8983
```

Keep this terminal containing the Solr log data open; you may need to refer to it later in order to troubleshoot issues with loading the data.

Now that you've successfully started Solr, you need to edit the data import handler configuration to reference the file you'll be using for training data. Edit the file $TT_HOME/apache-solr/solr-tagging/conf/dih-stackoverflow.properties and change the URL value from /path/to/stackoverflow-training-posts.xml to the full path to the training data on your system. Although the property is named `url`, it's fine to provide it a regular path. After you've modified that setting, save dih-stackoverflow.properties and exit your editor.

Visit the page at http://localhost:8983/solr/admin/dataimport.jsp, click the link to DIH-STACKOVERFLOW, and you'll be greeted by the Solr data import handler development console screen. You've edited the data import handler configuration since you started Solr, so you'll need to click the Reload-config button at the bottom edge of the left-side frame in your web browser to reload the changed configuration.

When the configuration has been reloaded successfully, you're ready to load the training data. Click on the Full-import button near the Reload-config button and Solr will start chugging away while it loads the training data. You can click the Status button to display the current status on the right-side frame of your browser in XML format. In a few minutes you'll see the following as the status response:

```
Indexing completed. Added/Updated: 100000 documents. Deleted 0 documents
```

You'll also see the following message in the Solr log's output in the terminal where you issued the start command:

```
Mar 11, 2011 8:52:39 PM org.apache.solr.update.processor.LogUpdateProcessor
INFO: {add=[4, 6, 8, 9, 11, 13, 14, 16, ... (100000 adds)],optimize=} 05
```

Now you've completed the training phase, and the Solr instance is ready to produce tag recommendations.

### 7.6.4   Creating tag recommendations

The `solr-tagging` instance has been configured to use Solr's `MoreLikeThisHandler` to respond to queries. As with the `MoreLikeThis` categorizer presented earlier, this query handler will take a document as input and use the index to identify the terms in the query most useful for retrieving matching documents. The next listing shows how the `MoreLikeThisHandler` is configured in solrconfig.xml.

**Listing 7.20   Configuring the `MoreLikeThisHandler` in solrconfig.xml**

```
<requestHandler name="/mlt" class="solr.MoreLikeThisHandler">
  <lst name="defaults">
    <str name="mlt.fl">title,body</str>
    <int name="mlt.mindf">3</int>
  </lst>
</requestHandler>
```

The approach we'll use to recommend tags is similar to the k-NN classification algorithm described in section 7.3.6. Instead of counting the categories assigned to the documents returned by a `MoreLikeThisQuery`, we count tags, which are then used to provide recommendations. The `TagRecommenderClient` takes care of delivering the input document to Solr and postprocessing the results in order to aggregate, score, and rank the tags. The next listing describes this process at a high level.

**Listing 7.21   Using the `TagRecommenderClient` to generate tag recommendations**

```
public TagRecommenderClient(String solrUrl)
      throws MalformedURLException {
  server = new HttpSolrServer(solrUrl);                    ←─❶ Solr client.
}

public ScoreTag[] getTags(String content, int maxTags)
    throws SolrServerException {
  ModifiableSolrParams  query  = new ModifiableSolrParams();  ←─┐ Query
  query.set("fq", "postTypeId:1")                             ❷ │ parameters.
    .set("start", 0)
    .set("rows", 10)
    .set("fl", "*,score")
    .set("mlt.interestingTerms", "details");          ❸ Create and
                                                         execute
  MoreLikeThisRequest request                         ←─┘ request.
```

```
   = new MoreLikeThisRequest(query, content);
QueryResponse response = request.process(server);

SolrDocumentList documents = response.getResults();
ScoreTag[] rankedTags = rankTags(documents, maxTags);
return rankedTags;
}
```

❹ Collect
and rank
tags.

First you must set up your connection to Solr. At ❶ you create an instance of Http-SolrServer which, despite its name, is a Solr client that uses an HTTP client library to send requests to your Solr server. The URL of the Solr server is provided as a parameter.

After you've created the client, you need to build the query you'll use to retrieve the documents that match your query. You'll use the tags on these retrieved documents to build tag recommendations. In the Stack Overflow data, only questions have tags, so when you set up your query parameters in ❷ you use a filter query to limit the results that are questions having a postTypeId of 1. You'll also notice that the query requests the top 10 matching documents; you should experiment with different numbers of results to determine what produces the best recommendations for your data.

When you create the request that will be sent to the Solr server at ❸, you use a custom MoreLikeThisRequest instead of the standard Solr QueryRequest. The MoreLikeThisRequest will use HTTP POST to deliver the potentially long query document directly to the Solr /mlt query handler. The content parameter of this request is used to hold the content for which you want to recommend tags.

Now that you have the results, you need to extract and rank the tags found within to provide recommendations. At ❹ you collect the counts for each tag and rank the tags by score. The ScoreTag class is used to store each tag found in the results set along with the number of times it appeared and its score. We examine this further in the next listing.

**Listing 7.22 Collecting and ranking tags**

```
protected ScoreTag[] rankTags(SolrDocumentList documents,
                              int maxTags) {
  OpenObjectIntHashMap<String> counts =
        new OpenObjectIntHashMap<String>();

  int size = documents.size();                          ← ❶ Count tags.
  for (int i=0; i < size; i++) {
    Collection<Object> tags = documents.get(i).getFieldValues("tags");
    for (Object o: tags) {
      counts.adjustOrPutValue(o.toString(), 1, 1);
    }
  }
  maxTags = maxTags > counts.size() ? counts.size() : maxTags;
  final ScoreTagQueue pq = new ScoreTagQueue(maxTags);    ← ❷ Rank tags.
  counts.forEachPair(new ObjectIntProcedure<String> () {
    @Override
    public boolean apply(String first, int second) {
      pq.insertWithOverflow(new ScoreTag(first, second));
      return true;
```

```
    }
  });
  ScoreTag[] rankedTags = new ScoreTag[maxTags];                    ⟵ ③ Collect ranked tags.
  int index = maxTags;
  ScoreTag s;
  int m = 0;
  while (pq.size() > 0) {
    s = pq.pop();
    rankedTags[--index] = s;
    m += s.count;
  }
  for (ScoreTag t: rankedTags) {                                    ⟵ ④ Score tags.
    t.setScore(t.getCount() / (double) m);
  }
  return rankedTags;
}
```

You begin the ranking and scoring process by first counting tags. At ① you scan through the documents in the result set, extract tags from the tags field, and collect a count for each tag.

When you have counts for all of the tags, you rank tags by count. At ② you collect the set of tags in a priority queue that will hold the most frequent tags. You extract the results from the priority queue at ③ and calculate the tags' scores in ④. Each tag's score is based upon the number of times it appeared in the result set divided by the total number of tags that appeared in the result set after cutoff. This way, the score ranges between 0 and 1, with a score closer to 1 indicating that the tag in question was particularly important in the result set. A set of tags where the top-ranked tag scores are higher indicates a smaller set of tags was returned, whereas lower scores mean that a variety of tags were returned for the result set. This could be used as a measure of certainty. Through experimentation it's possible to arrive at a cutoff score below which tags are unsuitable for recommendation.

### 7.6.5    *Evaluating the tag recommender*

Evaluating the output of the tag recommender is not substantially different from what you've done previously to evaluate categorizer output. You'll use a portion of the Stack Overflow data that you didn't train on as your test set, obtain tag recommendations for each of the questions in this set, and compare them with the tags assigned to them. The significant difference here is that each training document is accompanied with multiple tags, and the result of each query recommends multiple tags. As a result, the tests you perform here will collect two scores: the first is a measure of the number of test documents tagged where at least a single tag was correct. The percentage of documents you hit where at least one tag is correct will allow you to determine if the classifier is performing correctly. The second metric will be based on the number of cases where 50% of the tags recommended are correct. For example, if a test document is assigned four tags and the recommender produces a set of tags that contains at least two of those tags, the document is judged as being correct. This gives you an idea of how accuracy drops as the match requirements become more strict.

In addition to these metrics, you'll be collecting percentage correct metrics for a subset of the tags you encounter in your training and test data. You'll identify top most frequent tags in your test set and generate independent accurate metrics for these.

Let's dive right into how this is done by looking at the code. First you need to be concerned with extracting the Stack Overflow data from the XML files it's stored in. For this you use the StackOverflowStream class. This uses the StAX API to parse the XML documents and produce StackOverflowPost objects containing the fields for each post, including those that you're interested in: the title, body, and tags. Much of the code for StackOverflowStream is boilerplate related to parsing XML and iterating over a number of posts, so we won't reproduce that here as it's available in full in the sample code accompanying this chapter.

In order to collect metrics for individual tags, you must extract a set of tags for which to collect data from the Stack Overflow data. The following command will extract the 25 most frequent tags in the test data, with a cutoff for tags that appear in less than 10 posts:

```
$TT_HOME/bin/tt countStackOverflow \
  --inputFile stackoverflow-test-posts.xml \
  --outputFile stackoverflow-test-posts-counts.txt \
  --limit 25 --cutoff 10
```

The result will be a text file containing three columns: rank, count, and tag. The following excerpt shows a portion of this output where *c#* is shown to be the most popular tag, appearing in 1480 posts, followed by *.net* in 858, *asp.net* in 715, and *java* in 676:

```
1      1480     c#
2      858      .net
3      715      asp.net
4      676      java
```

Now that you have your category counts, you can feed them into your testing process. The following command is used to execute the test class TestStackOverflow. This class will read the text data and extract the necessary fields from the Stack Overflow XML format, use the TagRecommenderClient to request a set of tags from the Solr server, and then compare the tags assigned to the test data with the recommended tags. As it runs, it collects metrics that describe how the recommender is performing:

```
$TT_HOME/bin/tt testStackOverflow \
  --inputFile stackoverflow-test-posts.xml \
  --countFile stackoverflow-test-posts-counts.txt \
  --outputFile stackoverflow-test-output.txt \
  --solrUrl http://localhost:8983/solr
```

While testStackOverflow is running, it'll write metrics every 100 posts it processes. These will let you know how well the recommender is tagging test posts while the evaluation is running. The following excerpt shows how well the recommender is doing after tagging 300 and 400 test documents:

```
evaluated 300 posts; 234 with one correct tag, 151 with half correct
    %single correct: 78, %half correct: 50.33
```

```
evaluated 400 posts; 311 with one correct tag, 204 with half correct
   %single correct: 77.75, %half correct: 51
```

Here, between 77 and 78 percent of all documents tagged had a single tag correct, and roughly 50% of the documents had half or more tags correct. You'll notice as more documents are tagged, these percentages tend to stabilize. This suggests that although there's more than enough test data available in the Stack Overflow dataset, testing with 10,000 documents might be overkill. In this case it probably makes more sense to test with fewer documents.

When `testStackOverflow` completes, it'll also dump metrics for individual tags to the specified output file. This file includes the final percent-single and percent-half correct measures along with correctness measures for each tag found in the counts file:

```
evaluated 10000 posts; 8033 with one correct tag, 5316 with half correct
        %single correct: 80.33, %half correct: 53.16

-- tag  total    correct pct-correct --
networking       48      12       25
nhibernate       70      48       68
visual-studio   152      84       55
deployment       48      19       39
```

For each individual tag, you count the number of test documents it appears in, and then the number of cases where it was recommended for that particular document. From this you derive a percentage correct that indicates how well the recommender is doing for any particular tag. In this case, it doesn't do well for *networking* but does reasonably well for *nhibernate*. As you tweak the data used to train the recommender, you can track how these values change for individual tags.

There's also no reason to stick to the top X tags. If you're interested in how the recommender is performing on other tags, modify the counts file by hand to include them. As long as the tags are present in the test set, you'll see metrics for them in the output file.

## 7.7  *Summary*

In this chapter we explored some ways classification algorithms are used to automatically categorize and tag text documents. Along the way we discussed the process of creating automated classifiers: preparing input, training the classifier in order to produce a model for classifying documents, testing the classifier in order to evaluate the quality of the results it produces, and ways classifiers are deployed in a production system. We identified the importance of selecting an appropriate categorization scheme and choosing the right features for training a classification algorithm, and explored techniques for obtaining test data, including using publicly available resources, bootstrapping a training set using an existing set of categories, or adapting human judgments to create a training set. We explored a few different evaluation metrics and discussed the uses for accuracy, precision, recall, and confusion matrices to present slightly different views of the performance of a classification algorithm. We explored different ways the inputs or parameters that control the algorithm are modified to improve the results of the classifier, and demonstrated how each of our classifiers are integrated into Solr in order to provide categorization capabilities in a production environment.

This chapter has also introduced a number of basic concepts in classification and text categorization so that you should now be able to begin your own explorations into other algorithms. As you investigate the research and software available, you'll find that there are numerous approaches to solving text categorization problems. Now that we've discussed some of the basic algorithms, k-nearest neighbor, naive Bayes, and maximum entropy, you have a foundation of knowledge that will allow you to explore the ways text is tamed using classification, categorization, and tagging. Numerous other choices are available to you as a developer or researcher. Each algorithm has different characteristics that may make it suitable for your application's requirements. Here are a couple more that you should consider exploring as a follow-on to those demonstrated in this chapter.

The Mahout project also includes a logistic regression algorithm implemented using stochastic gradient descent as a learning technique. Generally, this is similar to the existing logistic regression classifier from OpenNLP, but Mahout's implementation is interesting in the numerous ways in which features may be interpreted, providing mechanisms for incorporating number-like, word-like, and text-like features into a single model. Ted Dunning has led the implementation of this classifier in Mahout and has written extensively about it in *Mahout in Action* (2011), also published by Manning.

Support vector machines (SVMs) have also been used extensively for text classification. A significant amount of research is available covering various approaches to modeling text using SVMs, and a number of open source implementations are used to implement working SVM-based text classification systems. These include the SVM-LIGHT (http://svmlight.joachims.org) by Thorsten Joachims and LIBSVM (http://www.csie.ntu.edu.tw/~cjlin/libsvm) by Chih-Chung Chang and Chih-Jen Lin. Through each of these libraries, text classification is implemented using a variety of languages.

There are countless other variations and combinations of these and other techniques to explore further. We'll discuss some of these alternatives later in this book in chapter 9, "Untamed text."

## 7.8   References

Lewis, David; Yang, Yiming; Rose, Tony; Li, Fan. 2004. "RCV1: A New Benchmark Collection for Text Categorization Research." *Journal of Machine Learning Research*, 5:361-397. http://www.jmlr.org/papers/volume5/lewis04a/lewis04a.pdf.

Owen, Sean; Anil, Robin; Dunning, Ted; Friedman, Ellen. 2010. *Mahout in Action*. Manning Publications.

Rennie, Jason; Shih, Lawrence; Teevan, Jaime; Karger, David. 2003. "Tackling the Poor Assumptions of Naive Bayes Text Classifiers." http://www.stanford.edu/class/cs276/handouts/rennie.icml03.pdf.

# Building an example
# question answering system

**In this chapter**

- Applying techniques for automatically tagging documents
- Enabling document and subdocument tags to be leveraged in search
- Reranking documents returned by Solr based on additional criteria
- Generating possible answers to users' questions

In the previous chapters, we've looked at different technologies and approaches independently. Though we've still managed to build useful applications focusing on one or two technologies, often you need to combine several of the tools we've described so far to get the job done. For instance, search and tagging (classification) with faceting are a natural fit, as are clustering and search, when it comes to helping users find and discover new and relevant content for their information needs. For the purposes of this chapter, you'll build a question answering (QA) system capable of answering fact-based questions from users (written in English) using search, named-entity recognition, and string matching, among other techniques.

Though most of the other chapters stand on their own, in this chapter, we assume you've read the previous chapters and so we don't explain the basics of Solr and other systems again here.

Before we move ahead and build a question answering system, let's look back at what we've covered previously. You'll see how all of these items provide the conceptual underpinning for this chapter. In chapter 1, we discussed the importance of text to different applications, and covered some of the basic terminology around search and natural language processing, as well as some of the challenges you face in building such systems. Much of this foundation is used both implicitly and explicitly in this chapter, even if we don't call it out.

In chapter 2, we focused on the foundations of text processing, including things like parts of speech, parsing, and grammar, perhaps reminding you of your high school days. We also took time to look at how to get content out of its raw format and into the format needed by leveraging Apache Tika. Though we don't explicitly use Tika for this example, we'll be doing preprocessing on the content to get it in shape for our task. We'll also make extensive use of tools for tokenizing, parsing, and part of speech tagging content in order to leverage it to answer questions.

Chapter 3 introduced search and Apache Solr as a powerful search platform with which you can quickly and easily index text and retrieve it via a query. We'll again leverage Solr here as the foundation for the question answering system along with some of the more advanced capabilities of Apache Lucene.

Chapter 4 dealt with fuzzy string matching, which is useful in many of the day-to-day operations of text processing. This chapter uses what you learned there to perform automatic spelling correction, as well as other techniques for fuzzy string matching such as *n*-grams. Some of these string techniques are used at the low level of Lucene, and we could easily hook a spell-checking component into our system, although we choose not to.

In chapter 5, we used OpenNLP to identify and categorize proper names in text. Here, we'll use OpenNLP again to perform this task as well as to identify phrases. This is useful both in analyzing the query and in processing the underlying content we use for the lookup of answers.

In chapter 6, we delved into the world of clustering and showed how we could automatically group together similar documents using unsupervised techniques. Though we won't demonstrate it in this chapter, clustering techniques can be used both to narrow the search space when looking for answers and to determine near-duplicates in the results themselves.

Finally, chapter 7 showed you how to classify text and use a classifier to automatically associate keyword or folksonomy tags with new text. We'll also use these techniques to assign incoming questions to a category in this chapter.

Now that you have a sense of where we've been, let's bring all of these things together to build a real application. Our goal in building a sample QA system is to demonstrate how many of the moving pieces that we've talked about up until now hook together to form a real working system. We'll build a simple QA application designed to answer factual questions utilizing Wikipedia as the knowledge base. To achieve our goal, we'll use Solr as a baseline system due not only to its search capabilities for passage retrieval, but also for its plugin architecture that allows for easy extension. From this baseline, you can plug in analysis capabilities during indexing as well as hook in search-side capabilities to parse users' natural language questions and to rank answers and return results. Let's begin by looking into QA and some of its applications a bit more.

## 8.1 Basics of a question answering system

As the name implies, a question answering (QA) system is designed to take in a natural language question—say, "Who is the President of the United States?"—and provide the answer. QA systems alleviate the need for end users to search through pages and pages of search results or click and browse their way through facets. For instance, IBM's Watson DeepQA system (http://www.ibm.com/innovation/us/watson/) used a sophisticated question answering system to play against humans on *Jeopardy!* (http://www.jeopardy.com). Did we mention it beat two of the greatest *Jeopardy!* players of all time? This system used a very large number of machines to process answers (remember, *Jeopardy!* requires the "answer" to be in the form of a question) based on a very large collection of world knowledge as well as ancillary systems for playing strategy (selecting clues, betting, and so on; see figure 8.1).

Note that an automated QA system shouldn't be confused with any of the popular crowd-sourced QA systems on the web today such as Yahoo! Answers or ChaCha, even if some of the technology that powers those systems (identifying similar questions, for instance) is also useful in building automated QA systems. In many ways, question answering is like a search application: you submit your query, usually consisting of a set of keywords, and look at the documents or pages that are returned for an answer. In question answering, you typically submit a full sentence as your query instead of just keywords. In return for your greater specificity, expect a piece of text considerably smaller than a document to be returned. In general, question answering is hard, but in particular applications or genres it can be effective. Many questions have complex answers and require a great deal of understanding to answer. As such, we're setting the bar for our question answering lower than full understanding, and instead will build a system that will perform better than a standard search for fact-based questions such as "Who is the President of the United States?"

**Figure 8.1  Screen grab of IBM's Watson Avatar as seen during the Jeopardy! IBM challenge**

**IBM's Watson: going beyond Jeopardy!**

IBM's Watson system was demonstrated on Jeopardy! as a means of bringing attention to the problem, but its deeper intent is obviously not to compete on Jeopardy! but to help people sift through information much more quickly and cost effectively. To quote the IBM website:[1]

> DeepQA technology provides humans with a powerful tool for their information gathering and decision support. A typical scenario is for the end user to enter their question in natural language form, much as if they were asking another person, and for the system to sift through vast amounts of potential evidence to return a ranked list of the most compelling, precise answers. These answers include summaries of their justifying or supporting evidence, allowing the user to quickly assess the evidence and select the correct answer.

Though the depth of the system is beyond what can be covered here, readers are encouraged to check out IBM's DeepQA project (see http://www.research.ibm.com/deepqa/deepqa.shtml) to find out more.

A full-fledged QA system might attempt to answer many different types of questions, ranging from fact-based to more esoteric. Keep in mind, also, that it's perfectly reasonable for a QA system to return multiple paragraphs and even multiple documents as the answer, even though most QA systems try to return answers that are much shorter. For example, a highly sophisticated system (which doesn't exist, as far as these authors are aware) might be able to answer questions that require deeper analysis and responses, such as "What are the pros and cons of the current college football bowl system?" or "What are the short- and long-term effects of binge drinking?"

Digging deeper, fact-based question answering can be thought of as a fuzzy matching problem at the level of words and phrases. As such, our approach here bears some resemblance to the strategy we took in performing record matching, with some additional twists that center around understanding what the type of the answer (referred to as the *answer type*) should be for a given question. For instance, if a user asks "Who is the President of the United States?" we expect the answer to be a person, whereas if the user asks "What year did the Carolina Hurricanes win the Stanley Cup?" the answer should be a year. Before we dig into how we built the system, let's spend a moment setting up the associated code so that you can follow along.

## 8.2 Installing and running the QA code

As we mentioned earlier, we'll use Solr as the base of our system, so installing and running the QA code means leveraging our existing Solr packaging much like we did in the clustering chapter. For this case, we'll use a different Solr setup. If you

---

[1] Retrieved April 12, 2011: http://www.research.ibm .com/deepqa/faq.shtml.

haven't already, follow the instructions in the README file on GitHub (https://github.com/tamingtext/book/blob/master/README). Next, run `./bin/start-solr.sh solr-qa` from the TT_HOME directory. If all goes well, you should be able to point your browser at http://localhost:8983/solr/answer and see a simple QA interface. With the system now running, let's load in some content so that you can answer some questions.

QA systems that are built on top of search engines (most are), as you might imagine, require content in the search engine to act as the source for discovering answers, since the system doesn't have some intrinsic knowledge of all questions and answers. This requirement brings with it the complication that a QA system can only be as good as the content that it uses as its source. For instance, if you fed the engine documents from Europe written in the era before Christopher Columbus (surely they are all digitized, right?) and asked the system "What shape is the Earth?" it likely would answer with the equivalent of *flat*. For our system, we'll use a dump of the English Wikipedia taken on October 11, 2010 (the first 100K docs are cached at http://maven.tamingtext.com/freebase-wex-2011-01-18-articles-first100k.tsv.gz; 411 MB zipped.) Note that this file is large, but this is necessary, as we wish to demonstrate with real data. After it's downloaded, unpack it using gunzip or a similar tool. If that file is too big or your want to try a smaller version first, you can download http://maven.tamingtext.com/freebase-wex-2011-01-18-articles-first10k.tsv, which consists of the first 10,000 articles of the larger file. This file isn't compressed, so there's no need to unpack it.

After you have the data, you can index it into your system by running the following steps:

- Type `cd $TT_HOME/bin`.
- Run `indexWikipedia.sh --wikiFile <PATH TO WIKI FILE>` (*NIX) or `indexWikipedia.cmd --wikiFile <PATH TO WIKI FILE>` (Windows). This will take some time to complete. Use the `--help` option to see all available indexing options.

After the index is built, you're ready to explore the QA system. You can start by pointing your browser at http://localhost:8983/solr/answer, where we've put together a simple QA user interface utilizing Solr's built-in `VelocityResponseWriter`, which takes Solr's output and applies an Apache Velocity (see http://velocity.apache.org) template to it. (Velocity is a templating engine mainly used for creating websites backed by Java applications.) If all went well with these steps, you should see something like the screenshot in figure 8.2.

Assuming this all worked correctly, we'll proceed to take a look at the architecture and code to build the system.

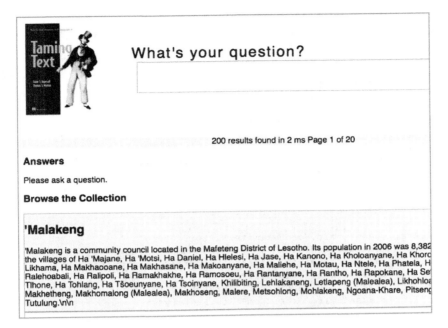

**Figure 8.2   A screenshot from the Taming Text fact-based QA system**

## 8.3    *A sample question answering architecture*

Much like our earlier work in search, our QA system needs to handle indexing content as well as searching and postprocessing the results. On the indexing side, most of our customization centers around the analysis process. We've created two Solr analysis plug-ins: one for detecting sentences and one for identifying named entities. Both rely on OpenNLP for the desired capabilities. Unlike most analysis processes in Solr, we elected to tokenize directly into sentences since it allows us to send those sentences directly into the named-entity token filter as well as avoid having to do extra tokenization, once in Solr and once in OpenNLP. Since both sentence detection and named-entity detection were described earlier, we'll point you at the classes here (Sentence-Tokenizer.java and NameFilter.java) and show the declaration for the text field type in schema.xml (located in the solr-qa/conf directory and edited here for space). Take note that we violated the usual rule of doing the same analysis during both indexing and searching, since we don't need to detect sentences on the query side because we assume a single input question. What matters most is that the output tokens are equivalent in their form (same stemming, for instance) when output and not how they arrived at that form. Here's the field type declaration:

```
<fieldType name="text" class="solr.TextField" positionIncrementGap="100"
        autoGeneratePhraseQueries="true">
  <analyzer type="index">
    <tokenizer
```

```
            class="com.tamingtext.texttamer.solr.SentenceTokenizerFactory"/>
        <filter class="com.tamingtext.texttamer.solr.NameFilterFactory"/>
        <filter class="solr.LowerCaseFilterFactory"/>
        <filter class="solr.StopFilterFactory"
                ignoreCase="true"
                words="stopwords.txt"
                enablePositionIncrements="true"
                />
        <filter class="solr.PorterStemFilterFactory"/>
    </analyzer>
    <analyzer type="query">
        <tokenizer class="solr.WhitespaceTokenizerFactory"/>
        <filter class="solr.StopFilterFactory"
                ignoreCase="true"
                words="stopwords.txt"
                enablePositionIncrements="true"
                />
        <filter class="solr.WordDelimiterFilterFactory"
                generateWordParts="1" generateNumberParts="1"
                catenateWords="0" catenateNumbers="0" catenateAll="0"
                splitOnCaseChange="1"/>
        <filter class="solr.LowerCaseFilterFactory"/>
        <filter class="solr.PorterStemFilterFactory"/>
    </analyzer>
</fieldType>
```

Though we'll skip over the details of the analysis process since it was covered in earlier chapters, it's important to note that the NameFilterFactory outputs both the original tokens and tokens indicating any named entities. These named-entity tokens occur at the exact same position as the original tokens. For instance, running the sentence "Clint Eastwood plays a cowboy in *The Good, the Bad and the Ugly.*" through Solr's analysis.jsp page (http://localhost:8983/solr/admin/analysis.jsp) produces a total of four tokens occupying the first two positions (two tokens at each position) of the resulting output, as shown in figure 8.3.

On the search side, there are more moving parts and we had to write more code, which we'll detail in the upcoming sections of this chapter. The crux of the system relies on two key capabilities:

- Parsing the user question to determine the expected answer type and generating an appropriate query
- Scoring the documents returned by the generated query

| com.tamingtext.texttamer.solr.NameFilterFactory {luceneM | | |
|---|---|---|
| position | 1 | 2 |
| term text | NE_person | NE_person |
| | Clint | Eastwood |
| keyword | true | true |
| | true | true |
| startOffset | 0 | 6 |
| | 0 | 6 |
| endOffset | 5 | 14 |
| | 5 | 14 |

**Figure 8.3    An example of how named-entity tokens overlap the original token positions for the sentence "Clint Eastwood plays a cowboy in The Good, the Bad and the Ugly."**

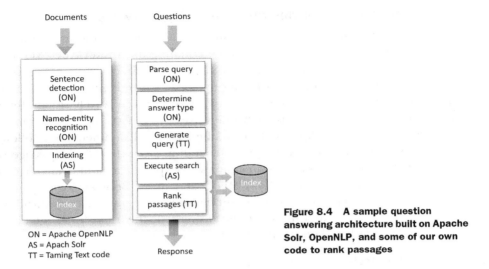

Figure 8.4 **A sample question answering architecture built on Apache Solr, OpenNLP, and some of our own code to rank passages**

Tying indexing and searching together, our architecture can be seen in figure 8.4.

As we stated earlier and as shown in figure 8.4, the indexing side is pretty straightforward. The query side has five steps, which will be covered in the sections following this one:

- Parse (chunk) the user's query.
- Determine the answer type so that when we search, we can find candidates that will best answer the question.
- Generate the Solr/Lucene query using a combination of the parsed query and the answer type.
- Execute the search to determine candidate passages that *might* contain the answer.
- Rank the answers and return the results.

To understand these five steps properly in context, we'll break this down into two sections: understanding the user's query and ranking the candidate passages. We built these two pieces using two of Solr's well-defined plugin mechanisms:

- A QParser *(and* QParserPlugin)—Processes the incoming user query and creates a Solr/Lucene query.
- A SearchComponent—Chains together with other SearchComponents to do the work of creating an appropriate response. See chapter 3 for background.

We'll examine the code more closely shortly, but for now it might be worthwhile to revisit the chapter on search and Solr (chapter 3) as well as the Solr documentation to see how these two pieces work in Solr. Assuming you're familiar with the relevant mechanisms, let's take a look at how we understand the user's question.

## 8.4    Understanding questions and producing answers

We're concerned with three components of understanding the user's question and producing results. They center around determining the answer type (AT), using that AT to generate a meaningful search engine query, and finally, ranking the results from the query. Of these three, determining the answer type is the crux of the problem, after which query generation and passage ranking are relatively straightforward. In our case, determining the answer type involves three parts: training, chunking, and the actual AT determination. All three of these parts are outlined in the following sections as well as our approach to query generation given the AT and passage ranking. Also note that, in our case, we assume the user is typing in a natural language question such as "Who was the Super Bowl MVP?" and not a Boolean logic query like we described in chapter 3. This is important because we've trained a classification system to determine, given a user question, the answer type the user is interested in and our training data was based on natural language questions.

### 8.4.1    Training the answer type classifier

For this system, the training data (located in the dist/data directory of the source) consists of 1,888 questions, each hand-labeled by Tom Morton as part of his PhD thesis (see Morton [2005]). The training questions look like this:

- P Which French monarch reinstated the divine right of the monarchy to France and was known as "The Sun King" because of the splendour of his reign?
- X Which competition was won by Eimear Quinn with "The Voice in 1996," this being the fourth win in five years for her country?

In the training questions, the first character is the answer type of the question, and the remaining text is the question. Our training data supports many different answer types, but our system currently only handles four for simplicity's sake (location, time, person, organization). The supported answer types, along with examples, are outlined in table 8.1.

**Table 8.1    Training data answer types**

| Answer type (training code) | Example |
| --- | --- |
| Person (P) | Which Ivy League basketball player scored the most points in a single game during the 1990s? |
| Location (L) | Which city generates the highest levels of sulphur dioxide in the world? |
| Organization (O) | Which ski resort was named the best in North America by readers of *Conde Nast Traveler* magazine? |
| Time point (T) | What year did the Pilgrims have their first Thanksgiving feast? |
| Duration (R) | How long did *Gunsmoke* run on network TV? |
| Money (M) | How much are Salvadoran workers paid for each $198 Liz Claiborne jacket they sew? |

**Table 8.1   Training data answer types** *(continued)*

| Answer type (training code) | Example |
|---|---|
| Percentage (C) | What percentage of newspapers in the U.S. say they are making a profit from their online site? |
| Amount (A) | What is the lowest temperature ever recorded in November in New Brunswick? |
| Distance (D) | What is the approximate maximum distance at which a clap of thunder can be heard? |
| Description (F) | What is dry ice? |
| Title (W) | In which fourteenth-century alliterative poem by William Langford do a series of allegorical visions appear to the narrator in his dreams? |
| Definition (B) | What does the postage stamp cancellation O.H.M.S. mean? |
| Other (X) | How did the banana split originate? |

To train the answer type classifier, we leverage the main method of the `AnswerType-Classifier` class, like this:

```
java -cp -Dmodels.dir=<Path to OpenNLP Models Dir>
        -Dwordnet.dir=<Path to WordNet 3.0> \
        <CLASSPATH> com.tamingtext.qa.AnswerTypeClassifier \
        <Path to questions-train.txt> <Output path>
```

We'll skip the testing phase that's normally associated with building a classifier model since Tom tested it as part of his thesis. If you're interested in the testing phase, refer back to chapters 5 and 7 on classification.

The code for the training process is fairly simple, relying on OpenNLP to chunk (shallow parse) and part of speech tag the training set, and then to feed into OpenNLP's MaxEnt classifier. The key pieces of code are in listing 8.1. Training the answer type model is similar to the training we did in early chapters on OpenNLP (named-entity recognition and tagging).

**Listing 8.1   Training the question model**

```
AnswerTypeEventStream es = new AnswerTypeEventStream(trainFile,
        actg, parser);
GISModel model = GIS.trainModel(100,
                        new TwoPassDataIndexer(es, 3));
new DoccatModel("en", model).serialize(
                        new FileOutputStream(outFile));
```

> Using the event stream, which feeds us training examples, do the training using OpenNLP's MaxEnt classifier.

After the model is trained, we need to write some code that can use this model. To do this, we wrote a Solr `QParser` (and the factory class `QParserPlugin`) named `Question-QParser` (and `QuestionQParserPlugin`). Before we go into what the code looks like, the configuration of the `QuestionQParser` looks like this:

```
<queryParser name="qa" class="com.tamingtext.qa.QuestionQParserPlugin"/>
```

As you can see, the primary thing Solr cares about for configuration isn't the QParser itself, but the QParserPlugin.

The primary thing the QuestionQParserPlugin needs to do is load the AT model and construct a QuestionQParser. As with any QParser and its associated factory, we want to try to do any expensive or one-time calculations in the initialization of the QParserPlugin and not in the QParser itself, since the latter will be constructed once for each request, whereas the former is only constructed once (per commit). In the case of the QuestionQParser, the initialization code is responsible for loading up the AT model as well as one other resource—WordNet. The code is straightforward initialization code and is shown next.

**Listing 8.2  Initialization code**

**Model directory contains all OpenNLP models that we use throughout the book.** →

**WordNet is a lexical resource used to assist in identifying answer types.** →

**Treebank chunker works with a Parser to do shallow parsing of questions.** →

**Create actual model and save it for reuse, because it's thread safe, but the containing class isn't.** →

**Create the AnswerTypeContextGenerator, which is responsible for feature selection.** →

```
public void init(NamedList initArgs) {
    SolrParams params = SolrParams.toSolrParams(initArgs);
    String modelDirectory = params.get("modelDirectory",
        System.getProperty("model.dir"));
    String wordnetDirectory = params.get("wordnetDirectory",
        System.getProperty("wordnet.dir"));
    if (modelDirectory != null) {
      File modelsDir = new File(modelDirectory);
      try {
        InputStream chunkerStream = new FileInputStream(
            new File(modelsDir,"en-chunker.bin"));
        ChunkerModel chunkerModel = new ChunkerModel(chunkerStream);
        chunker = new ChunkerME(chunkerModel);
        InputStream posStream = new FileInputStream(
            new File(modelsDir,"en-pos-maxent.bin"));
        POSModel posModel = new POSModel(posStream);
        tagger =  new POSTaggerME(posModel);
        model = new DoccatModel(new FileInputStream(
            new File(modelDirectory,"en-answer.bin")))
            .getChunkerModel();
        probs = new double[model.getNumOutcomes()];
        atcg = new AnswerTypeContextGenerator(
            new File(wordnetDirectory, "dict"));
      } catch (IOException e) {
        throw new RuntimeException(e);
      }
    }
  }
}
```

← **Tagger is responsible for part of speech tagging.**

WordNet (http://wordnet.princeton.edu/) is a lexical resource for English and other languages created by Princeton University containing information about words such as synonyms, antonyms, and hyper- and hyponyms, as well as other useful information about individual words. Its license allows for commercial use. You'll see its use later in helping us understand questions better.

Given the creation of these resources, the primary task of the factory is to create our QuestionQParser, which can be seen in the next listing.

**Listing 8.3   Creating the `QuestionQParser`**

Construct map of answer types that we're interested in handling, such as locations, people, and times and dates. ▷

Construct chunker (parser) that will be responsible for parsing user question. ▷

Create QuestionQParser by passing in user's question as well as the preinitialized resources from the init method. ▷

Use this if clause to create a regular Solr query parser when the user hasn't entered a question or entered the \*:\* query (MatchAllDocsQuery).

The AnswerTypeClassifier uses the trained answer type model (located in the models directory) to classify the question.

```
@Override
public QParser createParser(String qStr, SolrParams localParams,
                            SolrParams params,
                            SolrQueryRequest req) {
  answerTypeMap = new HashMap<String, String>();
  answerTypeMap.put("L", "NE_LOCATION");
  answerTypeMap.put("T", "NE_TIME|NE_DATE");
  answerTypeMap.put("P", "NE_PERSON");
  answerTypeMap.put("O", "NE_ORGANIZATION");
  QParser qParser;

  if (params.getBool(QAParams.COMPONENT_NAME, false) == true
              && qStr.equals("*:*") == false) {
    AnswerTypeClassifier atc =
            new AnswerTypeClassifier(model, probs, atcg);
    Parser parser = new ChunkParser(chunker, tagger);
    qParser = new QuestionQParser(qStr, localParams,
            params, req, parser, atc, answerTypeMap);

  } else {
    //just do a regular query if qa is turned off
    qParser = req.getCore().getQueryPlugin("edismax")
            .createParser(qStr, localParams, params, req);
  }
  return qParser;
}
```

The primary areas of interest in this code are the construction of the answer type map and the `QuestionQParser`. The answer type map contains a mapping from the internal code generated by the `AnswerTypeClassifier` (as described in table 8.1) and the type of named entity we tagged during indexing. For instance, *L* gets mapped to `NE_LOCATION`, which matches how we tagged location-named entities during the indexing process in the `NameFilter` class. We'll use this map to later construct an appropriate clause in our Solr query. The `QuestionQParser` is the class that actually parses the question and creates the Solr/Lucene query. On that note, let's peel back a layer and look at the `QuestionQParser` in more detail.

The `QuestionQParser` is responsible for three things, all of which are handled in the parse method of the class:

- Chunk the query into a `Parse` object
- Compute the answer type
- Create the Solr/Lucene query as a `SpanNearQuery` (more on this in a moment)

### 8.4.2   Chunking the query

*Chunking* is a light-weight form of parsing (sometimes called *deep parsing*) and is useful for saving some CPU cycles while focusing on key pieces of the sentence, such as verb and noun phrases, while ignoring other parts, which fits perfectly with what we're trying to accomplish. We don't need a deep parse, just enough to help us get at key parts of the question. The code in the QParser to do the parsing is rolled up into a single line, as can be seen here:

Parse question using
TreebankParser. The resulting
Parse object can then be
utilized by the classifier to
determine answer type.

```
Parse parse = ParserTool.parseLine(qstr, parser, 1)[0];
```

Note that in this parsing example, we pass in a Parser reference. This parser reference is an instance of ChunkParser, which we wrote to implement OpenNLP's Parser interface. The ChunkParser creates a shallow parse of the submitted question by using OpenNLP's TreebankChunker, which, as the name somewhat implies, uses the Penn Treebank resources (see chapter 2) from the 2000 Conference on Computational Natural Language Learning (see http://www.cnts.ua.ac.be/conll2000/chunking/) chunking task and a ParserTagger to create a Parse object. The ParserTagger is responsible for tagging the words of the question with part of speech (POS) tags. This class is a prerequisite of the chunker since the chunker model was trained using part of speech information. In other words, part of speech tags are a necessary feature for chunking in this case. Intuitively, this should seem reasonable: it should be easier to identify noun phrases if we first identify all the nouns in a sentence. In the example code, we seed the POS tagger with an existing model named tag.bin.gz, which is available from the OpenNLP models. Similarly, the TreebankChunker instance uses the EnglishChunk.bin.gz model that's included in the downloaded models to take the output of the POS tagger and produce the parse. Though this is a lot of work (all rolled up into a single method), it provides us the ability to figure out what kind of answer the user is after in their question, which we'll look at next.

### 8.4.3  Computing the answer type

The next step is to identify the answer type and then to look up the mapping from the internal, abbreviated answer type code and the label we used when indexing named entities. The code for this is shown next.

**Listing 8.4  Identifying the answer type**

```
String type = atc.computeAnswerType(parse);
String mt = atm.get(type);
```

Obviously, a significant amount of work is happening in the AnswerTypeClassifier and its delegated classes, so let's take a look at that class before we move on to the generation of the Solr/Lucene query.

As the name implies, the AnswerTypeClassifier is a classifier that takes in questions and outputs an answer type. In many ways, it's the crux of our QA system, since without the correct AT, it'll be difficult to find passages that not only mention the required keywords, but also contain the expected kind of answer. For example, if the user asks "Who won the 2006 Stanley Cup?" an appropriate AT indicates that the answer would be people or an organization. Then, if the system encounters a passage containing the words *won*, *2006*, and *Stanley Cup*, it can rank that passage to determine whether a matching word or phrase of the appropriate answer type is in the passage. For instance, the system might encounter the sentence "The 2006 Stanley Cup finals went to 7 games." In this case, no people (or organizations) are mentioned, so the system can discard the candidate because it lacks the answer type.

Upon construction, the AnswerTypeClassifier loads up the answer type model that we trained earlier in the chapter and also constructs an AnswerTypeContext-Generator instance. The AnswerTypeContextGenerator relies on WordNet and some heuristics to determine the features to return to the AnswerTypeClassifier for classification. The AnswerTypeClassifier code that calls the AnswerTypeContext-Generator is in the computeAnswerType and computeAnswerTypeProbs methods and looks like the next listing.

**Listing 8.5   Computing the answer type**

**Given the probabilities generated, ask the model for the best outcome. This is a simple calculation that finds the maximum probability in the array.**

```
public String computeAnswerType(Parse question) {
    double[] probs = computeAnswerTypeProbs(question);      ◁ 
    return model.getBestOutcome(probs);
}


public double[] computeAnswerTypeProbs(Parse question) {
    String[] context = atcg.getContext(question);      ◁ 
    return model.eval(context, probs);      ◁ 
}
```

**Get probabilities of an answer type by calling computeAnswerTypeProbs.**

**Ask AnswerTypeContextGenerator for the list of features (the context) that should be predictive of the answer type.**

**Evaluate the generated features to determine the probabilities for the possible answer types.**

The key to this code is the two lines of the computeAnswerTypeProbs method. The first line asks the AnswerTypeContextGenerator class to select a set of features from the parse of the question, and the second line then hands those features to the model for evaluation. The model returns an array of the probabilities for each possible outcome, from which we select the top value and return it as the answer type.

As you may have noticed in earlier chapters, feature selection is often a difficult problem as well, so it's worthwhile to examine more closely the work the AnswerType-ContextGenerator class is doing. Feature selection in the AnswerTypeContext-Generator is handled via the getContext() method. This method implements a few simple rules aimed at choosing good features based on the type of question that's being asked. Most of these rules are premised on finding the key verb and noun phrase in the question, and can be summarized as follows:

- If a question word is present (who, what, when, where, why, how, whom, which, name)
  - Include the question word and label it as *qw* (qw=who).
  - Include the verb to the right of the question word, label it as verb, and also concatenate it with question word and label that as *qw_verb* (verb=entered, qw_verb=who_entered).

- Include all words to the right of the verb and label them with *rw* (rw= monarchy).
- If a focus noun is present (the key noun of the question)
  - Add the head word of the noun phrase and label with *hw* (hw=author) and its part of speech with label ht (ht=NN).
  - Include any words that modify the noun, labeled as *mw* (mw=European), and their part of speech with label *mt* (mt=JJ).
  - Include any WordNet synsets (a synset is a grouping of synonyms for a word) of the noun, labeled as *s* (s=7347, the synset ID).
  - Indicate whether the focus noun is the last noun of the phrase and label it as *fnIsLast* (fnIsLast=true).
- Include the default feature, called def. The default feature is an empty label that's included for normalization purposes. Every question will have it regardless of the other features selected, and thus provides a baseline feature for the system to learn on.

Before we discuss some of the key components of this list, let's look at the features selected for the question "Which European patron saint was once a ruler of Bohemia and has given his name to a Square in Prague?" Its features look like the following:

```
def, rw=once, rw=a, rw=ruler, rw=of, rw=Bohemia, rw=and,
rw=has, rw=given, rw=his, rw=name, rw=to, rw=a, rw=Square, rw=in,
rw=Prague?, qw=which, mw=Which, mt=WDT, mw=European, mt=JJ, mw=patron,
mt=NN, hw=saint, ht=NN, s=1740, s=23271, s=5809192, s=9505418,
s=5941423, s=9504135, s=23100, s=2137
```

You can see this example and many others in action by running the demonstrateATCG test in AnswerTypeTest, whose code can be seen in the following example:

```
AnswerTypeContextGenerator atcg =
        new AnswerTypeContextGenerator(
                new File(getWordNetDictionary().getAbsolutePath()));
InputStream is = Thread.currentThread().getContextClassLoader()
        .getResourceAsStream("atcg-questions.txt");
assertNotNull("input stream", is);
BufferedReader reader =
                    new BufferedReader(new InputStreamReader(is));
String line = null;
while ((line = reader.readLine()) != null){
  System.out.println("Question: " + line);
  Parse[] results = ParserTool.parseLine(line, parser, 1);
  String[] context = atcg.getContext(results[0]);
  List<String> features = Arrays.asList(context);
  System.out.println("Features: " + features);
}
```

Going back to the feature selection, most features are selected by a few simple rules or regular expressions, as can be seen in the code of the AnswerTypeContextGenerator class. The question of finding a focal noun (or the head noun) stands out from the other rules, due to it having a number of features that it adds, and also because we do a fair amount of work to identify it. The focal noun depends on the type of question word (who, what, which, and so on) and is important in defining what we're looking for. For example, in our question about the ruler of Bohemia, our focal noun is *saint,* meaning we're looking for a person who's a saint. We can then use this noun, along with WordNet, to get synonyms for saint that might be helpful in identifying other questions that might ask the same or similar questions in different ways. In our travels through the question, we also apply certain rules for eliminating false matches for the focal noun. These are again based on simple rules and regular expressions. In the code, most of this work is done in the `AnswerTypeContextGenerator`'s `findFocus-NounPhrase` method, which won't be included here due to length.

Finally, keep in mind that this feature selection process is based on Tom's analysis of the questions as to the important things to consider when building a model. This doesn't mean it's the only way. Moreover, given more training data, it may be possible to have the system learn the model without any of this feature selection process. In some regards, this human-in-the-loop feature selection is a trade-off between time spent collecting and annotating examples and time spent doing up-front analysis of the existing queries for patterns. Which works best for your system will depend on how much data and time you have available.

### 8.4.4   Generating the query

After we've determined the answer type, we need to generate a query that will retrieve candidate passages from our search index. The candidate passages we retrieve need to have several things in order to be useful for QA:

- One or more words that are of the appropriate answer type must occur within the passage window.
- One or more of the key terms from the original query must occur within the passage window.

In order for us to construct a query that will retrieve candidate passages that meet these requirements, we need to know exactly where in a given document matches take place. In Solr (and Lucene), the mechanism to do this is via `SpanQuery` and its derivative classes. Specifically, `SpanQuery` classes match documents similar to other queries in Lucene, but they also, at the cost of extra compute time, can access position information, which we can then iterate over to produce a more focused passage for ranking than a larger document. Finally, we specifically need to construct a `SpanNearQuery` class for finding passages, because we want to find the specified terms and answer type together. A `SpanNearQuery` can create complex phrase-based queries that are composed of other `SpanQuery` instances. The code for creating our query is shown in the next listing.

**Listing 8.6   Query generation**

```
List<SpanQuery> sql = new ArrayList<SpanQuery>();
if (mt != null) {
  String[] parts = mt.split("\|");
  if (parts.length == 1) {
    sql.add(new SpanTermQuery(new Term(field, mt.toLowerCase())));
  } else {
    for (int pi = 0; pi < parts.length; pi++) {
      sql.add(new SpanTermQuery(new Term(field, parts[pi])));
    }
  }
}
try {
  Analyzer analyzer = sp.getType().getQueryAnalyzer();
  TokenStream ts = analyzer.tokenStream(field,
          new StringReader(qstr));
  while (ts.incrementToken()) {
    String term = ((CharTermAttribute)
            ts.getAttribute(CharTermAttribute.class)).toString();
    sql.add(new SpanTermQuery(new Term(field, term)));
  }
} catch (IOException e) {
  throw new ParseException(e.getLocalizedMessage());
}
return new SpanNearQuery(sql.toArray(new SpanQuery[sql.size()]),
                    params.getInt(QAParams.SLOP, 10), true);
```

In the code for generating the query, we undertake three steps:

- Add the answer type(s) to the query using one or more `SpanTermQuery` instances. If more than one answer type is used, we bind them together using a `SpanOrQuery`.
- Analyze the user query with the query analyzer for the given field to create `SpanTermQuery` instances for each term.
- Construct a `SpanNearQuery` that glues all of the terms together using a slop factor passed in by the user (or default to 10).

This approach isn't the only way we could construct the query. For instance, we could try to produce more selective queries by doing deeper analysis on the query to identify phrases or part of speech tagging to match only those terms that have the same part of speech in the passage. Regardless of the query approach, we hand off the query to Solr and get back a list of documents that we can then rank using our `Passage-RankingComponent`, which we'll cover in the next section.

### 8.4.5   *Ranking candidate passages*

Compared to the query parsing and feature selection process, ranking the passages is much more straightforward in our case—we're using a straightforward ranking process that was first outlined (Singhal 1999) at the TREC-8 conference on question answering. Though this approach has been passed by in other systems, it's still a

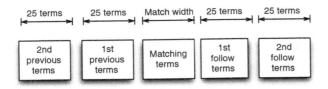

**Figure 8.5  The passage scoring component constructs a series of windows around the matching terms from the query and then ranks the passage.**

reasonable approach that's easy to implement and relatively effective for a fact-based system. In a nutshell, the approach looks for the matching terms in a series of windows around the location where the query matched; hence our use of the SpanQuery and its derivatives. Specifically, the approach identifies the start and end positions of the query term matches and then constructs two windows of a given number of terms (25 by default in our code, but can be overridden using Solr's request parameters) on each side of the match window. This can be seen in figure 8.5.

To build the passages efficiently, we utilize Lucene's term vector storage. Simply put, a *term vector* in Lucene is a data structure that keeps track, per document, of the terms and their frequency and positions within the document. Unlike the inverted index used for searching, it's a document-centric data structure instead of a term-centric structure. All this means is that it's good for doing operations that require a whole document (such as highlighting or passage analysis) and not good for operations that require quick term-by-term lookup (such as searching). Given the passage, which we codify in a class named Passage, we can then begin the scoring process, which is shown next.

**Listing 8.7   Code for scoring a candidate passage**

```
protected float scorePassage(Passage p,
                             Map<String, Float> termWeights,
                             Map<String, Float> bigramWeights,
                             float adjWeight, float secondAdjWeight,
                             float biWeight) {
  Set<String> covered = new HashSet<String>();
  float termScore = scoreTerms(p.terms, termWeights, covered);
  float adjScore = scoreTerms(p.prevTerms, termWeights, covered) +
        scoreTerms(p.followTerms, termWeights, covered);
  float secondScore =
        scoreTerms(p.secPrevTerms, termWeights, covered)
      + scoreTerms(p.secFollowTerms, termWeights, covered);
  //Give a bonus for bigram matches in the main window, could also
  float bigramScore =
              scoreBigrams(p.bigrams, bigramWeights, covered);
  float score = termScore + (adjWeight * adjScore) +
        (secondAdjWeight * secondScore)
      + (biWeight * bigramScore);
  return (score);
}
```

**Score terms in main window.** → float termScore = scoreTerms(p.terms, termWeights, covered);

**Score terms in windows immediately to the left and right of main window.** ← float adjScore line

**Score terms in windows adjacent to the previous and following windows.** ← secondScore line

**Score any bigrams in the passage.** → float bigramScore line

**The final score for the passage is a combination of all the scores, each weighted separately. A bonus is given for any bigram matches.** ← float score line

What's your question?

what is trimethylbenzene?

1 results found in 95 ms Page 1 of 1

**Answers**

- **Doc Id**: 4547829
  **Field**: body
  **Answer**: 1,2,4-Trimethylbenzene is a colorless liquid with chemical formula CH. It is a flammable aromatic hydrocarbon with a strong odor. It occurs naturally in coal tar an
- **Doc Id**: 4547829
  **Field**: body
  **Answer**: Approximately 40% of this fraction is 1,2,4-trimethylbenzene.\n\n1,2,4-Trimethylbenzene dissolved in mineral oil is used as a liquid scintillator. It is also used as a sterilizing agent and in the manufacture of dyes.
- **Doc Id**: 4547829
  **Field**: body
  **Answer**: isolated from the C9 aromatic hydrocarbon fraction during petroleum distillation. Approximately 40% of this fraction is 1,2,4-trimethylbenzene.\n\n1,2,4-Trimethylbenzene dissolved in mineral oil is used as a liquid scintillator. It is also use

**Figure 8.6   An example of the *Taming Text* QA system in action, answering the question "What is trimethylbenzene?"**

The scoring process is a weighted sum of the scores for each of the windows in the passage, with the most weight going to the main match window and decaying the further away from the main window that we go. We also give a bonus to any time there's a match of two words in a row (the *bigram bonus*). The final score is then used to rank the passage using a priority queue data structure. When we have a ranked set of passages, we write out the results to Solr's response structure; they're then passed back out to the client system. An example of the output can be seen in figure 8.6.

At this point, we now have a working system, based on first processing the user's question and then generating a search query that will bring back candidate passages. Finally, we ranked those passages using a simple scoring algorithm that looked at a window of terms around the matching parts of the query. With this basis in mind, let's take a look at what we can do to improve the system.

## 8.5   Steps to improve the system

If you've followed along in the code so far, you'll no doubt realize there are many more tasks that could be done to make the system better. Some ideas are highlighted in the following list:

- Many QA systems analyze the question and select a predefined question template that's then used as a pattern to identify the appropriate candidate based on passages that match the template.
- Create more restrictive Lucene queries in your system by requiring that the answer type be within a certain number of terms or even within a specific sentence.

- Not only identify the passage containing the answer, but extract the answer from the passage.

- If two or more passages produce the same or very similar answers, deduplicate these items and boost the result.

- Handle the case where you can't identify the answer type better by falling back on search or other analysis approaches.

- Show confidence levels or explanations of how you arrived at an answer and give the user a mechanism to refine the results.

- Incorporate specialized query handling for specific types of questions. For instance, questions like "Who is X?" could use a knowledge base resource of famous people to find an answer instead of searching in the text.

These are just a few things that could be improved. More importantly, we'd encourage you, the reader, to add your own insights.

## 8.6   Summary

Building out a working question answering system is an excellent way to see many of the principles of this book in action. For instance, the question analysis phase requires us to apply many string matching techniques as well as tasks like named-entity recognition and tagging, whereas the passage retrieval and ranking tasks require us to leverage deep search engine capabilities to not only find documents that match, but find where exactly in the documents the matches take place. From those matches, we then applied more string matching techniques to rank the passages and to produce an answer. All in all, we have a simple fact-based question answering system. Is it going to win on *Jeopardy!?* Of course not. Hopefully, it sufficiently shows how a working system can be built using readily available open source tools.

## 8.7   Resources

Morton, Thomas. 2005. *Using Semantic Relations to Improve Information Retrieval.* University of Pennsylvania. http://www.seas.upenn.edu/cis/grad/documents/ morton-t.pdf.

Singhal, Amit; Abney, Steve; Bacchiani, Michiel; Collins, Michael; Hindle, Donald; Pereira, Fernando. 1999. "AT&T at TREC-8." AT&T Labs Research. http:// trec.nist.gov/pubs/trec8/papers/att-trec8.pdf.

# Untamed text: exploring
## the next frontier

Whew! We've come a long way, and we don't just mean in terms of your patience in waiting for this book to be complete. (It's very much appreciated!) A few years back, search was all the rage and social networking was just taking off. Ideas that we felt were just coming into their own in the search and NLP space are now powering a wide range of applications, from very large-scale Fortune 100 companies on down to freshly minted startups and everything in between.

At the book level, we started by understanding some of the basics of working with text, searching it, tagging it, and grouping it together. We even looked into a basic question answering system that ties many of these concepts together into a single application. And though these capabilities constitute the large majority of practical text applications, they by no means constitute the entirety of the fields of information retrieval (IR) or natural language processing (NLP). In particular, higher-level language processing that looks at things like user sentiment toward entities (brands, places, people, and so on) is a rapidly growing area thanks in part to the current obsession with stream-of-consciousness tweets and updates.

We'll examine sentiment analysis along with many other advanced techniques in this chapter in hopes of providing both enough information to get started as well as inspiration to tackle some of the harder problems in the space. We'll also introduce the concepts behind each subject, provide resources for readers to explore more, and where appropriate, provide pointers to open source libraries and tools that may help during implementation. But unlike prior chapters, we won't be providing working code examples.

We'll kick things off by looking at working with higher levels of language including semantics, discourse analysis, and pragmatics, before transitioning into discussions on document summarization and event and relationship detection. Next, we'll look at identifying importance and emotions in text, and then finish up the chapter (and the book) with a look at searching across multiple languages.

## 9.1 Semantics, discourse, and pragmatics: exploring higher levels of NLP

Most of this book is structured to help users—living, breathing human beings—to find meaning in text by doing things like parsing it, labeling it, searching it, and otherwise organizing it into consumable units of information. But what if we asked the computer to discern the meaning of the text and tell us the result? At the simplest, we might ask the meaning of a particular set of words (phrases, sentences), but what if the computer could determine deeper meaning in text? For instance, what if the computer could tell you what the author's intent was or that the meaning of one document is similar to the meaning of another? Alternatively, what if the machine was able to use its knowledge of the world to "read between the lines"?

These ways of thinking about meaning, and others, are generally grouped into three different areas (see Liddy [2001] and Manning [1999]):

- *Semantics*—The study of the meaning of words and the interactions between words to form larger units of meaning (such as sentences).
- *Discourse*—Building on the semantic level, discourse analysis aims to determine the relationships between sentences. Some authors group discourse in with the next level of meaning: pragmatics.
- *Pragmatics*—Studies how context, world knowledge, language conventions, and other abstract properties contribute to the meaning of text.

**NOTE**  Though these three areas are primarily focused on meaning in text, all levels of language contribute to a text's meaning. For instance, if you string a bunch of characters together at random, they'll likely not be a word, which will most often render their use in a sentence as meaningless. Alternatively, if you change the ordering (syntax) of the words in a sentence, you may change its meaning, too. For instance, as "Natural Language Processing" (see Liddy [2001]) points out, the sentence "The dog chased the cat," and "The cat chased the dog," use all the same words, but their ordering significantly changes the meaning of the sentences.

With these definitions in place, let's dig deeper into each of these areas and look at some examples and tools that can be used to process text to find meaning.

### 9.1.1 Semantics

From a practical standpoint, applications interested in semantic-level processing typically care about two areas of interest (semantics as a whole is broader):

- Word sense, such as synonyms, antonyms, hypernyms/hyponyms, and so on, and the related task of *word sense disambiguation (WSD)*—picking the correct sense of a word given multiple meanings; for example a bank could be a financial institution or a river bank.
- Collocations and idioms, which are also related to *statistically interesting/improbable phrases (SIPs)*, are groupings of words that infer more meaning together than they do separately. In other words, the meaning of the whole is either greater than or different from the meaning of the parts. For example, the phrase *bit the dust* is about something dying/failing and not about literally eating particles of dust.

In the first area of interest, working with word sense, using synonyms, and so forth effectively can be beneficial for improving search quality, especially if you can disambiguate between senses of a word to select only those synonyms pertinent to the context of the query. That being said, disambiguation in general is often difficult and slow, making it impractical in the real world of search. But knowing your domain and what your users are most likely to type can often help improve the results without deploying a full-fledged disambiguation solution. To get started on WSD, check out chapter 7 of Manning and Schütze's *Foundations of Statistical Natural Language Processing* (1999). Disambiguation is also often a requirement for machine translation applications that translate one language into another, say French into English. For software that does WSD, check out the following:

- *SenseClusters*—http://www.d.umn.edu/~tpederse/senseclusters.html.
- *Lextor*—http://wiki.apertium.org/wiki/Lextor. Note that Lextor is part of a larger project; it may require some work to use it as a standalone system.

Many users will also find Princeton University's WordNet, introduced in chapter 8, useful for this type of task.

Collocations and SIPs also have many uses, ranging from search to natural language generation (the computer writes your next essay or report) to building a concordance for a book or simply for better understanding a language or field of study. For instance, in search applications, collocations can be used both to enhance querying and to build interfaces for discovery by showing users, for a given document, the list of collocations and links to other documents containing those phrases. Or imagine an application that took in all the literature for a particular field and spit out the list of SIPs from the literature along with definitions, references, and other information that made it easier for you to get up to speed. For software that does collocations, look no further than Apache Mahout. To learn more, see https:// cwiki.apache.org/confluence/display/MAHOUT/Collocations.

Other areas of interest at the semantic level can be useful to understand, especially as a part of the other levels of processing. For instance, assessing the truth of a statement involves having a semantic understanding of the words in a statement, as well as other knowledge. Semantics are also often difficult to discern given the role of quantifiers and other lexical units in a sentence. For instance, double negatives, misplaced modifiers, and other scoping issues can make it difficult to understand a sentence's meaning.

There's much more to learn about semantics. Wikipedia's article on semantics (http://en.wikipedia.org/wiki/Semantics) gives a good list of places to start learning more as should any decent introduction to linguistics.

### 9.1.2 Discourse

Whereas semantics usually operates within a sentence, discourse goes beyond the sentence and looks at relationships between sentences. Discourse also looks at things like utterances, body language, speech acts, and so forth, but we'll primarily focus on its use in written text. Note also that discourse is sometimes bundled in with the next area of discussion, pragmatics.

As far as natural language processing is concerned, the use of discourse tools is usually focused on anaphor resolution and defining/labeling structures (called *discourse segmentation*) in text. For instance, in a news article, the lead, main story, attributions, and the like could be split apart and appropriately labeled. *Anaphors* are references to other pieces of text, usually nouns and usually preceding the anaphor. For example, in the sentences "Peter was nominated for the Presidency. He politely declined," the pronoun *He* is an anaphor. Anaphors may be other than pronouns, as the following sentences demonstrate: "The Hurricanes' Eric Staal scored the game winning goal in overtime. The team captain netted the winner at 2:03 in the first overtime." In this example, *team captain* is an anaphor for Erik Staal. Anaphor resolution is a subset of a more general topic called *co-reference resolution*, which often also relies on discourse analysis as well as other levels of processing. Co-reference resolution's goal is to identify all mentions of a particular concept or entity in a piece of text. For example, in the following text,

> New York City (NYC) is the largest city in the United States. Sometimes referred to as the Big Apple, The City that Never Sleeps, and Gotham, NYC is a tourist mecca. In 2008, the Big Apple attracted over 40 million tourists. The city is also a financial powerhouse due to the location of the New York Stock Exchange and the NASDAQ markets.

*New York City, NYC, Big Apple, Gotham,* and *the city* are all mentions of the same place. Co-reference resolution, and thus anaphor resolution, are useful in search, question answering (QA) systems, and many other places. As an example in the QA context, suppose someone asked the question "Which presidents were from Texas?" and we had the following document (from Wikipedia's article on Lyndon Baines Johnson (http://en.wikipedia.org/wiki/Lyndon_B._Johnson) as a source in our QA system:

> Lyndon Baines Johnson (August 27, 1908–January 22, 1973), often referred to as LBJ, served as the 36th President of the United States from 1963 to 1969...
> Johnson, a Democrat, served as a United States Representative from Texas, from 1937–1949 and as United States Senator from 1949–1961...

We could use co-reference resolution to determine that the 36th president, Johnson, was from Texas.

To learn more on co-reference and anaphor resolution, a book on discourse analysis is likely a good place to start, as is the Wikipedia article on anaphora (http://en.wikipedia .org/wiki/Anaphora_%28linguistics%29). Implementation-wise, OpenNLP supports co-reference resolution.

Discourse segmentation has uses in search and NLP applications. On the search side, identifying, labeling, and potentially breaking larger documents into smaller segments can often lead to more precise results by driving users to the exact area within a document where matches occur, as well as providing more fine-grained weights of tokens. The downside is that it may take extra work to piece the document back together as a whole or to determine when a result that spans multiple segments is better than an individual segment.

Discourse segmentation can also be useful in document summarization techniques to produce a summary that better covers the topics and subtopics contained within a text (we'll cover more on summarization in a later section). See "Multi-Paragraph Segmentation of Expository Text" (Hearst 1994) as an example of approaches in this area. The MorphAdorner project (http://morphadorner.northwestern.edu/ morphadorner/textsegmenter/) has an implementation of Hearst's TextTiling approach in Java (be sure to check the license for commercial use) as well as a Perl version in CPAN at http://search.cpan.org/~splice/Lingua-EN-Segmenter-0.1/lib/ Lingua/EN/Segmenter/TextTiling.pm. Beyond that, it's often possible to do a more basic level of segmentation in Lucene and Solr through appropriate application-time decisions either during indexing or during querying (by using SpanQuery objects that allow for fine-grained positional matching). Many articles have also been written on passage-based retrieval, which may prove informative in this area. For now, we'll move on to talk about pragmatics.

### 9.1.3   *Pragmatics*

Pragmatics is all about context and how it affects the way we communicate. Context provides the framework and foundation for us to communicate without having to explain every bit of information necessary for understanding. For example, in the proposal stage of this book and throughout its development, one of the key questions for us authors to answer was, who is the target audience of the book? At the business level this is useful in determining the size of the market and the expected profit, but at the author level it's critical for setting much of the book's context.

At the end of the market analysis process, we decided the audience was developers who are familiar with programming, most likely in Java, but are likely not familiar with the concepts and practice of search and natural language processing, and who needed to use these tools and techniques at work. We also decided to avoid complex mathematical explanations and to provide working examples based on open source tools that already implement commonly used algorithms. With this context in mind, we assumed our users were comfortable working on the command line and with the basics of reading Java or another programming language, thus allowing us to avoid the tedious descriptions of setup and basic programming principles.

At a simpler level, pragmatics is about the combination of our knowledge of linguistics (morphology, grammar, syntax, and so forth) with our knowledge of the world around us. Pragmatics studies how we "read between the lines" to overcome ambiguity or understand people's intent. Pragmatic systems often need to be able to reason about the world in order to make inferences. For example, in our discourse example earlier about Lyndon Johnson, if the question was "What state was Lyndon Johnson from?" the QA system would have to identify that Texas was a proper noun and that it's a state.

As you can guess, encoding broad swaths of world knowledge into an application is nontrivial and why pragmatic processing is often difficult. Many open source tools are available that can help, such as the OpenCyc project (http://www.opencyc.org), Word-Net (http://wordnet.princeton.edu), and the CIA Factbook (https://www.cia.gov/library/publications/the-world-factbook/), to name a few. With any resource, application developers often get the best results by focusing on just those resources that prove useful to helping solve the problem via a fairly rigorous evaluation process instead of trying to boil the ocean by using any and all resources available.

Other areas of pragmatics might look into the use of sarcasm, politeness, and other behaviors and how they affect communication. In many of these cases, applications build classifiers that are trained to label such acts as sarcasm so that they can be used in downstream applications such as sentiment analysis (discussed later in this chapter) or an inference engine. In these cases, our earlier chapter on tagging is an appropriate starting place to dig deeper.

At the end of the day, pragmatic-level processing is often hard to incorporate into many applications. To learn more about pragmatics, try *Pragmatics* (Peccei 1999) or an introduction to linguistics text. See also http://www.gxnu.edu.cn/Personal/szliu/definition.html for a good introduction as well as pointers to other reading materials.

Our next topic, along with several others that follow, puts many of these higher levels of language to work in an effort to make it easier for people to deal with the massive amounts of information available today. To get started, let's look at how NLP can be used to significantly reduce the amount of information you need to process by summarizing documents and even whole collections.

## 9.2 *Document and collection summarization*

By Manish Katyal

Document summarization techniques can be used to give readers a quick overview of the important information in a long document or a collection of documents. For example, figure 9.1 shows a summary of an article from the *Washington Post* about unrest in Egypt (from *Washington Post* article dated February 4, 2011; since removed).

The summary was generated using Many Aspects Document Summarization from IBM's AlphaWorks (see http://www.alphaworks.ibm.com/tech/manyaspects). The left pane shows the sentences central to the story and gives a good overview of the article, which was copied and pasted from the *Washington Post*. This is an example of single document summarization. A summarizer could also be used to generate a summary of related news articles about the story of unrest in Egypt. The generated summary could include important information such as "Riots in Egypt. President Mubarak under pressure to resign. US government urges Mubarak to react with restraint." Each of these sentences can be from different news sources that are talking about the same story. This is referred to as *collection summarization* or *multidocument summarization.*

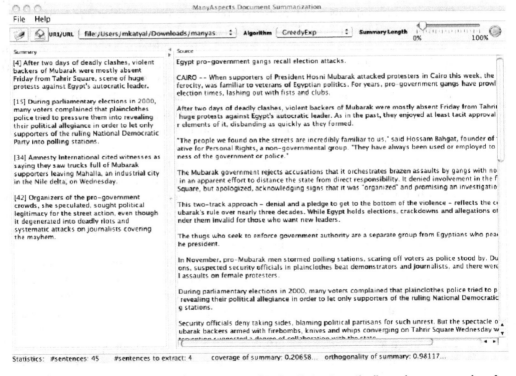

**Figure 9.1   The image shows an example of an application that automatically produces summaries of larger documents.**

Some other applications of summarization include generating a blurb for each link on a search page, or a summary of tech news by coalescing similar articles from Techcrunch, Engadget, and other tech blogs. The key objective of all these applications is to give readers enough information so that they can decide whether they want to drill down and read the details.

There are three tasks in generating a summary. The first task is content selection. In this task, the summarizer selects a list of candidate sentences that are vital to the summary. There's typically a limit on the number of words or sentences that can be selected.

There are multiple approaches to the task of selecting candidate sentences. In one approach, the summarizer ranks sentences by their importance or centrality in the documents. If a sentence is similar to a lot of other sentences, then it contains common information with other sentences and therefore is a good candidate to be selected in the summary. Another approach could be to rank sentences by considering their position in the documents, by the relevance of the words that they contain, and also by looking for cue phrases such as "in summary," "in conclusion," and so on. A word is considered informative or relevant for summarization if it occurs frequently in the document but not as much in a general document collection. A weighting scheme such as TF-IDF or log-likelihood ratio can be used for determining a word's relevance to a document. A third approach is to compute a pseudo-sentence that's the centroid of all sentences and then look for sentences that are as close as possible to the centroid.

For summarizing document collections, since groups of documents might overlap a lot, the summarizer must ensure that it doesn't select identical or similar sentences. To do this, the summarizer can penalize sentences that are similar to ones that have been already selected. In this way you can remove redundancy and ensure that each sentence gives the reader new information.

In our opinion, content selection is a relatively easy task in comparison to the next two tasks: *sentence ordering* and *sentence realization*. The sentence ordering task must reorder the selected sentences so that the summary is coherent and information flows smoothly for the reader. For a single document summarization, you retain the original order of the selected sentences. Unfortunately, this becomes a much harder task for document collection summarization.

In the final task, the ordered sentences may have to be rewritten for readability. For example, a sentence might have abbreviations or pronouns that have to be resolved to make it understandable to the reader. For example: "Mubarak promised to deal with the rioters with a firm hand" might need to be rewritten as "The President of Egypt, Mubarak, has promised to deal with the rioters with a firm hand." In our opinion, this task may be skipped, as it requires sophisticated linguistic analysis of the text.

As with most of these technologies, a few open source options are available for document and collection summarization. The MEAD project, located at http://www .summarization.com/mead/, is an open domain, multidocument text summarizer. An online demo of LexRank, an algorithm used in MEAD for content selection, can be found at http://tangra.si.umich.edu/~radev/lexrank/. We'll revisit some of the approaches that LexRank takes later in the section on importance. Another solution is Texlexan, located at http://texlexan.sourceforge.net/. Texlexan performs summarization, analysis of text, and classification. It works with English, French, German, Italian, and Spanish texts.

To learn more about text summarization, see *Speech and Language Processing* (Jurafsky [2008]). For research papers in this area, see the publications of the Document Understanding Conference (DUC) located at http://www-nlpir.nist.gov/projects/duc/pubs.html. DUC was a series of competitions in text summarization.

Similar to summarization, our next topic, relationship extraction, is aimed at extracting key bits of information out of text. But unlike summarization, it's more about adding structure to text that can then be used by downstream tools or consumed by end users.

## 9.3    *Relationship extraction*

By Vaijanath N. Rao

The *relation extraction (RE)* task aims to identify relations mentioned in the text. Typically, a *relation* is defined as a function of one or more arguments, where an argument represents concepts, objects, or people in the real world and the relation describes the type of association or interaction between the arguments. Most of the work related to RE has been focused on binary relations, where the relation is a function of two arguments, but you can see that it could be extended to more complex relationships by linking together common entities. As an example of a binary relation, consider the sentence "*Bill Gates* is the cofounder of *Microsoft.*" An RE system might extract the cofounder relation from the sentence and present it as: *cofounder-of (Bill Gates, Microsoft)*. In the rest of the chapter, we'll focus on binary relation extraction unless otherwise specified.

Another example of an RE system is the T-Rex system. Its general architecture and an example can be seen in figure 9.2. T-Rex is an open source relation extraction system from the University of Sheffield and further details can be found later in this section. The input text documents are fed to the RE engine which performs the relation extraction task.

The RE system in T-Rex consists of two main subsystems: the *Processor* and the *Classifier*. The subsystems are explained in detail in a later section. The right side of the figure contains an example that was run through the T-Rex system. Consider the sentence "Albert Einstein was a renowned theoretical physicist, was born in Ulm, on 14th March 1879." The RE system extracts the relations *Occupation, Born-in,* and *Born-on*. Hence, the relations extracted are *Occupation (Albert Einstein, Theoretical Physicist), Born-in (Albert Einstein, Ulm), Born-on (Albert Einstein, 14th March 1879)*.

Relation extraction has a number of applications because it describes the semantic relations between entities, which helps in deeper understanding of the text. RE is commonly used in question answering systems as well as summarization systems. For

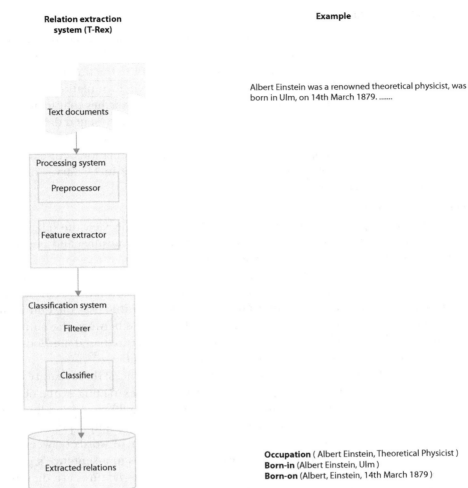

**Relation extraction system (T-Rex)**

**Example**

Albert Einstein was a renowned theoretical physicist, was born in Ulm, on 14th March 1879. .......

Text documents

Processing system

Preprocessor

Feature extractor

Classification system

Filterer

Classifier

Extracted relations

**Occupation** ( Albert Einstein, Theoretical Physicist )
**Born-in** (Albert Einstein, Ulm )
**Born-on** (Albert, Einstein, 14th March 1879 )

**Figure 9.2   T-Rex is an example of a relation extraction system. In this image, the output of RE shows several relations were extracted from the sentence.**

instance, "Learning Surface Text Patterns for a Question Answering System" (see Ravichandran [2002]) proposed an open-domain question answering system using text patterns and a semisupervised approach, which we'll discuss in a moment. For example, to answer a question like "When was Einstein born?" they suggest patterns like "$<$NAME$>$ was born in $<$LOCATION$>$." This is nothing but the relation \bf born-in}(\it Einstein, Ulm}), which could be extracted by a relation extraction system. With these examples in mind, let's look at some of the different approaches to identifying relationships.

### 9.3.1 *Overview of approaches*

A plethora of work has been done related to relation extraction. Rule-based approaches like those used by Chu et al. (Chu 2002) and Chen et al. (Chen 2009) have been proposed, where predefined rules are used for extraction for relations. But this requires a lot of domain understanding for rule formulation. Broadly, the approaches to RE can be categorized into supervised approaches that formulate relation extraction as a binary classification task learning from annotated data, semisupervised approaches mainly using bootstrapping methods, unsupervised approaches that involve clustering, and approaches that go beyond binary relations. An excellent survey on relation extraction approaches in detail is available in "A Survey on Relation Extraction" (Nguyen 2007).

#### SUPERVISED APPROACHES

The supervised approaches (such as Lodhi [2002]) generally view the relation extraction task as a classification problem. Given a set of tagged positive and negative relations examples, the task is to train a binary classifier.

For instance, given a sentence, you can use named-entity recognition (NER) tools such as those in OpenNLP introduced earlier in the book. Given these entities and the words that link them, you can then train another classifier that uses the entities to create a new classification model that recognizes relationships between the entities.

Supervised approaches can further be divided into feature-based methods and kernel methods based on the data used for learning the classifier.

Feature-based methods extract features from the sentences; these features are then used for classification. They employ different ways for extracting syntactic features (see Kambhatla [2004]) and semantic features (GuoDong 2002). Examples of syntactic features include named entities, type of the entities (for example person, company, and so on), word sequence between the entities, number of words between entities, and more. Examples of semantic features include entities in a sentence's parse tree, such as whether it's a noun phrase or a verb phrase. These features are then used for training the classifier. Naturally, not all features are equally important and sometimes it can be difficult to arrive at an optimal feature set. Kernel methods, which we'll introduce next, are an alternative approach that remove the dependency upon the optimal feature selection.

A *kernel* is a mapping function between two objects into a higher dimensional space and defines the similarity between them. Generally a variant of a string kernel (see Lodhi [2002]) is used for relation extraction. A string kernel computes similarity between two strings based on the common subsequence between them. The two most commonly used kernels are the *bag-of-features kernel* and the *convolution kernel*. Figure 9.3 shows an example of a sentence and different kernel representations.

A bag-of-features kernel defines the number of times a particular word occurs in two strings. For example, as can be seen in figure 9.3, the bag-of-features kernel shows the number of times each word in the sentence has occurred. If you follow "Subsequence Kernels for Relation Extraction" (Bunescu [2005]), you can subdivide into

**Sentence** : A spokeswoman says John heads XYZ company

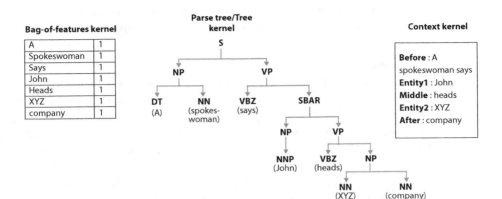

**Figure 9.3   An example of a bag-of-features kernel and a context kernel**

three subkernels. For the example given in the figure, two entities, *John* and *XYZ*, are identified. A *context kernel* identifies three areas of context that we're interested in:

- *Before*—Words occurring before the entity *John*
- *Middle*—Words occurring between the entities *John* and *XYZ*
- *After*—Words occurring after the entity *XYZ*

*Convolution kernels* (see Zelenko [2003]) measure the similarity between two structured instances by summing the similarity of their substructures. An example of a convolution kernel is a tree kernel that defines a relation between the two entities using the similarities between the subtrees. For the example given in figure 9.3, the relation between the entities *John* and *XYZ* is computed using the similarity between the respective subtrees containing them.

Though this treatment is short, see the referenced citations for more information. For now, we'll move on to look briefly at some semisupervised approaches.

**SEMISUPERVISED APPROACHES**

Supervised methods require a lot of training data as well as domain expertise for good performance. In contrast, you can use partially supervised methods with bootstrapping for RE in new domains. Bootstrapping methods proposed in the literature can be broadly divided into three types. The first approach (see Blum [1998]) uses a small set of training data called *seeds*. Using this seed data, an iterative bootstrapping process of learning is employed for further annotation of new data that's discovered. The second approach (see Agichtein [2005]) assumes a predefined set of relations. A small amount of training data is used in the training process. An iterative two-step bootstrapping process is employed to discover new examples holding the relations defined. In the first step, entities are identified and patterns are extracted, which are used for discovering new patterns in the second step. The third approach (see Greenwood [2007]) uses only a group of documents classified as relevant or nonrelevant to a particular relation extraction task. Patterns are extracted from the document pertaining to relevant and nonrelevant, respectively, and ranked appropriately. These ranked patterns are later used in an iterative bootstrapping process for identifying new relevant patterns containing the entities.

UNSUPERVISED APPROACHES

In the cases of supervised and semisupervised, there are an inherent cost of adaptation for new domain as well as requirement of domain knowledge. These costs can be overcome using the unsupervised approaches, which don't require any training examples. Hachey et al. (see Hachey [2009]) proposed an approach that uses similarity and clustering for generic relation extraction. The approach consists of two phases called *relation identification* and *relation characterization*. In the relation identification phase, pairs of associated entities are identified and extracted. Different features are used like co-occurrence windows, constraints on entities (like allowing only person-person relation or person-company relation), and so forth. Entities need to be appropriately weighted. In the relation characterization phase, top relations are clustered and the cluster label is used to define the relationship. For further details, see Hachey's detailed report.

### 9.3.2  *Evaluation*

In 2000, the United States National Institute of Standards and Technology (NIST— http://www.nist.gov/index.html) initiated the Automatic Content Extraction shared tasks program to help technologies that automatically infer meaning from text data. Five recognition tasks are supported as part of the program, including recognition of entities, values, temporal expressions, relations, and events. Tagged data is also made available as part of the shared tasks along with ground truth data (data annotated with labels).

Since its inception, this data has been widely used for evaluation of relation extraction tasks, and most of the supervised methods discussed in this section make use of the same. Some of the relation types that the data contains are organization-location, organization-affiliation, citizen-resident-religion-ethnicity, sports-affiliation, and so forth. Another rich source of data is the Wikipedia (http://www.wikipedia.org) data, as it contains hyperlinked entities in most of its pages and has been used for relation extraction in Culotta et al.'s work (Culotta [2006]) and Nguyen et al.'s work (Nguyen [2007]), among others. For the biomedical domain, the BioInfer (see http://mars.cs.utu.fi/ BioInfer/) data and MEDLINE (see PubMed) have been used in earlier work.

The most widely used metrics for performance evaluation are precision, recall, and F-measure. Precision and recall are as we defined them in the chapter on search. F-measure is a simple formula that takes into account both the precision and the recall to produce a single metric. See http://en.wikipedia.org/wiki/F1_score for more information. Most of the semisupervised approaches we saw in the earlier sections operate on large amounts of data. Hence, an estimate of precision is only computed using the relations extracted and the ground truth data available. With large datasets, it's difficult to compute recall since the actual number of relations are difficult to obtain.

### 9.3.3　*Tools for relationship extraction*

In this section, we list some of the commonly used relation extraction tools. As mentioned earlier, the T-Rex system consists of two phases: a processing task and a classification task. In the processing task, the input text is converted to features. In the classification task, first the features are extracted and then a classification is trained on the features extracted. It's available for download at the T-Rex project page at http://sourceforge.net/projects/t-rex/.

Java Simple Relation Extraction (JSRE) uses a combination of kernel functions to integrate two information sources. The first is the sentence where the relation occurs, and the second is the context surrounding the entities. It's available for download at the JSRE project page at http://hlt.fbk.eu/en/technology/jSRE.

The relation extraction algorithm in NLTK (Natural Language Toolkit), a Python-based NLP toolkit, is a two-pass algorithm. In the first pass, it processes the text and extracts tuples of context and entity. The context can be words before or after the entity (which can also be empty). In the second phase, it processes the triples of the pairs and computes a binary relation. It also allows you to specify constraints on entities, like *organization* and *person*, and to limit the relation type, such as *lawyer, head*, and so on. NLTK can be downloaded from its project page at http://code.google.com/p/nltk/.

Just as with all of the sections in this chapter, we've only touched on the surface of what's involved in doing a good job at relationship extraction. Hopefully your mind is already thinking of the uses for such extractions in your application. We'll leave the topic and look at algorithms for detecting important ideas and the people that relate to them.

## 9.4　*Identifying important content and people*

Given the explosion of information, social networks, and hyperconnectivity in today's world, it's increasingly useful to have help separating content and people according to some notion of priority or importance. In email applications, the notion of spam detection (filtering unimportant messages out) has been implemented for some time, but we're just now starting to use computers to identify which messages are important. For instance, Google recently launched, via their Gmail service, a feature called Priority Inbox (see figure 9.4) that attempts to separate important email from unimportant email.

In social networks such as Facebook and Twitter, you may want to promote

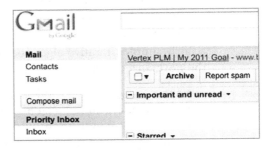

**Figure 9.4　Google Mail's Priority Inbox is an application that attempts to automatically determine what's important to the user. Captured 1/3/2011.**

posts from people who you rate as of higher priority than others, setting aside lower-priority ones to be read later or not at all. On different levels, the notion of importance can be applied to words, websites, and much more. As a final example, imagine getting the day's news and being able to focus on just the articles that are critical to your job, or being able to quickly and easily find the most important papers in a new research field. (We could've used such a tool for writing this chapter!)

The question of importance is a difficult one, and the approaches to solving it depend on the application and, often, the users. Importance also overlaps areas such as ranking/relevance, as well as authoritativeness. The primary distinction is that something that's important is also relevant, whereas something that's relevant isn't necessarily important. For instance, information on the antidote for a poison and where to get it is far more important to someone who just swallowed said poison than information that describes the way antidotes for poison are developed. It's unfortunately not clear and fairly subjective when something crosses the threshold from being relevant to being important.

In researching this section, it quickly became clear that there's not yet a notion of "importance theory," but instead there's a growing body of work around solving specific problems relating to importance. There are also some related areas in information theory, such as surprise (see http://en.wikipedia.org/wiki/Self-Information), mutual information (see http://en.wikipedia.org/wiki/Mutual_Information), and others. It's also useful to think about two levels of importance: global and personal. Global importance is all about what the majority of people in a group think is important, whereas personal importance is all about what you, the individual, think is important. There are algorithms and approaches that work for each level, which we'll explore in the next two sections.

### 9.4.1  *Global importance and authoritativeness*

Probably the single largest application that leverages global importance (or at least attempts to) is Google's search engine (http://www.google.com). Google's search engine harnesses the votes (via links, words, clicks, and more) of millions of users worldwide to determine what websites are the most important/authoritative (it returns relevant sites as well) to a given user's query. Google's approach, which they call *PageRank* and describe in its early form in "The Anatomy of a Large-Scale Hypertextual Web Search Engine" (http://infolab.stanford.edu/~backrub/google.html), is a fairly simple, iterative algorithm that "corresponds to the principal eigenvector of the normalized link matrix of the web."

> **NOTE**  Though beyond the scope of this book, interested readers will do well to learn more about eigenvectors and other matrix mathematics, as they come up often in the day-to-day work of NLP, machine learning, and search. A respected linear algebra text is a good starting point for such an undertaking.

This realization about eigenvectors has led to their use in other areas. For example, you can see similar approaches used in keyword extraction (TextRank—www.aclweb .org/

anthology-new/acl2004/emnlp/pdf/Mihalcea.pdf) and multidocument summarization (LexRank—http://www-2.cs.cmu.edu/afs/cs.cmu.edu/project/jair/pub/volume22 /erkan04a.pdf), as well as other graph-ranking strategies. (Grant sometimes calls them *Rank strategies.) Such approaches are also often used in understanding the dynamics of social networks, because they can quickly find important people and connections. The iterative algorithm is simple to implement and can fortunately be scaled fairly easily. The more difficult part is acquiring the content, at scale, in the first place.

### 9.4.2   Personal importance

Calculating what's important to an individual is, in many ways, harder than calculating global importance. For starters, what's important to user A is often not important to user B. Second, depending on the application, the cost of being wrong (either with false positives or false negatives) can be expensive. Personal importance applications also have a bootstrapping problem, since it's fairly hard to understand what an individual thinks is important if the individual has never interacted with the system!

To date, most personal importance applications treat the problem as a classification problem, often with a twist discussed earlier in the book. The application trains/ tests *n+1* models, where *n* is the number of users in the system. In other words, each user has their own model and the extra model is a global model that's trained with the notion of global features related to importance. The per-user model is typically just the differences the user has as compared to the global model, which has a number of benefits in terms of compactness and scalability. To read more about this in action, see "The Learning Behind Gmail Priority Inbox" by Aberdeen, et al., at http:// research.google.com/pubs/archive/36955.pdf.

### 9.4.3   Resources and pointers on importance

Unfortunately, as alluded to earlier and unlike most of the other subjects here, there's no one place to go for the theory and concepts of what makes something important. Even Wikipedia, the default place to start with many subjects in the internet age, has little more than a placeholder page for the word *importance* (at least it did as of January 21, 2001; see http://en.wiktionary.org/wiki/importance). Interested readers shouldn't be disheartened, as there are still plenty of places to put together the pieces:

- Google's PageRank paper (http://infolab.stanford.edu/~backrub/google .html) is a good start for understanding authority and graph ranking strategies.
- Any good textbook on information theory (start at Wikipedia—http:// en.wikipedia.org/wiki/Information_theory), mutual information, entropy, surprisal, information gain, and other topics can help.

Importance and prioritization work are undoubtedly among the hot topics of the day due to their significant role in social networks and dealing with the information deluge. Similarly, sentiment analysis, our next subject, is also an area of active research, thanks in no small part to the rapid rise of services like Facebook and Twitter.

## 9.5　*Detecting emotions via sentiment analysis*

By J. Neal Richter and Rob Zinkov

*Sentiment analysis* is the identification and extraction of subjective information from text. Often referred to as *opinion mining*, it generally involves the usage of various NLP tools and textual analytics software to automate the process. The following simple example is from the movie review website RottenTomatoes.com and was rephrased for clarity.

> "The movie *Battlefield Earth* is a disaster of epic proportions!"
>
> —Dustin Putnam

This is clearly a negative movie review. The basic form of sentiment analysis is polarity classification, and might assign this sentence a score of -5 out of a normalized range of [-10,10]. Advanced sentiment analysis techniques would parse the sentence and deduce the following facts:

- *Battlefield Earth* is a movie.
- *Battlefield Earth* is a very bad movie.
- Dustin Putnam thinks *Battlefield Earth* is very bad movie.

The complexity of the task is also evident. Software would need to recognize the entities {Battlefield Earth, Dustin Putnam} and have a database of phrases containing "disaster" with a negative score. It might also have the ability to recognize that the prepositional phrase "of epic proportions" is acting as an adjective of the noun "disaster" and is roughly equivalent to "big disaster" and should thus accentuate the negative value attached to "disaster." With the rapid proliferation of user-generated content on the web, it's now possible to gauge the opinions of large numbers of people on topics (politics, movies) and objects (specific products). The desire to find, index, and summarize these opinions is strong among corporate marketers, customer service divisions within corporations, and financial, political, and governmental organizations.

### 9.5.1　*History and review*

The survey papers by Pang and Lee (see Pang [2008]) and Liu (see Liu [2004]) provide excellent reviews of the history and current status of sentiment analysis. This area has deep roots in the NLP and linguistics communities. Early work in this area was done by Janyce Wiebe and co-workers (1995-2001), which they termed *subjectivity analysis*. The goal of the research was to classify a sentence as subjective or not based upon the adjectives used and their orientation.

Within the software industry, the year 2000 was interesting in sentiment analysis. Qualcomm shipped a Mood Watch feature in its 2000 release of the Eudora email client. Mood Watch performed a simple negative polarity analysis of emails into the range [-3,0] represented by icons of chili peppers on the screen. The system was designed by David Kaufer of Carnegie Mellon's English department (see Kaufer [2000]). Internally the algorithm categorized the emails into eight categories of common discourse patterns found in Usenet "flame wars."

In early 2000 the first author (Neal Richter) began work on an emotional polarity analysis system for a CRM software vendor specializing in email processing for customer service. At the time we used the term *affective rating* rather than sentiment analysis to describe the area (see Durbin [2003]). The feature shipped in 2001 and has been processing hundreds of millions of customer service inquiries per month since then. The system has also been translated into 30-plus languages. Though there were pockets of academic work prior to 2001, this year can be regarded as the arrival of sentiment analysis as a formal research area in natural language processing.

The first phase of research centered around using basic grammar rules and structure of English plus a dictionary of keywords to arrive at heuristic assessments of the polarity of a snippet of text. The dictionary of keywords was often manually constructed from human judgments on polarity. These techniques can achieve reasonable accuracy; for example, Turney (see Turney [2002]) achieved 74% accuracy in predicting the polarity of product reviews. These types of techniques are easy to implement yet fail to capture higher-order structures present in English. In particular these techniques can fail to take into account the way that words modify the meaning of those around them, sometimes on the far side of a sentence. As such algorithms extract only small phrases (two to three words), they may miss more complex constructs. These techniques often have bad recall: they often fail to give a classification.

A limitation of the heuristic algorithms is the enumeration problem. Given the complex nature of language, it's somewhat of a fool's errand to attempt to manually construct all possible sentiment-expressing patterns. Instead, the next phase of research used the growth of available internet data from product reviews to induce sentiment patterns or simply emit predictions. An early supervised learning technique was "Mining the Peanut Gallery: Opinion Extraction and Semantic Classification of Product Reviews" (Dave 2003). Starting with basic stemming techniques and preprocessing, usage of TF-IDF, Laplace transforms, and similar metrics, they fed the processed and scored reviews into various classifiers. The binary +/- classification was as high as 87% on a dataset with a naive Bayes' algorithm.

A more recent high-performing heuristics-driven approach is described by Ding et al. (Ding 2009). Highly recommended reading, they fuse a large data-driven opinion-word lexicon with rich preprocessing and transition state accounting. In particular, they use a rule grammar (in the compiler's sense) to extract inferences. The rules engine is applied multiple times to transform the tagged text into inference statements defining the association between a word and part of speech pair and a sentiment polarity. They achieved upward of 80% accuracy in both recall and precision.

A recent simple unsupervised approach is used by Hassan and Radev (Hassan 2010). They bootstrap on the WordNet database and perform a "random walk" starting from an unknown polarity word. The walk stops when it encounters a word with known polarity. The polarity prediction is averaged over multiple random walks from the same starting word. No attempt at utilizing higher-level structures is made. This method is fast; no corpus is needed other than the relatively short list of "gold standard" positive and negative terms. It achieved an accuracy of 92–99% on a very small list of seed starting words. Given that this is a non-corpus-based method and WordNet doesn't contain all English terms, this idea might be best utilized to bootstrap a sentiment keyword dictionary.

### 9.5.2  *Tools and data needs*

Most approaches to sentiment analysis require a few basic tools and data. The first is a *part of speech tagger,* a software package that parses and labels words in a sentence with their part of speech. A few common taggers are listed here:

- OpenNLP tagger, discussed previously in the text.
- Eric Brill's tagger—http://gposttl.sourceforge.net/ (C code)
- Lingua-EN-Tagger—http://search.cpan.org/~acoburn/Lingua-EN-Tagger/ Tagger.pm
- Illinois POS Tagger—http://cogcomptest.cs.illinois.edu/page/software_view/3
- Demo—http://cogcomp.cs.illinois.edu/demo/pos/

In addition to a part of speech tagger, a database of keyword/phrase polarity ratings is crucial. These can either be gathered from annotated sources or learned from a corpus. Whissell's *Dictionary of Affective Language* (DAL) (see http://hdcus.com/ and http://www.hdcus.com/manuals/wdalman.pdf) and the WordNet-Affect (see http://wndomains.fbk.eu/wnaffect.html and http://www.cse.unt.edu/~rada/affectivetext/) are two sources of data. Note that some extraction is required for usage of DAL data. A semantic dictionary might look like the one in table 9.1.

In addition, basic textual analysis tools are needed such as tokenizers, sentence boundary determination, stopword marking, word stemmers, and so forth. See chapter 2 earlier in the book for more info on these items.

**Table 9.1  An example semantic dictionary**

| Lexical entry | POS | Sentiment category (+ is positive; - is negative) |
|---|---|---|
| happy | JJ | + |
| horror | NN | - |
| dreadful | JJ | - |
| fears | VBZ | - |
| loving | VBG | + |
| sad | JJ | - |
| satisfaction | NN | + |

### 9.5.3 *A basic polarity algorithm*

The best way to think of sentiment polarity is as a fluid flowing through a document. Sentiment is expected to stay consistent across a document. As an example, here's a snippet of a review on Amazon of a blender:

> This was a good price and works well however it is very loud. Also the first 10-15 uses I noticed a very pronounced electric smell after running it. But hey, you get what you pay for. The thing works, blends well, and I like that I can stand the jar up and take it with me.

Notice how the sentiment shifts from positive to negative on the *however*. The review then shifts from negative back to positive upon reaching "But." This shift allows us to infer that *loud* has negative sentiment in the context of this review. The sentiment of loud will usually depend on the document. In discussing a rock concert, loud is usually a positive feature. In discussing a blender, loud is usually a negative feature.

Two early polarity algorithms were by Yi et al. (Yi 2003) and Turney (Turney 2002). Here's Yi's algorithm, reframed for clarity of implementation:

- Tokenize the text.
- Find sentence boundaries with heuristic or other approach.
- POS tag each sentence.
- Apply a set of patterns to each sentence to find verb phrases, noun phrases.
- Construct any binary or ternary expressions found.
- Look up verbs and adjectives and their modifiers in the Semantic DB—use stemming variants as needed.
- Output association expressions found.

An example ternary (target, verb, source) expression is "the burrito," "was," "too messy," and an example binary expression (adjective, target) is "quality," "camera." Pulling this all together, here's an example of the Yi algorithm on the sample text: "This recipe makes excellent pizza crust."

- *Matching sentiment pattern*—<"make" OP SP>
- *Subject phrase(SP)* —This recipe
- *Object phrase (OP)*—pizza crust
- *Sentiment of the OP*—positive
- *T-expression*—<"recipe," "make," "excellent pizza crust">

Turney's algorithm is another example of a basic pattern extractor that applies point-wise mutual information (PMI) theory to approximate the polarity of a given keyword based on its proximity to known positive and negative words in a large corpus of text. In basic terms, PMI states that two terms are highly related when they co-occur more often than their individual frequencies would predict. Otherwise it's similar to the preceding: it tokenizes and POS tags sentences and then extracts two- and three-word tagged phrases (bigrams and trigrams) as patterns. It then uses the PMI method to classify words based upon their co-occurrence with any known positive/negative word in that bi-/trigram.

### 9.5.4   *Advanced topics*

One of the more advanced ways to detect sentiment analysis is by using a technique called *conditional random fields* (CRF; see Getoor [2007]). A key benefit of CRFs and other data-driven techniques is their ability to model dependencies and structures between words. Consequently, they have much better recall performance. Many of the previously stated techniques treat the sentiment of each term independent of the terms around it. For many natural language problems this usually doesn't affect performance too significantly. Unfortunately, the sentiment of a word is heavily determined based on the words around it. One of the best ways to take into account this dependency is through modeling the problem using a conditional random field.

CRFs allow you to model data with internal structure that constrains what labels terms can take on. Sentiment classification tasks can use a CRF to take advantage of the structure latently available within human language to achieve state-of-the-art results.

The particular details of the learning and inference algorithms for CRFs are beyond the scope of this book. Instead, we'll concentrate on outlining how we'll define the features for the CRF. We may then use an open source library to train our models. We define a CRF by specifying what features we'd like to take into account when determining the sentiment of a term. Some of the common features discussed earlier will be relevant:

- POS of the word.
- Is this word an entity?
- Is this word describing an entity?
- Synonyms of the word.
- Stem of the word.
- Is this word capitalized?
- The word itself.

Now we can take into account features that aren't just about the given word, such as these:

- The POS of the previous word and following word.
- Is the previous word *not?*
- Is the previous word *but?*
- If this word is an anaphora, features of the word it refers to.

More importantly, we can now link features by defining features that have elements of the current term, surrounding terms, or even terms that are further away such as the anaphora feature. As an example, we may have as a feature, the POS of the current word, and the anaphora it refers to if it does. When we have these features we feed them through a tool like CRF++ (http://crfpp.sourceforge.net/). Keep in mind that some preprocessing will be necessary to get your features into a format CRF++ likes. Some postprocessing will be necessary to use the learned model, but there's little magic going on.

Another common operation you'll want to perform is to aggregate opinions across multiple terms or documents. In these situations, the aggregations will be in terms of documents or entities referred to within the document. You may, for example, want to know the average opinion people have of Pepsi. This can be achieved by averaging the sentiment of every entity that belongs to or refers to Pepsi.

In many situations, we want something less well defined. We want to know the themes of the document. There are natural clusterings of terms that people will have coherent and consistent opinions about. These clusters are sometimes called *topics*.

Topic modeling (which we covered briefly in chapter 6) refers to a family of algorithms designed to find these clusters in a collection of documents. They tend to organize important terms in the documents into different topics that are most representative of the documents. If it makes sense for your domain to ascribe sentiment to these topics, you may acquire it through a myriad of ways. The simplest is to average the sentiment of each word weighted based on how strongly it's associated with a particular topic. You may also learn your sentiments and topic at the same time. This allows you to force the choices of topics to have coherent sentiment across the words within them. The intuition behind this is that you want the words in your topics to have roughly the same sentiment. Approaches that do this are called *sentiment-topic models*.

## 9.5.5  *Open source libraries for sentiment analysis*

Though many classification libraries can be used to build a sentiment analysis model (keep in mind, classification is a general approach not specifically geared towards the sentiment analysis task), there are a few libraries that are already set up to do sentiment analysis, including these:

- *GATE* (http://gate.ac.uk/)—General-purpose GPL-licensed NLP toolkit that contains a sentiment analysis module
- *Balie* (http://balie.sourceforge.net/)—GPL-licensed library providing named entity recognition and sentiment analysis
- *MALLET* (http://mallet.cs.umass.edu/)—Common Public–licensed library that implements conditional random fields, among other algorithms

A variety of commercial tools (such as Lexalytics), APIs (such as Open Dover), and shared source (such as LingPipe) libraries are available for doing sentiment analysis. As with any tool we've discussed in this book, make sure you have the tools in place to check the quality of results before making a purchase or implementing an approach.

Though sentiment analysis is one of the hot topics of the day (circa 2012), our ever-increasing connectivity that spans the globe (Facebook alone has 500 million-plus users as of this writing, encompassing much of the world) creates the need to cross the language barrier more effectively. Our next topic, cross-language search, is a crucial part of the solution that makes it easier for people around the world to communicate regardless of their native tongue.

## 9.6    Cross-language information retrieval

*Cross-language information retrieval (CLIR)* is a search system that allows users to input queries in a given language and have results retrieved in other languages. By way of example, a CLIR system would allow a native Chinese speaker (who doesn't speak English) to enter queries in Chinese and have relevant documents returned in English, Spanish, or any other supported language. Though those documents are, on the surface, often still meaningless to a nonspeaker, most practical CLIR systems employ some sort of translation component (automated or manual) for viewing documents in the user's native language.

> **CROSS-LINGUAL VERSUS MULTILINGUAL SEARCH**   In some search circles, you'll hear people say they want multilingual search and sometimes you'll hear a need for cross-lingual search. Multilingual search, in our view, deals with a search application that has multiple indexes containing different languages and users only query the system using their chosen language. (English speakers query English resources, Spanish speakers query Spanish resources, and so on.) In CLIR, users explicitly ask to cross the language barrier, such as an English speaker querying Spanish resources.

In addition to all of the barriers to overcome in monolingual search, as detailed in chapter 3, CLIR systems must also deal with crossing the language barrier. Given the difficulty for most humans to learn a new language, it should be obvious that good cross-language search is no small task in a software application.

CLIR applications are traditionally built by either translating the user query to the target language and then performing retrieval against the target documents in their source language, or by translating, during preprocessing, all of the documents of a collection from the target language to the source language.

Regardless of the approach, the quality of the system often hinges on the ability to do translation. In all but the simplest of systems, manual translation is out of the question, so some type of automated approach must be used. The simplest programmatic approach is to acquire a bilingual dictionary and then do word-for-word substitution in the query, but this suffers from problems of disambiguation and semantics due to the fact that most languages use idioms, synonyms, and other constructs that make word-for-word substitution difficult at best.

Several commercial and open source tools are available which provide higher-quality automated translations based on statistical approaches that analyze parallel or comparable corpora and can therefore automatically learn idioms, synonyms, and other structures. (Parallel corpora are two collections of documents where each document is a translation of the other. A comparable corpus would be two collections of documents that are about the same topic.) The best-known automated translation system is likely Google's online translator, located at http://translate.google.com and shown in figure 9.5, but there are others including Systran (http://www.systransoft.com/) and SDL Language Weaver (http://www.languageweaver.com/). On the open source side,

**Figure 9.5    Example of translating the sentence "Tokyo is located in Japan" from English to Japanese using Google Translate. Captured 12/30/2010.**

the Apertium project (http://www.apertium.org/) appears to be fairly active, but we haven't evaluated it. The Moses project (http://www.statmt.org/moses/) is a statistical *machine translation (MT)* system that needs only parallel corpora to build your own statistical MT system. Finally, Mikel Forcada has put together a decent-sized list of free/ open source MT systems at http://computing.dcu.ie/~mforcada/fosmt.html.

In some CLIR cases, no direct translation capabilities exist and so a translation may only be possible via the use of a pivot language (assuming such a language exists) that acts as an intermediate step. For example, if translation resources exist to go from English to French and from French to Cantonese, but not directly from English to Cantonese, then you could pivot through French to get to Cantonese. Naturally, the quality would suffer, but it *might* be better than nothing.

Even in a good translation engine (most are useful as a starting point to get the gist of the concept), the system often produces multiple outputs for a given input, and so a CLIR system must have the means to determine when to use a translation and when not to use one. Similarly, many languages also require transliteration (to transcribe from one alphabet to another, not to be confused with translation) to take place between alphabets in order to deal with proper nouns. For instance, in an Arabic-English CLIR system that Grant worked on, trying to transliterate English names into Arabic or vice versa often resulted in many different permutations, sometimes hundreds or more, from which you had to decide which to include as search terms based on the statistical likelihood of the result occurring in the corpus.

**NOTE**    If you've ever wondered why some articles spell the name of the Libyan leader as Gaddafi while others spell it Khadafi or Qaddafi, it's primarily due to differences in transliteration, as there isn't always a clear-cut mapping between alphabets.

In some cases, the translation system will return a confidence score, but in other cases the application may need to use user feedback or log analysis to be effective. Finally, and unfortunately, in many cases, no matter how well the search part of the CLIR equation is implemented, users will likely judge the system based on the quality of the automated translations of the results, which is almost always mediocre in the general case, even if it's sufficient to get the gist of an article with some practice.

To learn more about CLIR, see *Information Retrieval* by Grossman and Frieder (Grossman [2004]) as a starter, and Doug Oard's site at http://terpconnect.umd .edu/~oard/research.html. There are also several conferences and competitions (similar to TREC) focused on CLIR, including CLEF (http://www.clef-campaign.org) and NTCIR (http://research.nii.ac.jp/ntcir/index-en.html).

## 9.7    Summary

In this chapter, we've lightly covered many other topics in search and natural language processing. We started with a look at semantics and the quest for finding meaning automatically, and then proceeded to look at areas as diverse as summarization, importance, cross-language search, and event and relationship detection. Regrettably, we didn't have the time or space to dig into these areas deeper, but hopefully we left with you some pointers to go find out more if you wish. As you can see, the areas of search and NLP are filled with challenging problems that can fill a career with interesting work. Making significant inroads on any of these subjects will unlock a multitude of new applications and opportunities. It's our sincere hope as authors that the contents of this book will unlock new opportunities for you in your career as well as life. Happy text taming!

## 9.8    References

Agichtein, Eugene. 2006. "Confidence Estimation Methods for Partially Supervised Relation Extraction." Proceedings of the 6th SIAM International Conference on Data Mining, 2006.

Blum, Avrim and Mitchell, Tom. 1998. "Combining Labeled and Unlabeled Data with Cotraining." Proceedings of the 11th Annual Conference on Computation Learning Theory.

Bunescu, Razvan and Mooney, Raymond. 2005. "Subsequence Kernels for Relation Extraction." *Neural Information Processing Systems.* Vancouver, Canada.

Chen, Bo; Lam, Wai; Tsang, Ivor; and Wong, Tak-Lam. 2009. "Extracting Discriminative Concepts for Domain Adaptation in Text Mining." Proceedings of the 15th ACM SIGKDD International Conference on Knowledge Discovery and Data Mining.

Chu, Min; Li, Chun; Peng, Hu; and Chang, Eric. 2002. "Domain Adaptation for TTS Systems." Proceedings of IEEE International Conference on Acoustics, Speech, and Signal Processing (ICASSP).

Culotta, Aron; McCallum, Andrew; and Betz, Jonathan. 2006. "Integrating Probabilistic Extraction Models and Data Mining to Discover Relations and Patterns in Text." Proceedings of the main conference on Human Language Technology Conference of the North American Chapter of the Association of Computational Linguistics.

Dave, Kushal; Lawrence, Steve; and Pennock, David. 2003 "Mining the Peanut Gallery: Opinion Extraction and Semantic Classification of Product Reviews." Proceedings of WWW-03, 12th International Conference on the World Wide Web.

Ding, Xiaowen; Liu, Bing; and Xhang, Lei. 2009. "Entity Discovery and Assignment for Opinion Mining Applications." Proceedings of ACM SIGKDD Conference (KDD 2009). http://www.cs.uic.edu/~liub/FBS/KDD2009_entity-final.pdf.

Durbin, Stephen; Richter, J. Neal; Warner, Doug. 2003. "A System for Affective Rating of Texts." Proceedings of the 3rd Workshop on Operational Text Classification, 9th ACM SIGKDD International Conference.

Getoor, L. and Taskar, B. 2007. *Introduction to Statistical Relational Learning.* The MIT Press. http://www.cs.umd.edu/srl-book/.

Greenwood, Mark and Stevenson, Mark. 2007. "A Task-based Comparison of Information Extraction Pattern Models." Proceedings of the ACL Workshop on Deep Linguistic Processing.

Grossman, David A., and Frieder, Ophir. 2004. *Information Retrieval: Algorithms and Heuristics (2nd Edition).* Springer.

GuoDong, Zhou; Jian, Su; Zhang, Jie; and Zhang, Min. 2002. "Exploring Various Knowledge in Relation Extraction." Proceedings of the Association for Computational Linguistics.

Hachey, Ben. 2009. "Multi-document Summarisation Using Generic Relation Extraction." Proceedings of the 2009 Conference on Empirical Methods in Natural Language Processing: Volume 1.

Hassan, Ahmed and Radev, Dragomir. 2010. "Identifying Text Polarity Using Random Walks." Proceedings of the 48th Annual Meeting of the Association for Computational Linguistics (ACL). http://www.aclweb.org/anthology-new/P/P10/P10-1041.pdf.

Hearst, Marti. 1994. "Multi-Paragraph segmentation of Expository Text." Proceedings of the Association for Computational Linguistics.

Jurafsky, Danile, and Martin, James. 2008. *Speech and Language Processing, 2nd Edition.* Prentice Hall.

Kambhatla, Nanda. 2004. "Combining Lexical, Syntactic, and Semantic Features with Maximum Entropy Models for Extracting Relations." Proceedings of the Association for Computational Linguistics. http://acl.ldc.upenn.edu/P/P04/P04-3022.pdf.

Kaufer, David. 2000. "Flaming: A White Paper." Carnegie Mellon. http://www.eudora.com/presskit/pdf/Flaming_White_Paper.PDF.

Liddy, Elizabeth. 2001. "Natural Language Processing." *Encyclopedia of Library and Information Science, 2nd Ed.* NY. Marcel Decker, Inc.

Liu, Bing, and Hu, Minqing. 2004. "Opinion Mining, Sentiment Analysis, and Opinion Spam Detection." http://www.cs.uic.edu/~liub/FBS/sentiment-analysis.html.

Lodhi, Huma; Saunders, Craig; Shawe-Taylor, John; and Cristianini, Nello. 2002. "Text Classification Using String Kernels." *Journal of Machine Learning Research.*

Manning, Christopher D, and Schütze, Hinrich. 1999. *Foundations of Natural Language Processing.* MIT Press.

Nguyen, Bach and Sameer, Badaskar. 2007. "A Survey on Relation Extraction." Literature review for Language and Statistics II.

Pang, Bo, and Lee, Lillian. 2008. "Opinion Mining and Sentiment Analysis." *Foundations and Trends in Information Retrieval* Vol 2, Issue 1-2. NOW.

Peccei, Jean. 1999. *Pragmatics.* Routledge, NY.

PubMed, MEDLINE. http://www.ncbi.nlm.nih.gov/sites/entrez.

Ravichandran, Deepak and Hovy, Eduard. 2002. "Learning Surface Text Patterns for a Question Answering System." Proceedings of the 40th Annual Meeting on Association for Computational Linguistics.

Turney, Peter. 2002. "Thumbs Up or Thumbs Down? Semantic Orientation Applied to Unsupervised Classification of Reviews." Proceedings of the 40th Annual Meeting of the Association for Computational Linguistics (ACL).

Yi, Jeonghee; Nasukawa, Tetsuya; Bunescu, Razvan; and Niblack, Wayne. 2003. "Sentiment Analyzer: Extracting Sentiments About a Given Topic Using Natural Language Processing Techniques." Third IEEE International Conference on Data Mining. http://ace.cs.ohiou.edu/~razvan/papers/icdm2003.pdf.

Zelenko, Dmitry; Aone, Chinatsu; and Richardella, Anthony. 2003. "Kernel Methods for Relation Extraction." *Journal of Machine Learning Research.*

# *index*